# Caroline's Dilemma

BETTINA BRADBURY is a New Zealand-born historian who spent most of her career at York University, Canada, writing women's and family history. Her most recent book, *Wife to Widow: Lives, Laws, and Politics in Nineteenth-Century Montreal*, has won multiple awards. She has now retired to Wellington but spends considerable time in Australia where one of her two daughters lives. Great-great grandparents on both sides of her family migrated to the Pacific in the 19th century, spending some time in the same colonies as Caroline Kearney. On her father's side Priors and Fordhams left England and became Methodist missionaries and ministers in Fiji, South Australia, and then New Zealand. On her mother's side, three German Jewish Hallenstein brothers provisioned miners during the gold rush in Victoria before sending Bendix and his wife, Mary Mountain, to set up business during the Otago gold rush in New Zealand.

# Caroline's Dilemma

A COLONIAL
INHERITANCE SAGA

Bettina Bradbury

**UBC**Press

29 28 27 26 25 24 23 22 21 20     5 4 3 2 1

First published in Australia by NewSouth, an imprint of UNSW Press.

Published in 2020 by UBC Press. UBC Press gratefully acknowledges the financial support for our publishing program of the Government of Canada (through the Canada Book Fund) and the British Columbia Arts Council.

*Caroline's Dilemma* is available in Australia and New Zealand (print and e-book) from NewSouth and in the rest of the world (print and e-book) from UBC Press.

Printed in Canada on FSC-certified ancient-forest-free paper (100 post-consumer recycled) that is processed chlorine- and acid-free.

**Library and Archives Canada Cataloguing in Publication**

Title: Caroline's dilemma : a colonial inheritance saga / Bettina Bradbury.
Names: Bradbury, Bettina, author.
Description: Includes bibliographical references and index. Identifiers: Canadiana (print) 20200258559 | Canadiana (ebook) 20200258664 | ISBN 9780774865609 (hardcover) | ISBN 9780774865319 (softcover) | ISBN 9780774865326 (PDF) | ISBN 9780774865333 (EPUB) | ISBN 9780774865340 (Kindle)
Subjects: LCSH: Kearney, Caroline, 1834-1886. | LCSH: Kearney, Caroline, 1834-1886 – Family. | LCSH: Women – Australia – 19th century – Biography. | LCSH: Widows – Australia – Social conditions – 19th century. | LCSH: Widows – Legal status, laws, etc. – Australia – History – 19th century. | LCSH: Inheritance and succession – Australia – History – 19th century. | LCSH: Australia – History – 1788-1900. | LCGFT: Biographies.
Classification: LCC HQ1822.5.K43 B73 2020 | DDC 305.420994 – dc23

Canadä

Printed and bound in Canada
Cover design: Gerilee McBride

UBC Press
The University of British Columbia
2029 West Mall
Vancouver, BC V6T 1Z2
www.ubcpress.ca

# Contents

# The Bax and Kearney families – three generations

William Margery Bax (1805-85) married (1827) Caroline Frances Steele (1808-71)

**William Thomas** (1828-1909) married (1865) Helena Edwards (1848-?)

**Eleanor Margery** (1831-1910) married (1860) James Hamilton (1836-1927)
- Amelia Frances Jane (1861-1946) married (1880) William Philip (1857-1933)
- Francis Lennox (1862-1926) married (1889) Mary Ellen Smith (1870-1947)
- James Charles (1865-1940) married (1891) Jane Harriet Hateley (1865-1950)

**Caroline Anne** (1834-86) married Edward Kearney (c.1819-65)
- Maria Ellen Kearney (1854-66)
- Edward (1856-1925) married (1879) Anna Cooke (1852-1929)
  - Anna Violet (1880-1954)
  - Ida Ellen (1881-1920)
  - Edward Frances (1892-97)
- Frank Henry (1856-1933) married (1881) Margaret Kearney (1857-1929)
- William (1860-1940) married-1 (1885) Mary Therese Sheridan (1860-89) married-2 (1899) May Emily Isabella Moutray (1874-1931)
  - Edward Moutray Kearney (1901-54)
- Patrick Edgar (1862-1936)

**Robert, 1837-?**

**Mary (1837-95)** married-1 (1875) William Robert Catt (1826-84), married-2 (1890) Alfred Pain (?-1894)
- Charles James (1864-1915) married-1 (1889) Harriet Elizabeth Burnell (1869-1903) married-2 (1906) Rachel Naomi Margaret Tasker (1883-1944)
  - May Burnell (1890-1966)
  - Elizabeth Lockhart (1891-?)
  - Winnifred Laura (1894-?)
  - Kenneth Ignatius (1897-97)

**Esther Jane (1836-61)** married (1854) James Allen (1815-65)
- James (1855-1942)
- Charles Joseph (1856-88)

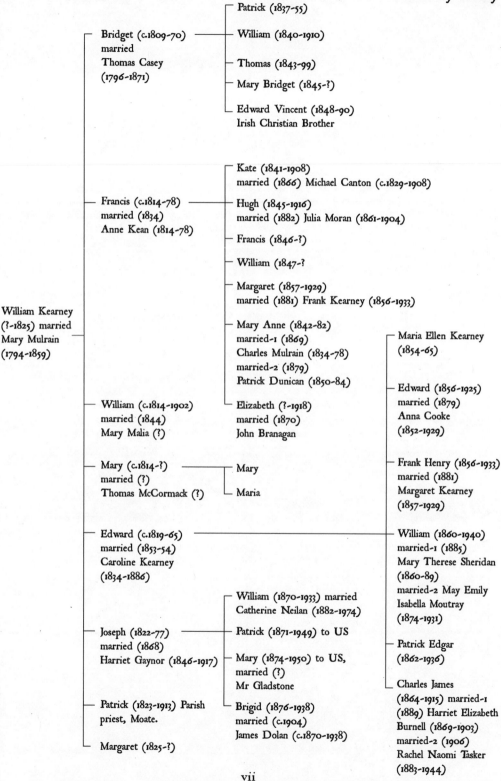

Bridget (c.1809-70)
married
Thomas Casey
(1796-1871)

- Patrick (1837-55)
- William (1840-1910)
- Thomas (1843-99)
- Mary Bridget (1845-?)
- Edward Vincent (1848-90)
  Irish Christian Brother

Francis (c.1814-78)
married (1834)
Anne Kean (1814-78)

- Kate (1841-1908)
  married (1866) Michael Canton (c.1829-1908)
- Hugh (1845-1916)
  married (1882) Julia Moran (1861-1904)
- Francis (1846-?)
- William (1847-?
- Margaret (1857-1929)
  married (1881) Frank Kearney (1856-1933)
- Mary Anne (1842-82)
  married-1 (1869)
  Charles Mulrain (1834-78)
  married-2 (1879)
  Patrick Dunican (1850-84)

William Kearney
(?-1825) married
Mary Mulrain
(1794-1859)

William (c.1814-1902)
married (1844)
Mary Malia (?)

- Elizabeth (?-1918)
  married (1870)
  John Branagan

Mary (c.1814-?)
married (?)
Thomas McCormack (?)

- Mary
- Maria

Edward (c.1819-65)
married (1853-54)
Caroline Kearney
(1834-1886)

Joseph (1822-77)
married (1868)
Harriet Gaynor (1846-1917)

- William (1870-1933) married
  Catherine Neilan (1882-1974)
- Patrick (1871-1949) to US
- Mary (1874-1950) to US,
  married (?)
  Mr Gladstone
- Brigid (1876-1938)
  married (c.1904)
  James Dolan (c.1870-1938)

Patrick (1823-1913) Parish
priest, Moate.

Margaret (1825-?)

- Maria Ellen Kearney
  (1854-65)
- Edward (1856-1925)
  married (1879)
  Anna Cooke
  (1852-1929)
- Frank Henry (1856-1933)
  married (1881)
  Margaret Kearney
  (1857-1929)
- William (1860-1940)
  married-1 (1885)
  Mary Therese Sheridan
  (1860-89)
  married-2 May Emily
  Isabella Moutray
  (1874-1931)
- Patrick Edgar
  (1862-1936)
- Charles James
  (1864-1915) married-1
  (1889) Harriet Elizabeth
  Burnell (1869-1903)
  married-2 (1906)
  Rachel Naomi Tasker
  (1883-1944)

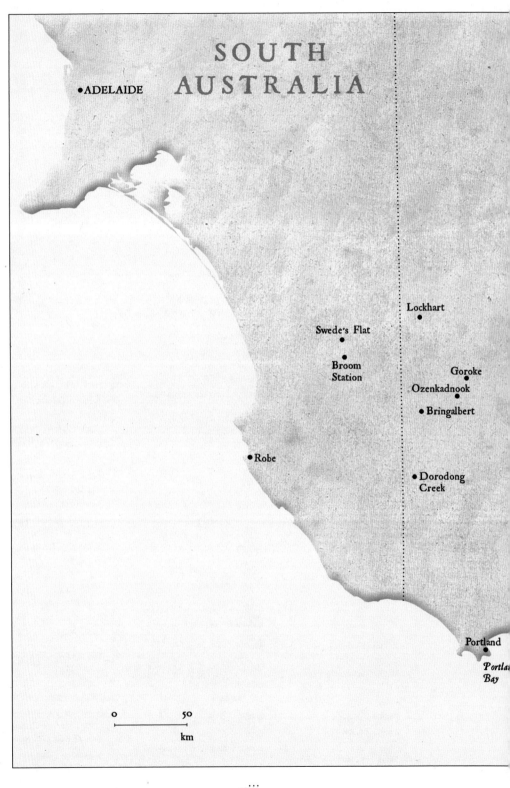

SOUTH
AUSTRALIA

•ADELAIDE

Lockhart
●

Swede's Flat
●

Broom
Station
●

Goroke
●

Ozenkadnook
●

● Bringalbert

● Robe

● Dorodong
Creek

Portland
●

Portla[n]
Bay

0        50
├───────┤
km

# Location of Bax family and relatives, 1837–70

VICTORIA

MELBOURNE

Geelong

# Introduction

Caroline Kearney (née Bax) had much to worry about as her husband hovered near death in a Melbourne hotel room in October 1865. She and Edward Kearney had been married for twelve years. They had six children aged from not yet two to nine. Caroline was 31. Unlike her older sister, Eleanor, she had little if any experience in earning a living. How would she manage as a widow and sole parent? What would happen to the sheep station, Lockhart, they had worked so hard to improve over the last seven years? Might her eldest son, Edward, inherit it one day? Could her brother-in-law have sought to influence the provisions of Edward's will, just as he had meddled in so many aspects of their lives in the last year?

Caroline, Edward and his brother William had set out for Melbourne from Lockhart in the western Wimmera country of Victoria in late August as Edward's health deteriorated. The six children remained in the care of station hands, or perhaps of her sister or parents. This was a bone-rattling, long and uncomfortable trip at the best of times. For a man dying and in pain it would have been excruciating. It took days to travel the 200 kilometres by coach or bullock cart along the rough, old droving and gold rush tracks from Lockhart, on the border of South Australia and Victoria, south-west to the small port of Robe. There they boarded the coastal clipper *Penola*. After a rough voyage they docked in Melbourne on 11 September.[1]

They took rooms at the Washington Hotel on the corner of Collins and William streets. Edward secured the services of a Melbourne law firm to draft his will. He signed the final copy on 30 September. Caroline had good reason to dread its contents, but what she learned when the will was read following his death on 20 October undoubtedly came as a complete shock.[2] Edward wanted her and their six children removed not only from their station but also from Australia. He instructed his executors to use the assets of his estate to send his family to Ireland, his birthplace. There they were to live in a house that two of his brothers and a brother-in-law would choose and furnish for them. He promised an annuity of £100 a year for Caroline and their only daughter. Funds for the maintenance, education and support of his five sons were to be made available from their future one-seventh of the estate until they reached 24. Then they would receive their portion. Caroline was also to receive one-seventh. However, if she refused to take the children to Ireland, refused to live in the house chosen for her, or remarried, the trustees were to pay her £150 for just two years. After that she would receive nothing.[3]

Edward bequeathed Caroline a heart-breaking dilemma. In most British settler colonies, as in England and most of the American states, the English common law gave husbands vast power to do what they wished with their property. Anything Caroline had brought to their marriage and all the property they had acquired during their lives together was understood to belong to Edward. Few if any other legal systems allowed men such a claim on virtually all family assets, or so much liberty to avoid sharing these with their widows and their children. Edward's will dramatises the immense power that the English law gave husbands over all family property. In England and across the colonies British men understood their right to decide what to do with their own property in a final will as fundamental, akin to trial by jury or the right to contest unlawful detention, habeas corpus.[4]

The prominent Australian legal scholar Professor Rosalind Croucher (formerly Atherton) has aptly described testamentary freedom as the 'power to disinherit wives'.[5] Yet Edward was not proposing to cut Caroline off. He did not seek to leave her or the children penniless. One hundred pounds was a much more generous amount than working-class widows could dream of, and more than many lower to middling middle-class widows could hope for. But to claim that support Caroline would have to leave the colony she had lived in since she was seventeen and sever her ties with her parents and siblings. Caroline was English. She had never been to Ireland.

What could she do? Remain in Australia with her six children and try to raise them with help from her family? Then she would lose her claim on the promised economic support from the assets that were understood to belong to Edward alone. Or would she have to agree to this forced family migration?

I first learned of the tragic choice she faced as a widow when I read a legal account of her fight against Edward's final wishes. At the time I was planning to write a broad history highlighting the importance of issues of marriage, property, and especially inheritance, in 19th-century settler colonies of the British Empire. Kearney's attempt at testamentary extradition struck me as one of the most draconian provisions I had encountered in 19th-century wills.[6]

Why was this his final wish? How did Caroline react? I knew from the legal report of the case that she contested this aspect of his will. What decisions had the courts and judges made? What had happened to her and the children? Did she go to Ireland? If so, did she stay there? These are questions I have been pondering and seeking to answer ever since I first encountered the case. I began to think of wills in part through the words that the Irish novelist Colum McCann attached to a very different situation. Could final testaments be read as 'the collision point of stories?'[7] I wanted to discover the colliding threads ultimately expressed in Edward's final wishes. I started trying to write Caroline's story, thinking it might merit one or two chapters in my book. I began building family trees using the genealogical sources available online and elsewhere. I visited archives and contacted relatives. Caroline's history and her predicament seduced me. As I gathered more information I decided that their history deserved a whole book. So I put aside my broader study and began to explore the Kearney and Bax family histories as settler colonisers in 19th-century Australia.

Settlers in Victoria in the 1860s may have taken a cursory interest in the 'will case of some singularity' that was involving some of the colony's leading legal minds and reported on in the colonial newspapers.[8] Today, apart from a few of Caroline and Edward Kearney's descendants, who pieced some of the threads together, her history is unknown. I have found no copious archives of letters or diaries written by members of the Kearney or Bax families that might help interpret the motives, emotions or characters of Edward, Caroline and their children. Her great-great-granddaughter Rosalind McLeod remembers that there was a large trunk in an old outbuilding next to the farmhouse at their grandmother's house at Nana Glen, New South Wales. This was forbidden and hence fascinating territory for them as children. They believed it contained letters, diaries and photographs that might help them better understand some of their family history. After their grandmother died they sought to satisfy their pent-up curiosity and opened the trunk. Rosalind told me sadly that the entire contents 'had been eaten by white ants!'[9]

Edward junior, Caroline's eldest son, left a handwritten account of his early years that has survived. Joe Palmer, his great-great-grandson, transcribed it for me. This 'memorandum', as Edward junior called it, was written to explain the travails of his childhood and youth to his future wife (see image 1 in the picture section). It combines the romantic hopes of a young man looking forward to a loving marriage with reflections on his perceptions of his parents' failings. Read carefully, it offers glimpses into his parents' relationship and the children's upbringing that are unavailable in other sources.[10] Caroline's brother-in-law, James Charles Hamilton, an early colonist on the Victorian frontier, penned a revealing memoir late in life. It provides vivid accounts of pioneering, of generous assistance from Aboriginal peoples, and includes a few references to Edward and Caroline.[11] In Ireland there is a Kearney genealogy written by a descendant. It makes no mention of Edward.[12] His life and death are almost invisible in Irish sources, just as they are in the family memories of the descendants of his Irish siblings today.

The Kearney's family conflicts burst into the public record most often when they went to court. The resulting legal records are the richest sources I have found. Newspaper reports, and the genealogical traces family members left as they lived, moved and died, have been equally essential. The digitisation of documents, and especially projects that have facilitated name searching, have revolutionised access to many sources over my career as a historian. In writing this book, genealogical tools, and the wonderful websites of digitised and indexed newspapers of Australia, New Zealand, Ireland and occasionally England, have been indispensable. So too were traditional historical digging, following leads in small town libraries, local history societies and state and town archives, and discussions with locals.

This book shares what I have been able to find out about

Caroline, Edward and their children. It follows Caroline's struggles against her husband's final wishes. And it tracks Caroline and the children over the rest of their lives. Paralleling the narrative of their lives is the story of my research discoveries, surprises and disappointments. I have had eureka moments and disappointing hours of digging with few results. Frustrating gaps and silences in the documentary evidence remain. Though this is true of all historical research, it is more obvious when recounting a life. I have sought to connect information that seems certain, and to share my thinking about missing evidence and what might have happened. I invite readers to share my surprise and puzzlement about missing information and to use their own imaginations when concrete evidence is missing. A fiction writer could enrich the account. A scriptwriter could definitely turn it into a profoundly moving film. But the story of Caroline, Edward and their children is dramatic, indeed often melodramatic, enough without fictionalising. This is a work of non-fiction.[13]

Caroline's quandary not only led me to archives in multiple locations, but also into Australian history for the first time. This has been a richly rewarding experience. I am a New Zealander who moved to Canada in my early adulthood and became a historian of 19th-century Montreal. In my previous work I have sought to place women, children and families at the heart of major historical transformations, including the industrial revolution, political conflicts and legal changes. My last book traced the transition of hundreds of women in 19th-century Montreal from their status as wife to that of widow. Here I follow one woman, Caroline, contextualising her life as a daughter, then wife, mother and widow in the times and places she lived. Over recent years I have been enticed by the richness of piecing together biographies of individuals and families in much the same way that genealogists do. This book reflects my growing interest, shared with other scholars, in blending biography, narrative and genealogy to reveal new and surprising aspects of a time, a place, power dynamics or historical processes.[14] Individual and family stories compel us to grapple with the complexities of the past in new and often unexpected ways. They take us across and beyond the boundaries of cities and regions, and colonies, and back and forth from metropole to colony. And they force historians across the artificial lines that divide different areas of expertise.

This story of Caroline, Edward and their children builds on and traverses what are often separate historical fields examining migration,[15] settler colonialism,[16] gender and women's history,[17] intimacy, marriage and family life,[18] sectarianism, inheritance[19] and the law.[20] *Caroline's Dilemma* adds the extraordinary story of one fairly ordinary middle-class woman and her family to the rich and growing cast of characters now peopling the history of colonial Australia and the wider British Empire.

The lives and actions of Edward, Caroline and her children offer different glimpses into the dynamics of settler colonialism and the 19th-century British Empire from works focusing on more prominent men and women.[21] Both Edward and Caroline were in many ways privileged immigrants. They came to Australia freely, of their own accord, unlike convicts, indentured workers and other involuntary labourers. The spouses shared literacy and a reasonable education and came from different, but compatible, class backgrounds. Both families might have been considered of the middling classes. They were neither rich nor desperately poor. Edward came from an Irish family of tenant farmers who had done reasonably well. He left Ireland on his own in 1842 or 1843, without government assistance. The Baxes left England in 1851 as a family, travelling as assisted emigrants. As colonisers from England, they were assumed to share the capacities that placed 'white Anglo Saxons' at the top of contemporary hierarchical understandings about race and civilisation and Australian Aboriginal peoples near the bottom.[22] Not so for Irish Catholics like Edward Kearney. In some strands of contemporary thinking the Irish were a race apart, not really white. Anti-Catholic prejudice added to these understandings the idea that Catholics would always do as their priests told them and so lacked the independence of thought and person necessary for full participation in colonial self-government. In the Australian colonies, as elsewhere in the British Empire, long-held British ideas of the Irish as backward, barbarous, lazy, stupid and quick to fight shaped daily interactions and had an impact on immigrants' prospects in life.[23]

Caroline and Edward participated directly in the dispossession of Indigenous peoples that characterised settler colonialism in Australia as in New Zealand, the Americas and elsewhere. They ran sheep stations on the hunting and gathering grounds of local Aboriginal peoples. They hoped they might succeed and perhaps pass a station on to their eldest son. Edward's early death highlights the precariousness of such hopes and dreams.[24] Successful or not, such ordinary people were critical to the making of white settler colonies. Yet until recently historians have paid more attention to the governors and other officials who circulated around the British colonies, to missionaries, and to European men who had sex – both consensual and forced – with Indigenous women.[25] Without white settlers who occupied land and procreated there could be no settler colonies.

The book's structure is simple. The chapters move chronologically from the separate and different histories of Caroline and Edward's migration and arrival in the colony through their lives together, first on a station in South Australia, then in Victoria, and then to his death. They then focus on the legal and other challenges of Caroline's widowhood. The last chapters explore Caroline's final years as well as those of her siblings and her children as they moved into adulthood. Hers and theirs are stories of individual settlers seeking to shape their lives under conditions that were not of their making. Few families have uncomplicated histories. Digging back invariably reveals that past lives were as complicated as any today. We find joy and sorrow, pride and shame, hopes and despair, love and hatred, sectarian zeal, racism, faith, fatalism and foolishness, vengeance and violence. These are all part of the story of Caroline, Edward and their children.

Caroline's fights in the courts against the will's contents, the actions of the executors and the wishes of Edward's family show one woman's remarkable tenacity in the face of the patriarchal power of her husband, his brothers, the law, its officers, and the society and culture in which she lived. The children also showed remarkable resilience and determination. As a woman and as minors they were subject to the conditions of Edward's will. As adults the siblings sought their own ways to surmount the challenges of their childhoods and upbringing. Their success at remaking their lives in the aftermath of their forced migration varied.

# Part One

# Migration, marriage and station life: Becoming Australian colonisers

# 1

# Migrations and marriage

Caroline Anne Bax had recently turned seventeen when in mid-June 1851 she boarded the 571-ton barque the *Earl Grey*, bound for Port Jackson, New South Wales. Behind her lay the Port of Plymouth and her life as a young girl in the south-east of England. Ahead lay the long and potentially dangerous voyage to Australia and an unknown future. She did not travel alone as a single woman seeking a new life in the colonies, as did the thousands of female migrants who have long fascinated historians. Hers was a family migration.[1] What say did Caroline have in the decision to migrate to Australia? Had her mother and father and five siblings debated their options, shared information gleaned from the posters, handbills, circulars, handbooks and gazettes that proliferated in the 1840s and 1850s promoting Australia, other colonies and emigration? Did the hopes and fears of these eight family members converge or conflict as they contemplated the radical possibility of uprooting themselves from their home and moving elsewhere? And why did they choose the lengthy trip to far-away Australia rather than head for the much closer colonies of the United States or the British colonies that later became Canada, as so many emigrants were doing?

Few records of any such family deliberations have survived. We have none for the Baxes. The broader context is clear. Emigration from Great Britain had accelerated over the three previous decades. Publicity spread like wildfire. Parishes assisted their poor to leave, saving the cost of their support. Organisations and colonies promoted emigration. Colonies competed for migrants. Rural workers dreamed of land in the colonies. Working-class men and women sought to throw off the shackles of wage labour. Educated men and women hoped for better futures. Emigration was in the air – talked about in pubs and shops and on the streets and made tangible by the absence of former neighbours, customers and fellow church members who no longer occupied houses, shops and pews.

Caroline was the third child of Caroline Frances and William Margery Bax. She was born in Ninfield, Sussex, and baptised there on 1 June 1834. In 1851, the year of their departure, the family was living in the small Sussex market town of Cuckfield, 63 kilometres south of London. Its origins dated back as far as the 13th century. Their house was on Church Street. Hardly a minute's walk down the road was the Holy Trinity Church, some parts of which were equally old. The town and surrounding parish were home to just over 3000 people. At the apex of local class and social relations were the gentry. Minor local officials included the postmaster, inspector of the constabulary, the master and matron of the union workhouse, a schoolmaster and -mistress, and William Bax, the area's excise officer. The town had a couple of surgeons, one lawyer and a chemist. Most of their fellow villagers followed occupations only lightly touched by the industrial transformations underway elsewhere. Townsmen worked as grocers, drapers, stationers, tailors, bakers, plumbers, builders, shoemakers and ran inns and posting houses. Several women ran shops and hairdressing establishments, and produced clothing. Farmer was the leading occupation. Around the village the rural population produced crops and raised animals on fields whose boundaries had changed little since medieval times.[2] But much else had changed. Growing numbers of rural families were dependent on wages earned as agricultural labourers or on parish relief. In the 1830s Kent, Surrey and Sussex were among the hotbeds of protest as rural followers of Captain Swing burned property, smashed threshing machines and rioted in the face of poverty and the growing degradation of their lives, livelihoods and rights. Government investigations, repression and trials followed. Some of those convicted were transported to Australia.[3]

Australia was on the minds of the Bax family two decades later as economic turmoil and class warfare continued to wreak havoc across England. In March 1851, English household heads were required to fill out the schedule left at their homes providing specific information about every member of their family. The details that Caroline's father, William Bax, inscribed offer us a snapshot of the family three months before their departure. Here are potential hints at aspects of their lives that might have influenced their decision-making about their future. Questions about places of birth required more precision that year than in previous English censuses. The children's birthplaces show that the Baxes had moved often over the 24 years since their parents, William and Caroline Frances (née Steele), married in South London in 1827. Their eldest child, William Thomas, aged 22 in 1851, was born in Godalming, in south-western Surrey. He was working as a journeyman baker. Both nineteen-year-old Eleanor Margery and sixteen-year-old Caroline were born in Ninfield, Sussex. Eleanor was listed as a dressmaker. Family hearsay suggests she wanted to become a doctor and had acquired considerable nursing skills prior to leaving England. Esther, aged fifteen, was born in Deal, Kent. Neither she nor Caroline were working steadily enough for their father to report an occupation for them. They may well have taken on odd jobs and certainly would have helped their mother around the house. Their two youngest, the thirteen-year-old twins, Mary and Robert, were born in Beckley in eastern Sussex. They were still attending school.[4]

Such frequent moves often reflect unstable work histories, a potential reason to emigrate. But this was not the case for William Bax. In 1825 at the age of 20 he had sought training as an excise officer. For centuries, excise men had estimated the taxes due on locally manufactured goods. These provided the government with a major source of revenue. He was deemed a 'likely man to make a good officer'. His mathematics and writing were strong and his character considered to be good. He was then single, debt-free, healthy and active. And, perhaps more importantly, he was 'well affected to' the government of the time – the Tories. William chose to train in his home town of Canterbury. After four months his instructor had informed the Board of Excise that he was qualified to determine excise taxes on a wide range of manufactured products, including those made by brewers, maltsters, tanners, tobacco dealers and chandlers. He, like others in his position, was transferred frequently to avoid any possibility of corruption.[5]

Adding information from his employment record to the places of his children's births shows that this couple and their growing family had been compelled to change their place of residence at least seven times since they married. No novelty for them in contemplating another move! However, no previous relocation had taken them beyond the counties of Kent, Surrey and Sussex in south-eastern England. Two months after the census was taken, William was informed that he was to be transferred once again, this time some 40 kilometres north-east to Tunbridge Wells in Western Kent.[6] Might this proposed transfer have been the final straw for him and his family, pushing them to embrace the idea of migration? Or were their plans to head to Australia already well underway?

Though William's job had been quite a good one, his work conditions had always been challenging. Local producers resented the power of excise officers to set tax rates on their goods, so they were often unpopular within their villages.[7] Between the time of his appointment in 1826 and the 1850s, the significance of excise duties – previously a major source of government revenue – fell dramatically, while customs duties and other forms of revenue production for the government rose. The government response was to restructure. The Board of Excise lost its independent bureaucracy and was merged into the Board of Inland Revenue. The possibilities and prospects in William Bax's profession were changing, and not for the better. Within a month of the news of his proposed transfer, he sought permission to relinquish his position. This was officially granted on 4 June 1851, just before their departure.[8]

Ultimately it was William Bax senior who had the power to decide the family's future. As women and/or minors Caroline, her sisters and her younger brother had no legal grounds to contest their father's decision to emigrate. Nor did her mother. Alongside losing their independent legal capacity on marriage, wives were obliged to take up the residence of their husbands. In that sense this was not a voluntary migration for all family members, though it's possible they discussed it together at length and eagerly embraced the opportunities it offered. At 43 years old, William Bax was no longer a young man. The children had all reached their teens or early twenties. Theirs was a family economy in which older sons and daughters were expected to contribute wages – a pattern most frequent in working-class families, but common too among families of the lower middle classes like theirs. With William Thomas and Eleanor working, they were likely better off than when the children were all younger. Perhaps they had been able to make some savings.[9]

But what of their future? The publicity about the Australian colonies suggested that the boys would be able to secure land or well-paid employment. The prospects for Caroline and her sisters finding independence as domestics or even governesses – or, more likely, finding husbands – were better than at home. For while English observers were increasingly worried about that country's 'surplus women', the Australian colonies had the opposite problem. Authorities were keen to promote policies that encouraged marriage and the migration of families as well as of female domestic servants.[10] If the Baxes were to take the drastic step of leaving the country, sooner was better than later.

Migrating to Australia was expensive. Even for migrants opting to travel independently in steerage it cost £20 to £25 per passenger – around £200 for the Bax family. Over the previous decades the Australian colonial governments had ramped up their attempts to attract colonists otherwise tempted by the much cheaper costs of travel to North America by offering assisted passages. Emigrants did not travel free. They had to contribute a mandatory deposit of around £2 each, with a further £1 to £2 each for kits of bedding and utensils. These expenses made the price competitive with sailing to North America.[11]

As the Baxes calculated costs and devoured informational pamphlets, more personal connections and stories are likely to have influenced their choice of destination. Mrs Bax came from a large family. The sixteen Steele siblings were all born in Reigate, Surrey where their father had practised as a doctor prior to his death in 1838. Few of her brothers and sisters had moved far beyond Kent and Surrey as they reached adulthood and started their own families. Emigrating would cut her off from this large group of kin, except for her younger brother, Robert. He had run away from home as a youngster, joined the royal navy, worked in the early 1830s on ships suppressing the slave trade off the coast of West Africa, then sailed to Australia. He jumped ship in Hobart and moved to Melbourne in 1837, where he met and married Mary Duane. After two babies died they moved briefly to Portland Bay, securing pastoral leases first at Poolaijelo, then Dorodong Creek Station, in the south-west of the area that became the colony of Victoria in 1851. Information from them surely influenced the family as they considered their futures, for it was to that area of the colonies that they would head soon after arriving in Australia (see map, page ix).[12]

In a perplexing move for a man of his class and education, William Bax sought an assisted passage for himself and his wife and children. Candidates had to send their applications to the Colonial Land and Emigration Commission in London, either independently or through local clergy or emigration societies. The well-educated Baxes no doubt had little trouble completing the complicated paperwork or finding three people willing to provide character references. They had to secure medical certificates as well. Eligibility criteria included health, character, age, marital status and family status. Specific occupations were favoured. None of the Bax males could claim experience in the favoured categories – agricultural labourers, shepherds, herdsmen or country mechanics. Young William and Robert would pass muster as potential farm workers. Caroline, her sisters, indeed almost all female migrants, were seen as potential female servants – a category in high demand. Their application was accepted, so they had to send half the required deposit to London. The rest would be paid on arrival in Australia. Things could move quickly after that. Embarkation orders were issued. Emigrants scrambled to get to their assigned vessels in time.[13]

Plymouth, the main departure port for assisted emigrants, was far from Cuckfield. No direct road or single railway line covered the 380-kilometre trip west from their home, though the expanding network of local railways was making the trip easier. The first step was a short one – east by carriage to the Haywards Heath station on the Brighton to London line. Then a 75-kilometre trip north to that company's terminus in London. There they had to make their way to Paddington Station. Great Western trains took passengers the 170 kilometres west to Bristol. Another change, and on to the recently completed South Devon Railroad, which carried emigrants south to Plymouth. As assisted emigrants the Baxes were eligible for shelter in the emigrant depot on the departure pier in Mill Bay at government expense. Plymouth's depot had been built in 1847 to house the thousands of Irish fleeing the potato famine. On arrival, assisted emigrants presented their embarkation orders and were inspected by the ship's surgeon.[14] When all the passengers bound for Australia on the *Earl Grey* had been prodded and probed and found healthy and Captain Urquhart deemed the ship ready to sail, the Baxes and other passengers could embark.

All the 257 emigrants on this vessel charted exclusively for emigrants travelled in steerage. Here, with little privacy and less comfort, passengers lived cheek by jowl for the four-month voyage. The Baxes seem to have stood out like sore thumbs. They were all literate. Many others passengers could read but not write. More could do neither. Most male passengers were recorded on the passenger list as farm labourers. William Bax's identification as a 'late excise officer' stands out, but so do the listings for young William as a baker and Eleanor as a milliner/dressmaker. Caroline and her other sisters blend in with the other single women emigrants identified as domestic servants. Caroline's parents were among the eldest of the 37 married couples on board. Only one other couple, two of the three widows and the one widower were close to them in age. Most other couples were in their thirties or younger and either childless or had only young children. The 57 single men and 27 single women were predominantly in their late teens or twenties. Among them the Bax girls might find some congenial companions. The vast majority of their shipmates were Irishmen and -women, virtually all Catholic. The Baxes belonged to the Church of England. There were a few Presbyterians, dissenters of diverse kinds and the odd unbeliever.[15] Distinguished by their class, religious denomination, age and literacy, it is unlikely that they mixed easily with the other passengers.

One hundred and nineteen days at sea. South from Plymouth on the Atlantic to the equator, further southward around the Cape of Good Hope, then east across the southern Indian Ocean, taking advantage of the prevailing westerly winds. Always the risk of high winds, massive waves and sometimes icebergs. All depended on the weather and the condition of the ship.[16] Few of these lengthy sailing trips were free of troubles, and the Baxes were travelling before 1855, when a new Passenger Act tightened up the regulation of safety conditions on board, making the trip less of a 'gamble with survival'.[17] They were reasonably lucky. The *Earl Grey* took roughly the average amount of time to complete the voyage. Their four months at sea were marked by an outbreak of scarlet fever that lingered, spread and killed six young children. One pregnant woman died during childbirth at sea. On the final stretch of the journey they struck 'foul weather'; the captain claimed this was the cause of the dirty state of the vessel, which shocked the immigrant agent when they arrived in Port Jackson.[18] These were relatively minor complaints compared to the scandals and dangers that provoked investigations of some voyages.[19]

Caroline and her fellow passengers sailed into Port Jackson on 15 October 1851. On arrival the passengers again had to undergo the bodily intrusion of a medical examination. All received a clean bill of health. The medical officer also offered the newcomers the chance to make any complaints 'respecting treatment on board this ship'. Neither Caroline's family nor others had any. The final instalment of their deposit was due on arrival. They paid £19. Most family groups on the *Earl Grey* owed similar amounts.[20]

The Baxes had landed unwittingly on a continent infected with gold fever. Since their departure from England news of gold finds in Australia had burst into newspapers across the colonies, in England and around the world. Information travelled slowly. The first mention of Australian gold did not appear in the *Times* of London until 2 September 1851. It reproduced a *Sydney Morning Herald* article of 20 May, entitled 'Gold Fever in Australia', that confirmed the discovery of gold in New South Wales and described the numbers of people of all ages, sexes, denominations and callings who were heading for the diggings. More significant discoveries were made at Ophir in mid-July that year. The movement of people within, across and into the colonies exploded. New areas opened up. Dramatic transformations were underway. For their own reasons, the Bax family had been swept into this watershed moment in the history of the Australian colonies.[21]

On arrival in Port Jackson, the single women travelling without family members were whisked off to the immigration barracks, where eager Australian colonials competed to secure domestic servants. Squatters from miles away rode into town, desperate to replace workers who had deserted their farms to seek their luck in the goldfields. Within days the *Sydney Morning Herald* was informing readers that 'almost all the families' on the *Earl Grey* had been hired at 'high rates of wages'. Remaining families would be available for engagement that day between 10 am and 4 pm.[22] Within a week most of the married men had been hired as farm servants at between £20 and £24 a year. Just eight married men with families were still at the depot.[23] I suspect the Baxes and the other older family heads were among them, though their two sons may have found work. It is unlikely that William Bax senior would stoop to, or be chosen for, labouring work.

I have found no traces of what happened to them over the following two months. On 4 January 1852 all the Bax family except one of the boys boarded the 123-ton brig *Essington* at Circular Wharf in Sydney. Formerly a whaling boat, this coastal sailing ship carried a few passengers and their belongings, as well as cargos of tea, flour, sugar, alcohol and various other goods, between Sydney, Port Fairy and Portland Bay on the south-western coast of the new colony of Victoria.[24] This was the Baxes' first experience sailing along this treacherous coast. It was not a good one. The *Essington* hit such bad weather that ten days after leaving Sydney Captain Mills sailed her far south into Hobart's harbour to escape the 'stress of weather', before heading north again from Van Diemen's Land.[25]

They were bound for Portland Bay. Why this small coastal town? Indigenous peoples of that area had encountered Europeans first when whalers and sealers made it a base decades earlier. From the 1830s on, settlers keen to run sheep over their hunting grounds began taking up the best grazing lands in the wider region. In 1840 it was laid out as a township. It briefly became one of the colony's main centres as the numbers of pioneer squatters taking up vast tracts of land far to the north and west increased. Among those purchasing land there was James Allen, the man Caroline's sister Esther would marry a few years later. For a while it was the main market town for the young James Hamilton and his family, whose stations Bringalbert and Ozenkadnook were some 200 kilometres almost due north. Later, he married Caroline's elder sister, Eleanor. In 1848, when he was twelve, James and his father took ten days to take their years' wool clip there by bullock cart, camping and staying with other squatters along the way. He described it as a 'nice compact town built mostly of stone'. They sold their wool to George Henty, a member of a family recognised as pioneers in the region. There were several other wool merchants, an iron merchant, a draper, a saddler and a tanning yard as well as a doctor and chemist's shop. James Hamilton had taken up rooms at the small, square and mediocre London Inn, facing the sea.[26]

It was to Portland that Caroline's mother's younger brother, Robert Steele, and his wife had moved briefly in 1846 after leaving Melbourne. The Baxes' decision to sail there was surely no coincidence. Letters from relatives were among the strongest influences on emigrants' decisions to migrate, sometimes initiating chain migrations that led to clusters of kin in particular locations. Perhaps this was the latest address the Baxes had for Robert. Or they may have known that he now ran a sheep station at Dorodong Creek, some 150 kilometres north-west of the Bay, and sought to travel there, or to catch up with him when he came to town to sell his wool and secure supplies. They certainly renewed their links with Robert Steele over subsequent years. Portland Bay was their first foray into the broad southern border region between the new colony of Victoria and South Australia that would soon become home to Caroline, her parents and most of her siblings. How long they remained there, I don't know.[27]

❧

Gold was luring men young and old, and some women, from cities, small towns and stations across Australia to Clunes, Castlemaine, Ballarat, Buninyong, Bendigo and the other successive finds. Caroline's two brothers, William and Robert, and even her father were surely tempted to try their luck in the goldfields. William junior disappears from the Australian records I have unearthed for the period between their arrival in late 1851 and his marriage fourteen years later. I have not found a single trace of young Robert's movements after they left the *Earl Grey* in Sydney. Sadly for historians, there is remarkably little record of the names and activities of goldminers, in contrast to the detailed information kept on convicts in Australia or slaves in the Americas. But we know that gold lured at least one married man named William Bax. The 'Messages to the Diggings' section of the *Adelaide Observer* in September 1852 included a plea from the wife of a 'William Bax', 'anxious to hear from him as she intends to leave Adelaide for Melbourne'.[28] Bax was a relatively common name. This might have been written by Caroline's mother, or by the wife of one of the several other William Baxes in and around Adelaide at the time. Shreds of evidence do connect the Bax family to the Norwood region, south-east of Adelaide, before they moved to the town of Robe, where Caroline's parents lived out the rest of their lives. A William Bax is listed in the *Biographical Index of South Australians, 1836–1885* as residing in both Norwood and Robe. Later, the births of the two sons of Caroline's sister Esther were registered at Norwood, and her sister Mary would marry a man whose father lived in that area.[29]

Robe, then known as Robetown, occupied the territory of the Buandig peoples. It sits in the large arc of Guichen Bay on the coast of the Great Australian Bight, some 340 kilometres south of Adelaide and about 250 kilometres up the coast from Portland Bay. In the early to mid-1850s this coastal town eclipsed Portland Bay as the main port and supply centre for sheep stations in western Victoria and south-eastern South Australia. Europeans interested in settling arrived only in the 1830s. In 1846 the governor, Frederick Holt Robe, selected it as the main port and administrative centre for the South-East. A rectangular township was then carefully planned in the bay. 'Sea locked on three sides, accessible by land only from the east', it was laid out like an English village, with a village green at its centre and a small grid of streets, five leading up the gentle rise from the seashore intersecting with six running parallel to the bay. Within a few years there were some 20 local families, a population of over 70, and resident 'stonemasons, quarrymen, carpenters, blacksmith, a butcher' and numerous carriers and other transportation workers.[30]

When members of the Bax family arrived in the early to mid-1850s it was a small, bustling town that served as a pastoral port, an administrative centre, and above all a service centre for the growing hinterland of sheep and cattle runs stretching east and over the border and north as far as the Murray River and the Tatiara country. The government resident for the South-East, Captain Charles Philip Brewer, presided over the town from his gracious sandstone house. He was the second military man to hold this position. Brewer had 'served in South Africa, Ireland and Corfu' before sailing to South Australia in 1839 with his wife, four children, a 'collapsible timber house and a milking cow'. Brewer also served as the local magistrate. His other duties included distributing rations of flour and meat and blankets to local Aboriginal people to prevent them starving – awful testimony to the profound disruption settler colonists were making to their former ways of life. The gold rush offered some reprieve. Aboriginal men and women moved into positions as shepherds and bullock drivers, vacated by men departing for the goldfields, surprising some colonists with their valuable contributions.[31]

The region's courthouse, customs officer, police station and barracks were in Robe. By the 1850s, residents and visitors could find pubs, hotels, a few shops and later a gaol, school and a telegraph office.[32] The town lots sold quickly. Houses built from the attractive golden limestone quarried in the area began to give an air of permanency to the place: a stark contrast to other shacks, and the rows of bullock-drawn carts carrying wool bales along the rough track that became known as Victoria Street to the offices of its leading merchant and the port. Despite its 'oft-noticed atmosphere of an English village', I imagine it seemed new, rough, raw and utterly different from Cuckfield and the other ancient villages in which Caroline and her family had lived.[33]

I have found no traces of how Caroline's father made a living over their first years in the colony. Nor can I pin down exactly when they arrived in Robe. William's mathematical skills and experience as an excise officer in England could have opened up job possibilities in what was then South Australia's second most important port. Robe needed men with his credentials and experience. However, colonial coffers could only support one full-time customs officer, and that position was already filled. William turned instead to teaching. In 1858 he was officially appointed to replace Betty Hamshaw as Robe's only licensed teacher. Her marriage had made her ineligible to continue in the role.[34]

The town grew rapidly as the number of sheep stations sending their wool to the port increased. More and more people opened businesses and services for the squatters and the growing number of men, women and children who lived in and around the town. Within months there were 30 boys and girls attending the school 'under the superintendence of Mr. and Mrs. Bax' – though government pay rates did not recognise the contributions of wives in such teaching teams. Robe historian Kathleen Bermingham reports that William's annual stipend was £60. At least one newspaper report considered it an 'excellent preparatory school', noting funding support from the government. Caroline's parents are said to have also held evening classes for illiterate adults.[35]

The Baxes' school sat 'on the rise to the side-rear of the first house in Syleham', fronting the main route into town, Victoria Street. Syleham was one of three new subdivisions, then referred to as 'villages'. As the town expanded, men who had been granted land around the original central area profited by subdividing and laying out lots on tracks that awkwardly joined and extended existing streets. The lots sold at auction in late 1858. William Bax purchased a lot, and probably built its first residence – the typical early settler's cottage that still sits there today. Soon they started adding more space so they could accommodate a small number of boarding pupils.[36] Mrs Bax's daughters surely helped their mother with the additional cooking, washing and domestic labour that housing live-in students entailed.

Bermingham writes that William Bax was 'not brilliant, but gave his pupils a good grounding in the 3 R's'. Captain Brewer, in his capacity as school inspector, was more generous. He noted that the organisation, supply of requisites, quality of instruction and discipline were all good. Bermingham also reports that Bax was one of the town's 'Red coats', and that every afternoon after school, he donned his red military coat and marched the children out to the Fellmongery Corner before dismissing them. 'Military training and military bearing' mattered to him.[37] This is puzzling, as I have found no evidence that William Bax ever served in any military capacity. Such very British behaviour was hardly likely to endear him to his future son-in-law, Edward Kearney, whose eldest son later described as 'hating all English'.[38]

⁂

Around the time that Caroline arrived in Australia, Edward Kearney began working the lease known then as Campion's

28

Run on the Mosquito Plains in the South-East district of South Australia. This land lies close to where the old Padthaway homestead still sits today. Padthaway was the name Robert Lawson, the most successful pastoralist in the area, gave to his station. After Robe was developed as a port, squatters from stations on the 'Mosquito Plains and the intervening country' as well as western Victoria took their wool clips there rather than to Portland for export to London. They left with six months' to a year's worth of supplies. Local historian Alan Jones reminds us that 'these early sheep stations were very isolated and had to be almost completely independent'.[39] The 120-kilometre ride on horseback or bullock wagon south-west to Robe from Edward's lease was shorter than attempting to travel to the colony's capital, Adelaide, over 300 kilometres to the north-west, or to Portland Bay. Robe's most prominent merchant, George Ormerod, who soon monopolised the wool export trade, held several leases on the Mosquito Plains, including one close to Campion's Run and another that later became the town of Naracoorte. When Edward arrived on the plains, Ormerod had recently moved permanently to Robe, married and was devoting his attention to his growing complex of businesses there.[40]

In Robe, the government resident took care of legal and political matters. Ormerod was vital to the town's and region's economy. His entrepreneurial energy boosted Robe's expansion. Virtually every bale of wool and other merchandise passed through the hands of George Ormerod's company. He built a jetty when government attempts were slow, monopolised imports and exports, and after 1857 owned the *Ant*, an early iron screw steamship that traded along the coast and played an important role in the development of trade in South Australia, Tasmania and Victoria.[41] Ormerod purchased numerous sections in Robe, in addition to those that he held on the Mosquito Plains and elsewhere in the colony. He was at the heart of the complex networks of trade, lending, borrowing and social and cultural connections of the wider area. Cash was scarce. Before the first bank opened in 1859, his 'company's promissory notes constituted perhaps 40 per cent of the currency used in the region'.[42]

By all accounts Ormerod was both an excellent businessman and a kind, caring and generous person. It was 'not uncommon for him to grant free passage on his ships to people with little money, including clergymen of all denominations, and he was said to carry many of his clients through hard times'. He earned the confidence, custom and 'respect of South Australian settlers'.[43] Caroline and Edward's brother-in-law, James Charles Hamilton, recalled in later life that Robe 'was a great business centre in those days, and Ormerod was the reigning Monarch'.[44] Ormerod's centrality to commerce and his ownership of land on the Plains placed him in a position to inform Kearney that Campion planned to return to Ireland, so that the lease to his run was available. Both Edward Kearney's future brothers-in-law, James Allen and James Hamilton, already resident in the area, might have also passed on such news.[45]

Perhaps Ormerod introduced Edward to the Bax family. He and Captain Brewer, the government resident, both liked to welcome newcomers of standing to town. Caroline's future neighbour Frances Jones harboured fond memories of the reception the Ormerods gave her and her husband, Henry, when they arrived in Robe in 1857. Finding domestics and potentially brides for the single male settlers of the South-East was definitely among his many interests. A few years after Caroline arrived, Ormerod was involved in caring for 80 women who were sent to Robe as part of a broader South Australian scheme to set up depots for the large number of single migrant women arriving in the colony. They were chaperoned by the wife of one of his employees, guarded by the police, sheltered in one of his wool stores and the courthouse, and then distributed on bullock wagons – like commodities – to stations across the area, including on the Mosquito Plains.[46]

Robe was a marriage market too! In 1853 Eleanor was 21, Caroline nineteen, Esther seventeen and young Mary sixteen. Bachelor squatters would have received word of the newly arrived Bax family and their four daughters. There were 165 men but only 95 women aged 21 to 44 in the whole of Robe County, which stretched from the Victoria border to the coast and north through the Mosquito Plains, and many of these women were already married.[47] Within a decade of arriving in Australia, the three eldest Bax girls would marry men who ran stations in Robe's hinterland and shipped their wool and secured their supplies there. Caroline's, Esther's and Eleanor's husbands had all spent many years as bachelors, working their leases, seeking gold and accumulating land, cattle, sheep and experience before deciding to marry. Edward Kearney was fifteen years older than Caroline. James Allen was 21 years older than Esther. Eleanor, in contrast, remained single longer. She was 29 when she married James Hamilton in 1860. He was five years her junior, but had many years of experience as the son of a pioneering family. Mr Ormerod's wife, Mary, was only seventeen when she married the 27-year-old George. Frances Eliza Caton was also seventeen when she agreed to marry 43-year-old Henry Jones of Binnum Station and leave Wales to join him on the Mosquito Plains. Such large age differences were not as unusual then as they would become in the 20th century. Still, they heightened the power differentials and challenges of married life.[48]

Kearney had migrated to the colonies some ten years before he met Caroline. He left Ireland before blight hit Irish potato crops in 1845 intensifying the long history of exploitation, misery and hunger among tenant farmers and leading to widespread starvation and death. Relatively few Irish migrated voluntarily to Australia then. Voyages to the United States or British North America were shorter, cheaper and often subsidised or paid by landlords keen to rid themselves of unwanted tenants.[49] Some were sent as convicts. Others were assisted by the emigration commissioners of one colony or another. Edward does not appear among these two groups of well-documented migrants. Indeed, locating verifiable information on exactly when he migrated has proved challenging. His death certificate and later court evidence place his arrival in 1843.[50]

Edward, like so many Irish emigrants, came from a tenant farming family. Yet unlike many of his countrymen, his family had done reasonably well. In County Westmeath, where he and his siblings were born and raised, the land was better than in many parts of Ireland. Cattle rearing and beef exports along with textile production from this region helped feed and clothe the growing urban working classes of British cities. Landlords rewarded good tenants with long-term leases. The Kearneys were 'strong' farmers – that small minority of families who had the security of long-term leases because their productivity benefitted their landlords.[51] Edward's father, William, and then his elder brothers had accumulated leases to a growing number of agricultural plots around Athlone as well as holding some sections in the town. Williamstown, the farm named after his father, was in the townland of Ballykeeran, to the north-east of the town of Athlone. They leased it from Lord Castlemaine, the main local landowner and politician. An 1837 Ordnance Survey map shows a substantial farmstead and three outbuildings facing onto a common farmyard.[52] This was probably Edward's birthplace. Dwellings on the farms of tenants of their status were usually well built and might be two storeys high, with stone walls and roofs made of slate rather than thatch.[53]

So Edward was not a poverty-stricken Irish tenant farmer, but he was the third son. His father, William, died in November 1825 when Edward was just five and a half years old. His mother, Mary (née Mulrain), raised at least eight children beyond childhood. Incomplete baptismal records mean that there may have been others who did not survive and that their exact ages are unclear. Edward definitely had two elder sisters, Bridget, born around 1809, and Mary, who was baptised in January 1814 but born earlier. His two elder brothers, Francis and William, were both baptised later in 1814. Edward was baptised in June 1820, Joseph in May 1822 and Patrick in 1823. Mary's youngest child, Margaret, was born in the year their father died. Mary Kearney became a widow while still in her early thirties, with eight young children to raise.[54]

It was important to keep the farm productive if they were to retain their lease with Lord Castlemaine. Francis and William would have already worked alongside their father as they moved into their teens. They could play their part in the family labour that kept such farms going. Hired herders spanned labour deficits until the sons were able to take over.[55] William Kearney senior's death might diminish their chances of securing more good leases to set up all the boys on the land. Yet it also meant that Edward's older brothers, Francis and William, could become independent, marry and take control of the lease and homestead while still quite young, rather than waiting until middle to late life, as elder sons of Irish farmers often had to do.[56] The widow Mary and William junior retained the lease on the properties surrounding Williamstown. William remained single until the age of 30. Francis, in contrast, married at 20 in 1834. He either took over or secured the lease to a farm named Renaun in Ballinahown wood to the south-east of Athlone. The family genealogist reports that the couple lived in Athlone for a while, perhaps while the Renaun house was being built on the farm. That property has been passed down through generations of Francis's descendants, proof of the capacity of such strong farming families to 'continue in occupation of the same holding over a number of generations'.[57] The growing commercialisation of agriculture, the significance of exports from such areas and the resultant exposure to overseas price fluctuations left even such relatively privileged farm families vulnerable to economic swings well before the Great Famine dramatised the colonial economy's dangerous fragilities in the 1840s.

Edward's departure left one less mouth to feed. He was in his early twenties when he headed for Australia around 1843.[58] Some personal issue, trouble with the law, or particular dreams or demons may have precipitated his move. Some of the Kearney boys were heavy drinkers, quick to use their fists and physical force to settle arguments or apply rough justice. Excessive drunkenness, dangerous use of firearms and several assaults in the community led several Kearney brothers into brushes with the police.[59] In the rough local economy of words and blows, they were probably little more or less prone to violent behaviour than most of their neighbours. Some such occasion that got out of hand may have precipitated Edward's departure. Most likely he left as a 'superfluous son': Irish farmers sought to avoid subdividing their holdings. Francis and William were established. Edward was highly unlikely to inherit, or to earn access to the leases necessary to maintain the standard of living he hoped for. Migration to Australia offered the promise of land and better material prospects.[60]

Unlike Caroline, Edward migrated alone. His siblings remained in Ireland, most within County Westmeath. His invisibility among the carefully listed assisted immigrants like the Baxes suggests he was among that small minority of Irish migrants who could afford to pay their own way.[61] He might well have been the

Mr Edward Kerney (sic) who sailed to Australia on the *Haidee* in 1842. It left Belfast on 1 May and London on 9 May and arrived in Hobart, Tasmania, on 30 August that year. A year later there was an Edward Kearney managing a property for the prominent Tasmanian pastoralist Simeon Lord junior. His workforce comprised at least eighteen men, including former and current male convicts on tickets of leave employed as shepherds, stockmen and general labourers on the property. Edward Kearney's common name and the lack of any concrete corroborating evidence make it impossible to know if this was the man that Caroline later married. Yet it seems likely. In such a position the skills he had learned farming and raising stock in County Westmeath would serve him well. Later, Hobart newspapers reported on Edward's purchase of a sheep station in Victoria, which suggests that he was known in Tasmania.[62]

To move from manager to owner of a run, Edward had to secure significant funding. Henry Jones suggested that a minimum of £6000 capital would provide a good down payment on an existing station, allowing that amount again to be paid off over four or five years.[63] In 1851, gold made all dreams seem possible. Surely Edward was tempted. One lucky find could furnish some of the capital needed to start farming independently. If he went to the diggings, he, like so many others, left no traces in the documents that have survived. If he struck it lucky, he used it well. In 1853, while many men were still seeking their fortunes in gold, Edward Kearney looked to sheep and the land for his future. The first time we can pin him down with certainty is in 1853 as the owner of Campion's sheep run in the South-East region of South Australia, near where the town of Padthaway is today. Sheep were gold on legs. Prices and demand had soared with the gold rush. His lease was not far from the border and the routes to the diggings in Victoria.[64]

South Australia was established in 1835, centred on Adelaide. The founders of the South Australian Association were strongly influenced by the humanitarian movement sweeping England. The slave trade within the empire had been successfully abolished and now they sought to protect Indigenous peoples from the worst ravages of colonialism and to encourage conversion to Christianity. Unlike in other Australian colonies, Aboriginal peoples in South Australia were designated legally as British subjects.

Following the principles of Edward Gibbon Wakefield, the sale of land to settlers was supposed to finance the migration of a population of small yeoman farmers. Settlers would in turn fund their land purchases by working initially as wage labourers. They would bring wives or marry in the colonies.[65] This yeoman farmer ideal never worked in the Australian colonies. This was as clear in this south-eastern part of the colony as elsewhere on the continent. In 1838 legislation allowed farmers to take out leases on the lands from which local Aboriginal peoples had secured their food for centuries. Soon European occupiers were running sheep on vast tracts of land.[66] Prior to 1850, licences involved only a small fee but the government could take back the land and put it up for sale. Aspirant pastoralist squatters, overrepresented in the colony's legislative council, had some success in making tenure more secure, without requiring purchase. Legislation in 1851 replaced occupation licences with fourteen-year leases secured at an annual rental of between ten shillings and one pound an acre, depending on the quality of the pastures. In return for such a lease, squatters were obliged to stock each square mile with sixteen cattle or 100 sheep.[67]

It was two years after this change in the ways pastoral land was secured, and the careful mapping of boundaries that it initiated, that Edward was working the lease numbered Run 156, commonly known as Campion's Run. Roland Campion was also an Irish immigrant. He had grazed sheep there in the late 1840s and secured the lease in 1851. It occupied 88 square kilometres at the north-eastern end of the Mosquito Plains – later renamed the Padthaway Plains. This region sits to the east of the broad, swampy plain that stretches inland from the lagoons, sand hills and marshes of the Coorong Coast, east of the rows of low coastal inclines left by former seashores, and just to the west of the rolling hills that stretch eastward to the border with Victoria. It merges to the north with the dryer area known as the Tatiara, or 'good country'. The Tatiara straddles both sides of the border between Victoria and South Australia. Later, Caroline and Edward will move to the other side.[68]

Edward Kearney arrived in the area too late to choose prime land in the 1851 scramble for leases. On the Mosquito Plains, as throughout the South-East region, men who arrived in the 1840s had identified and claimed the best stretches of country. George Ormerod, Robert Lawson, William McIntosh and John Robertson had owned or worked leases in the area for a decade. All were immigrants from Scotland. All made sure to formalise their holdings when the fourteen-year leases were initiated in 1851. Because squatters drew their own boundaries to incorporate the better bits of land, the resulting maps resemble crazy patchworks of oddly shaped properties. Some of today's roads follow those old property lines. Robert Lawson formalised his claim to lease 157, which bordered on Campion's Run, number 156. James Allen, future husband of Caroline's sister Esther, took up number 154, then known as Swede's Flat – about 10 kilometres north-east of Campion's run – as well as co-ownership of Mount Monster, to the north-west.[69] Newcomers interested in farming in the area would have few good choices, unless they could purchase an existing run.[70] (See image 2 in the picture section for a map of Tatiara Country, Mosquito Plains and Robetown, showing Edward's and James Allen's leases.)

Edward was lucky. Campion appears to have sold him his run when he decided to return to Ireland around August 1853. It is possible that Edward had already worked for him as a supervisor or manager for a while. It was a good time to raise sheep. This was pretty good grazing land – dryer than most of the Mosquito Plains and indeed most of the South-East region. Campion had cleared enough trees and scrub by 1848 to run 4000 sheep and some 70 cattle. A gold find, a mortgage from George Ormerod or both may have placed it within Edward's reach. From then on Edward was recognised as being in charge of the lease in correspondence and in newspaper reports, though the official listing of leaseholders was never updated to include his name.[71] He and the other squatters of the area travelled the long journey to Robe once or twice a year to arrange export of their wool clips, secure supplies, dispatch letters, connect with other squatters, down a pint or more, 'let their hair down' and perhaps even find a wife.[72]

Many pioneers ran stations for a while without a helpmate, wife or family. It was hard work to establish a run and build even the rudimentary huts from bark, twigs or rough timber that served as the earliest dwellings. But life on the isolated stations on the late frontier could be eased by the presence of a woman. Wives promised female companionship, domestic comforts, good cooking and sex. They could tend gardens and care for cows or pigs, freeing men up to patrol their borders, keep track of their sheep and construct fences and buildings. In 1853 Edward was 34 years old. Like many Irish immigrants, he likely waited to marry until he had 'decided to stay in Australia', 'felt like settling down', and had 'sufficient wealth to keep a wife and family' in the style he wished. Many Irish immigrants married much younger women. If he looked anything like his sons, he was a dashing man with an aquiline nose, dark hair and piercing blue eyes. His eldest son later described him as a man of contradictions – 'good hearted to the last degree … but … if he was thwarted on anything, he would be as obstinate as the native animal of his own country (pig)'.[73]

Somewhere he and Caroline Bax crossed paths. Did this older Irishman sweep the nineteen-year-old Caroline off her feet? Seduce her – emotionally, sexually, or both? Much later his brothers claimed that the couple married in 1853. I have found no official record of their union. No registration. No newspaper announcement. Though this is not very surprising, it still puzzles me. Historian of Irish migration to Australia David Fitzpatrick has noted that many alliances 'were never recognized by church or state, and that these irregularities had to be veiled from upright Irish readers'.[74] In Margaret Kiddle's superb study of the squatting period in the western district of Victoria, she argues that many 'men died and were buried without benefit of clergy, the form of marriage was often dispensed with, and children remained unbaptized'.[75] Ministers were rare in such new areas of colonisation. And yet there were visiting ministers and occasionally a priest in Robe at the time. The town's only doctor acted as the registrar of marriages. Local historian Roland Campbell reports that in 1853 he married three couples whom the registrar-general then refused to accept. A mixed marriage – as unions of Protestants and Catholics were called – could provoke such a response. If Caroline and Edward were among them, this might explain the lack of evidence of their marriage.[76]

Later, Edward's brother William presented a different account of their union from Caroline's. William Kearney claimed that Edward had been 'married first by a Protestant, then by Catholic clergy'. Caroline's rebuttal that they were married by a minister

39

of the Established Church and that there was no subsequent Catholic marriage seems more credible. This was her family's denomination and there were more Anglican ministers in the area than Catholic priests. Mixed marriages were widely discouraged by Protestant ministers, Catholic priests and often parents too. Catholics considered them scandalous. Some bishops refused to allow them. At the very least it would have required a special dispensation and Caroline's conversion. None of this was easy anywhere, let alone on the frontier. Anyway, Edward apparently 'cared very little about' 'cultivating the faith of his fathers', in his early years in the colony, so it is unlikely that he insisted on a Catholic marriage.[77] The very English and Protestant William Bax may well have disapproved of his daughter's union with an Irish Catholic. However, she was a minor, and he had to give his consent.[78] Perhaps the lack of publicity is not an accident. Catholic–Protestant conflict was as virulent in the Australian colonies as in England and elsewhere. A quiet wedding would keep this 'mixed marriage' out of the public eye for a while.

William Bax did not set any property or money aside for Caroline in a pre-nuptial agreement, as wealthy fathers often did. He presumably provided some furniture, plates and other household items to set up the new couple. Edward may well have expected a more significant dowry. In Ireland, parents gave marriage portions to their daughters well into the 20th century to help with setting up their new households or purchasing farms.[79] Unless William Bax had been lucky in the goldfields, it is unlikely that in their two years in the colony he had accumulated much to launch any of his four daughters in married life. Nor might it matter. With twice as many single men as women in the county of Robe there was no shortage of men seeking wives.[80] Women's assets were their domestic skills, labour power, and ability to produce children and potential heirs.

Caroline never achieved the independent legal status that single woman over the age of 21 attained. On marriage she ceased to be a minor, legally subject to the wishes of her father, and became subject to Edward's. As a wife her identity and rights were subsumed, buried, in his. The technical term applied to wives' legal state – *coverture* – captures this covered state of identity. So too the British custom of referring to them by their husband's name – Mrs Edward Kearney or, worse, simply Mrs Kearney. 'Husband and wife are one person ... the husband is that person', the great English jurist Blackstone is said to have explained. Marriage to Edward meant that anything Caroline already owned, anything she might earn through her own labour and any wealth they accumulated together belonged to him. In South Australia Caroline would be just as subject to these common law rules of husband and wife as her mother had been in England.[81]

This did not change across the British Empire until the 1870s and 1880s, and in South Australia until 1884, when legislation allowed wives to keep their own property separate. But few married women had much property or earned wages then. Wives would not have a claim on assets accumulated during their marriage until the 1970s. Marriage law thus served as a powerful instrument of male accumulation. Men gained more than ownership of the fruits of their wives' labour, their earnings and property at marriage. The law made them owners of their wives' bodies – and hence gave them the right to all the services those bodies performed, including domestic labour, sex and the children they produced. Edward would later exercise those rights fully when he wrote the will that sought to extradite his whole family from Australia.

For now, Caroline's future was largely in his hands. She would learn more about this man she had married as they settled into their new life together on his lease on the remote Mosquito Plains of South Australia.

# 2

# Broom Station, Mosquito Plains, South Australia, 1853–57

Two years since leaving the medieval town of Cuckfield with its ancient church, footpaths, bridleways and turnpikes. Months and months of ocean voyage, turbulent coastal sailing and rough, body-shaking, headache-inducing travel on tracks and trails over vast distances of unfamiliar, empty-looking land-scapes. Everywhere strange, noisy birds and odd-looking animals. So many changes. And now, at nineteen, a new life ahead as wife, pioneer and probably mother. A husband. Another new home. The trip to the forebodingly named Mosquito Plains. How would Caroline negotiate the complicated gender, sexual and emotional relations of marriage with Edward, a man fifteen years her senior and with vastly different life experience? Would there be churches there? Neighbours? Female company?[1]

And what of the dangers of life on the frontier where Edward's run was located? Caroline had been in the colony long enough to hear settlers' horror stories about fires, bushrangers, ex-convicts and other male marauders who terrorised the occupiers of the rough outback country. Long enough too to know about violent murders of Indigenous people by colonisers who almost always got off scot-free. Her uncle, Robert Steele, must have regaled her family with his own largely positive stories of the Aboriginal men and women whom he employed to tend his ewes at lambing time and the youths who had served them on several stations. Perhaps they had all laughed together over the tale that his family shared over the years and memorialised after his death: 'Mrs Steele was left alone in the bark-roofed hut they first had on the station. A wild black fellow, in a state of nature, came into the room, and catching sight of himself in the looking-glass, looked behind it several times, cautiously, and then not solving the mystery of the *alter ego*, executed a war whoop and a jump, and cleared away, to the intense relief of Mrs Steele.' Stories of encounters both friendly and violent circulated widely. They furthered European convictions about the superiority of their civilisation and the inferiority of Aboriginal peoples and their cultures.[2] In England Caroline's whiteness was commonplace, unremarkable. Here it marked her as different from this continent's many first peoples, homogenised most frequently simply as 'blacks'. Caroline's sense of herself and her identity would shift as she began thinking of herself as a white, civilised Australian settler and a frontier wife.

Marriage led her far from civilisation.[3] Caroline and Edward would have travelled to her new home on horseback or in a wagon or dray pulled by bullocks. Horse-drawn carriages could not navigate the rough terrain from Robe to Edward's lease on the Mosquito Plains. A few years later, Frances Jones decided she would much rather 'go up country' slowly, but surely in a dray, than in a four-in-hand horse-drawn carriage driven by her husband. He was 'a wild and reckless driver'. So was Edward.[4] Rough networks of trails crisscrossed the region, worn by graziers droving sheep and stock, riding their horses and driving their bullock carts between and across the stations and to Robe and back. Some became well-travelled routes to gold rush sites across the border and, in later times, roads. Most were little more than tracks.[5] Dry, dusty and rutted in hot weather, the tracks of south-eastern South Australia turned to bog or flooded completely after rain. When the surveyor-general sought to map the station boundaries and tracks of the region, he was utterly frustrated by the 'impassable roads', the submerged flats and the damage they wrought on his bullocks and carts alike.[6] In a bullock-pulled cart Caroline and Edward would be lucky to make it in a week or two. Riding, they might make it in three to four days.[7]

The tracks to the Mosquito Plains skirted swamps, traversed 'desolate, jolting, never-ending' flats, and crossed low, scrubby limestone ridges and high tussocks of grass. Travel demanded constant bowing and bobbing to avoid overhanging branches that could knock you off a dray or horse. To Caroline, used to the dense networks of farms in south-east England, the swamps, the vast, apparently unpeopled spaces, the eucalyptus trees, strange scrub and grasses, the noisy birds, black swans and kangaroos must have seemed bizarre. Like her contemporary Frances Jones, she surely found it remarkable that they went 'for miles and miles', without hearing any 'sound of human voices save their own', with hardly a dwelling in sight.[8]

Maps from that time show several tracks from Robe to the Mosquito Plains (see maps, picture section, images 2 and 4). The most direct followed the mail route north from Robe towards Mount Benson, then north-east, dividing near James Brown's station, Avenue Range. A northern branch traversed the upper edge of the Mosquito Plains, crossing Edward's lease and then James Allen's before swinging up into the Tatiara country and to the border with Victoria. A more southerly branch headed less sharply north then eastward, passing through George Ormerod's former main holding on the plains, Naracoorte. From there several tracks led north-west, crossing Robert Lawson's lease just to the east of Kearney's run before hooking up with trails into the Tatiara.[9] Edward would have chosen which route to follow. By then he knew how to avoid the soggiest sections, and where to stop for food, to refresh his animals, and to camp. He would decide whether he wished to stop at particular stations and introduce Caroline to other squatters or seek overnight shelter and hospitality. Where there were no inns, station owners expected to feed and shelter passing travellers.

All routes traversed the lands of Aboriginal peoples. North of Robe they passed from the territory of the Buandig peoples, which covered much of this southern part of the south-east, and into that of the Meintangk or Ngarrindjeri peoples. Their lands stretched north up the Coorong coast and inland across the swamps, wet fields and scrubby rises east towards Naracoorte. To colonisers' eyes much of this area seemed barren, hopeless for farming.[10] For the local Ngarrindjeri peoples the coast, inland lagoons and scrub had long provided abundant food. As the summer's good fishing dwindled, the weather worsened and some areas flooded, they moved inland and onto the Mosquito Plains to hunt and gather. Caroline and Edward would meet some of them there later.[11] Inland, their winter excursions led at times to conflict with other tribes, including the Bindjali peoples on whose ancestral lands Edward's lease sat. Their homelands included the Mosquito Plains stretching 'north to Tatiara, Bordertown, Wirrega, and Keith' and east into the Wimmera country. They were also known as Bedaruwidj, or Potaruwutj, names that mean 'wandering' or 'travelling' men. Tindale, the influential early-20th-century South Australian ethnographer, described these Indigenous Australians as 'highly nomadic', living in 'constantly shifting campings' in the low scrubby areas of mallee eucalyptus trees, supporting themselves in good times on the abundant food sources in this area.[12]

Caroline would soon be mistress of a station in a colony and region in which Indigenous peoples had been exposed to new diseases, hunted, raped and murdered. Their sources of food were rapidly disappearing as settlers transformed the land to graze their sheep. They were renegotiating their relationships to the colonisers, to the land, to other groups and to each other as well as their ways of providing for themselves. It was not yet five years since James Brown had shot and killed nine Aboriginal men, women and children, angered by his ongoing loss of sheep and cattle from Avenue Range station. Despite solid evidence against him Brown had been acquitted because the only testimonies came from 'Blacks'. This brutal massacre became 'part of the frontier folklore of South Australia's South East'.[13] When Caroline arrived it was raw, recent history. Closer to her new home, their neighbour Robert Lawson had set up an Aboriginal station on his run sometime after his arrival.[14] Just one year earlier a 'hostile tribe' attacked eight Aboriginal men, women and children living there, raping and abducting the women and killing at least four people. Caroline had surely heard of these tragic events. That attack troubled one local settler enough to write to the colonial secretary seeking justice for the wronged group. He pointedly argued that as South Australia had proclaimed its Indigenous peoples British subjects, they had 'a right to its benefits'. Instead, they seemed only to 'endure the wrongs of British law'.[15] His was one of few such voices.[16]

❧❀❧

The rolling, grassy Mosquito Plains were surely a welcome sight for Caroline. The 'low hills and extensive plains without any timber, exquisitely green and luxuriant', and 'the grey curling smoke of household fires' certainly pleased Frances Jones.[17] Here, sheep and cattle grazed on tall native grasses and swamp reeds among the she-oak, honeysuckle and blackwood trees. The

English promoter of agriculture Ebenezer Ward imagined cantering pleasantly across this 'well-grassed and lightly-timbered country', so evidently 'good grazing country'.[18]

At the heart of the plains was Ormerod's former lease, Naracoorte, by then owned by Thomas Margery. Nearby, William McIntosh had built a store and an inn, anticipating a growing population in the area. He then founded a small township which he named Kincraig, after his birthplace in Scotland. Here Caroline and Edward might have stopped to take a cup of tea, have a drink, refresh their horses or spend the night. It was hardly an English village. Like so many early townships across Australia it comprised little more than the inn, the store, a blacksmith's establishment and a few huts. The Merino Inn was so unimpressive from a distance that Frances Jones mistook it for a hut. The tea was so awful she didn't drink much of it.[19] But this was the closest cluster of buildings to Padthaway and to Edward's lease. Fifty more kilometres and Caroline would see her new home.

The track from Naracoorte ran north-west on the slightly higher ground where the eastern edge of the plains meets the rolling hills. Today the Riddoch Highway follows the same route through Padthaway, Robert Lawson's lease. It stretched up the gentle slopes rising from the plains, avoiding some of the worst flooding that plagued the whole area until massive drainage schemes were initiated in the 1860s. Edward's run abutted on his northern and western boundaries, doubtless wetter, but less so than the rest of the swampy plains. With some clearing this made very good sheep country, except in rainy seasons when the water sat on the land, creating ideal breeding grounds for the mosquitos for which the plains were named and for other diseases that ravaged flocks of sheep. Caroline's brother-in-law James Hamilton thought it 'a good block'.[20] Considering that he was a latecomer to the region, Edward had managed to secure a lease to pretty good land. At only ten shillings per square mile, the lowest rate for leases at the time, the annual rent of £17 was affordable. This rate signalled that the land was considered suitable only for grazing.[21]

The Lawsons would be Caroline's closest neighbours – just under 11 kilometres away. Like so many of the squatters in the area Robert Lawson was a Scot. He arrived in South Australia in 1839 and took up his lease in 1844 after working land near Mount Barker for several years. Four years before Caroline arrived he married Eliza Bell, also born in Scotland. Her father ran the Mount Barker station so, unlike Caroline, she was used to frontier life. Eliza and Robert were made of stern stuff. They are said to have ridden on horseback 'through the wilds of the unknown bush' from Adelaide to the South-East, then lived in a primitive camp at first. In 1850, 6000 sheep and 30 cattle grazed on the Lawsons' 52 square miles (135 square kilometres) lease. When Caroline arrived they had three daughters aged between three months and three years. What a relief to have a female neighbour, though one might well wonder whether this Scot who would be lauded for her 'stamina and grit' would take to the nineteen-year-old Englishwoman and her Irish Catholic husband.[22]

The Lawsons already lived in a 'civilised' stone cottage. Said to be the first in this area, this squat, two-chimney building still stands today, though it is dwarfed by the imposing mansion, Padthaway, which Robert and Eliza had built later. Building a house or homestead to replace the reed huts and camps in which frontier graziers first lived was often the moment when owners gave a name to runs until then identified either by their surname or the number of the lease. Some names evoked memories of home. Others drew on Aboriginal names. Many of these names remain today, attached to small towns or discrete areas. Eliza and Robert chose an Aboriginal name, calling their homestead Padthaway, which meant 'good water'.[23]

Had Edward described the housing that awaited Caroline? She was not moving into a luxurious dwelling. Most local histories suggest that the house on Edward's run was unfinished at this time, and much later too. Perhaps she moved first into a hut. These could be snug, Frances Jones noted, as she travelled to her new home. Some women made them comfortable and attractive, with green baize (a soft woollen material something like felt) on the walls and calico ceilings. One local historian suggests the walls of a solid house were erected in 1856; others date it slightly later. I suspect that Edward was still building a cottage when Caroline arrived. Later photographs show a fairly standard bush dwelling: a four-room house with one front door, two windows and two chimneys. Unlike most station cottages it had no verandah to shelter residents from the bright South Australian sun. Establishing decent dwellings was slow, costly and labour-intensive. One settler's wife related repeatedly putting off plans to build a house. There wasn't 'much time for improving the homesteads', given the other demands of station life. Instead they added rooms to structures, built huts, and joined them with verandahs.[24]

Brothers might help each other build homesteads. James Hamilton's uncle and father had done this when they first took up their two stations in 1846. Edward may have had assistance from his future brother-in-law James Allen. When James and Esther Bax signed their marriage papers in Portland in May 1854, they reported their place of residence as Broom Station, Edward's run. This is the first reference I have found naming Kearney's run Broom Station, rather than Campion's run, a hint at more substantial housing, confirmed perhaps a year later in the mention of a home station on Kearney's lease. James Allen's main run, Swede's Flat, was an easy ride away. I assume the newly married couple moved in with Caroline and Edward for a while. The name did not stick. In later years it was known as Yallamurray.[25]

Caroline began her life as a wife in this isolated setting, in rudimentary housing. Despite their age, religious and cultural differences, she later claimed that her relationship with Edward was initially a happy one. Her son Edward, who remembered later times, was not so sure. Looking back, he wanted to believe that his father was 'a fine man, such a one as any woman with a tender trusting heart could deserve', and 'good hearted to the last degree'. He was a man 'whom a woman could lead to anything if she went about it in a proper way'. He did not believe that his mother had achieved this. Managing her strong-willed, hard-working, hard-drinking Irish husband was one of the major challenges Caroline would face as a new wife.[26]

The arrival of her eigthteen-year-old sister Esther within nine months of settling in on Broom Station offered Caroline companionship and surely pleasure. They might share the tasks and travails of their new roles as mistresses of outback stations, wives and, soon, mothers too.[27] There was much to learn. Equestrian skills were essential to getting around independently. You could not walk to visit neighbours. Neighbours! That ancient middle-English word for people living in proximity fails to evoke the 100-mile (160-kilometre) rides some women made to visit women on other stations, and to welcome newcomers.[28] My hunch is that Caroline and Esther were already competent riders. If not, they would soon have learned. Gardening skills mattered too. Vegetables and fruit would not travel well from Robe and were unlikely among the array of goods that the hawkers who crisscrossed the plains sold. Little about the climate of Mosquito Plains resembled south-eastern England. The seasons were topsy-turvy. Local almanacs offered horticultural wisdom in sections curtly advising what should be done month by month on the farm, in the 'kitchen garden', the flower garden or the vineyard. They might proffer hope or despair. January advice included to sow cabbage seeds and cauliflower in 'shaded situations', sow celery seed, 'keep marrows, melons and cucumbers clear of weeds, watering when needed. Lift late crops of onions, sow radishes, mustard and cress.' No detailed directions here. No assumptions that anything about the seasons or soils might be unfamiliar! With persistence some women learned to grow roses and other flowers reminding them of home, as well as 'vegetables of every conceivable kind'. With proper care, peach, apricot, apple, pear and plum trees produced abundantly, as well as gooseberries, currants, grapes and other vines.[29]

Caring for fruit trees, growing vegetables and cleaning, preparing or preserving them all took time and knowledge. So did the care of chickens, pigs and cows for food and milk. Milking cows, churning butter or making cheese, even raising pigs or cows, are tasks that Caroline is unlikely to have mastered in the English villages where she grew up. Cuckfield had a butcher, three bakers and numerous grocers. The only store on the Mosquito Plains was McIntosh's, 50 kilometres south. Edward would secure most of the vast supplies of staples the station needed when delivering his wool in Robe. In 1855 their stores included 200-pound (91-kilogram) bags of flour, 90-pound (41-kilogram) bags of sugar, and large quantities of tea and potatoes.[30] Caroline's tasks would include cleaning and sifting sugar, flour, tea and grains for rodent droppings, weevils, husks and other impurities before they could be used. There was no running water. Washing clothes was a herculean task. Meals were cooked on wood-fired stoves, or in open fireplaces. Firewood had to be found, chopped and the fire fed – even on the hottest summer days when temperatures sometimes soared into the high thirties. The rudimentary stoves and open fireplaces used for cooking in frontier dwellings were likely unfamiliar too. These tasks fell mostly to Caroline, assisted perhaps by the wife of one of the station hands.[31]

And there was sex and then babies. The historian Margaret Kiddle notes that wives and mothers on some stations insisted on family prayer. They were, she suggests, particularly in need of prayer. 'Not only were there blacks, bushrangers, fires, snakes, and all manner of real and fancied dangers to contend with; there were also their own life processes.' Many children were born without medical assistance, or even the help of other women.[32] I imagine the two sisters, Caroline and Esther, helping each other through their pregnancies, morning sickness, miscarriages and the births and care of successive children. Their sister Eleanor, later widely respected for her skill as a midwife, may well have come up from Robe to help. Local Aboriginal women might have assisted too, sharing birth practices and sometimes standing in as wet nurses.

Pregnancies, births and babies would shape Caroline's and Esther's adjustments to life and work on the plains. Caroline's first child was born on 7 November 1854. Local newspapers announced the birth of 'Maria Ellen Kearney to Mrs. Edward Kearney of Brown's station (sic), Mosquito Plains'.[33] Esther was by then pregnant with James, who was born in February 1855. Shortly after his birth Caroline was pregnant again with Edward junior. He arrived in February 1856. Within a month or two Esther was also again pregnant. Charles Joseph was born in September that year, followed quickly by Caroline's second son, Frank, in November. Five cousins born in a two-year period! Kiddle suggests that 'the first few children were welcomed, but as one year of struggle succeeded another weary mothers feared not only the birth itself but the extra work and anxiety afterwards'.[34] Every pregnancy and birth raised worries. Deaths in childbirth were common. Living conditions, diseases and diverse dangers meant that many newborns and children failed to survive. In late December 1855, Eliza Lawson's little Mary died at the age of eight months.[35]

Eliza, Caroline, Esther and their children contributed to the transformation of this area from one occupied by Aboriginal peoples, then by male European squatters forging enormous sheep runs, 'almost exclusive of women and concerned almost wholly with work', to one that included some women and families.[36] That transformation was slow. When the non-Aboriginal population of the whole county of Robe, from the town up through the Mosquito Plains and north into the Tatiara country, was counted in 1855, enumerators located only 149 children under the age of fourteen. There were fewer than 100 married couples among the area's 532 colonisers. Station workforces remained predominantly male. White wives were understood as essential to the civilisation of these new areas of settlement across the British Empire. They would civilise men, curbing the drinking and fighting and sexual relations with Aboriginal women or each other, and other practices of outback homosocial cultures. Wives' very presence could be read to signal that the colonisers' superior civilisation – rooted in a gendered division of labour, and husbands' power over wives and children – was in place.[37]

James Charles Hamilton remembered Edward as a 'hard-working, industrious man', who would spend all day at 'ordinary station work', come home, have his tea, then go out in the moonlight and 'work till all hours of the night'.[38] Campion had been running around 4000 sheep and ten cattle on Broom prior to selling the lease and probably most of the stock to Edward. Edward expanded the flock. In 1857 he had 6000 sheep. Edward benefitted from the clearing and building that Roland Campion had completed, but it would still take heavy labour and considerable capital to purchase more sheep, complete the house, clear scrub, ringbark and fell the eucalyptus trees, and pay and feed workers, shearers and shepherds and his growing family.[39]

These large stations required both seasonal and permanent hired labour to function. The men of shearing gangs were indispensable seasonal workers. First in importance among permanent workers, Kiddle reports, was a bullock driver, possibly with a wife who could help with cooking and housekeeping. The Kearneys' workers included a Mrs Macfarlane and at least two Aboriginal workers, 'Jemmy and his Lubra', who were described as old servants of both Mr Allen and Mr Kearney.[40] A 'native man' named George was one of his shepherds. Edward shared the prevailing understanding that it was important not to be 'soft' with Aboriginal employees and visitors.[41] He made sure that George and his other employees 'black and white' understood they were not to kill his sheep for the 'natives', and that he would 'discharge them if they killed wethers for rations'. Broom Station was a contact zone in which Caroline, Esther and other women would learn to negotiate the hierarchical relations of gender, class, age and race largely in the domestic sphere of station power dynamics.[42]

⁂

Much of Edward's work took him away from the home station, often for days on end – inspecting his sheep, securing supplies, seeing to other business. Most masters rode around the outstations on their land at least once a week, checking on their sheep and distributing rations to their shepherds. Even at a gallop it could take several days to patrol the perimeter of Broom Station or traverse its ridges and hollows, checking ewes at lambing time, moving them to grassier areas, or making sure all the sheep were herded for shearing. Some squatters' wives learned to help shepherd sheep, drive cattle or cook for the large numbers of men required at shearing times. A few widows in the area ran stations for a while after their husbands died.[43] Caroline's village background, successive pregnancies and childbirths, and the age of her children meant she was unlikely to ride far from the area around the home station for very long.

On 11 April 1855 Edward left Caroline and five-month-old Maria Ellen for several days to see to business. While he was away, a group of 'Coorong natives' camped near the hut where George watched the sheep. When he learned of this on his return, Edward rode out to check. Newspapers reported later that he found 'a party of about forty blacks' slaughtering some wethers fattening for market. Under oath, Edward only mentioned finding several men cooking meat from one sheep they had killed. He was furious. He 'demanded of them the reason that they robbed' him and why they camped on his run without his permission. He was not impressed by the response of a man known as Frank that 'he only took one fellow for he was very hungry'. The group left when Edward threatened to ask George whether he had given them the sheep as they claimed. He then counted the flock and found seven missing. Within days George had lost his job.[44] Edward ignored Frank's hungry plea. He could not accept the possibility that Indigenous peoples might view sheep as 'lawful game', 'just the same as kangaroos, or emus or any animal'. Like many squatters he showed no respect for those clauses of the squatting provisions of 1851 that required their holders to give Aboriginal inhabitants and their descendants 'full and free right' to move across the land, take food and water, build dwellings and hunt birds and animals.[45]

Settlers like Edward saw their leases as confirming their ownership of the land and debated the best ways to prevent Aboriginal people from congregating on their stations. Frank and his companions, like their Ngarrindjeri and Bindjali ancestors, had historically headed inland from their summer camping grounds on the coast to avoid winter weather and flooding. Old pathways linked summer camps with winter foraging areas.[46] Now they were hungry. Indigenous ways of managing the land through the judicious use of fire, which facilitated travelling, hunting and the regrowth of plants used for food and medicine, had been curtailed. Settlers disrupted the habitat of their traditional food sources and sought to exterminate others. Kangaroos and sheep did not mix well. Two kangaroos could eat as much grass as three sheep; squatters trapped or shot them. Some paid Aboriginals sixpence a head to kill them and gave them guns and ammunition to do so – guns to wipe out one of their own main sources of food.[47] Guns that some settlers would later regret handing over. Guns some settlers would use to kill Aboriginal interlopers.[48]

Caroline and her sister (Esther, I presume, though it might have been Eleanor) were alone two days later when some of the Ngarrindjeri returned. Their visitors were armed 'not only with spears and other weapons ... but also with guns and pistols'. Coquata, known to settlers as King Henry, demanded food from the two women. They replied that they 'could not afford to feed so many'. Newspapers report that after 'threatening some injury to Mrs Kearney' and much swearing 'the females being unprotected at the moment were obliged to comply with their demands'. Caroline may have actively chosen to share food with them. Newspaper reporters were not keen to recognise female agency. The group then moved on to Swede's Flat, Esther and James Allen's station, unsuccessfully seeking more supplies there. The following night they returned to Broom Station. On this third visit there was no confrontation. Their arrival and departure went unnoticed. The next day, Caroline discovered that several slabs that protected their food store had been moved and that a bag of flour weighing some 91 kilograms, a bag and a half of sugar weighing about 40 kilograms and some tea and potatoes were missing.[49]

No reporters came to the scene. Newspaper information was based on testimony Edward gave later, and perhaps on conversations with him, Caroline, Esther or James Allen. Reporters shaped their stories to suit their agendas. The melodramatic press reports were usually entitled 'Depredations of the Blacks'. They deployed gender and the language of civilisation to highlight the dangers that roving Aboriginals posed to squatter families and to women in particular. 'Something must be done,' one report concluded, 'or our wives and families as well as ourselves may fall a sacrifice to their barbarity'. Canadian historian Kathryn McPherson refers to similar stories of First Nations' visits to settler women's homes on the Canadian prairies as 'domestic intrusion narratives'. These 'spatially fixed' white women are shown 'within the domestic sphere' when, in reality, much of their time was spent working outside in gardens and on the land, thus emphasising 'white settler women's claim to domesticity'.[50]

Such vocal and often exaggerated complaints about the risks of Aboriginal 'depredations' were common in South Australia. They failed to acknowledge the numbers of Aboriginal men, women and children whose hunger made Edward's fattened ewes, flour, sugar and tea so welcome.[51] Similar food stories lay behind numerous skirmishes and conflicts between colonisers and Aboriginal peoples across the Australian colonies. They spread understandings of the dangers Aboriginal peoples posed for settlers and fuelled the thread of settler discourse that represented Aboriginal people as hindrances to progress and 'trespassers on European land'. Such selective reporting contributed to what Foster and Nettelbeck refer to as the 'culture of secrecy' that surrounded the frontier war in South Australia in which much of what happened was 'clothed in euphemisms, and the knowledge transmitted with all the accuracy of a Chinese whisper'.[52] One of the widely republished reports concluded that 'these fellows have been getting more abusive and daring every season'. They had stolen from Mr Kearney's stores a year earlier and were taking advantage of 'the temporary absence of the masters or men', to intimidate females to get 'flour etc'. Local residents were said to be considering writing to the lieutenant governor of South Australia to prevent such a 'set of barbarians' from 'using firearms'.[53]

Of course, colonisers' right to use firearms was seldom questioned, whatever the target. On returning to the station the day Caroline discovered the theft, Edward double-checked the losses, then sought vengeance. As he described it under oath, first he sent for 'a native by the name of Paddy Smith', who 'pointed out to me the tracks of six men and told me one … was King Henry'. 'I was well acquainted with five of the six natives whose names were told to me by Paddy Smith.' Appunwoonile, known to Edward as Paddy Smith, was an Aboriginal tracker working with the police.[54] Newspaper reports invariably identified Aboriginal peoples by their European names. Court records offer some sense of how they named themselves. Appunwoonile had skills that Edward did not and on which Edward depended. By reading their tracks he could identify the individuals involved as well as what they were carrying. He could navigate and interpret the land, drawing on the knowledge practices of his people. Trackers acted as cultural intermediaries, translating differences between languages, cultures and world views. They were 'indispensable to the police patrols that worked … to pursue and punish Aboriginal people for attacks on settlers' stock'.[55]

Once he was sure that the thieves were the same people who had killed his sheep, Edward rode to the newly established headquarters for the plains police at Naracoorte to request assistance.[56] One of the key roles of the police was to 'capture Aboriginal people suspected of stock theft and escort the prisoners to the nearest magistrate or police court for trial'.[57] Police Constable Scott arrived at Broom Station. Edward was more determined to play an active role and to punish those involved than worried about leaving Caroline and their daughter again. He packed his firearm and for two days Edward, the trooper Scott, Appunwoonile and another Aboriginal man followed the fleeing party's tracks. They led westward and north for over 100 kilometres towards Salt Creek, the territory of the Ngarrindjeri of the Coorong coast.[58] Edward testified as to what followed.

> On the following Friday we came up with them, a few
> miles behind Thomson Station at a fresh water lagoon. It
> was quite dark at the time on arrival at the Native's Camp.
> I crawled up to the worley and saw the prisoner there ...
> returned and sent Paddy Smith to go and speak with him
> and to bring me word if that was King Henry. He returned,
> said it was, then in company with Scott and the Native
> Smith, went to apprehend him. I told him to stand that
> we would not hurt him he resisted and broke away twice,
> and ran into the lagoon. I ran after him to the edge of the
> Lagoon. Scott and the Native Smith also followed, I being
> in advance ... and knowing that if the Prisoner got into the
> Lagoon we would lose him I fired at him and wounded him
> which caused his detention till the trooper came up.[59]

King Henry's Indigenous name was transcribed as Coquata. Edward had raised his gun and fired at him as he escaped from Appunwoonile's grasp and was seeking to hide in the swamp. Edward could have missed his target; he could also have killed him. Finding this information in the archives was a shock. I hesitated to inform his descendants. I had read widely about frontier violence, but was not expecting to find it in this family whose history I was tracing for other reasons. That I did speaks to how widespread it was. Edward, with masculine bravado, represented his own role as central. He was likely such a good shot that he believed he could be sure of harming rather than killing his mark. Yet one could never be sure. Such 'recklessness' was deplored by Edward Eyre, the British farmer, coloniser, explorer, and later notorious governor of Jamaica, who had depended on Aboriginal skills to survive in his epic explorations of South Australia and beyond. He condemned the attitude that led European settlers in Australia 'to think as little of firing at a Black, as at a bird and which makes the number they have killed, or the atrocities that have attended the deeds, a matter for a tale, a jest or boast at their pothouse revelries'.[60] Whether Edward Kearney bragged or jested about shooting Coquata will remain unknown, though the masculine and racist culture of this pastoralist frontier makes it likely that he did. Such boasts might mitigate the stain of his Irish Catholicism.

His shot injured Coquata's arm, making it easy for the troopers to capture him. Scott charged him with stealing flour and sugar, and escorted him to Robe to appear before the magistrate. Few settlers 'wanted the trouble of a court hearing'. But, just as Edward had not trusted the troopers to catch his man, he deemed his intervention necessary to secure a conviction. Captain Brewer, the Robe resident and magistrate, recorded his testimony on 25 April. Coquata was there listening. Judging that there was insufficient evidence for the theft charge based on Edward's testimony alone, Brewer remanded the case until 10 May to give Edward time to procure witnesses. He also issued arrest warrants for the other Aboriginal men involved.[61]

Meanwhile the injured Coquata languished in Robe's temporary stone gaol, awaiting sentencing. On 10 May, having failed to secure a conviction for the theft of foodstuffs, Edward accused Coquata and Frank of the theft of his sheep. His deposition described finding them cooking the sheep. Depositions by Appunwoonile and trooper Scott described only their pursuit of the culprits. Despite the legislation according Aboriginal peoples the right to move across leases, despite Frank's simple admission of hunger, despite Edward's shooting, this evidence was sufficient to convince Brewer. He convicted Coquata and sentenced him to three months' imprisonment in the Adelaide gaol, with hard labour – the usual punishment at this time for such thefts. For Aboriginal prisoners, time in gaol was devastating. Their health deteriorated. Many could not survive long periods of incarceration. Coquata's status as a British subject offered him no protection in the face of Edward's uncorroborated testimony.[62]

When news of Coquata's injury and conviction reached the protector of Aborigines for South Australia, Matthew Moorhouse, in Adelaide, he was not impressed. This position had been created in the Australian colonies following the recommendations of the humanitarian-influenced 1838 Select Committee Report on Aboriginal Peoples in the British Colonies. Though lacking sensitivity to the wide range of Indigenous cultures across the empire, the British humanitarians driving the investigation were determined to curtail the violence of settlers against the Aboriginal peoples in colonies of settlement.[63] Moorhouse requested an inquiry into Kearney's conduct. He also castigated Captain Brewer for the impropriety of having 'convicted this man with his arm broken, and with a full knowledge of the cause'. Brewer defended himself, asserting that Coquata's arm was healing well under 'the skilful treatment' of the district surgeon when he left Robe for gaol in Adelaide. No inquiry into Edward's conduct was ever instigated. Brewer had successfully delayed and parried this possibility, considering it 'useless', given all the publicity the case had received. Like most European men who committed crimes against Aboriginal people, Edward faced no trial for his shooting.[64] Caroline and Edward's involvement as settlers running sheep on Aboriginal land in this frontier region located them at the heart of Aboriginal strategies of resistance and survival that included stealing sheep or other foodstuffs.[65]

Hungry Aboriginal people were only one source of worry for young station wives like Caroline and Esther in what remained predominantly male space. Vast numbers of unattached men passed through the area. Some gold seekers followed the track heading east from Salt Creek inland across the Mosquito Plains, past their neighbour Lawson's station and on to the border. Newspaper readers were warned that this route was not 'safe for travellers unaccustomed to the Bush'. Kincraig and Naracoorte expanded as stopping places for gold seekers travelling north-east from Robe. After the colony of Victoria imposed a racist £10 poll tax on Chinese gold seekers in 1855, boatloads turned to the South Australian port of Robe instead. Over the next few years some 14 000 Chinese walked from Robe through the Mosquito Plains and across the border. Some later returned and set up market gardens. Gold escorts, set up to ensure that gold from the Victorian goldfields enriched South Australia's coffers, passed to the north of Broom Station through Bordertown.[66]

Other roving strangers, almost all male, included bushrangers and diverse outlaws, convicts, ex-convicts, gangs of shearers, hawkers, occasional ministers and, later still, priests. Many were feared. Some were welcomed. Caroline and Edward would surely have sought images of themselves from the photographer Robert McClelland as he stopped at stations across the plains promising 'pictures as quick as lightning', including ones of 'children and animals in motion'. What excitement too when the enterprising Mrs Mary Ann Bryan arrived in her buggy pulled by a borrowed horse or sent her drivers into 'the bush' with samples of millinery, drapery and jewellery from her haberdashery shop in Robe. Gossip was that her husband had deserted her but returned occasionally to claim her income as his own – as indeed the law deemed it was. She was said to command 'nearly the whole of the squatter trade in the feminine department'.[67]

After the establishment of a police presence on the plains in 1854, the mounted police circulated the area, stopping at the different stations seeking the perpetrators of robberies, escaped prisoners, madmen and rapists. Later in the year that Caroline gave birth to her first son, Edward, they searched for a man charged with attempting to rape a married woman on McKinnon's run to the south-east of Broom Station. Over several days in mid-October 1856, Corporal Hunt and PTs Wren and Hunter rode from station to station seeking information on the man. On Sunday 19 October, Corporal Hunt rode some 114 miles, stopping at the Kearneys' after the Lawsons'. Such visits might produce information leading to arrests or misinformation leading nowhere. They would also spread fear among the women of the stations, reminding them of the range of dangers they faced.[68]

Mobile men raised fears. So did mobile sheep. Some carried human diseases that could be fatal to Aboriginal people and settlers alike. Some transmitted animal diseases that endangered sheep and cattle. 'Worst of these was scab' – the mite-spread disease that heralded ruin, loss, and 'endless torment to all concerned, of medicated drippings, dressings, deaths and destruction innumerable'.[69] As the value of sheep increased with the gold rush, squatters increased the size of their flocks. Only healthy sheep earned a profit. Scab-infested flocks imported from

New South Wales and Tasmania had long caused problems. From the 1840s on, legislation sought to control this disease. As a result, sheep and their owners were under heavy surveillance from sheep inspectors – another category of mobile males in these pastoral areas.[70]

In the 1850s, the chief inspector of sheep for South Australia had his hands full overseeing the inspection of the 1.5 million sheep on stations across the colony.[71] The South-East region was among the worst hit by scab, but rigorous inspection was producing results. In May 1857, Allan McFarlane, inspector for the South-East district, found only two stations left with scabby sheep. Nearly 4000 of Kearney's sheep were diseased. As required, Edward had branded them to indicate they had scab, applied for a lease to cure them, and paid the sixpence penalty per head set out in the recent revisions to the *Scab in Sheep Act* of 1852. He was given six months to cure them and appeared to have done so when the inspector called again in August that year.[72]

It was no easy task to rid sheep of scab. It spread readily and rapidly, especially in damp areas and the rainy season. The plains were notorious for holding water in the winter months. Early solutions were primitive and toxic. Tobacco, arsenic and 'corrosive sublimate' (mercuric chloride) made the remedies worse than the disease. Yet the inspector of sheep was convinced that most stations had the necessary equipment to treat some 3000 to 6000 sheep a day without much labour. Dunking the sheep in a tobacco wash, mixed sometimes with sulphur, was working. Most farmers throughout the region successfully cured their sheep. Risking spreading scab to neighbours' sheep was something akin to taking a child to school today without treating them for a severe infection of head lice. It made pariahs of pastoralists.[73]

Scab soured Edward's career as a South Australian sheep farmer. In November McFarlane found 'only one settler' who still had active disease in their flock. It was Edward Kearney. All of his 6000 sheep were infected. None were branded 'with the letter S as required by clause 3' of the Act. McFarlane informed him that he would have to proceed against him. Edward offered to pay the fine on the spot. McFarlane insisted it had to be recovered before the magistrate in Robe.[74] When Constable Thomas Budd arrived at Broom Station to deliver the summons requiring Edward to appear in court on 30 December to answer the charges against him, Edward was elsewhere. It was Caroline who signed for the summons. The price for Edward's non-compliance and failure to control scab was mounting: £97 5s for the April lease that had bought him time to cure his sheep, £50 for not branding them and an additional massive £245 for the November infraction. In contrast with his determination to appear in the Robe courtroom when he was charging Coquata with theft, Edward did not attend the hearing of his case.[75]

Within six years, the chief inspector of sheep, Henry Thomas Morris would be feted by the colony's squatters for having eradicated the disease completely from South Australia. They attributed this early English pioneer farmer turned official's success to his strict impartiality, honesty and forbearance.[76] Between 1857 and 1858 Edward and his scabby sheep tested that forbearance. Morris proclaimed it strange that anyone would 'so neglect their sheep', especially as it was in his own interest that they be healthy. In a stinging report republished in the *South Australian Register*, he disparaged Edward as the rare kind of farmer who defied the law and disregarded alike 'their own and their neighbours' property by neglecting their sheep after they know them to be diseased'.[77]

Kearney's subsequent actions compounded Morris's evaluation of his character. His failure to appear in court to acknowledge his 'wilful neglect' was bad enough. Worse, Morris asserted, he had had his sheep shorn, sold them to Robert Lawson, and the wool from the station was sold 'with other persons' brands' on them without their authority. Adding to these failures, he had again demonstrated his unmanliness by removing 'to a station … on the Victoria side of the border', beyond the reach of South Australian authorities. The inspector publicly expressed his belief that this move was undertaken to evade paying his fines.[78]

Edward Kearney had his failings. Neither laziness nor a lack of interest in farming improvements were among them.[79] He was impetuous, easily angered and did not hesitate to use his whip. He had coolly raised his gun and shot at the escaping Coquata. Quick to contact or write to authorities when he felt slighted, he could be sloppy with paperwork and the bureaucratic demands of the colonial state.[80] His failure to control the highly contagious scab among his sheep surely tested his relationships with neighbouring squatters. Had the considerable publicity of the inspector of sheep's critiques ended Edward's desire to remain in that area? Did this quick-tempered Irishman feel out of place among the Scots who predominated in the area, or was he perhaps being targeted as an Irishman by the Scottish and English sheep inspectors?[81]

Kearney's response to the sheep inspector, like that of the Aboriginal men who had slaughtered his sheep and sought food at his station, appears, indeed, to have been to flee. Just after the deadline to eradicate scab from his flock, he had arranged to sell both the station lease and his sheep to his nearest neighbour, Robert Lawson. Edward agreed to deliver the sheep after shearing was complete.[82] This would allow him to make some profit from the sale of their wool. The sheep inspector was correct. By early 1858 he had removed himself from South Australia and begun working at Lockhart station in the Western Wimmera country, just over the border, in the colony of Victoria. At some point in 1857 he was hired as superintendent by John Pearson, the fourth holder of that run, apparently with the understanding that he could purchase the lease later. The Mosquito Plains and Tatiara Country in South Australia and the Tattyara stations of the Wimmera on the other side were a natural geographical and social region, artificially divided by the mis-surveyed border. The station holders knew each other, socialised, witnessed each other's marriages and shared stories. Most used Robe to export their wool. Lockhart sat some 70 kilometres north-east of Broom Station.[83] For a while in 1857 and early 1858, Edward was stretched thin, trying to run two stations a considerable distance apart. Little wonder his sheep were neglected. Doubtless his wife and children were too.

Why did Edward decide to leave the well-watered area of the Mosquito Plains for the dry western Wimmera plains? When the pastoralist J. Wood Beilby visited the Lockhart area in 1849, seeking potential land for a new run, he saw only 'narrow sandy ridges covered with heaths, prickly honeysuckle and stunted scrub'. He considered the land so monotonous and so poor that no-one would ever want to farm it.[84] Had the Kearneys' encounters with sheep inspectors, the hungry Ngarrindjeri people, the dangers of roving rapists, bushrangers and escaped criminals on Mosquito Plains scared them away? Yet they would face many similar challenges across the border.

I suspect that the sheer size of Lockhart and the challenge of running it appealed to Edward's ambition to make it as a pastoralist in Australia. Lockhart and the adjoining Coniay lease were immense. At about 65 000 acres, or roughly 260 square kilometres, this was three times Broom Station's 88 square kilometres. It was over ten times larger than the Kearneys' leases in Ireland. Beside it the 320-acre (130-hectare) sections that selectors would soon be able to purchase for small family farms in Victoria were tiny. So too the 160 acres (65 hectares) that homesteaders could secure a decade later on the Canadian prairies.[85] Perhaps Robert Lawson made Edward an excellent offer for his land, his scabby sheep, and the still unfinished house. He might have wished to rid himself of his scab-tainted neighbour, or simply have coveted this adjacent property. Edward would need significant capital to embark on this new venture.[86]

Ambition was surely part of the attraction of Lockhart for Edward. But there were other reasons to contemplate leaving Broom Station, and in these, perhaps, Caroline had her say. Her sister Esther became seriously ill following her second son Charles's birth in late September 1856. Allen decided to sell his runs and leave the country. In April 1858 he belatedly registered his two boys' births, identifying himself as a squatter, 'late of Tatiara', then residing in Norwood, near Adelaide. The family sailed to Dunedin, New Zealand. Gold discoveries in Central Otago made Dunedin a magnet for investors and hopefuls alike. In early February 1861, Esther died. The cause was listed as consumption. James purchased a plot in the Southern Cemetery and arranged to erect a headstone listing 'his beloved wife' Esther's death on one side, with space for the details of his own death on the other. Unable to envisage raising his two young boys without a wife, he sent them to England to live with an uncle and to get an education. James senior died in 1865. The orphaned boys later returned to New Zealand, where the young James embarked on a distinguished career in politics and the army.[87] Caroline had lost the sister with whom she could share the joys, sorrows and worries of frontier station life, as well as contact with her two nephews. She may also have lost her desire to remain on the Mosquito Plains.

A move to Lockhart would put Caroline closer to two of her other siblings. James Hamilton, who was then courting her elder sister, Eleanor, was running Ozenkadnook station, roughly

90 kilometres south-east of Lockhart. (See image 3 in the picture section for photographs of Eleanor and James Hamilton.) James's extended family were, as noted earlier, pioneer settlers in the area. After his father's and then uncle's deaths he, his siblings and his mother inherited equal claims to the family holdings, which they ran as a shared family business. His widowed mother, Janet, would be the mistress of the comfortable homestead at Bringalbert (see image 4 for the locations of Lockhart and Bringalbert) for decades to come, running a strict but caring household that sheltered her disabled daughter, successive sons and daughters-in-law, children and grandchildren. James and Eleanor were married in April 1860 at the Merino Inn in Naracoorte. The prominent local squatter James Affleck was one of the witnesses, the town's storekeeper the other. Eleanor became mistress of Ozenkadnook. Over time she won the admiration of family and neighbours for her skills as a midwife, her musical abilities and the wise advice she provided to many. Caroline's intelligent, kindly older sister would also offer shelter and support to several of her siblings over subsequent years.[88]

Caroline and Eleanor's elder brother, William, had moved into the region around 1857, staying at Ozenkadnook at times, and settling permanently in Goroke, just 23 kilometres to the east. His wedding with Helena Edwards in 1865 was celebrated at Ozenkadnook. The three siblings would hardly be next-door neighbours, but in outback terms they were close. One urban contemporary claimed it would 'occupy a Man and Horse about three days' to travel between Lockhart and the Hamilton's station. A good rider could cover the distance much faster.[89] Caroline and some of her siblings would be close enough to socialise and support each other in good or difficult times. In a few years Caroline would need their support.

Moving to the western Wimmera would take Caroline further

from her parents and sister in Robe. It was some 200 kilometres away, but remained the closest port and service centre. William and Caroline Bax and Caroline's youngest sister, Mary, were set-tling into life there. They had their small stone cottage and school in the suburb of Syleham. The school was going well. Soon they would move to larger teaching quarters, taking up three rooms in the town's Temperance Hotel. William became active in the local Anglican St Peter's Church, completed in 1859, working alongside Ormerod and other more prominent citizens to place the parsonage in the hands of local trustees rather than the distant synod. He became a member of the local volunteer lifeboat crew – an important role on this treacherous, shipwreck-prone coast.[90] Caroline Bax assisted him in running the school. Robe had become a family metropole for the Bax siblings living north-east of the town. They might visit for many reasons: bringing their clips of wool to be shipped by George Ormerod and company; seeking supplies; attending court, as Edward had done; seeing to other business; or simply for the pleasure of seeing family. In Jan-uary 1858 Edward was in town seeing to many bureaucratic mat-ters. He sent off letters finalising the transfer of Broom Station. He registered the births of Edward junior and Frank Henry, who had come into the world two years earlier, and paid the fines due for his scabby sheep.[91]

I imagine that Caroline and the children accompanied him to Robe following the sale of Broom Station to Lawson and that they stayed there for some time while he secured the stock and the significant workforce needed to successfully run a station as large as Lockhart. Caroline may well have been relieved to spend time away from her volatile, hard-drinking, obstinate and sometimes harsh husband. Perhaps Edward and Caroline were apart for quite a long time. For while there were only nine months between Edward's birth in February 1856 and Frank's in November that year, their next son, William, was born 44 months later, in July 1860, well after they arrived at Lockhart. Caroline later testified that she had gone to Lockhart station in 1859. This was at least a year after Edward.[92]

Caroline and Edward's time as South Australian settlers left very few traces. His name never appeared officially in the colony's listings of leases. Early maps and local historians alike refer to lease 156 as Campion's run, or as part of Padthaway. Later some of this land was sold to selectors. The homestead, if remembered at all, is not referred to as Broom Station but as Yallamurray, the name assigned by later occupiers. Today, 'Edwards Line' still traverses the former lands of Broom Station, and the most direct route from Padthaway to Swede's flat, where Caroline's sister, Esther and James Allen lived, follows 'Edward's Road'. Edward failed to control scab, but his move does not mean he failed as a pastoralist. Many of his fellow squatters moved several times before legislation pushed them to purchase land, or disease, debt or death ended their careers.

There were good reasons to leave the Mosquito Plains then. As in much of the South-East, a few prominent squatters were increasing their pastoral properties by buying runs from smaller farmers. Edward could hardly compete with such men. The costs of raising sheep were mounting too as pastoralists built fencing to contain their sheep to prevent the spread of scab and improve the quality of their wool and the breeding of their stock. Fences would keep out kangaroos too. They were multiplying as the numbers of Aboriginal people fell through disease, deaths and departures. The quality of the soil was deteriorating. Soon expensive fertilisers and grass seed would be necessary to provide good grazing for sheep. Other squatters, including two of James Hamilton's brothers, decided to head to Southland and Otago in New Zealand, attracted by the possibility of securing licences to run sheep there.[93] Moving to Lockhart meant Edward could run a large station. He could avoid some of these changes and their associated costs. It had an established homestead, surely an attraction for Caroline. Yet the move was a gamble. How would the couple and their growing family fare on the vast acreage of Lockhart Station, on the hot and often dry lands of the Western Wimmera country?

# 3

# Lockhart Station, Western Wimmera, Victoria, 1858–65

When Caroline and the children settled into Lockhart, she had six years' experience of life in the outback as a wife, station mistress and mother. Time to adjust to the demands of her volatile, determined husband; time to reframe her own hopes and fears. This most western part of the Wimmera was also frontier and predominantly male space, through which gold-diggers, fortune seekers, bushrangers and other males roved. Here, too, there were no churches, no schools nearby and few visiting ministers or priests.[1] In the census taken in 1857, the year of Edward's move, enumerators found and counted 4066 males, but only 1518 females in the vast Wimmera district. These figures included 517 Chinese, almost all male, and 417 of the area's Aboriginal inhabitants. Most men worked on stations as overseers, stockmen, shepherds and labourers. Most single women found employment in some form of domestic service. Virtually all the women aged 20 or older were married, while over half the men that age were single or widowed. Well over one-third of non-Aboriginal and Chinese inhabitants lived in canvas tents rather than wood, brick or stone houses.[2]

Edward's decision was an expensive one. Newspapers reported in January 1858 that he had paid John McKellar £13 000 for the leases to the Lockhart and Coniay runs along with existing buildings and some 10 000 sheep. McKellar did well. He had recently purchased the leases with the same number of sheep for £10 000.[3] A wise investment? It was certainly an ambitious one. Thirteen thousand pounds was surely more than any surplus he had received from selling his scabby sheep and the lease to Broom Station. Presumably he needed to secure a loan to proceed. It took three more years before his name appeared as the official lease-holder. Until then, John McKellar and the entrepreneurial Robe merchant George Ormerod were listed as Lockhart's owners in the official lease registers, suggesting that Edward initially secured mortgages or loans from them.[4]

The Western Wimmera was settled later than the prosperous Western District of Victoria to the south. It was remote, but it offered chances to latecomers like the Kearney family as well as investment opportunities for others who had already accumulated significant assets and who could help fund newcomers. Edward might have hoped to become part of the pastoral elite of the area. He might well have dreamed of doing better than his Irish brothers had, and returning to visit and lord it over them. Looking ahead, he contemplated passing the land on to his children. Edward, his eldest boy, recalled that 'he used to say that if I was to succeed him, I was to know how to rough it, and earn my daily bread as he had to do'. If he could make a go of it, Lockhart would be a good legacy for his children. Caroline likely shared some of these aspirations. It was not a bad gamble. Yet there were warning signals that might have dissuaded him from the move had he not been so impetuous. To be fair, some of them are probably clearer in retrospect.[5] His land-savvy brother-in-law, James Hamilton, considered Lockhart a 'grand block of country', and thought Edward might have pulled through, despite the challenges posed by the 'glittering gold of stations in a waterless country'.[6]

In contrast to the Mosquito Plains, where water sat on the land in the wet seasons, exacerbating potential footrot and other diseases among the sheep, Lockhart lay in a drought-prone area. To the south was the dry, sandy, flat Little Desert. To the north, sandy forested areas and then dense mallee scrub of *Eucalyptus dumosa* and porcupine grass extended on and on up to the Murray River. Here the environment – along with bureaucratic bungling – had challenged Henry Wade and Edward White, the surveyors commissioned to mark the border between New South Wales and South Australia before the establishment of the colony of Victoria. Wade faced horrific problems when he sought to survey what he believed was the 141st meridian longitude in 1847. First, the bullock carts bogged down in the Mosquito Plains, then the dryness, heat and topography forced him to stop the survey just to the north of Lockhart Station. Two years later, Edward White's attempt to continue the survey faced similar problems. He and his team consolidated and regrouped at Lockhart Station, then headed north into the 'dreaded mallee'. Here, lack of water killed their bullocks and nearly killed the men in the survey team. When the squatter James Beilby met up with the expedition he was shocked at their depleted state and critical that they had not employed an Aboriginal person who might have helped them locate places to dig for water.[7] Beilby made a sketch of the area. Just below the names of Lockhart's first leaseholders, Baird and Hodgkinson, he inscribed the words 'Box (eucalyptus) forest badly watered'.[8]

Previous owners of Lockhart had soon discovered the problem. Baird and Hodgkinson informed officials in 1847 that their lease was 'almost without water', and in 1850 that they had been obliged to move their flock because there was insufficient water for 500 sheep.[9] The frequent turnovers of leaseholders might have served as a warning to Edward: Baird and Hodgkinson from 1847 to 1851; Hunter, Young and Lloyd in 1852; John McKellar in 1853; James Shanks for a short time in 1854; John Pearson later the same year; then John McKellar again. One after another they had sought to sell their leases, not always successfully.[10]

Lockhart Station sat on a slight rise in big, wide-open country to the north-west of the Little Desert. No major hills break the view. The land's flatness is punctuated by low ridges and hollows, natural water soaks and, in some areas, by creeks and swamps. Today the small border town of Serviceton and its railway station lie within its former perimeter. When Edward secured the lease, the boundaries of the Lockhart and Coniay runs formed a huge, rough parallelogram. The northern border was just under 13 kilometres long. It began roughly 2.5 kilometres north of the trail that Alexander Tolmer had established as the armed escort route for gold bound for Adelaide from the Victoria goldfields. That route 'followed Aboriginal tracks through the Ninety Mile Desert and crossed the Wade–White Line near the old Lockhart homestead'.[11] Today's Dukes and Western highways retrace much the same course. The western boundary extended 14.5 kilometres south along the line that Wade and Wright had wrongly marked as 141 degrees longitude, the border. They were roughly 3 kilometres too far to the west. Later, when their mistake was discovered, Victoria and South Australia would fight for years about which line should constitute the legal border. Eventually in 1914 the Privy Council in England decided on the true measurement. South Australia lost near 1500 square kilometres. Lockhart was at the heart of this disputed territory.[12]

Such borders and lease boundaries meant little to the local Bindjali peoples, whose ancestral lands stretched across the

Mosquito Plains and eastward into the Wimmera country, over-lapping to the east of Lockhart with those of the Wergaia peo-ples.[13] Caroline and Edward had left the jurisdiction of South Australian sheep inspectors but not the lands of the Bindjali. They might not meet Coquata, Edward's Ngarrindjeri nemesis, again but they remained within the travelling radius of their former Aboriginal employees. Here, too, Aboriginal naming practices marked the land. Among the many names some Bindjali called themselves, or were given by others, was the Tatiaras.[14] European colonisers applied that name to the border area, with spelling variations: Tatiara on the South Australian side and Tattyara in Victoria. It meant 'the good country', and had proven so for gen-erations of its Aboriginal owners, who knew how to find water, and hunt and forage for roots, fowl and mammals. 'Before the white man came, the creeks and swamps … teemed with wildlife: possums, kangaroos, wild cats and turkeys.'[15] Local historian Les Blake reports that part of the Lockhart run was known by the Aboriginal name of Dinyarrak, which might have referred to the home of Aboriginal song-makers, suggesting that 'this locality was the starting point of a native myth path that stretched across the country to … the place of the spirits of the dead'.[16]

Like the Mosquito Plains, this was an area of relatively recent and relatively late colonisation and of ongoing challenges for its original inhabitants. Aboriginal men and women had certainly not disappeared. When 'the worst bushfire ever to hit Victoria' devastated the area in 1851, one of White's surveying party was saved when he managed to stumble as far as an Aboriginal camp near Lockhart Station. Many left the areas that colonisers were taking. Kiddle argues, 'if they stayed where the white men set-tled they had to take sheep because the kangaroos and other game they depended on were slaughtered'.[17] To prevent this, and the kinds of domestic intrusions that Caroline and Edward had experienced, some settlers provided voluntary 'gifts of food'. At some point a rudimentary shelter made of branches was constructed on Lockhart Station. An undated photograph in a local history book describes it as a 'Storeroom for Aborigines' Provisions', a physical reminder of their continued presence. It appears to sit apart from the homestead, making it possible for the station's owners to avoid contact with any Aboriginal people seeking food supplies, and vice versa.[18]

The first wave of squatters cleared some of the land and began erecting fences. By the time the Kearneys arrived, much of the Wimmera 'was a huge sheep run'. Its stations were immense. At 260 square kilometres when he purchased the lease, Lockhart was one of the larger ones in this western part of the Wimmera. Cove, on their northern boundary, covered 146 square kilometres; to their east, Tattyara covered 132 square kilometres; Bunyip some 271 square kilometres. Further south-west, Eleanor's new husband's two family stations covered 98 000 acres or nearly 400 square kilometres.[19] Others around them were equally large. Ebenezer Ward described parts of the Mosquito Plains as a place 'you may canter pleasantly enough'; around Lockhart Station the flatness and sheer size of the country and stations called for galloping rather than cantering. It took days to patrol the outstations on these large runs on horseback. Caroline would have seen little of Edward most days.[20]

A small, but solid homestead awaited Caroline and the three children when they arrived.[21] It sat on a slight rise at the north-western corner of Lockhart's lands. Not far away was a natural water soak, long known to local Aboriginal peoples, and rediscovered by the surveyor, White, when he camped there. Today a small grove of trees behind the current house on the site marks where the original homestead was built. It was a four-room dwelling with 46-centimetre thick limestone walls, log rafters and a roof made of iron tiles. 'Native pine logs laid on the ground' supported the floorboards of the house and the verandah. Two of the four rooms had open fireplaces and chimneys. The thick walls would keep it cool for a while in the scorching heat of Wimmera summers. A later photograph shows a wide verandah. It would offer shade and perhaps a cool place to sit on hot summer days – if there was time to sit.[22] The house appears small for a growing family. When they arrived, Maria Ellen, Edward and Frank were all under the age of five. Caroline gave birth to William in July 1860 and to Patrick Edgar in March 1862. Their sixth child, Charles James, came over two years later in July 1864. Edward oversaw considerable improvements both to the housing and to the farm facilities. They added a 'five-roomed, weather-board cottage', perhaps to give the family more room, or for married staff with families. And they developed a good, 'well enclosed garden'.[23]

Caroline's responsibilities as a station mistress included supervising cooks, other domestics and governesses. Lockhart would require many more workers than Broom Station had. Shearing gangs, other workers and visitors had to be housed and fed. Women juggled these tasks with their responsibilities as wives and mothers to growing families. Mothers often provided the only education their children received. While her children were young Caroline gave them 'religious instruction herself' and oversaw their education. There are no signs that over these years Caroline's and Edward's differences of faith mattered. Looking back later, Caroline claimed that he 'had no strong religious bias, and never interfered with her, and they always lived happily together'. She taught her children prayers from the Church of England prayer book. They did not use a Roman Catholic prayer book or a Catholic version of the Bible in their home. Every five weeks or so Caroline, those children who were old enough and a governess went to Cove, the McLellans' station six kilometres away, for a Presbyterian service. Edward sometimes went in the carriage with them.[24] As the children grew older, a series of governesses assisted Caroline in feeding, clothing and educating them: Miss McDonald in the early 1860s; Miss Cunningham in 1866; Mrs Brown in 1868; and probably others.[25] High turnover among the women employed to try to instruct children in the outback was common. Another pioneer in the Wimmera recalled that she and her siblings had 'governesses from an early age'. She feared 'that we gave some of them an unpleasant time'.[26]

While Caroline saw to the children's education, the boys learned to ride, shoot and farm sheep from their father. Young Edward's recollections of his childhood at Lockhart offer precious shards of insight into the children's lives and family dynamics. He remembered having worked since before he was six years old and thought he had never really been 'a boy'. Seeing the children of other squatters playing made him jealous of them.[27] Yet Edward's experience of having to work hard from an early age was common on these large stations, as it was on farms in other colonies and among urban working-class children at the time. His uncle James was driving bullocks from at least the age of seven or eight, and later in life reminded readers that 'the boys on stations sixty years ago had a full share of the hard work entailed in forming and building up a home. There were no parties – no fun of any sort such as the young people of the present day enjoy.'[28]

The children were 'made' to ride at an early age. Edward junior travelled hundreds of miles across the station with his father while still very young. Edward senior was a passionate rider, like his brothers in Ireland. He surely relished the freedom and exhilaration of the long rides around Lockhart's perimeter and beyond. Horse raising and horseracing were passions shared by many of the pastoralists on the Mosquito Plains, in the Tatiara country and the Western Wimmera. From around 1860 races were held on Lockhart every year after shearing time. The course is said to have run from the 'dam near the west end of the property, around the foot of the sand rise, to finish where the five soaks were, or between the house and the road'. A few posts on the property still mark where these early races were held. The event was formalised later in the 1860s with the creation of the Lockhart Race Club. For a century it attracted shearers, other hands and riders from each side of the border to the races and a picnic at the end of the shearing season.[29]

The youngsters took part. Young Edward later told his future wife that he

> was counted the best rider for miles round. Everyone used to look for young Kearney at races time to ride their horse for them. I was also a pretty good athlete having been trained to walk and jump. In fact I was considered as a very smart young fellow, and the old squatters used to pat me on the head and say that I was a little brick, and that I would be a big man someday, meaning a wealthy one, and so perhaps I might, but an old saying is 'make hay while the sun shines', else if you wait till tomorrow, you will lose your chance.

He too became 'passionately fond of hunting, shooting and horse racing'.[30]

Teaching a love of riding or hunting and sharing knowledge about farming and stock were significant legacies from Edward to his children. He also scarred their lives with the harsh physical punishments he imposed, and his rages when he drank. He did not hesitate to whip them, often 'bringing blood'. Young Edward recalled fearing for his life when his father drank heavily. Neither heavy drinking nor strict discipline were unusual in this colonial frontier context. Hotels and inns did a brisk trade in drink when squatters stopped to refresh their horses or pass the night. Station owners served wine to passing visitors.[31] Alcohol was among the stores purchased in towns like Robe and stored on stations. But excessive use of alcohol combined with explosive violence increased the chances of family abuse and violence. Did Edward beat Caroline too? His workers? His son's strong memory of his father hating 'all English', and threatening to 'knock all the English blood out of' him, suggests tumultuous relations between this English wife and her Irish husband. Remembering this period of his parents' marriage, young Edward did not think it 'was one of love on his part at least'.[32] To whom could Caroline turn if her marriage was dangerous, or just disappointing? Young Edward remembered with disapproval that she 'made confidants of her servants'.[33] Yet one can well imagine that she welcomed any female company and conversation.

Marital and family tensions and power struggles played out in the context of the broader dynamics of life and work on these huge, isolated outback stations. They were rather like small feudal villages, with clear social hierarchies and clusters of buildings. No-one could run them alone. The squatter or supervisor was the lord and master, ruling co-resident workers, transient male shearers and labourers and family members alike. At peak season, especially during the shearing, well over 30 men were employed, housed and fed on the site.

We can get some idea of the residents and larger workforce on Lockhart from two contemporary documents. In 1862 men and women at Lockhart joined people from other Australian stations, from across the empire and indeed the globe to respond to the severe plight of Lancashire weavers, whose employment was devastated by the cotton famine caused mostly by the American

Civil War. The newspaper report on recent contributions from the country districts identified donations from fifteen Lockhart workers as well as Caroline and Edward, totalling £12 5s. The amounts they gave reflect the social and economic hierarchy of the station workforce. Edward gave £3, Caroline £2, and a Miss Lecamp, probably a governess, gave £1. Mr and Mrs Burge contributed £2 and £1 respectively. Later evidence shows that William Burge was the overseer. Mary Campbell and William Roebuck, the bullock driver, each gave 10s. Seven other men, likely all station hands, donated 5s each, as did a Mrs Earthem, possibly a cook and the wife or the mother of R. Eartham, another worker.[34] The historian Angela Woollacott has shown that Australian settlers also raised funds for the relief of the families of those killed in the Indian uprisings of 1857, as well as for the families of 'British soldiers and sailors killed or incapacitated' in the land wars between Māori and imperial forces in New Zealand in the 1860s. She argues that these relief efforts demonstrate the ties colonists felt for their counterparts facing threats of violence and loss of property and life in other colonies. Clearly Edward, Caroline and their staff and workers knew and were concerned about the challenges that workers in England were facing as their ways of making a living were transformed by the ongoing industrial revolution.[35] Another glimpse of the station's workforce comes from accounts submitted to settle Edward's estate. Lockhart's workers still included William Burge, the manager, and Roebuck, the bullock driver. There were also several boundary riders, a well attendant, a saddler and many permanent and casual male labourers as well as seasonal shearers, fleecerollers, wool carriers and a boy who picked up the fleeces. There was a male cook to provide their meals.[36]

It was costly to staff these large stations and feed and shelter family, workers and passing wanderers alike. The significant improvements Edward had made to increase their comfort and productivity might pay off in the long run, but they increased their debts. By the time he died in 1865 the buildings included the four-room cottage, the five-room wooden house nearby, and a men's hut that could sleep up to 30 men. The woolshed was large enough for fourteen shearers. He had invested in the latest technology – a 'horizontal wool press with a large screw-type monkey' to press the wool. These machines revolutionised the process of packing wool bales. They could cost up to £100. A 'store shed and stable, roofed with straw thatch laid on native pine rafters' were the other main buildings on the station.[37] Like other squatters, Edward began the expensive task of enclosing much of his vast station 'with post and rail and wire fencing'. He created seven paddocks around soaks and large dams to hold water. Within a few years the gross rateable value of the property was assessed at £558 and the improvements at £60. The station was more valuable than their neighbours the McLellans' Cove and Brimble runs, or that of Brewer, who had purchased Lillimur, but half the value of some of the larger Western Wimmera stations like Nihil or Mount Elgin.[38]

Sheep would pay the bills. 'There goes our breakfast, lunch, dinner and clothes,' a New Zealand pioneer told his children as his bales of wool were taken away to market.[39] But returns, as Edward had already learned, depended on the vagaries of disease, the world market and the weather.[40] Lockhart's original owners had estimated the station's carrying capacity at 9000 sheep.[41] Edward had purchased 10 000 sheep from McKellar when he took over the station. He had hardly arrived when drought hit. The summer of 1858 was hot. Grass drooped, then fried to a crisp. On Lockhart the five soaks that provided water for stock would have turned to mud then to caked, cracked dirt.[42] By early May 1858 up-country squatters were said to be despairing of 'ever having grass again', as their cattle and sheep began to feel the effects of a long drought.[43] By the end of that year the worst drought since 1839 was being widely proclaimed. Nearly 60 years later some observers still assessed the severity of droughts in relation to that of 1858.[44]

Only a reliable supply of water would get them through such prolonged dry periods. In addition to the usual costs of setting up, stocking and running any station, Edward had to deal with the water problem. He began sinking wells. James Hamilton estimated that a station the size of Lockhart required six wells. It was expensive and difficult work 'as the water was in many instances, 200 and even 250 feet [61 and 76 metres] below the surface'. The costs of drilling, building lumber shafts, and the huge wooden casks, increased with the depth of the water. Each well cost roughly £200.[45] By the time of Edward's death in 1865, three wells had been dug.[46] With some assurance of water in dry seasons, Edward increased the size of his flock. By 1862 he was running nearly 12 000 sheep as well as pasturing 24 cattle and six horses. Three years later there were closer to 20 000 sheep, 60 cattle and eight working bullocks.[47]

Edward's dreams were greater than his assets. As a hard-working man from a farming family who had experience running Australian sheep stations, he possessed many of the skills that might have led to success as a squatter raising sheep.[48] Virtually all pastoralists required credit to carry them through the period before their wool was sold, and many had to mortgage their properties for a while. Edward's first solution to the financial challenges he faced was to sell some of this vast block of land. In 1860 he sold the lease to a 37.5 square kilometre rectangle on Lockhart's north-eastern border to the neighbouring squatters, Donald and Nicol McLellan of Cove Station. That became the Brimble run.[49] Still financially strapped two years later, he had a huge 89 square kilometre block surveyed as a new run covering much of the eastern side of Lockhart and sold the lease to John Brewer, who named it Lillimur. Lockhart had shrunk from 260 square kilometres to 145. And yet Edward increased the size of his flock.[50]

James Hamilton thought that Edward might have pulled through were it not for a serious accident. Accidents haunted Lockhart's history; Edward's jeopardised their future as a family and as pastoral settlers. How it occurred was remembered in different ways. In his brother-in-law's memory, Edward was injured in one of the deep wells he had paid so much to have dug on the station. According to James Hamilton he burst a blood vessel. A newspaper article about the old Wimmera stations described him as having 'nearly lost his life sinking a well' when a 'bucket fell down on him in the shaft', nearly killing him, but only breaking a leg.[51] Young Edward's recollections were different. He believed his father's reckless driving had led to him falling out of a trap, breaking his collarbone and three ribs. The doctor set his arm, but not the ribs. They became 'deeply embedded in his lungs'.[52] These varied stories about Edward's injury, passed on by family and through local lore, highlight the ways settlers grappled with the complexities of risk and misfortune as part of the colonial experience.[53] There definitely was an accident towards the end of 1863, or early in 1864, and it left Edward with lung problems which affected his health and eventually caused his death.[54]

The timing was terrible. Edward was badly injured. The family was growing. There were no children old enough to step into his shoes. Edward had invested heavily in improvements to the station, but it would take several years of good wool clips to eliminate his debts. Edward needed money. He turned to a man with one of the murkiest reputations for business dealings in the Australian colonies: William John Turner Clarke. Clarke had migrated from England in 1825. By the mid-1860s he owned extensive blocks of sheep-raising country on stations in Victoria, Tasmania and South Australia as well as across the Tasman Sea in New Zealand. He already held one run in the Wimmera area, and had recently purchased the Mount Schank Estate near Mount Gambier in South Australia from its bankrupt owner. 'Known generally as "Big" Clarke and "Moneyed" Clarke, he was widely feared for his ruthless land hunger, but respected for consummate ability in pursuit of fortune.'[55] He swooped in on people in trouble, and purchased their livestock and land at a price that he set. A contemporary noted that he seemed 'to possess an innate power of quick calculation which in matters of business is worth all the acquired powers in the world. Such men strike while the iron is hot; others ponder and waver until it cools.' When Edward secured the mortgage for his station, infirmities and obesity had taken their toll on Clarke. One biographer notes that by 1862 he 'was beginning to show his years physically. He had put on considerable weight and could no longer cover long distances on horseback.' He left the pastoral management side of his investments to his sons, and focused on moneylending and investments. In early March 1864 Clarke agreed to mortgage the station, its stock and animals for £8000 and interest.[56]

No doubt Edward hoped to recover, but in case he did not, he asked Clarke not to sell the station to secure repayment. They agreed that 'the said Station should be carried on and worked for the benefit of the persons entitled to the said Testator's estate', and that the income from the station should be applied as it came in to reduce the mortgage.[57] In this agreement Edward senior clearly envisaged the station remaining in the family's hands. Something changed before he wrote his will. Edward junior notes that after his accident, his father 'felt a sort of longing to visit the place of his birth'.[58] Edward senior decided to return to Ireland. In March or April 1864, he left Lockhart, taking their third son, William, who was then not quite four years old, with him. They would not return until February 1865.

Caroline was used to Edward being absent for several days or even weeks at a time as he patrolled the shepherds' huts, rode the perimeter of the station or travelled to town for supplies. She may have relished these absences, even dreaded his returns. But this was to be a much longer departure than usual station business required. Given the dangers of travel, Edward's poor health and the children's frequent illnesses, Caroline may well have wondered whether her husband and third son would return at all. She was aged 30 and about five months' pregnant. Edward would have known he would miss this child's birth. She remained on the station with the other four children and their domestic staff and farm workers. Maria Ellen was nine and a half years old and without doubt well used to assisting with domestic work in the house, the garden and on the station. Young Edward had recently turned eight. Later he told his future wife that his father had beaten both him and Maria Ellen 'with a whip' on the day he left. He also claimed to be the main person in charge while his father was away. Frank was seven, and Patrick Edgar just two.[59]

Caroline's baby was born in July 1864. His name, Charles James, suggests her gratitude to her sister Eleanor and Eleanor's husband James Charles Hamilton, who surely helped her while Edward was away. His absence may have left her free to choose her son's name herself – all the other boys were named after Edward and his brothers. The memoir that young Edward penned about twelve years later offers insights into his father's departure, and family life while he was away, filtered through his sensitivities and wish for sympathy from the woman he hoped to marry. Supervising the station staff on these large sheep stations demanded authority and respect that few women could command in this male-dominated world. Caroline does not seem to have been one of those women. One suspects that Edward ruled his men and family as he rode horses – insisting on control and his power through the whip if necessary. The manager, Mr Burge, and other station hands would have kept the station running during his absence. Yet as young Edward later presented this grim turning point in his life, he was the one in charge of superintending the men 'all day', and 'working from daylight until after dark', even though he was not yet nine years old.[60]

This was a time of transition in Caroline's life too. If Edward junior's memories are reliable it was during his father's absence that 'drink which used to be consumed moderately by mother began to increase'. He thought that this explained fights she had with 'a common hawker', though haggling over prices with the men and occasional woman who traded their wares from station to station might often have led to disagreements. He blamed her for letting the garden go to 'wrack and ruin'. Young Edward had inherited the class vision that fed his father's ambitions and had a keen sense of how he should have been treated, as Edward's firstborn son. And he blamed Caroline's close relationship with the servants for their neglect of their work. Particularly upsetting to this troubled eldest son was returning in the evenings to find

No hot dinner or drink, only the remains of the dinner, and sometimes not that. I am of a very sensitive nature, and it used to hurt me awfully when I would ask for it. I used to be told to go to the cook and get it. 'A nice thing' I used to say, 'for the master's eldest son to go to his kitchen and get his meals, or to the men's dining room, whom he had been superintending all day'. No I would not do it. I used to go to bed supperless sometimes.[61]

Edward's young male view could not empathise with Caroline's pregnancy or the exhaustion and work involved in caring for a newborn along with the other children. Nor could he understand the need for the female companionship which led her to chat with women servants. Edward senior was gone for eleven months. Was it that Caroline relaxed in his absence, relieved that her children would no longer be whipped, or relieved that she too might escape his wrath? Had she learned to love the Wimmera bush – the 'attractive vistas of hill and dale … and the ever-changing hues of the various shrubs' that lent an 'attraction to the observant eye'? Sunsets in the relative cool of autumn are beautiful from the site of Lockhart homestead. Did she enjoy the sounds and sight of the stunning red-tailed cockatoos that were so numerous in that region, or the marvellous xanthorrhoea grass trees that sent their strange white flowering spikes up to 5 metres high when they bloomed after fires scorched them? Or was she brooding about her future, wondering if her husband would survive, fretting about how she might manage as a widow with six young children? Did she take a glass of wine or two as she contemplated the challenges she might soon face?[62]

More can be ascertained about Edward's movements after his departure than about Caroline's hopes and fears. After leaving Lockhart, Edward senior and young William stopped first in Melbourne. Edward arranged for doctors to mend his ribs. They planned to sail on the *Great Britain*, but William caught scarlet fever, so they had to wait. Once he had recovered they boarded the *True Briton* for London on 7 May 1864 (see image 5 in the picture section). It was then a new packet, 'built expressly' for the Australian trade, and offering 'a comfortable passage to London'. The Money, Wigram & Sons advertisement for this particular voyage announced proudly that the two previous outward passages had completed the voyage in 66 and 72 days. William was only four, yet some things made an impression on his young mind. It must surely be through conversations with him that his oldest brother Edward became convinced that his father 'spent a great deal of money' during the trip and led 'a very fast life, so much so that he signed his own death warrant'. Beyond the squandering of what he saw as his rightful inheritance, what Edward junior meant by this – like much else in Caroline and Edward's story – is puzzling. I am particularly intrigued by the listing of the passengers on the *True Briton*. A 37-year-old 'Mrs Kearney' is recorded in the same cabin as Edward and young William.[63] Who was she? Had he taken another woman with him who was travelling as his wife? The order of the names implies a marital relationship. Had someone arranged for a relative to chaperone them, or care for William? Were this true, it seems unlikely that she would have slept in the same cabin. I have found no evidence of any other Mrs Kearney who might have travelled with them from Melbourne to England.

From London they proceeded to Ireland. Edward returned to a country, a county and a family that had been dramatically transformed over the two decades since he emigrated. He had missed the mass starvation that spread from late 1846 as potato crops failed, English food imports ceased and exports of other foodstuffs continued. Mass evictions and massive emigration had followed. Nor had he been involved in the resurgence of Catholicism and nationalism and the expansion of educational and occupational opportunities for Catholics that were changing Irish society and culture. County Westmeath was a hotbed of agitation, intimidation and destruction as secret societies sought to prevent evictions and liberate land for the Irish from the hated landlords. The British parliament was so concerned about this county that it set up a special Select Committee on Westmeath to investigate the actions of the Ribbon societies – the secret groups of poor Irish tenants who organised to fight evictions – and of the Fenians, the increasingly international movement contesting British rule.[64] Perhaps some of the Kearneys were involved. Later Edward's brother Patrick became president of the local branch of the National Land League. And the family was rapidly becoming 'noted for its zeal in the cause of Religion and Fatherland'.[65]

Edward's mother, Mary, had died five years before his return. She had spent 34 years as a widow living on their family holding at Williamstown, Ballykeeran, County Westmeath with some of her children. Her sons' life trajectories reflect wider practices among rural Irish families seeking to avoid excessive land division. Some remained celibate; several married late; two seem to have inherited land; and one, Edward, had chosen emigration. His youngest brother, Patrick, joined the Church. Joseph, the second to youngest boy, was in his early forties and still single when Edward returned. He married four years later at the age of 46. William seems to have married Mary Malia in 1844, when he was 30, but I have found no further traces of her, nor any evidence that they had children.[66]

The Irish Kearneys were doing well in the improving economy of post-famine Ireland. They had built on their father's success in securing long-term leases, and continued to accumulate leases, land and capital, social and religious as well as financial. William had taken over the leases to four parcels of land around the Williamstown property where they grew up. These totalled 135 acres (55 hectares). He also held a few smaller separate parcels and four houses around the town of Athlone. Edward's eldest brother Francis now had six surviving children aged from their teens into their twenties. He had moved away from the family home, taking up holdings totalling 444 acres (180 hectares), mostly in and around Ballinahown Wood, about the time of his marriage in 1834. He also owned several valuable houses or businesses in the town of Athlone. The family seem to have lived in one of these substantial houses or shop premises before making the farm in Renaun, Ballinahown their main residence. This property remains the home of Francis's descendants today.[67]

Edward's mother died knowing that at least two of her sons were well placed on the land. She was surely also proud that she had been able to ensure that Patrick received a good education locally and then at the seminary in Maynooth. She was still alive when he was ordained as a priest in 1854. Between then and the time of Edward's arrival Patrick had served as a parish priest in several locations, and as an administrator in colleges in County Longford and Westmeath. Two years after Edward's visit he was appointed as the parish priest of Moate and Mount Temple. Moate is a small village, close to his brothers' holdings. Patrick was rising quickly within the local Catholic hierarchy, and would eventually be remembered in his region as the most 'able and colourful' of the 'dedicated band of Catholic clergy, who realised that landlordism was bad and decided to fix it' through a strong, disciplined resistance movement.[68]

Canon Kearney was a passionate man. His great passions included his Catholic faith and rebuilding Catholicism in his home parish; the struggle to liberate Irish land and its tenants from the grip of the landlords; horseriding and hunting. Many years later, when he died, his life work was described as 'practically a history of the agrarian struggle'. He organised his parishioners to rally to prevent tenant evictions, fought to retain land for commons in his parish, and raised money successfully enough to build impressive churches in three small towns, including his parish of Moate. Temperance was another of his pet projects. Kearney was said to sit on a horse 'like Wellington', and was later remembered as having ridden around his parish, dismounting upon meeting parishioners, whom he then tested on their knowledge of the catechism. If they made mistakes, he whipped them.[69]

Edward and his younger brother shared a love of riding and of horses, as well as excessive use of whips. Their opinions surely differed on the question of drink. If Edward had been hoping to play the part of the successful returning emigrant running a vast sheep station in the colonies, the impact of his return visit to Ireland was the opposite. Some members of his Irish family, with Patrick taking the lead no doubt, were clearly shocked when they realised that he had not been practising his faith properly in Australia. Worse, he had married a Protestant and did not seem to have insisted on her conversion or on raising his children as Catholics. Poor little William, who turned five shortly after arriving in Ireland, could only have failed to display adequate knowledge of Catholic doctrine and the catechism. Perhaps Patrick played on Edward's illness and religious guilt, and convinced him to donate money that would help him as he funded the building of local churches. Edward junior believed that while in Ireland his father 'bought a parish and built a chapel, and bestowed it on his brother, Pat, a priest'. Descendants of Francis also suspect that family money went into Patrick's church construction projects.[70] I have not found evidence to confirm or to refute these family stories. Patrick certainly became a vigorous and successful money raiser, travelling to the United States five years later to raise funds among Irish emigrants from the region for his parish regeneration and church-building projects in Moate and beyond. He attributed his success at building St Patrick's church in Moate to that campaign.[71]

Patrick and possibly some of his other brothers doubted Edward's ability to ensure the Catholicism of his family alone. They may also have understood that in his weakened state he needed help on the station, and help to die a good Catholic death, and generously offered assistance. Or they may have sought to ensure Lockhart's profitability, in the hope that they might benefit from it. They made a plan. When Edward and young William boarded the luxury screw-propelled steamship the *Great Britain* in Liverpool to sail to Melbourne on 16 December 1864, they were not alone. Edward's elder brother William had been delegated to return to Australia with them. The ship's register records Edward as travelling with 22-year-old Mary Anne Kearney, one of the daughters of his brother Francis, a Mrs McLaughlin and a Miss Kelly, also both in their twenties. They were to serve as Catholic governess and servant respectively. Edward's brother William, aged 50, and little William were listed separately. The Irish Kearney brothers later claimed that among the baggage was 'a suit of priest's vestments and other requisites for the celebration of Catholic services at Lockhart Station'. There may well have been other Irish friends and relatives who travelled with them, expecting work as servants and labourers at Lockhart.[72]

The return voyage took 68 days. In mid-February 1865, this retinue of relatives arrived in Melbourne, then travelled to the station. Edward met his new son, Charles James, for the first time. Caroline met his brother William and the Catholic relatives and servants who accompanied them for the first time. She had sought to raise her children as good Protestants. As noted earlier, she later claimed that she had done so 'with the full knowledge of their father, who never made the slightest objection'.[73] Brother William as the family emissary now sought to change that. Edward junior later explained that his father brought 'a lot of minions of his own to eat up what was mine. Poor mother got an awful persecution from them, and they made a wide breach between husband and wife, and wanted to make us all Catholics, which I would not be.' Religious zeal combined with the Kearney brothers' tendency to resort to violence. Young Edward claimed he had 'seen them nearly kill a man on our run for courting a servant that they brought out from home'.[74] 'Them', I assume, was William Kearney. If Caroline had found her final pregnancy and childbirth and her time as mistress of the station in Edward's absence demanding, she was about to face the greater challenge of dealing with the actions and influence of his brother William and Edward's rapidly declining health.

Edward survived nearly nine months after his return from Ireland. In April he wrote to his family back in Ireland, reassuring them that a 'Miss Cunningham, a Catholic governess, was teaching the family, and that a Roman Catholic Clergyman, the Rev. Julian Woods ... the best of all doctors had given him the rites of the church and had comforted him much.'[75] Edward's chances of survival may have been in question when he decided to visit Ireland again. Soon after his return it was clear that he would not live. William took over the management of his brother's station at least four months before his death.[76]

The new role of Catholicism in his life, whether genuinely embraced or insisted upon by William, made Catholic support and presence when the end came critical. Father Julian Tenison-Woods, whom Edward mentioned to the family in Ireland, had arrived in Robe in 1857 as parish priest for the entire South-East district of South Australia. Within a year of Woods' arrival, Edward had been among the Catholics of the wider area who contributed to the building of the first Catholic Church in Robe. Woods' circuit extended across the border from the Mosquito Plains and the Tatiara country to the Western Wimmera stations. His occasional visits may have allowed Edward to renew his Catholic faith from around this time. This inquisitive, independent-thinking, scientist–priest had already published his first book, *Geological Observations in South Australia*, in 1862. He was friends with the Australian nun Mary MacKillop, with whom he would shortly set up an order of teaching Catholic sisters in the area. He could visit and comfort Edward and other dying Catholics in his massive parish, but the vast distances meant there was no guarantee that he would be present to perform the final rites that were so important to Catholics. Nor at Lockhart was there any guarantee of medical assistance for Edward. The absence of facilities and the distance from services compounded the challenges of his illness.[77] They decided to take Edward to Melbourne, where religious and medical support and legal advice were more readily available.

It was in late August 1865 that Edward, Caroline and William travelled the 180 or so kilometres south to Robe, possibly following the route that passed near their former station on the Mosquito Plains. They may have left the children at Lockhart with the governess, with her sister Eleanor at Ozenkadnook, or in Robe with her parents. In Robe they boarded the new coastal steamship the *Penola*, bound for Melbourne via Port MacDonnell and Portland. Their former neighbour George Ormerod had recently purchased this Glasgow-built iron steamship, designed for the trade between Melbourne and Adelaide. It was captained by Frederick Peter Snewin, who had garnered significant public acknowledgment for his role in saving passengers when the *Admella* was shipwrecked south-west of Port Gambier in 1859. They took the four-day trip in the relative comfort of the saloon. By the time they left Portland all the cargo had been delivered, and the ship was sailing with ballast. A strong westerly gale on the final stretch past Port Fairy and Cape Otway doubtless made it a particularly uncomfortable trip for the dying Edward. The *Penola* reached Melbourne on 11 September. A month later, a Miss Kearney – likely their daughter, Maria Ellen, who was about to turn eleven – arrived in Melbourne. Three days later, Edward died.[78]

The Washington Hotel sat at the corner of Collins and William streets. The exclusive Union Club of Victoria was on the opposite side of the street. A few blocks to the east was the section of Collins Street that historian Penny Russell has described as the only street of the city considered respectable and safe by and for the city's elite women, although she points out that prostitutes 'sometimes plied their trade there'.[79] The hotel had recently been taken over by a William Kennedy. He seemed intent on erasing its bad reputation. His publicity in the *Argus* claimed it as the 'nearest first class house to Spencer Street Station' and promised excellent accommodation at moderate charges. In the month prior to Edward's arrival he began advertising a *table d'hôte* (fixed-price menu) each day at 1 o'clock. He subsequently sought the services of a nurse, suggesting that Edward was not the only sick person who took advantage of this hotel, located relatively close to the outpatient clinics of the Royal Melbourne Hospital.[80]

The proximity of priests to administer the final sacraments was likely an even more important consideration than the availability of doctors in their choice of location. Medical experts could offer Edward little hope at this stage. St Francis' Church, the first Catholic church built in the colony, was within easy walking distance. The ringing of its bell, imported from Dublin a decade earlier, was surely audible in Edward's room at the Washington Hotel. As the hotel also sat in the city's legal precinct, medical, spiritual and legal assistance were all nearby.[81]

Two and a half weeks after arriving in Melbourne, Edward confirmed his final wishes. His last will and testament was witnessed by a law clerk, James Fairhurst, and the hotel's proprietor, William Kennedy. Edward, or more likely William, had engaged Fairhurst's boss, the solicitor Thomas Pavey, whose law office was a short block away at 60 Collins Street West, to draw up his final will and testament. Normally solicitors met at least once with their clients to offer advice and to take notes to ensure that their wishes were properly framed. They then returned some time later with a draft of the will, and read it to the testator. Only when they were sure that the document reflected the person's intentions did they get it signed and witnessed. To be valid, the person signing the will had to be in full control of their capacities. If they were delirious or demented, the validity of the will could be contested.[82] It doubtless took some time to prepare Edward's will, for his wishes for his family had become very complicated since the time he had talked to Clarke about keeping Lockhart for the family.[83] Transcribed in small, neat handwriting, the final version filled ten pages. Kearney was not well. His hand was clearly shaking as he scrawled his signature at the end of the document on 30 September.[84]

Much later Caroline claimed that 'from the time [Edward] became ill he fell under the influence of his brother, Mr. William Kearney'.[85] One can well imagine William playing on Edward's religious guilt, guiding, manipulating and bullying him about the provisions he should make. Edward surely worried about the future of his widow and six young children, especially if her drinking had escalated, as his eldest son suggested. The law placed few constraints on what Edward could decree. Most European inheritance rules favoured family support over testamentary freedom. A father was obliged to give a certain proportion of his property to his children. European legal systems also recognised that some of a wife's property remained hers, or in her family line, and that some portion of property accumulated during marriage should pass to her and the children. Not so the English common law as followed in most of the United States, Canada, New Zealand and the Australian colonies. At this time a man could do pretty well what he wished with property of all kinds, including any his wife had earned, gained or saved. Only wives who had signed a private, ante-nuptial agreement might retain control over property carefully specified in the document. Caroline and Edward, like most couples outside the upper middle classes, had made no such agreement. Earlier, widows could claim dower rights – a widow's third – the right to live off the proceeds of a third of their husband's property. This ancient widow's claim had been largely whittled away over the previous century.[86]

At the time of Edward's death, advocates of women's rights were proposing legislation across the British Empire and in many American states to give married women the right to retain control of their own property. Early laws in some jurisdictions gave deserted wives the right to retain their earnings and savings, but only if they secured a protection order through the courts.[87] As one Victorian politician noted, a wife could support 'herself and her children by keeping cows and selling milk', only to lose that source of income when a 'husband, in a fit of drunkenness' sold off the cow. Five years after Edward's death, wives in Victoria became the first married women in the Australian colonies to gain the right to own real estate, savings, wages and inherited property in their own names. Politicians speaking in favour of the change decried the fact that 'a woman has no separate existence from her husband; all that she possesses, the very shoe on her foot, is his property'. Modelled quite closely on the British *Married Women's Property Act* passed earlier that year, Victoria's legislation helped wives who had independent assets, jobs or other ways of making money. Such acts changed little for the vast majority of married women who, like Caroline, had no income or other assets that could legally be considered theirs. It was not until the 1970s that family law began to acknowledge that women's contributions to family assets through domestic labour and childcare should give them a claim on men's earnings and savings.[88] So Edward was legally entitled to bequeath the Lockhart Station lease, its buildings and improvements, the thousands of sheep, the horses, farm machinery and their furniture as he wished in his will, subject to repayment of any debts.

Caroline had lived with Edward since her late teens, first for six years at Broom Station in South Australia and then for six more across the border in Victoria, on the vast lands of Lockhart Station. This village girl from England had endured many of the challenges that squatters' wives shared; isolation, hard work, rudimentary housing, cooking and washing facilities, and lack of religious, health and educational services were among them. Edward's trip home to Ireland with William had left her pregnant with four children to care for as well as her work as the station mistress. The circumstances of his return were unlikely to rekindle any remaining romance. She was now 31 – no longer young, yet still in the prime of her life. If the marriage had been a reasonably happy one early on, it had deteriorated in recent years, or so her son's memories suggest. Edward was close to death. Their six children were between one and eleven years of age. Caroline had no assets of her own. Her family was not poverty-stricken, but they were not wealthy either. How she would manage as a widow depended on the contents of the will that Edward signed in Melbourne on 30 September 1865.

# Part Two

# Widowhood: Contesting Edward's will and his brothers' influence

# 4

# Edward's death, his final wishes and religious warfare

Edward died in his room at the Washington Hotel on 20 October 1865, three weeks after completing his will. Doctor R. Tracy listed 'Phthisis Pulmonalis' as the cause and reported on the form registering his death that Edward had been ill for nine months. This version of tuberculosis is described by the historian Helen Bynum as one that followed a burst blood vessel. 'The blood transformed into purulent matter' and 'caused ulceration of the lungs'.[1] This was most likely the long-term result of Edward's accident. It fits both his brother-in-law's recollection that he had burst a blood vessel and his eldest son's belief that his broken ribs punctured his lungs. His was not the romanticised death at home surrounded by family so dear to Victorians, especially those of evangelical faiths. But the proximity of the hotel to Catholic institutions makes it likely that he received the final Catholic rites of confession, absolution, the last Eucharist and extreme unction which would have been so difficult to secure at Lockhart. William later swore under oath that his brother was visited by priests and nuns during his last illness.[2]

Other deaths recorded at the same time as his indicate that husbands, offspring and friends informed the registrar of deaths. Interestingly, the informant for Edward was not his brother

William, who as senior male in the family might have taken on this task, but the undertaker. Was Caroline present at his death? Was William? What were Caroline's emotions over this challenging period? To these questions I have no answers. Young Edward's recollections are hardly eloquent on this subject. 'Eventually father went to Melbourne and died,' he wrote years later.[3]

Convention dictated that Caroline enter a long period of mourning, displaying the external signs of grief in the clothing she wore. 'Women often responded immediately to news of a death by reviewing their clothes, and deciding whether to purchase new mourning dress or to dye existing clothes and hats black,' notes historian Penny Russell. Purchases were made 'as soon as possible after the death'. Melbourne offered special shops selling the dull, dark fabrics for dresses and the black crape for veils and trim that widows were expected to don for at least a year.[4] Though widows in the outback followed these rigid customs less rigorously than in cities, I suspect that Caroline did go shopping for her widow's weeds. As in most wills, Edward had directed his executors to pay all of his just debts and funeral and testamentary expenses. Later accounts of expenses over this period show that up to £500 was provided for 'the maintenance of the Wife and Children, and other necessary payments and outgoings' in the three months following his death.[5] It was quite proper for Caroline to seek support to purchase appropriate mourning clothing for herself and the children. Bereaved widows were expected to represent their dead husbands in ways that displayed both their grief and their new status as widows.[6]

They were not expected to attend funerals. Burial, Russell reminds us, 'was a public, male ritual'.[7] A prominent Melbourne undertaker was in charge. John Daley had organised the large, public funeral held in Melbourne two years earlier for the explorers Burke and Wills after they and many of their team had died on their foolish and fatal attempt to explore the country between Melbourne in the south and the Gulf of Carpentaria in the north, in order to find a route for an overland telegraph line. Daley placed the announcement of Edward's funeral in the papers the day after his death. It identified him as 'Edward Kearney Esq., of Lockhart, West Wimmera', and 'respectfully invited friends to follow his remains'. The procession was set to depart at 3 o'clock on Sunday 22 October from the Washington Hotel to the 'place of interment', Melbourne General Cemetery. A Reverend Marshall performed the ceremony.[8] I have not found records that indicate whether Edward's funeral was modest or lavish, as some funerals in this period were. It is unlikely he knew many people in the city. The costs were initially paid by Clarke, adding to the considerable mortgage he held on Lockhart and its stock.[9] Caroline or William ensured that two further notices spread the news of Edward's death. These gave his age as 46 and identified him as originally from Athlone, County Westmeath, Ireland. Such sparse details, listing age, sometimes occupation and often linking immigrants back to their place of origin were common in 19th-century death notices for relatively ordinary people.[10]

Caroline's anxiety about their future was surely compounded when she learned the content of Edward's will. Good husbands were expected to provide for their widows and children following their deaths, and his will confirmed his commitment to this responsibility. He was not seeking to leave them penniless. But the provisions were under conditions of his or his brothers' choosing. Earlier he had convinced Clarke not to sell his station, but to apply the income to the mortgage; and young Edward had grown up expecting to inherit the station and 'be a big man someday, meaning a wealthy one'. But Edward's vision of the future of his wife and children had changed following his trip to Ireland. It seems entirely plausible that he did not understand the details of his will and was heavily influenced by his brother William, as Caroline later claimed.[11]

Gone was his hope to keep the station in the family or pass it on to one or several of his sons. The will sought to Catholicise his children and to render them Irish. Edward's final wishes fully deployed his power as a male patriarch to dictate their future and to bequeath his property as he wished. As was usual in English wills, it placed his property of all kinds in the hands of executors/trustees, with instructions on how to dispose of it. His particular wishes meant that he needed trustees in both Australia and Ireland. So Edward named two Melbourne accountants, William McGann and William Noall, as the 'colonial trustees and the executors' of his will. How he knew these men is unclear, but both had offices on Collins Street near the hotel. Perhaps they were suggested by Thomas Pavey, the lawyer who oversaw the drafting of his will, or his clerk.[12] His Irish trustees, in contrast, were his close male relations: three of his children's uncles from his side of the family – his brothers William and Patrick, and his sister Mary's husband, Thomas McCormack. He named these three men, as well as Caroline, as guardians for the six children, all of whose names and birthdates he carefully listed in the will. He demonstrated sufficient faith in Caroline's mothering skills to appoint her as one of the guardians, but this role was to last only as long as 'she continues my widow'.[13]

The bequests and, especially, the instructions were lengthy and complicated. One of the earliest promises was to Edward's niece, Mary Anne Kearney, who had accompanied him and William back to Australia in 1864. She was to receive £200 sterling, should she agree to return to Ireland with his family. He left £100 each to two daughters of Mary and Thomas McCormack. And he promised William £100 over and above the £100 he was to receive as a trustee, specifying, rather mysteriously, that he was to use it 'according to the directions I have already given him'. William Kearney and James Hamilton, Caroline's brother-in-law, were placed in charge of Lockhart and its stock until the station was sold. The will specified that the Australian executors/trustees should sell his property by private contract and on terms that appeared 'expedient and best for the interest of my family'. Once it was sold and his debts repaid, they were to 'outfit my family for the voyage home and to pay the expenses of the voyage in a first class Vessel or Vessels', and 'ensure as far as possible the comfort and convenience of my family on such voyage'. Edward made it clear that he wanted Caroline and the children to go to Ireland 'as early as practical'. They were to remain there until the boys became eligible for a share of his estate at the age of 24, or earlier for Maria Ellen, if she married younger than that.[14]

Once in Ireland, the family's future was to be overseen by the children's uncles as both guardians and trustees. Edward gave little autonomy to Caroline beyond naming her one of the children's four guardians. His Irish trustees were to choose their accommodation and oversee its upkeep until his youngest son turned 24. Then they could decide to sell or dispose of it and the furniture. Edward placed conditions on every promise that involved Caroline. He instructed the trustees to provide her with the annuity of £100 to cover living costs for herself and Maria Ellen. More was to go to support the boys and their education. However, if she remarried, she was to cease to be a guardian to his children and would no longer receive the annuity. If she did not go to Ireland with all or some of the children, or did not reside in the house provided by the trustees, she was to receive £150 for two years, and lose all other bequests in the will. As long as she was a faithful widow, agreed to his terms, did not remarry or 'become the mother of another child except by me', she could hope to receive a proportion of his remaining assets equal to that of each of the surviving children once they were adults. If she remarried, half of her promised share of the estate was to be used to support his children's education. The other half was to be shared equally by his brother-in-law Thomas McCormack's family and his brother Patrick Kearney. Patrick could use this portion 'as he thinks meet for charitable purposes'. He instructed the trustees to use his assets to educate the children and to ensure that his sons – but not his daughter – should receive what was needed for their 'advancement' in the world. His final words enjoined the children to 'attend to their religious duties before all things so as to earn a share in the Kingdom of Heaven'.[15]

Edward's will continued the persecution of Caroline by his relatives that young Edward had complained of. It created a situation in which it was in the financial interest of his Irish trustees that Caroline should remarry, get pregnant or decide not to go to Ireland. And it furthered their moral and religious power to 'make us all Catholics', as young Edward put it.[16] The content supports Caroline's later claim that it was William who influenced what Edward envisaged. The intervention of his family was more critical in shaping its content than Edward's experiences in Australia. Edward may well have been disillusioned as a coloniser. Aboriginal invasions, scabby sheep, rigorous sheep inspectors and land that required deep, expensive wells were successive challenges that likely embittered and thwarted this headstrong man. His temper, use of violence and the heavy drinking both he and Caroline indulged in soured the childhoods of their offspring. He had good reason to worry about how Caroline would manage after his death. But it was the strong pressure of his family, keen to reshape his children's faith, that most shaped his final wishes. With whatever lucidity he brought to crafting the will, he may have weighed the advantages of a Catholic education and surveillance by his brothers against the love his children had for their horses, dogs and the country in which they were born. He opted for the former. The will sought to send Caroline away to a country she had never seen, cutting her off, likely for life, from her ongoing connections to her siblings and parents in South Australia and Victoria. Its provisions would take his children far away from their network of Protestant grandparents, aunts, uncles and cousins, and nip their emerging Australian identities in the bud.

What action could Caroline take? Women were expected to mourn privately, but things moved quickly in the days following deaths. Edward's was no exception. He died on Friday the 20th; the funeral was announced on the 21st and held on Sunday the 22nd. A day later, the solicitor, Thomas Pavey, arranged to place a notice in local newspapers as proctor for the executor, William Noall, announcing their intention to seek probate for the will. It appeared on the 24th, indicating that probate would be granted in fourteen days. This was the best time to contest a will, but there is no evidence that Caroline took any steps to do so. Had she consulted a lawyer, she would likely have been told that over-turning a will that was carefully constructed and signed by some-one of 'sound disposing mind' was difficult.[17] Still, her claim, years later, that Edward did not understand the conditions of the will might well have held up had she had the legal knowledge, financial resources, family support or stamina at the time to take action. Probate was granted to Noall as executor a month later, on 24 November. It took a further two months for the second executor, William McGann, to seek and receive approval. Both men swore that they would make an inventory of Edward's prop-erty and provide an account of their administration and that they believed the total value of his property fell below £7000.[18]

Caroline had few assets of her own beyond some furniture and 'personal chattels of very small value'. Her father, William Bax's teacher's salary of £60 was less than the £100 annuity

Edward had promised her, and certainly did not make him wealthy. Her sister Eleanor and her husband, James Hamilton, would help. At Ozenkadnook they accommodated relatives and passing strangers alike with generosity and the help of several servants, a cook and governess. Yet running their own station and household and raising their own three children, all under the age of five, surely limited their flexibility to absorb Caroline and her six children. Caroline could not claim the old widows' right of dower.[19] The Victorian courts recognised dower under some conditions, especially for women married prior to 1837, but there, as elsewhere, conveyancing strategies had eliminated most widows' claims. Anyway, as land held by lease, Edward's land would not have constituted a basis for dower.[20] His most valuable assets were his sheep and the improvements he had made to the station.[21] In the immediate aftermath of his death, Caroline's options were stark. She could refuse his final wishes and risk losing financial support beyond the first two years of her widowhood. Or she could submit to them.

After Edward's death and funeral, Caroline returned to Lockhart and the children. William Kearney and James Hamilton followed Edward's instruction to act as co-managers of the station until it could be sold. He had given them full authority to spend what was required to manage the station and its stock, hire and fire staff, and maintain Caroline and the children. They were not to sell anything. As Hamilton had his own station to oversee and William had effectively been running Lockhart for months, William took over. In that capacity he effectively stepped into Edward's shoes as the family patriarch and provider. He purchased the food and other supplies needed in bulk on the station. He controlled all financial transactions. If Caroline wanted money or needed credit to purchase clothes, books or anything else for herself or the children, she had to turn to him, to

Hamilton or to the executors. However, the executors were far away in Melbourne. At least one of them was increasingly aware of the messy financial situation and of the tense family relationships and divergent hopes dividing Kearney family members. Lockhart Station was mortgaged to W. J. T. Clarke for a considerable sum. Lockhart and Coniay were already listed in the Pastoral Register under his name. Shortly after Edward's death Clarke took possession of all the property except for some furniture and chattels that Caroline held on to. Initially, he left William Kearney and Hamilton in charge as managers and allowed the family to remain in residence. Hamilton appears to have contributed £100 personally every six months or so toward the family's maintenance between Edward's death and April 1867.[22]

William ran the station, overseeing the sheep and the first shearing season during the months that followed Edward's death. He sought to ensure that Caroline and the children were instructed in the Catholic faith. Miss Cunningham, the 'Catholic governess', remained until at least April 1866. Father Julian Tenison-Woods, who had ministered to Edward before his departure for Melbourne, made several return visits to the station in early 1866. William paid him for his services: £5 in January, £2 in February and £3 in April.[23] Later, William claimed that Caroline became a practising Roman Catholic over this time, attending mass and making confessions. This claim, like many that the Kearney brothers made under oath in court or elsewhere, rings false. Caroline denied it vehemently and swore that she had remained Protestant and always instructed the children in the Protestant faith.[24]

Conflicts between Catholics and Protestants and discrimination against Catholics had long roots in the law and culture of Britain and its Empire. Anti-Catholicism and Catholic–Protestant violence were common in Ireland, England, the settler colonies and beyond during the 19th century. The

Australian colonies were no exception. In the microcosm of Lockhart Station, the Kearneys' suspicion and hatred of English Protestant colonisers and landlords in Ireland pitted them against Caroline and her English parents and siblings. As we have seen young Edward believed that his father 'hated all English as most Irish do'. He described 'mother and father's relations' as being 'at drawn daggers, both sides holding different religious views'. Lockhart was a religious war zone, with Caroline, the children and their future at the heart of the conflict.[25]

Caroline may well have sought solace in the company of her servants and in drink, as she had done during Edward's eleven-month absence while in Ireland. She clearly agreed with her eldest son's determination not to be converted to Catholicism. Visits from or to members of her family offered a temporary escape from the tense climate and uncertainty about her future. In her tenth month of widowhood, in August 1866, she left Lockhart to visit Eleanor and James Hamilton at Ozenkadnook. Perhaps she rode alone on horseback or took some of the younger boys with her in a bullock cart or carriage. Or maybe she left them under the care of their cousin, Mary Ann Kearney, of a governess, or of the station manager's wife. Maria Ellen, by then aged twelve, certainly remained at the station.

Caroline was at Ozenkadnook when she received a letter with shocking news. Mary Ann Kearney had written to warn her that William had taken advantage of her absence to abduct her only daughter, Maria Ellen, from the station. She later found out that he had taken his niece hundreds of miles south-east to a convent in Geelong (see image 6 in the picture section), where, claiming his authority as one of the children's guardians, he placed her under the care of Mother Xavier.[26]

Mary Cecilia Xavier Maguire was the Mother Superior of the Sisters of Mercy. The nuns of this Dublin-based order were rapidly expanding across the British Empire, running schools, orphanages and other institutions for girls in parts of British North America and New Zealand as well as in Australia. The Bishop of Melbourne, James Alipius Goold, a native of County Cork, had been seeking to bring nuns to Victoria for some time. He hoped they would reproduce the services they offered to orphans, girls seeking education and the poor in Ireland among the Catholic population of the colony. The sisters set up their first institution in Perth. Goold convinced them to go to Melbourne in 1857. In 1859 Mother Xavier, then just finishing her term as Superior of the Dublin convent, agreed to start a new establishment in Geelong. The Sisters of Mercy in Ireland had also recently established a convent in Moate, Westmeath, Patrick Kearney's parish. When Patrick died, that convent was described as a 'tribute to his wise counsel, patronage and charity'. I believe that Patrick's close connection with this order played a role in William's removal and placement of Maria Ellen.[27]

Was William acting upon the unexplained clause in Edward's will that provided him with £100 'to be applied by him according to the directions' he had already given him? Did Maria Ellen willingly seek to escape the religious, personal or sexual tensions at the station, or the male world of station life? Had her uncle William bullied or bribed her to accompany him? She has left almost no records that might help determine her role in this. It was not a spur-of-the-moment decision on William's part. Later accounts show that he had bought clothes for 'going to school' for his niece, whom he referred to as 'Minnie', on 7 August. They did not leave until the 20th. This abduction of a young daughter whose father was Catholic and mother Protestant speaks poignantly to the power of his family's influence, and perhaps to a revival of Catholic faith having influenced the dying Edward's final wishes. Like his will and the retinue of Irish Catholic relatives who returned with him from Ireland, it sought to ensure that his children were raised Catholic and that Caroline's influence was minimised.[28]

To place Maria Ellen with these nuns was to assert both her Irishness and her Catholicism. At this time the Sisters had been in Geelong for less than six years. Housed initially in an existing orphanage in the suburb of Newtown, the community had pledged to raise money for a complex of buildings for them. Eventually, their institutions would include an orphanage, a boarding school, a day school, an industrial school, a lending library and a small farm. In early 1860 they began advertising for boarders at their new convent school. Fees paid by the families of relatively wealthy students would help fund the care of orphans and other work with the poor. The sisters began taking in orphans in 1860, though the official register of Our Lady's Orphanage began in 1862. By the time Maria Ellen and William arrived in late August 1866, the convent was complete. Both the orphanage and the girls' boarding school, Sacred Heart College, were admitting children. This impressive complex of classical buildings still sits on a large property with panoramic views across parts of the growing town of Geelong and the broad sweep of Corio Bay.[29]

William and Maria Ellen travelled there at considerable expense. They took a Cobb & Co. coach to Melbourne on 20 August. From there they travelled south-west to Geelong to what William called the 'Geelong Convent School'. The school was in the same large building as the beautiful chapel and the Sisters' living quarters. The school's current archivist explained to me that parents and children entered through the smaller of two north-facing doors. The gendered religious hierarchy of Catholic protocol dictated that only the bishop could enter through the other more elaborate doorway. Inside, a hallway led to the reception room where Maria Ellen and William likely met Mother

Xavier. Perhaps William brought greetings from his brother Patrick in Ireland. What passed between them and exactly what was agreed on about Maria Ellen's future may never be clear. He might have shared worries about his niece's soul, or her life on the station, or about Caroline's mothering skills. He made it clear that he was her legal guardian. And he paid Mother Xavier £20 towards Maria Ellen's maintenance from his brother's estate. Records produced later show a further immense £29 5s owing.[30]

Pupils' names were usually carefully inscribed in the school register. Sadly, or possibly strangely, the original register for the earliest years of the school no longer exists. At some point someone transcribed the names of pupils who entered between 1860 and 1873 into the following register, which began in 1874. Instead of the usual detail of their full names, those of their parents, and sometimes an indication about their death, they were listed simply as 'The Misses O'Malley', or 'Miss Foley'. There is no Miss Kearney among the thirteen girls listed for 1866.[31] Why not? Perhaps it was because she did not arrive at the beginning of term. Or, might Mother Xavier and William have sought to keep her presence a secret, given his actions in taking her from her Protestant mother, and Edward's enigmatic instructions? Could the first register have been destroyed and her name omitted from the later transcription of pupils to cover up her presence, or what happened next? This all remains a mystery.

It is easier to understand why the college appealed to William. The Sisters offered a Catholic environment and a solid Catholic education. Here girls could benefit from a liberal education that included mathematics, botany, astronomy, languages and ancient and modern history alongside tapestry and religious instruction. Among its pupils were the 'daughters of the wealthiest people in the land', who had until then relied on governesses. The number of girls at this 'high class educational establishment' grew rapidly

– from under ten initially to around 100 in the following years.[32]

Caroline had not taken immediate action to contest Edward's will, but now she moved quickly. Once she had determined the direction that William and Maria had travelled from someone at Lockhart, she and James Hamilton set off on the long trip to Melbourne. There they consulted the trustee, William McGann. Inquiries in Melbourne clarified that William had taken Maria Ellen to the convent. Their first tactic was to reason with the mother superior. Caroline, James Hamilton and McGann travelled to Geelong. On 8 September they saw Maria Ellen and met with the 'tall and commanding' Mother Xavier. They showed her the will that named both Caroline and William as guardians of the children, and asked her to return Maria Ellen. Unsurprisingly, this devout, energetic Catholic woman did not wish to relinquish one of her charges to a Protestant mother, and certainly not without William Kearney's consent. Newspapers report that 'the superioress, bound by her engagement with and duty to William Kearney and the child, declined to surrender her on the mother's sole demand'.[33]

Caroline Hamilton and McGann returned to Melbourne where they secured the services of Thomas Pavey, the solicitor who had overseen the writing of Edward Kearney's last will. To help Caroline retrieve her daughter he engaged the barrister George Henry Webb, a former journalist, who was admitted to the bar in 1860 and began publishing the first legal case reports in Victoria in 1861. If Caroline's understandings of legal possibilities and procedures had been minimal up to this point, she now began to experience the work and strategies involved in crafting affidavits for court with a solicitor. Pavey and Webb decided to apply for a writ of habeas corpus. This old English law, understood to lie at the very heart of English rights to liberty, had become part of the law in Victoria, as in the other Australian and most British colonies. It offered a mechanism for determining whether 'or not an alleged detention' was legal. Though it is best known and was most frequently used to remedy cases of arbitrary imprisonment, it has also been applied over the centuries in cases of disputed custody and guardianship. Caroline's claim was that her daughter was unlawfully detained by the Sisters. Her goal was simple: to get her back.[34]

Pavey prepared Caroline's affidavit. Webb appeared in the Supreme Court in Melbourne on 12 September on her behalf, requesting that a writ of habeas corpus be addressed to the mother superior 'commanding her to bring into court the body of Maria Ellen Kearney that she may be delivered to the lawful custody of her mother, Caroline Anne Kearney of Lockhart Station'. Caroline's affidavit outlined the date of Edward's death, the clauses of his will appointing her and the other guardians, and the events leading up to William's removal of her daughter. It also described her attempt to secure her daughter's release and Mother Xavier's refusal. One section of the affidavit claiming that she believed her daughter was being held against her will was crossed out. In its place this section simply noted that Caroline wished her daughter to return home and live with her and her other children.[35] The three justices directed that a writ of habeas corpus be delivered to the mother superior. It required that Mother Xavier bring Maria Ellen to the court in two days, or risk being proceeded against for not doing so.[36] The next day, James Hamilton and the solicitor Pavey delivered the writ to her in Geelong.[37]

*Re Maria Ellen Kearney* was heard in the colony's imposing courthouse in Melbourne on 14 September. When it was built in 1842, it was on 'the outskirts of town, high on the hill' north-west of the city, and 'visible to the settlement below'. By the time Caroline made her way up to the corner of La Trobe and Russell streets in 1866, the city had expanded around and beyond it.[38]

119

Three of the colony's four judges – Chief Justice Stawell, and Justices Redmond Barry and Edward Eyre Williams – heard the case. They were the elite of the legal profession in the young colony. All had played key roles in its political, legal and social formation, holding official posts and elected positions and shaping its laws and institutions.

Sir William Foster Stawell had arrived in Victoria in 1842 – about the same time as Edward Kearney. He too came from Ireland but, like a disproportionate number of early members of the bar, including Redmond Barry, was from an Anglo–Irish family. From County Cork originally, he trained in the law first at Trinity College Dublin, and then at Lincoln's Inn, London before emigrating. In the colony he had risen quickly within the legal profession and in politics. He personally shaped many of the administrative and legal structures of the new colony, including 'the system of responsible government' in Victoria after it separated from New South Wales. He was appointed as Victoria's first attorney-general in 1851, won a Melbourne seat in the first election for the colony's legislative assembly in 1856, then resigned to fulfil his ambition of becoming chief justice of the colony in 1857. He would hold that position until 1886. When Caroline's case was heard, he had been married for a decade and, in contrast to some of his contemporary legal colleagues, his private life was said to be 'impeccable'. Initially agnostic, and somewhat 'wild', he had become a devout Anglican by the time of this case, as well as a leader of the Anglo–Irish community in Victoria.[39]

Mother Xavier complied. She brought Maria Ellen and her own counsel to court. The justices later reported that they had considered consulting Maria Ellen herself, but decided against it. This practice was beginning to be more common in Australia, as elsewhere, particularly if children were nearly adult. But Maria Ellen was not yet twelve, and while boys legally reached the age of discretion at fourteen, for girls the age was sixteen. Stawell made it clear that they were not seeking her own 'desires as to the custody she would prefer, because she is not of an age to have any legal discretion or choice upon that point'. Anyway, the case seemed clear to this judge, who has been described as conscientious, very practical, and impartial. Caroline had been caring for her daughter since her husband's death. She asked for the return of her daughter. She was the mother. She was one of the guardians. She had not remarried. He concluded that there was

> not a shadow of a suggestion that the mother is of a
> character disentitling her to the custody of her child.
> The father who appointed her one of the testamentary
> guardians evidently thought her a proper person to have
> such custody. The child was taken away in an improper
> way ... The child is of an age, above all other ages, when
> she is most in need of a mother's care. In the absence of
> all suggestion of any special reason to the contrary, the
> mother has established her right at law to the custody
> of her daughter, and our duty is a simple one on this
> application.[40]

Mother Xavier was ordered to return Maria Ellen to her mother. Stawell may have been influenced by Caroline's Protestantism. Yet ultimately the processes of the law and gendered understandings about girls needing mothers worked against William's determination to stop the court returning the child to Caroline. William had engaged counsel and sworn an affidavit seeking a postponement that would allow him to contest any decision in Caroline's favour. This tactic was not legal. As Stawell repeatedly explained to Mr Billing, William's counsel, once a writ of habeas corpus had been accepted, as this one was, 'only the applicant for the writ, and the person to whom the writ was addressed, could be heard' regarding its content.[41]

This sad tale of a white mother separated from her child was published in several newspapers in Victoria and New South Wales, fuelling the existing discourses of sectarian strife. 'Detention of a Girl in a Convent' was the dramatic heading in the *Maitland and Hunter River General Advertiser*. The more detailed versions ended by reporting that after the solicitors for Mrs Kearney and the mother superior had conferred, 'the child was delivered over to her mother, and both with happy faces left the precincts of the court.'[42]

There is no indication in the court records or most newspaper reports that Stawell considered the Catholic–Protestant battle at the heart of William's actions. Melbourne's *Punch* certainly did. It published a satirical column headed 'A Case of Alleged Religious Kidnapping'. Maria Ellen, the author wrote, 'was brought from a Geelongese convent to the Supreme Court by train and habeas corpus, in order to be restored to her heart-broken mamma, who appeared to have a rooted repugnance to young girls wearing veils'. Their column named William Kearney as the 'cruel relative', and suggested that 'Mr. Webb was one too many for him, as he had enlisted everybody's sympathy in consequence of having, with an old quill pen, drawn a heartrending picture of a mother's misery, making any quantity of blots for tears, and little holes in the paper for sobs'.[43]

Yet Maria Ellen did not return to Lockhart with Caroline. Apparently she herself 'wished to go back to the convent'. Caroline allowed her to do so. The crossed-out clause in the affidavit of the habeas corpus case stating she was held against her will suggests that Caroline knew of Maria Ellen's desire before the case went to court. Perhaps having won her court case, and hence defeated her brother-in-law, she accepted her daughter's wish to remain there.[44] One can guess at good reasons why Maria Ellen might have opted to remain. The convent complex was a predominantly female space, regulated by the rhythms of Catholic prayer, set meal times and classes. What a contrast with the rough, largely male space of Lockhart Station, dominated by the rhythms of the day, the season, the weather and sheep farming! The male culture of outback stations made them dangerous places for girls on the edge of puberty. At nearly twelve she may already have experienced or feared sexual advances from men on the station, from the retinue of Catholic relatives or from males passing through. Peaceful and certainly pious, the convent may well have seemed a welcome refuge after the death of the father who had beaten her, the uncertainty about their future, and the religious conflict and general chaos of the previous months of her life. She may also have wanted a better education than the series of governesses and her mother could offer, and enjoyed the company of the daughters of the colony's Catholic elite. William and his relatives could well have encouraged her to favour Catholicism over Protestantism.

Less than three months later, Maria Ellen died. The death certificate indicates that she died on 29 November in the Geelong convent. Measles was listed as the cause. She had been ill for fourteen days. Her eldest brother, Edward, later told his future wife that he found it strange that some 100 girls in the school caught the measles, yet only Maria Ellen died. Indeed, much was strange about her death. I have found no evidence of a significant outbreak of measles at the school at the time, though this infectious disease was certainly in the area. A month after Maria Ellen's death, the Protestant Orphan Asylum in Geelong stopped taking in new children because of an outbreak of the infection. Some 100 of their children had contracted it – perhaps this number explains young Edward's mention of 100 girls. All recovered.[45] Outbreaks of infectious disease were most common in orphanages and industrial schools, not elite girls' schools. The government-run industrial school in Geelong was swamped with children brought from Melbourne that year. They were undernourished, dirty and infected with lice. Conjunctivitis, and occasionally measles, spread among them like wildfire. But the inspector of industrial schools, George O. Duncan, found no such problems at the industrial school run by the Sisters of Mercy at the Geelong convent when he visited just two weeks after Maria Ellen's death. He reported that all the children there were well cared for and healthy.[46] There was no legislation requiring any similar investigation of the Sisters' private school for girls.

Caroline later claimed that Maria Ellen died of tuberculosis. It is possible that the family history of consumption, to which Caroline repeatedly referred, had weakened her system, making her susceptible to complications from measles. Or the cause may have been wrongly listed. Death from measles was by then rare.[47] In the convent there was a small room that served as an infirmary for sick girls, beside the larger infirmary for the Sisters. Nursing sisters could move between the two. I imagine that Maria Ellen was cared for in this space and quarantined from the other students. Quarantining any mention of her death from a contagious illness while at the school was surely important too. Any news of infectious diseases in a school that was attracting the daughters of prominent Victorians could scare away the parents of current students, and potential future parents. A death might ruin their reputation. Maria Ellen's body was whisked away the day after she died to the Geelong cemetery and quickly buried by the undertaker, J. W. Hudson.

Hudson signed Maria Ellen's death certificate.[48] The missing details on that document add yet another perplexing thread to her brief and sad life story. Nuns normally kept excellent records about their charges. It is strange that no trace of her time with Mother Xavier appears in the current archives of the school or the orphanage, and even stranger that Hudson reported her mother's and father's names as well as the amount of time in the colonies as unknown. Mother Xavier clearly knew who her mother was. The two women had met at the convent and been in the same courtroom together less than three months earlier. Caroline's descendants today rightly question why Mother Xavier or other Sisters withheld information that should have been at their finger-tips about who her parents were. They wonder too whether she failed to inform Caroline about her daughter's illness. A decade later, young Edward recorded his conviction that there was 'some deep roguery at the bottom of it', rooted in the religious conflict between Caroline and the Kearneys.[49] I remain perplexed about why these details were not better recorded. Edward remem-bered his mother being 'much grieved' by Maria Ellen's death. Caroline surely blamed her brother-in-law William. Yet she her-self had agreed to Maria Ellen remaining with the Sisters. And now she had lost her only daughter.

The state of the estate was a nightmare. William Noall had renounced his position as executor soon after probate was granted. William McGann, who had helped Caroline search for Maria Ellen, was soon very keen to do so too. Working with William Kearney proved challenging for the executors. He failed or refused to properly explain many of the expenditures he was incurring as manager. Like his brother, he was obstinate, liti-gious and sloppy about records. McGann was careful and sus-picious enough in his role to request that an accountant go over William's accounts. He could track records for only £80 of the £264 William had spent. McGann made plaint in court for the £184 difference. William hired the prominent solicitor John Barter Bennett, of the firm Bennett & Taylor, to fight back. Bennett had migrated to Melbourne in 1842 from England, articled in Melbourne and practised there since 1847. He was a member of the legislative council of Victoria and served from 1856 until 1863, when he resigned. He worked with William to settle some matters regarding Edward's estate, and in the proceedings against him by McGann. William was quicker to turn to the legal profession than to pay for their services. Eventually Bennett had to pursue him for £55 13s William owed him.[50] The number of court cases concerning the Kearneys and Edward's estate was growing.

Executors' jobs were usually onerous. The distance between Melbourne and Lockhart, and William Kearney's actions and meddling, compounded the challenges that most executors faced. The mortgager, Clarke, was clearly worried about his investment. In September 1866, while William Kearney was away transporting Maria Ellen to Geelong, he installed his own manager on the station.[51] William, who was allowed £2 6s 8d a week for his services from the time he took over prior to Edward's death, was out of a job. Clarke did not kick Caroline and the children out of the station. He applied the balance of profits and expenses towards paying off the mortgage. But he refused to advance money for their maintenance or any other purposes on the security of the estate. The executors thought that Caroline's annuity was only to start once she and the children had removed to Ireland. If she needed money for clothing or to travel she had to ask her relatives or the remaining executor, McGann. As noted earlier, her brother-in-law James Hamilton appears to have contributed £100 personally towards the families' maintenance three times between Edward's death and August 1867.[52] Caroline might well have resented this demeaning dependency.

She had lost her only daughter. Her life and the lives of her five surviving children were in limbo. Edward's wish to send them to Ireland hung over them, threatening to rip them out of her network of kin and the only world the boys knew. Edward's promise of a £100 annuity was reasonably generous, especially when combined with the further provisions for the boys' education. Yet she could not access this support. It was the injunction to leave Australia and live in Ireland that was draconian, revealing the extent of a male patriarch's power over the bodies of his widow and children. Ireland was home for Edward; Caroline had never been there. Such a will would not hold up in courts today. But in jurisdictions of the English common law at the time, a testator's final wishes had the sanctity of a contract.

Caroline and the children remained at Lockhart, now run by the manager installed by Clarke. They also spent time at Ozenkadnook with her sister Eleanor. Caroline 'repeatedly' asked William McGann not to sell the station. The mortgage was slowly being paid off as sheep were sold, but the estate continued to be unsettled.[53] The trustees were based in Melbourne, far away from Lockhart. Distance compounded their tasks. To Caroline, they were clearly dragging their feet. The abduction of Maria Ellen ten months after Edward's death revealed the depth of William Kearney's determination to Catholicise the children at all costs. The 'drawn daggers' of the religious conflict that began on Edward's return from Ireland had escalated into family warfare.[54] Caroline determined to fight back. Her first foray into the courts, contesting Maria Ellen's placement with Mother Xavier, was successful legally, though it ended disastrously. Maria Ellen's decision to stay at the convent school and her subsequent death surely furthered Caroline's resolve to contest the conditions of Edward's will and the actions of his brothers. She did so shortly.

# 5

# Learning legal procedures

Visiting their uncle and aunt at Ozenkadnook Station offered comfort to the children and support for Caroline. It was there that a messenger sent by Thomas Pavey's law firm finally located her after travelling first to Lockhart in July 1867. There he had served William Burge, the manager, a subpoena duces tecum. He was seeking Caroline to deliver a subpoena ad testificandum. Caroline might not understand the Latin, but the message was clear enough. She and Burge were required to attend court in Melbourne. Burge was being asked to produce records that would justify or discredit the claim of one of Edward's Irish Catholic workers, Charles Mulrain, that the estate owed him a significant amount of money. Caroline was wanted to give oral testimony in that case, as well as in the two others underway pitting Edward's executor William McGann against William Kearney.[1]

It was not yet a year since Caroline had gone to court to seek the return of Maria Ellen with McGann's help. It was just eight months since her daughter's death. Caroline's knowledge of legal language and court-related processes was about to expand dramatically. Her movements and her hopes and fears over the next three years would be shaped by the slow, ritualised processes of the civil law in colonial Victoria. She would observe how lawyers crafted affidavits and cross-checked evidence. She would experience the tedious, expensive and frustrating workings of equity law, critiqued so scathingly a decade earlier in Charles Dickens' 1853 novel *Bleak House*. The detailed, careful accumulation of information that this process produced has been a goldmine for me. Virtually every payment of a bill, every hour of solicitors' and barristers' time, was tracked. Such civil cases lack the drama of criminal court proceedings with their oral examinations before a judge and jury. But the figures and other evidence that Caroline's suit generated, so carefully tallied, double-checked and sworn on oath, offer invaluable insights. They reveal the unfolding of the legal processes and decision-making that were critical to Caroline and the children's futures. And they provide some evidence of their movements and whereabouts from the time of Edward's death until the suit ended.

Maria Ellen's death had, I imagine, left Caroline grieving, seething with anger and struggling to develop a strategy to remain in Australia. The subpoena offered new possibilities. It obliged her to return to Melbourne. If she did not go she could be charged with contempt of court. If she did, the legal authorities would pay for her to travel from Ozenkadnook to Edenhope and then by coach and railway to attend court. They would also compensate her for her loss of time.[2] Here was a chance to return to the city, consult lawyers, and deal with the awful fact of her daughter's burial in the Geelong cemetery. She decided to go and to take her eldest son with her.

Caroline and young Edward arrived in Melbourne on 6 August. She gave evidence, as required in these three cases. She would have known Charles Mulrain. He was a relative of Edward and William on their mother's side. He probably began working at Lockhart when William and his retinue of Catholic relations arrived from Ireland. He had initiated this suit in the county court against William McGann in June 1867, claiming that over £215 was owed to him for back pay, at a rate of £100 a year, and that further money was owing to him for a horse he had sold the manager and for some of his sheep that had not been returned to him. Charles was sweet on William's niece Mary Anne Kearney. He could afford to marry her and return to Ireland if he could secure the money owed him. Because of the amount involved, the case was moved to the Supreme Court, which is where Caroline's evidence was heard. In the end, Mulrain received only £34 from the estate, and costs. McGann resented being charged by another member of the Kearney family for actions taken by the manager whom Clarke, the mortgage holder, had appointed. And his frustration with William Kearney was mounting as his case against him dragged on in the courts.[3] Litigation involving William Kearney, the executors and the estate more generally was beginning to make the Kearney troubles widely known among the legal community and the newspaper-reading public of the colony.

Melbourne offered many attractions to a young widow from an isolated sheep station. It had shops with the latest fashions, entertainment, restaurants with fine wine, saloons and a vibrant street life. Like other squatters' wives, Caroline might have shopped, window-shopped and asserted her gentility through her choices of accommodation, clothing and entertainment.[4] Caroline was surely tempted by some of these attractions. Yet her main goals concerned her family. She wanted to arrange a proper burial for her daughter. She contacted Hudson, the undertaker who had buried Maria Ellen, and arranged to have her body exhumed from Geelong, transported to Melbourne and reburied in Edward's grave in the Catholic section of the Melbourne Cemetery. Young Edward recalled that 'father's grave was opened, and the coffin that is supposed to contain sister's remains' was buried in it. A note was added to the registration of Maria Ellen's death indicating that this transfer occurred on 15 August, apparently with the authorisation of the registrar-general. Caroline also commissioned a painting of the grave (picture section, image 7). It evokes a rich green landscape, dramatically different from the yellow-brown colours of the Wimmera country. Romantic and conventional, it suggests that however strained Caroline's relationship may have been over the final years of their marriage, she retained an emotional bond with her deceased husband. Hudson charged £50 for his part in the transfer. Daley, who had buried Edward, charged a further £2 for reopening the grave. In addition to any amounts the court provided for her court testimony, the executors paid at least a further £17 for food, accommodation and other expenses on this trip. It was clearly important for Caroline to unite the two dead members of her family.[5]

Burying her dead daughter in the grave with Edward was not Caroline's only goal on this paid trip to Melbourne in August 1867. She also sought legal help to free herself from her financial dependence on distant and changing executors and on her brothers-in-law. She wanted to find a way to overturn the requirement that she and the children move to Ireland. Perhaps she talked with Pavey about her options while attending one of the other cases. He was by then only too aware of the fraught relationships in the family and heavily involved as solicitor for McGann. He may have suggested other law firms she could approach. She was now very familiar with Melbourne's legal precinct, in the south-west part of the city, framed by Collins, William, Lonsdale and Queen streets, where the majority of Melbourne's leading solicitors, barristers and attorneys had their offices. Edward had died at the Washington Hotel in the heart of the precinct. The office of Thomas Pavey was located at the corner of Collins and Queen streets. The chambers for most of the city's barristers were in the elegant, classical Temple Court building (see image 8 in the picture section), constructed in the 1850s in Chancery Lane between Collins and Little Collins streets. Solicitors' offices dotted the other streets of the precinct.[6]

The offices of Miller and Ireland at 100 Elizabeth Street were nearby and easy to find. Solicitor Walter Moore Miller agreed to assist in mounting a case for her and the children. This recent immigrant had been admitted to the English bar in 1854, then migrated to Australia. Men already admitted 'to a court in the United Kingdom' needed no further training to practise in Victoria.[7] If Caroline hoped for a speedy resolution of her problems, as had happened in her habeas corpus case, she would soon learn that there was little chance of that. Her complaints fell within the jurisdiction of the body of English law known as equity, administered in England by separate courts of chancery. In *Bleak House*, Dickens painted a particularly dark picture of conflicts over a will that dragged on longer than the lives of the original litigants. In Victoria, legislation passed in 1852 – shaped largely by Sir William Foster Stawell, who had heard Caroline's habeas corpus case – provided for one Supreme Court for the colony of Victoria, headed by a chief justice and two other judges. That court oversaw both civil and criminal cases, and administered all the main bodies of English law – common law, equity and ecclesiastical – rather than having separate courts for each, as was true in England before 1873. Its jurisdiction in Victoria included cases involving minor plaintiffs, along with those 'involving complex financial arrangements, execution of intestate estates where there was no apparent heir', interpretation of contracts, wills and inheritance contests. Caroline's complaints involved her children as minors. Tracking the financial state of the estate would prove complex. She was seeking to modify her husband's final wishes.[8]

Suits in equity had to follow a series of precise steps. The first involved the plaintiff outlining their grievance in a petition known as a bill. Evidence was presented in written form as numbered points rather than orally in court. This demanded the careful crafting of the plaintiff's bill, stating the facts and background history of the case, seeking specific goals and identifying the defendants. The court's master in equity, Frederick Wilkinson, oversaw all that was sent to court from the original bill through the collection of evidence, the wording of affidavits, the verification of accounts and all matters relating to the settling of estates, the careful lodging of documents, following up on evidence and eventually arranging costs. Walter Miller began the work of preparing Caroline's bill.[9]

Caroline and Edward junior remained in Melbourne for about ten days on that trip – long enough to give evidence in the court cases, rebury Maria Ellen, and to clarify the nature of Caroline's concerns in discussions with Miller. They then rejoined the rest of the family at Lockhart. Her actions appear to have precipitated some changes. McGann had had enough of the Kearney conflicts and his role as a trustee. Perhaps he had heard of Caroline's intentions. He encouraged Henry Wallace Lowry, an Irish-born accountant, to replace him as the sole colonial trustee. After some time Lowry agreed, and took over officially on 23 September, about five weeks after Caroline and young Edward had left Melbourne.[10]

It was nearly seven months before Caroline's bill was ready to present. This was partly because she had other worries. After their return to Lockhart young Edward had a bad fall from his horse. As he later described it, the fall led to serious internal bleeding and gastric irritation which lasted several months. He seemed to recover, but then relapsed with 'gastric fever'. He recalled being bedridden for seven months. Fearing the possibility of losing another child, Caroline took him again on the long trip to Melbourne late in December 1867. There they consulted two 'eminent' doctors. He later said that they held little hope for his survival, but he 'cheated the undertaker. If I had not done so, there would have been 3 Kearneys buried in the same grave in as many years.' Visits to the Collins Street doctors Garrard and James, and their care for Edward in Melbourne, cost over £15. Medicine purchased at William Bowen's chemist shop on Collins Street added £7 18s 6d. Lowry provided a further £35 to Caroline to cover their travelling expenses and board and lodging in the city. Caroline likely consulted her solicitor again while in Melbourne before they returned 'to the bush'.[11] Young Edward's illness surely reinforced Caroline's conviction that it would be dangerous for her sickness-prone children to travel to Ireland. Fighting for that outcome would take her away from the station and the children again and again before a decision was finalised. Eleanor and James Hamilton stepped in, offering support and shelter to the children, and to Caroline at times.

In February 1868 she and the solicitor, Miller, sorted out the final details of her suit. Late in March she officially authorised Miller to institute the 'suit and to use my name as the next friend to the infant plaintiffs'. Caroline and her boys had now officially entered the legal system as plaintiffs. The bill identified the defendants as her family adversary, William Kearney, and the new trustee, Henry Wallace Lowry. On 30 March William Foster Stawell, as chief justice, and Frederick Wilkinson, as master of equity, signed to acknowledge the court's receipt of Caroline's plaint. As finally formulated, it began, as was required in equity cases, with the background history. The first ten points carefully outlined the details of Edward's death and of what he had written in his will. It explained that William Noall had renounced his position as executor and that McGann had sought to replace himself with Lowry.[12]

Then, as required, it turned to her allegations. This part of a bill alerted defendants to the charges that the plaintiff, Caroline, believed were true, and to which they would have to respond. The eleventh point claimed that Lowry had neglected to collect monies due to the estate and was refusing requests for maintenance for her and the children. She then claimed that her daughter had died of consumption and that the other children were susceptible to the same disease. Caroline expressed her fear that moving to Ireland would 'prove fatal' to the health of her five remaining children. Finally she asserted her wish 'to remain in this country with her children'. Such suits concluded with what was known in English equity as a prayer – a delineation of the remedies sought. Caroline sought an account of Edward's estate; a suitable allowance for her and the children, backdated to Edward's death date; and directions from the court about the residence of the children, given 'their present state of health'. The conclusion asserted that Caroline was entitled to enjoy her legacy under the will even if she did not 'proceed to and reside in Ireland'. The defendants were required to prepare their responses to each point within 42 days.[13]

Caroline's solicitor had copies of her bill made. These were sent along with a summons to the defendants, Henry Wallace Lowry and William Kearney. Her official contestation of the will initiated a busy period for them. They had to go to the Equity Court and submit themselves to its jurisdiction. If they did not already have legal advice, they had to quickly engage a law firm to secure and present the evidence required to answer Caroline's charges.[14] Lowry wisely hired Thomas Pavey, the solicitor who was already deeply involved in the Kearney conflicts. Later, when the issues grew more complex, demanding the specialised knowledge and courtroom skills of a barrister, he again requested the services of George Henry Webb.[15]

Lowry responded quickly, with the help of Pavey. His answer was ready and sworn on 1 May. Such answers had to accept or reject each of the claims made in the plaintiff's numbered bill. Lowry accepted the summary of the content of Edward's will and added some details about William Noall's resignation as executor. Then he claimed that he not been able to pay any support to Caroline because the mortgage on the station and the lack of subsequent revenues from it meant he had only received £36 up to that point, £35 of which he had given to Caroline for maintenance for her and the children. He also noted that he had requested that the mortgage-holder, Turner, advance money to them that would be repaid with the mortgage, but he had refused. Finally, he asserted that his appointment as a trustee did not overturn the rights or liabilities of the former trustee, William McGann, and therefore that he was a necessary party to the suit.[16] Wilkinson, the master of equity, agreed. McGann became the third defendant. The suit's official title from then on was *Kearney and others versus Henry Wallace Lowry, William Kearney and William McGann*. The short title was simply *Kearney v. Lowry*.

It took William Kearney longer to craft his answer – a few days more than the 42 normally allowed. He may have had some trouble finding a solicitor willing to take on his case, given his ongoing conflicts with John Barter Bennett, the solicitor he had engaged in the suits the executors had taken out against him.[17] Over the course of Caroline's suit he would try the patience of his legal team with his constant interfering and obfuscations. In April 1868 he secured the services of Mr William Hughes, a much less prominent solicitor than Bennett. Hughes was then working as an agent for another Melbourne solicitor, R. R. Lees. Hughes's name does not appear among the solicitors and attorneys listed in the city's leading directory until 1870, when he had settled into an office on Elizabeth Street, which suggests he was not yet very well established. William worked with him over April and early May, and on 18 May his answer was deposited at the equity office.

William was determined that his Catholic family in Ireland

rather than Caroline's Protestant family in Australia would control the futures of Caroline and especially the children. 'The plaintiff ... should not be permitted to enjoy the bequest to her ... unless she proceed to and reside in Ireland pursuant to the direction in said will' was the final and key claim in his affidavit. He had no quarrel with most of the summary of Edward's will. He did highlight the clause that had required that the trustees sell the station by private contract and that prior to that he and James Hamilton were to be entitled to 'such sums' as were necessary to work and manage it. He anticipated compensation for his assistance running the station. William pleaded ignorance about whether Lowry had neglected to collect moneys or to support Caroline and the children. In his final paragraph he took care to counter Caroline's claim that her daughter had died of consumption. His evidence was Maria Ellen's death certificate, which listed the cause of her death as measles. Given that, he dismissed Caroline's suggestion that the other children were susceptible to consumption or that moving to Ireland would be harmful to their health.[18]

McGann's answer, also deposited on 18 May, was crafted with the assistance of another Collins Street solicitor, William Trollope. McGann supported Lowry's actions as trustee, dismissing the idea that Lowry had neglected to collect and receive monies as Caroline claimed. He confirmed William Kearney's claim that Maria Ellen had died of measles, offering her death certificate as proof. But McGann, who more than anyone else involved had experienced the frustrations of dealing with Edward's will and with his brother William, supported Caroline's other requests. He agreed that an account should be taken of the estate, that she be paid an allowance, and that the court should make a decision about whether moving to Ireland would compromise the children's health.[19]

Copies of the three defendants' answers were filed in the court and given to Caroline as the plaintiff. This precipitated the next stage of a suit in equity: evidence-gathering. Over the next three months the solicitors for each of the defendants met each other and their clients frequently, performing the routine information-gathering and close work with clients that distinguished their work days from those of the more educated barristers who undertook complicated legal tasks and presented cases in the courts.[20] William Kearney's sloppy bookkeeping compounded the task. Mr Pavey, as Lowry's solicitor, spent hours with Kearney's solicitor and his accountant, poring over the station bank books and vouchers. They identified discrepancies between the different records. Matters had to be verified with Clarke regarding the mortgage and his accounts. McGann's solicitor, Trollope, went over information for the period prior to his resignation as a trustee. Each solicitor began crafting affidavits for their client that would support their claims as plaintiff or defendants and provide evidence for their answers.[21]

Caroline had to wait until their answers and the collection of all the other necessary information was complete before the suit could go to court. Perhaps in anticipation of her appearance in court she had purchased some new clothes, two hats, ostrich feathers, a brooch, boots and some envelopes and papers in January 1868. Three months later she bought some red flannel, tweed, trimmings, some wincey fabric, and one wincey dress as well as a pair of stays. Later the draper would bill the estate for £33 14s 2d worth of goods for her and the children.[22] Postal deliveries had just been regularised into Lockhart. Mail was forwarded from Melbourne to Portland via Nhill, Lawloit, Yannock, Bullarook, Bunyip, Yarrack and Cove to Lockhart Station. In 1868 the post office directory named Lockhart's manager William Burge, as well as stockkeepers William Jones and J. O'Keefe, and W. Kearney as the receivers of mail at Lockhart.[23] The envelopes and paper and speedier mail communication would be essential for Caroline as she communicated back and forth with her solicitor reworking the wording of her bill and preparing for the case to be heard.

Waiting is awful. Caroline chafed at her dependence on station rations, relatives and others for financial support. Before William's response was submitted on 18 May she asked her solicitor to let the trustee know that she and the children were destitute. Lowry then finally succeeded in convincing Clarke to advance some money for support of the family on the security of the mortgage. Caroline's claim was somewhat disingenuous. Her brother-in-law James Hamilton was contributing to their support, and food supplies were available at the station. Certainly bills were mounting: lawyers' fees for her court case about Maria Ellen; doctors' bills for young Edward's illness and for other medical care at the station; merchants' bills for her clothing; costs of travel to Melbourne. But these were understood as debts against the estate. Creditors were willing, indeed obliged, to wait until the estate was settled. Caroline herself was not liable for these debts.

What Caroline lacked was the freedom that a steady flow of cash offered. And yet McGann's accounts show that he had advanced her some cash: £30 in October 1866; a further £10 for her expenses in Melbourne in August 1867; £5 on 4 September and the same again on 13 and 28 September; £10 on 2 October and £15 on 23 October; and £30 in November that year. These amounts totalled £110 over thirteen months. That was £10 more than the annuity Edward had promised her, and over double what a stockman – one of the best paid workers on a station – might receive in a year.[24] Travel from Lockhart to Melbourne was expensive. So were legal costs. Caroline had middle-class expectations about clothing, accommodation and food, and sometimes showed little sensitivity about the implications of her actions. In late June of 1868 she bought goods at a shop in Bordertown – the small town created during the gold rush, just across the border from Lockhart. She charged them to her brother-in-law James Hamilton's account without his permission.[25]

Bordertown was on the route from Lockhart to Robe. She stopped there that June on her way to Melbourne. She was heading back to the city expecting to be called on soon to give evidence in her suit and hoping that a successful outcome would liberate money to support herself and the children. She left the boys at Lockhart, 'under the care of a servant', and found accommodation on Bourke Street East, again within the legal precinct area. The process continued to be frustratingly slow. She arrived in early July and worked with Miller to produce further evidence to support her claims. They asked a Dr Robert Banks Perry, who had attended the children when they were ill at Lockhart, to come to Melbourne from the Tatiara area in South Australia to be examined about the children's health. He refused initially. The estate owed him £30. He would only attend if he was paid £10 for travel expenses. Lowry, as trustee, sent him £5 for expenses, and he agreed to appear.[26] But still nothing happened.

By early August Caroline was beside herself. Her expenses were mounting. She and Miller crafted a deposition which she signed on 6 August. In it she explained that she had been waiting in the city for six weeks, anticipating appearing in court. Lockhart Station was over 300 miles from Melbourne and she was 'anxious to return', as she was worried about the care and health of her children. Yet she claimed to fear leaving without any resolution, as all of her 'present available means are exhausted in paying for my board and lodging incurred up to the present time'. This was not an understatement. Later accounts show that her travel and maintenance costs on that trip amounted to £20. While in Melbourne on this or another visit she also took advantage of the city's shopping opportunities, purchasing £25 15s 2d worth of drapery goods for herself and the children.[27] Despairing of a hearing, Caroline returned again to Lockhart once her deposition was complete.

The suit was eventually filed in Melbourne's equity court on 4 September 1868. The solicitors for both sides now spent time providing details and instructions to the barristers who would argue their case in court. Barristers, or counsel as they were also called, were the elite of the legal profession. Legal historian Richard Harrison explains that candidates for admission as barristers were required to pass written exams in 'Greek and Latin; mathematics and algebra; ancient history; English history; universal history; real property and conveyancing; common law, pleading and practice; equity and insolvency; criminal law; and evidence and the law of contracts'. Because of the more extensive legal knowledge required of them, they were treated as 'the socially superior branch of the legal profession'. They could also charge higher fees. As equity cases did not involve juries, their task was to provide learned arguments that would influence the particular judge hearing the suit. The Melbourne legal community was small. Barristers and judges knew each other well, so counsel could shape their arguments in ways they believed would influence a particular judge.[28]

As noted, Webb had agreed to represent Lowry in court. William McGann's counsel was Thomas A'Beckett and William Kearney's was Mr John Atkins. Caroline's solicitor, Miller, had secured the services of two barristers: Edward de Verdon and William Edward Hearn. Hearn came from a Protestant, Anglo–Irish family, had studied logic and ethics as well as law at Trinity College, and been admitted to the Irish bar in 1853. He was attracted to Australia in 1854 with the offer of becoming the 'first professor of modern history and literature, political economy and logic' at the University of Melbourne. Although he was admitted to the Victorian bar in 1860, he practised little and was more widely recognised for his scholarly writings in law, but especially in political economy. Why Miller or de Verdon chose to engage him is unclear. Possibly it was Miller's colleague Ireland, with whom Hearn had collaborated on drafting the *Victoria Land Act* of 1862, who recommended him.[29]

*Kearney v. Lowry* was involving some of the most prominent barristers and legal experts in the colony. Most worked in close proximity within the legal district and in the courts. De Verdon, Atkins and Webb all had offices within the Temple Court building. That of Thomas A'Beckett, a member of one of the city's elite families, was close by in Chancery Lane.[30] By early October witnesses and documents were ready for the next stage of an equity case: the taking of evidence in court. The legal teams attended court in anticipation of being heard each day between 6 and 9 October, only to have the case adjourned until the next sitting. It was not until between late October and the end of November that evidence was finally taken in the equity court.[31]

By Tuesday 1 December 1868, Caroline's suit was ready for the hearing and decree. As required, local newspapers had announced the hearing. The judge was Robert Molesworth (see image 9 in the picture section). Like Chief Justice Stawell and Professor Hearn, he was an Irish Protestant immigrant. He had studied at Trinity College, Dublin and was called to the Irish bar in 1828. In 1852 he migrated to Australia, and moved to Melbourne in 1853 after a year in Adelaide. He was admitted to the bar in Victoria that same year. After developing a large practice, and serving briefly as acting chief justice, he was appointed as the fourth Supreme Court judge for the colony in 1856. Most of his work involved equity rather than criminal law. He was also the chief judge of the Court of Mines.[32]

Molesworth has been described as an admirable judge, noted 'for his industry, courtesy, learning and expedition'. Just four years earlier, however, his own personal life had burst into public scrutiny when he petitioned for a divorce for adultery. His wife had had at least two affairs, one of which led to the birth of a child. She had counter-petitioned for a judicial separation on the basis of cruelty. This was high, high scandal in Melbourne society. The divorce had been heard before Chief Justice William Stawell in the Supreme Court. The local newspapers, the *Argus* and *The Age*, reported in detail on the proceedings. One Melburnian described the Molesworth evidence as including 'the most disgusting and filthy details'. Following his divorce, and the public furore the evidence produced, Molesworth had refused to sit on the divorce and matrimonial dispute cases that had previously constituted a significant portion of his workload.[33] As a result, wills, estates, issues of custody and other civil matters made up the bulk of his daily work in the equity court. Caroline's plea thus fell into the hands of a man doubtless still smarting from the public humiliation of the evidence produced during his divorce. He, like other Melbourne residents, seemed to have learned to distrust 'female innocence'.[34]

Early that Tuesday Molesworth heard four cases as chief of the Court of Mines. *Kearney v. Lowry* was scheduled for 11 am. It took up the rest of the day.[35] On Wednesday details of the case appeared in the Melbourne newspapers. *The Age* gave a brief account in the 'news of the day' column. A much longer account introduced readers to Caroline's plight in its law reports section. Similar details appeared in the *Argus*.[36] Summaries followed in other local and colonial newspapers. The content was not as salacious as the Molesworth divorce, yet papers noted the case as one of 'some singularity'. Articles informed the public of most of the content of the plaintiff's and defendants' affidavits: the clauses of

Edward's will regarding his wish to send Caroline and the children to Ireland; the annuity he had promised; Caroline's claim that Lowry had neglected to collect and receive money due to the estate or to support her and the children; her claim that the children risked dying of consumption and were in a precarious state of health for travelling; her wish that the court direct an account of the estate, pay her maintenance, and direct as to where the children should reside given the state of their health. Readers might have some sympathy for Lowry's dilemma when he stressed that because the station was still mortgaged to Clarke, he had been unable to collect any monies beyond £36 he had already paid to Caroline. Clarke's ruthlessness as a moneylender was well known. They also learned of William Kearney's denial that the children's health would be compromised by moving to Ireland.[37] Readers might form their own ideas about the characters in this family melodrama, but it is hard to imagine that the women of the colony did not sympathise with Caroline's dilemma. The futures of this widow and her children were at stake. Could a dead husband force his wife to leave Australia against her will?

Dr Hearn drew on Dr Perry's evidence to argue that it would be 'extremely hazardous to take the children to Ireland, where the climate was unfavourable for such diseases'. Perhaps memories of his own childhood, growing up in the dampness of counties Cavan and Leitrim, shaped his response. More likely he anticipated that his wide learning and clarity of argument would win the day. His key point was that 'the whole tenor of the will was to benefit the children and provide for their care and protection'. He concluded that it would 'be acting contrary to the spirit of the will to send the children' to Ireland. Supporting Hearn, de Verdon drew on a range of cases to argue that some of the provisions of the will seemed contradictory. He reinforced Hearn's argument that Edward's desire to send the children to Ireland went against the overall intentions of the will, which sought to maintain and support them.[38]

Molesworth was not swayed. 'It is my business', Melburnians read in the *Argus* a day later, 'to carry out men's wills, and not to consider what will best benefit their families.' In a statement that hints that he still found it hard to avoid making judgments on the emotional content of marital relations, he claimed that the whole tone of Edward's will treated Caroline 'as if, in some respects, he mistrusted her, and did not wish her to be the sole manager of the estate'. Yet men with significant assets often sought to protect their widows from sole responsibility. Molesworth himself had judged many cases in which husbands placed estates in the hands of trustees rather than their widows. He dismissed the medical evidence as very unsatisfactory, insisting that the experts should have examined all the children but had only given evidence about one. And, using language that placed resisting a dead husband's wishes on a par with infidelity, Molesworth asserted that Caroline's actions induced him 'to think that there are other motives which lead this lady, contrary to her husband's intention, to violate her husband's will, under the pretence that she is acting out of regard for her children's health'.[39]

Ultimately he fully upheld the primacy of the testator's intentions and the sanctity of a will as a contract. 'It is my business to consider what persons require in their wills ... I will not be a party to any arrangement except the working out of this gentleman's will.' Neither he nor the barristers mentioned the presence of her family in the colony. Nor did they raise the issue of religious differences, though as a Church of England Irishman, Molesworth surely understood the challenges that such mixed marriages raised. He informed the court that he could see no reason to interfere with Edward's desire for the legatees to take up residence in Ireland in order to receive support from the estate.[40]

Caroline's worries about her children's health may have been strategically deployed in court to avoid the provisions of Edward's will. Yet other evidence confirms that these were genuine anxieties. Young William had caught scarlet fever when he and his father were on their way to Ireland. Her eldest daughter was said to have died of measles – usually a non-threatening infection. Edward had just survived a life-threatening illness following his fall from his horse. Her legal team could well have made a stronger case for the children's fragile health. Sources show that over subsequent months several of the other children contracted infectious diseases. Medical bills mounted alongside lawyers' fees.[41]

Could Molesworth or any judge have made a different decision? The jurisprudence regarding interpreting wills was pretty clear. A well-written will, and especially one already proved, was difficult to overturn. And when a will was not very clear, the key issue was determining the intention of the testator. Molesworth's statement was blunt, but not wrong. A judge could not refuse probate of a will just because he disapproved of a testator's conduct, as Rosalind Croucher cogently argued decades ago. Molesworth overtly sympathised with the testator, not his widow. Had Caroline's legal team sought to argue that Edward was not of sound mind, the law offered some hope. But this issue was not raised. As a judge, Molesworth was consistent in upholding testators' intentions – whether they were men or women. A year later, when trustees and the children of the widow Anne Neeson sought to secure money from her estate to place one of her children in an apprenticeship, Molesworth ruled against them. 'I may say generally, that when people make their wills and are aware of the circumstances of their children, they are far better judges than I can possibly be of the probabilities of their children finding support from their own exertions or otherwise,' he explained.[42]

Molesworth's decision was consistent with the jurisprudence of the times. Still, the case and the issues it raised were deemed of sufficient legal interest and importance to be published in the two collections of law reports then existing in the colony. Such case reports provide the legal profession with details of decisions deemed to set or reiterate a precedent and offer a thumbnail summary of the key lessons. *Kearney v. Lowry* was summarised as teaching that 'in interpreting a will, the Court considers the intentions of the testator, and not what may be best for those interested under it', and that trustees must 'conform strictly to the directions of the testator'. What might be best for a widow and her children was thus irrelevant.[43]

Caroline had wished to be in Melbourne to hear Molesworth's decision, but there is no evidence that she was able to attend. She had surely hoped for a decree that would settle the question in her favour. Instead, Molesworth had explicitly upheld Edward's right to determine his family's future against any dangers to her children's health. If she wanted access to the promised annuity and portion of Edward's estate, she would have to move to Ireland with the children. Molesworth was more sympathetic to the other parts of Caroline's bill. He reserved judgment on these until the documentation was assembled. He asked the trustees to explain their 'course of inactivity'; he castigated them for not having 'done what the will told them'.[44] In his formal decree, issued two weeks later, he declared that Edward Kearney's will had been 'well proved' and Henry Wallace Lowry properly appointed. He instructed Lowry, as the sole remaining colonial trustee, to carry out the trusts of the will as much as was then practical, keeping both Caroline and William Kearney informed in case they objected to any of his intentions. He instructed the master of the court, Wilkinson, to take account of all profits from the real estate and of all personal property in the hands of any parties in the cause, as well as of any encumbrances.[45]

Molesworth's decree initiated a further lengthy period of information-seeking, fact-gathering and account-tallying for the parties' solicitors and especially for Lowry. He was now legally compelled to settle the estate and to arrange the sale of Lockhart. William Kearney grew more and more impatient with the slowness of the case. He was keen to return to Ireland himself and to get Caroline and the children there as soon as possible. He sought to intervene in a range of ways in the process now being overseen by the solicitors and the master of equity. In early February he threatened to fire his solicitor, Hughes, and find a new legal firm. He complained to another lawyer about the delays but was told the case was progressing normally. On subsequent visits to Hughes later that month he learned that Miller had placed an advertisement in the *Argus* asking for all creditors to lodge their claims at the master of equity's office. He lodged his own claims. Later William informed Hughes that Clarke considered the mortgage repaid. In March he asked Hughes to apply to the court to give him sole custody of the children should their mother decide not to proceed to Ireland. He claimed that they were 'without tutor or governess and insufficiently looked after'. This request went nowhere.[46]

Calling in debts, adjudicating claims, tallying the bills and expenses that had accumulated since Edward's death and selling the station all took time. Edward's will had authorised the trustees to sell Lockhart 'by private contract only and upon such terms of credit' as his trustees, brother William and brother-in-law James Hamilton thought 'expedient and best for the interest of my family'.[47] An advertisement for the 'well known and superior station, Lockhart' appeared in the *Argus* and other papers between 20 March and 9 April. It itemised the station's buildings, equipment, 25 000 sheep, 60 head of cattle and 16 horses, and highlighted the 'three wells from 100 to 180ft [35 to 55 metres] deep, capable of supplying all the stock on the station', along with its 'eight good working bullocks and a dray, station implements and tools, saddles, &c.'. Early notices announced it as a private sale.[48] This provision of Edward's will irked both James Hamilton and William Kearney. Subsequently most of the parties agreed that it could be sold by tender, despite Hamilton's objections and the provision in Edward's will that his consent was necessary. Some wishes of will writers clearly carried more weight than others! Revised advertisements appeared in Melbourne and other papers over a two-week period in April requesting the submission of tenders prior to 3 May.[49]

On 4 May 1869, Lowry and McGann accepted the tender for the station and stock offered by James, John and Thomas Robertson. Since their arrival in Australia in 1840 these three Scottish brothers and their father had been securing leases to stations across Victoria and other Australian colonies.[50] Newspapers reported that the price was satisfactory, without naming an amount. James Hamilton objected. He maintained in his old age that after Edward's death, 'the mortgagees foreclosed, and the station was sold for half its value, which left very little for Kearney's wife and family'.[51] Hamilton may have been correct in thinking that the station and its stock could have attracted a better price. Yet it seems likely that his memories of the difficult times Caroline and the children faced in the aftermath of Edward's death shaped his sense of the propriety of the deal.

When all the bills, claims and accounts were settled, the remaining amount of the mortgage paid off and the wool clip sold, the net estate was worth a staggering £14779. This was over £1000 more than Edward was said to have paid for the larger station in 1858. His hard work on the station had left sufficient assets to pay off the mortgage and generate a sum that represents well over A\$1.5 million today.[52] The financial stakes in this suit and in the lives of Caroline and the five boys were much higher than I had imagined until I found these details. And for William and the Kearney family in Ireland, more was at issue than the soul of their departed brother or their nephews' religious upbringing. This money would be placed in the hands of Patrick, William and Thomas McCormack to manage for the family. If Caroline did not leave Australia, if she remarried, or if she refused to live in the house the Kearneys were to choose for her in Ireland, a portion of the estate would go to two of the three Irish trustees: Edward's brother Patrick and brother-in-law Thomas McCormack.[53]

For Caroline the choice remained grim: stay in Australia and forgo the support the will offered or accept Molesworth's decree and Edward's wishes. It was an impossible choice. Opting for the promised economic support would not only distance her from her family in Australia, it would distance the boys from the network of uncles, aunts, grandparents and cousins whose support had been so essential following their father's death. She had tried to overturn Edward's draconian wish through the courts, but the equity process had proven slow, expensive and ultimately disappointing. She had served an apprenticeship of sorts in legal procedures, and had succeeded at least in forcing the trustees to settle the estate. Lockhart was sold. Debts and claims remained to be settled. What now for her and the boys?

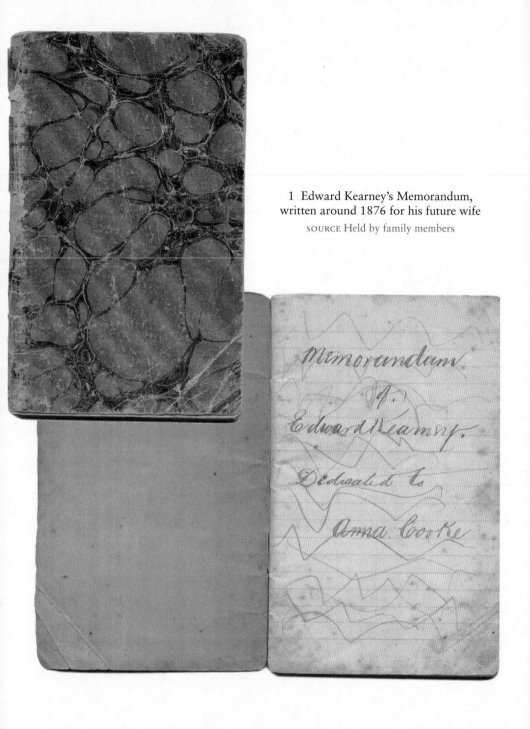

1  Edward Kearney's Memorandum,
written around 1876 for his future wife

SOURCE Held by family members

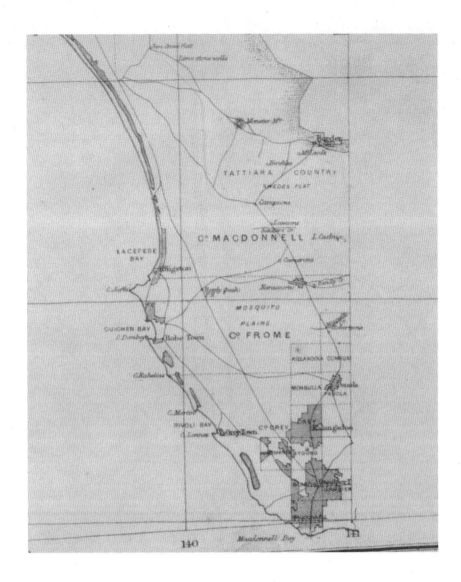

2  Tatiara Country, Mosquito Plains and Robetown, South Australia showing
Edward's lease (Campion's), James Allen's (Swede's Flat) and Robe Town,
where Caroline and William Bax lived

SOURCE SRSA, Extract from Map of Pastoral Leases in South-East, South Australia, c.1861
(Adelaide: Surveyor General's Office, 1865), original held by the South Australia Surveyor-
General's Office, Department of Planning, Transport and Infrastructure

3  Caroline's sister and brother-in-law, Eleanor (née) Bax
and James Charles Hamilton

SOURCE *Henderson's Australian Families: A genealogical and bibliographical record*,
Melbourne: Genealogical Society of Victoria 2004, 358

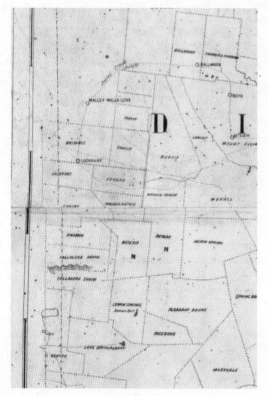

4  Locations of Lockhart and the
Hamilton's Station, Bringalbert

SOURCE W. Owen (1869), *Map of
Victoria including the pastoral runs
& c. with alterations to 1869–70*,
National Library of Australia

WIGRAM'S SHIP TRUE BRI

TRUE BRITON. ONE OF WIGRAM'S EARLY AUSTRAL

DERS.

5 Edward Kearney and four-year-old William boarded the *True Briton* in Melbourne on 7 May 1864, bound for Ireland, leaving Caroline pregnant at Lockhart with their four other children.

SOURCE Brodie Collection, La Trobe Picture Collection, State Library Victoria, Accession H99.220/3993

THE ROMAN CATHOLIC CONVENT & FEMALE ORPHANAGE.

Norton, Photo., Geelong.

6  The Roman Catholic Convent and Female Orphanage, Geelong, 1866

SOURCE J. Norton, photographer, 1866, State Library Victoria, accession no. H1238

7  Painting of Edward and Maria Ellen Kearney's grave,
Melbourne Cemetery

*Temple Court, Melbourne.*

9 Robert Molesworth, the supreme court judge who
presided over *Kearney v. Lowry*

SOURCE Print, wood engraving,
State Library Victoria,
accession no. IAN08/11/90/11

8 Temple Court, legal precinct, Chancery Lane
(now Little Collins Street), Melbourne

SOURCE Arthur Willmore 1814–88, engraver,
State Library Victoria,
accession no. 30328102131637/15

10  The French College, Blackrock, Ireland

SOURCE Robert French and William Lawrence Photograph Collection,
National Library of Ireland, L-ROY-00152

11 Thomas O'Hagan, First Baron O'Hagan, Lord Chancellor of Ireland, 1868–74, 1880–81, judge for *Re Kearneys, Minors*, 1871–74

SOURCE John Watkins, photographer, albumen carte-de-visite, c.1868, National Portrait Gallery, London, NPG AX17776

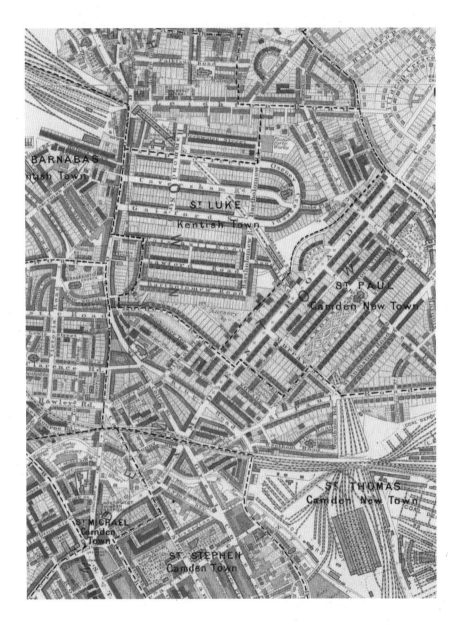

12  Extract from Charles Booth's 1889 map showing Stratford Place,
Camden, Kentish Town, and the railroad yards, London

SOURCE Charles Booth's London © London School of Economics
& Political Science Library

13 Caroline's sister, Eleanor,
as an older woman

SOURCE Held by
Helen Mulraney-Roll

14 Edward Kearney and Anna
Cooke, Dublin, circa 1876

SOURCE Held by family members

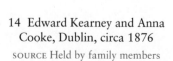

15 Grafton Hospital staff with Charles James Kearney, back row, far left, 1901

16  Anna, Anna Violet, Ida and Edward Kearney, Grafton, between 1898 and 1905

SOURCE Clarence River Historical Society, Grafton, NSW

17 Edward and Anna Kearney, with their daughter Vi (Anna Violet) standing behind them, and grandchildren (from left to right) Norah, Alice and Carrie (Caroline), in 1914

SOURCE Held by family members

18 Kearney family gathering, c.1925–26, Nana Glen, NSW. William Kearney would have been sixty-six when he visited his sister-in-law Anna Kearney. He is pictured here with (from left to right) Alice, George, Vi, Carrie, Anna Kearney and Norah

SOURCE Held by family members

# 6

# Leaving Lockhart Station

Young Edward was the first to leave Lockhart. His recollections suggest that he joined his aunt and uncle at Ozenkadnook around March 1869, when the station was put up for sale. He was thirteen. Ever since his father had gone to visit Ireland, he had felt that the station was his responsibility as 'the master's eldest son'. He had put in long hours of work and harboured hopes of succeeding his father. Now his life hopes were shattered: 'Our station was to be sold. I would not stop to see the sacrifice, for I loved my dogs, horses, and sheep, and they all knew my voice so well. I used to use them kindly. I could not bear to see them sold, so I parted with them whilst they were my own, and the parting was sad for me. I kept one horse only which I took to my uncle's.' He remained with Eleanor and James Hamilton for a few months and then went to stay with his grandparents in Robe. Relations with his mother seem to have been rocky. He blamed Caroline for not managing better when Edward was away, and following his death. Later he suggested that he had always isolated himself from his brothers and sister. Caroline claimed that she thought it best for him to stay in Robe until their future was settled, because she feared that the climate of Melbourne would be dangerous for his health.[1]

The selling of Lockhart Station was a watershed in the lives of Caroline and the boys. They were homeless. They had already lived through major upheavals since Edward's departure to visit Ireland in the early months of 1864. Young Charles James had been born while he was away. Edward's return with his brother William and the other Catholic relatives had initiated the religious war between Caroline and the Kearney brothers. Most of the children had remained at Lockhart when Edward went to Melbourne to die. A year later, their uncle William had taken their only sister, Maria Ellen, far away; she never returned. Since then Caroline had frequently been away in Melbourne, leaving them with governesses, servants and at Ozenkadnook with her sister. Lockhart was the only home the younger boys, William, Patrick and little Charles James, had known. These outback stations were more than homes and farms. They constituted a community of working people, a cluster of families; indeed, a way of life. Couples married there. People were buried there. Staff often remained when stations changed hands. Now Caroline and the remaining boys had to leave.

Away from the station there would be no supplies to rely on. They would need cash to pay for food and accommodation. Married at under 20, a mother for fifteen years and a widow by then for nearly four, Caroline's options were few. She had no work history, no skills to parlay. With five children aged between five and thirteen she could hardly hire herself out as a domestic servant. The possibility of not going to Ireland and losing the promised annuity and possibly her children too surely made life look bleaker and bleaker. The only bright side was that with the station sold she might hope for steadier maintenance from the estate. But she would still have to request every penny she wished to spend. And allowances to her and the children and every moment of lawyers' time would be tracked as *Kearney v. Lowry* moved towards the stage of settling debts and determining legal costs. Caroline clung on to the hope that she might be able to remain in Australia.

She decided that she and the other boys would go to Melbourne. In the city she might try again to influence the outcome of the suit, perhaps even change Molesworth's mind. She would certainly be closer to the trustee so she could seek maintenance for herself and the children. She arranged for any articles of furniture and other possessions that were understood to belong to her and the children to be transported to her parents' home in Robe. She and the four boys headed east, then south, taking advantage of the recently completed railway line to go overland and experience travel on a train. We can follow their itinerary and some costs through the expenses submitted: south-east for about 140 kilometres by coach to Horsham (£24) and a night in the Munro hotel; a 200-kilometre coach trip south to Ballarat (£9 9s), and a night there at Duffy's hotel (£5). Then a train trip over the final 150 or so kilometres, south and into Melbourne (£4). It was then a short cab ride from the station to the inner-city suburb of Fitzroy (4s), where Caroline had secured accommodation. They arrived around the end of May.[2]

Their lodgings were at 52 Gertrude Street, Glass Terrace, between Nicholson and Fitzroy streets. This architecturally designed row of two-storey attached houses in Colonial Regency style with 'verandas, French windows, upper casements and restrained internal joinery', was constructed during the gold rush boom of the mid-1850s. It is now considered Melbourne's oldest surviving example of the terrace housing that came to characterise buildings in the new expanding suburbs. When Caroline and the boys arrived it was a somewhat respectable, if not luxurious, place to stay.[3] The neighbours included several other widows and married women heading their own households. One made her living as a bookseller, another as a milliner. These female household heads moved often. More stable residents included a grocer, teacher and dentist, several watchmakers, a bricklayer and other craftsmen.

Their landlords were Frederick William Marsden and his wife, Sarah. For a brief time Frederick had had a promising career playing cricket for the Melbourne Cricket Club and for Victoria. James Hamilton's brother Tom was a very keen cricketer. He, another local station owner and local Aboriginal men had forged a hugely talented cricket team that made history as the first Australian sporting team to tour overseas,[4] and his connections might explain this choice of residence. The Marsdens surely needed money. In 1869 Frederick was very ill. He died in 1870. Taking boarders in to what appears to have been a nine-room home would help Sarah pay her husband's medical bills and compensate somewhat for his inability to earn wages.[5] For Caroline and the boys it was a good location. The Collingwood Common School was about a ten-minute walk from their lodgings – perhaps she sent the boys there. It was just a fifteen-minute walk or a shorter cab ride to the courthouse at the corner of Russell and Latrobe streets, and easy travelling distance to Miller's office at 100 Queen Street.[6]

Caroline and Miller began crafting yet another affidavit to support a motion to the court for maintenance. In equity suits, such a motion allowed the court to respond to matters requiring 'immediate relief' quickly, without going through a full court hearing.[7] Her affidavit was signed on 6 September. In it she claimed that since Edward's death she had 'not received any money' for her own maintenance; that the infant plaintiffs were without any means of support, and in need of clothing and education. She concluded by affirming that she had been obliged to go into debt as a result and that 'if it had not been for the kindness of persons who gave me credit' to the tune of some £300, the children 'would have gone naked'. Ever adversarial, William opposed the idea of her receiving the promised annuity or any money. He registered his belief that Lowry had already advanced her money. Again he pointed out that while at Lockhart Caroline had been able to avail herself of the station supplies. He argued that Lowry should have sufficient money on hand 'to provide passage to England'.[8]

Both Caroline and William were now residing in Melbourne. Their relationship remained toxic. He had taken lodgings on Swanston Street, not far from Caroline, but apparently did not know where she was. He sought to find her address through her solicitor. She tried to retrieve some pictures from the station that William claimed were his property.[9] He pushed again and again for her to be sent to Ireland. And he fretted, as the tallying and verifying of his expenses and other accounts continued. Her application for maintenance brought the barristers back into the courthouse and once again before Molesworth on 9 September. Molesworth had no patience with this request or with the family squabbles. Privately he told Miller that the trustees should deal liberally with the plaintiffs. Publicly, apparently as exasperated with the trustees and William as he was suspicious of Caroline, he suggested that the parties should arrange matters among themselves.[10]

Once again, her claim to Molesworth that she had received no maintenance for herself or the children was ingenuous at best. The affidavit presented a brilliant performance of a widow in need of support for herself and her children. It fitted the situation of many working-class widows following their husbands' deaths.[11] But it stretched the truth about Caroline's financial situation, as the evidence McGann and Lowry later produced for court shows. However, her acknowledgment of 'the kindness of persons who gave me credit' reflects reality. Her parents and sister were caring for Edward. Her brother-in-law had contributed to their support. Merchants had been patient in waiting to present their bills until the station was sold. Caroline might well have overspent any allowances she was given, but without her annuity, the promise of regular support or ready cash, she still had to have every bill sent to the trustees, or rely on personal loans, merchants' credit and family support.

Caroline was desperate. Bills mounted quickly with four children to feed. City living was costly. She had expensive tastes. Perhaps her reliance on alcohol was accelerating as she faced these ongoing challenges. Among her bills was £22 6s to the merchant Edward French for wine and groceries for her and the children. There were debts and experiences that she surely preferred to hide from Lowry, William and the Equity Court. Especially one. She could hardly ask that court to pay the £5 1s for damages awarded to Mary Jane McManus, who had successfully charged her with assault. Had Caroline lashed out at another woman as her worries mounted? Searches for further evidence of this incident and of the hearing before the District Court of Melbourne have led nowhere, though this evidence of aggression echoes young Edward's censure of 'her fighting with a common hawker' while at Lockhart.[12] The trace that alerted me to this assault was revealed as a result of another desperate act she committed at this time. On 23 September, before she received any further maintenance from the trustees, Caroline filed as an insolvent in Melbourne's insolvency court. At first I did not think this was her. The record lists her as a spinster, not a widow. It seemed to make no sense – especially given the value of Edward's estate. But the signature matches those on her affidavits and the timing fits with her move to the city and her worries about debt.

Caroline's insolvency application claimed the causes of her indebtedness as 'want of employment and ill health'. The only asset she listed was £3 worth of clothing apparel. The liabilities she identified to this court totalled £15 7s. The largest sum was the damages she owed Mary McManus. Others included £4 6s owed to a Mrs Coffey of Fitzroy for board and lodging from when she was in the city on one of her previous visits. A Mrs William Taylor of Sandridge had lent her £2 10s in 1866, while a Mr Henry Hartigan of Carlton, the suburb close to Fitzroy, had recently lent her £3. These were minuscule amounts compared to other bills for stores, board and clothing then being tallied by Lowry as trustee. For reasons both obvious and obscure, she chose not to submit them among documents that would pass through the oversight of the officials, solicitors and defendants in the Equity Court.[13]

In failing to note her right to support from Edward's estate she was not dissimilar to other Melbourne insolvents who attempted 'to hide superior assets'.[14] As historian John Weaver notes, one of the problems with Melbourne's insolvency files is that such explanations were provided by the insolvents themselves and they were not always 'completely candid. Accounts of accidents and illnesses, for example, never mentioned alcohol or alcoholism.'[15] Caroline's rather devious attempt to turn to another branch of the law failed. Though she was in the city, she did not appear at the meeting called for 5 October by the chief commissioner of insolvent estates at their office on Collins Street West. Nor did her creditors. Her debts were deemed unproven and the case closed.[16]

Caroline's interactions with the Melbourne courts and the law in her first few months away from the life she was used to at Lockhart suggest that anxiety about their future made her desperate, impetuous and even aggressive. The conflict between her desire to remain in Australia and William's determination that his brother's final wishes be respected escalated as the case in equity continued. Molesworth's suggestion in early September that the trustees and parties work out the issue of maintenance for Caroline and the boys among themselves was doomed to failure.

Caroline sought again to see whether she and the children might remain in the colony. When Pavey sought to broach the issue with William's solicitor he was informed bluntly that William would 'insist on the Will being carried out in its strict sense'. Pavey then began consulting with her solicitor and the barrister Webb to determine how to secure a fixed sum of support for her and the boys. William again contested any payment to her as against Edward's instructions. In early October, presumably to her great relief, Lowry paid Caroline £60 10s to cover the eight weeks of board and lodging she owed for her and the children between 23 May and 10 October. There were other bills for general stores, clothing and drapery for the plaintiffs, as well as the aforementioned £22 6s to French for wine, groceries and supplies.[17]

Over September the plaintiffs and their solicitors were scurrying to finalise documentation on the costs and expenses of the estate to present as affidavits to the master of equity so that he could produce the reckoning of accounts that Molesworth had requested. McGann and Lowry drew up lists detailing the amounts they had spent as trustees, including for the support of Caroline and the children. From early September through October, William saw his solicitor virtually every day. He and Hughes scrutinised his expense claims and double-checked figures with Clarke's clerk as they finalised his claims against the estate. They checked and rechecked Lowry and McGann's figures and noted Caroline's many expenditures. Each client and their solicitor then made copies of these as affidavits and submitted them to the other parties as well as to the court. These details provided the master of equity, Wilkinson, and Judge Molesworth with evidence about the management and state of the estate and the truth of Caroline's and the defendants' claims. Each solicitor also made a lengthy listing of the time they had spent with their clients drawing up briefs and affidavits and copying documents for the other parties, the court or the barristers. These would be tallied to remunerate them for their time and labour and serve as the basis for determining costs. Wilkinson's report on the estate and claims to costs was ready on 21 October. Molesworth ordered it ratified a week later.[18]

Molesworth now had sufficient information to make a full decree in the case of *Kearney v. Lowry*, including determining costs. Usually suits only reached the stage of settling costs when it was unlikely any further matters or evidence would arise.[19] The following week the parties were once again in court, represented by their barristers. First they went through all the affidavits and claims about costs. Then Molesworth turned to the ongoing issues. The decree sought this time represented the combined desires of the trustees and William, while acknowledging Caroline's requests for support. As publicised in the Melbourne papers, they sought to permit McGann and Lowry to pay the legacies of the will; to allow Lowry to maintain Caroline and the boys while they were in the colony and to defray the expenses of their outfit and passage to Ireland.[20] Molesworth supported these requests, offering specific instructions on what was required to place all monies in the hands of Lowry to pay the legacies specified in the will with interest, and to pay any outstanding maintenance to the plaintiffs during their stay, pending their departure for Ireland. He concluded by insisting that maintenance could not continue more than six 'months computed from the date of this order'. He instructed Lowry to transfer the balance of the estate to the Irish trustees in six months, or earlier if Caroline and the boys left before then. His decree followed the usual practice in equity cases regarding a will in specifying that Lowry and McGann should pay the 'costs of all parties' out of the estate.[21]

A reprieve of six months for Caroline, but no more. She would have an allowance, but must leave the country by 12 May 1870. There were farewells to say, and family members to see for one last time. Return to Australia doubtless seemed unlikely. Wanting to see her parents 'before leaving the Colony', she took the four boys to Robe in early December. Her plan, she later informed the court, was to live with them until she departed.[22] Caroline's parents were by then well settled into their lives in Robe and into the cottage and school on the main route into the town.

Robe had blossomed in the years since they arrived. Later these would be seen as its golden years. It now boasted two banks, three hotels and Catholic, Anglican and Presbyterian churches and chapels. Gracious one- and two-storey shops lined Smillie Street – the main street. There was a butcher, a baker, a blacksmith, a saddler and a dressmaking establishment. The enterprising Mary Ann Bryan, who sold her goods throughout the Mosquito Plains, had her shop near the Robe Hotel. Her Chinese silks, jewellery and haberdashery might not rival the shops of Melbourne, but Caroline might enjoy perusing her wares. The old bullock track, on which the Bax's house sat, was renamed Victoria Street, and enterprising men and women had built businesses along it too. Over the sixties the town had become quite a social centre, with 'races, kangaroo hunts, picnics, dinners, dances and balls, lasting sometimes till dawn'. By then Robe had developed a reputation as 'the sanatorium of the south'. Squatters from miles around, along with prominent Adelaide residents, were building gracious mansions and summer residences to escape the intense summer heat and enjoy the cool coastal breezes, dramatic cliffs and lovely beaches. These 'summer people' entertained 'Robe society and the local squattocracy in grand English style'.[23]

Much about life in Robe likely pleased Caroline. The sea air was good for their health. Edward could attend his grandparents' school. His brothers may have joined him there when they arrived. Her parents could help keep an eye on her boys. Robe offered them greater liberty to run or ride around than Melbourne had, though she might have worried about the dangerous cliffs that surrounded the bay. Again, she imagined remaining. In mid-March, with just two months left before the date Molesworth had deemed she should depart, she wrote to Lowry, refusing to go to Ireland 'as directed by the decree and advising him thereon'. His solicitor, Trollope, sought the opinion of counsel. All agreed 'that he was to write Mrs Kearney on the matter, insisting on her complying with the decree'.[24]

Caroline's extended family had supported her over the stressful years since Edward's death and Maria Ellen's removal and death. They remained her best potential asset. But her parents were aging. Caroline Bax was unwell; William was in his mid-sixties. His salary of £60 would hardly stretch to cover the expenses of raising these five grandchildren, let alone their widowed daughter. He was compensated with £44 from the estate for tuition, board and lodging of young Edward over the year he had been with them. His energy, income and inclination might not stretch much further. William Bax's future was not looking rosy. Robe's growth had brought competition for pupils. In 1869 the Sisters of Saint Joseph opened a Catholic school in the town. A Miss Dubois opened up a private school in the street then known as Rotten Row. Several of the churches were offering Sunday Schools. The following year Mr Hill, the teacher at the Bible Christian Chapel, informed Robe District Council that he intended to apply for the government stipend. William Bax remained the only teacher licensed by the Education Board of South Australia to teach in the town. But a Mr Allport was keen to secure a licence, or worse, Bax's post. For several years he had been writing to the board requesting a position. He continued to do so. Within a year the school inspectors, who had reported favourably on the school for many years, noted that the number of students enrolled was falling. A year later his licence was not renewed.[25]

The long-drawn-out court case, the rollercoaster of Caroline's hopes to remain and Molesworth's insistence that she leave, as well as her own behaviour, surely took their toll on her parents' health and on their teaching. They surely would have strained her relationship with members of her extended family, as well as with her growing boys. Eleanor and James continued to provide support, especially for young Edward and for her aging parents. Edward junior later described moving back and forth between Caroline's sister's station and Robe with his grandparents, taking his beloved horse and saddle with him. Perhaps it was after Caroline returned to Robe with his brothers that he and his grandparents went to his uncle's 'for a month or two'.[26]

These were difficult times. Drought hit again in 1869. Selectors were beginning to claim land in the area freehold, challenging squatters like the Hamilton extended family. James secured 2748 acres (1112 hectares) of freehold from the 32 860 acres (13 300 hectares) on Ozenkadnook, but the Hamilton family finances were precarious. They took out new mortgages and second mortgages on their family leases. Young Edward helped his uncle. Indeed, in his own description of this time he ran the farm while James Hamilton was 'called away on important business' and then fell sick. Edward reports that he tended the 'stock and saved them for him, for which he thanked me, and offered to keep me in Australia, educate, and give me a good start in life'. Edward declined. This was the moment when he finally parted with the 'last relict of former days my dear old saddle in which I had ridden hundreds of miles, nay thousands. I cried over it when leaving.'[27] The fourteen-year-old Edward had opted out of remaining in Australia. He accepted his duty to remain with his mother and brothers.

The deadline for their departure was 12 May 1870. Early in April Frank contracted typhoid fever. He was confined to his bed for the rest of the month. Or so Caroline claimed in her last desperate attempt to remain in the colony. Late that month she sent Lowry a telegram 'stating that one of her children was ill with a fever and that she could not comply with the decree'. Within a day William Kearney, who was determined not to leave Melbourne until his brother's wishes were fulfilled, was threatening proceedings if the monies and plaintiffs were not sent to Ireland immediately.[28] Then, in early May, Patrick caught typhoid too. Caroline now informed Lowry that he was in such a 'precarious state' that she had been advised by the Robe physician, Dr Mustarde, that he should not be moved. Furthermore, Peter Snewin, captain of the steamer that offered the most practical means of transit between Robe and Melbourne, had refused to transport the boys. He feared spreading this infectious disease among his passengers. Both these men later produced affidavits in court attesting to the ill health of the two boys. Dr Mustarde added that Caroline's chest seemed unsound and – supporting Caroline's earlier claim that the children were prone to tuberculosis – noted that he thought there was phthisis on both sides of the family.[29]

Caroline determined to head to Melbourne to sort things out. On 2 June she boarded the steamer *Penola*, leaving the children in Robe. She took up lodgings again in Glass Terrace and prepared to submit her future yet again to Judge Molesworth. Miller crafted yet another affidavit, outlining Frank's and Patrick's illnesses. The solicitors consulted at length about further delay. Lowry had made it clear that Molesworth's November decree meant he could not pay any support to her beyond the six months. Trollope, acting for both Lowry and McGann at this point, sought to make William understand the dilemma that the children's illnesses posed for Lowry. They finally agreed that Caroline would have to submit a further application to the court.[30]

Miller set out to draw up a motion to allow Lowry to maintain the plaintiffs for a further period from the trust funds. This meant securing an affidavit from Dr Mustarde – a somewhat complicated process as he lived in Robe, outside Victorian jurisdiction. On 17 June, Molesworth once again considered the claims of the parties in *Kearney v. Lowry*. There were two motions. De Verdon presented Caroline's request to remain in Australia until her children were healthy again. Mr Atkins, the barrister engaged by Hughes for William, presented the latter's request that the £100 legacies promised in the will to himself, McGann as trustee, Mary and Maria McCormack, his sister Mary's daughters, be paid with interest at 8 per cent from the date of Edward's death. Once again, the case hit the news. Molesworth agreed readily to the 8 per cent interest, though it seems usuriously high for the times. He had been dealing with Caroline's suit since October 1868. In the reporting of the case, his determination to uphold Edward's will and his frustration with her are palpable. 'This lady', he fumed,

seems determined not to submit to the will of her late husband. She desires to enjoy his property without submitting to his wishes; and she has got a matter which required no litigation involved in a very expensive suit, thus frittering away a good deal of her children's money. I suppose, however, the affair will soon settle itself, and she will be starved out. £12 000 has been sent to Ireland, and a small balance remains here; when that is all frittered away she must go to Ireland as best she may. The matter, however, is now in such a position that the children's health is in danger, and I must, therefore, yield to this application, and extend the time in which the colonial trustee is to pay maintenance for three months from the present time.[31]

Molesworth's frustration with Caroline was rooted in more than ongoing hurt from his own very public divorce. Yet from the perspective of the 21st century, it is important to acknowledge a time when a judge could assert that it was his 'business to carry out men's wills, and not to consider what will best benefit their families', and have equity on his side.[32] Molesworth's irritation with Caroline clearly had some basis. Her tenacity, facilitated by the extent of the estate's resources, was remarkable. She had contested Edward's will. She had extended the period she could stay in the colony. There were no more options. The £12 000 was sent to the Irish trustees in May.

Molesworth was correct that the litigation was expensive. But so were all equity cases. As the British jurist Sylvester Joseph Hunter noted, every step in such suits involved expenses: the solicitors' fees for their time and labour; fees for the counsels and court fees; and costs of travel and accommodation. The distance between the Australian trustees' workplaces and homes in Melbourne and Lockhart had compounded the weight of their responsibilities as well as costs. Caroline was not the only person responsible for the mounting legal claims on the estate. William's constant interference had increased costs and delayed the settling of the estate. And his determination that she and the children would leave the country had eliminated all possibility of compromise around the conditions of Edward's will, in or outside the courts.

The legal costs in *Kearney v. Lowry* were indeed massive. After Wilkinson had gone through the claims of all the solicitors except William's in early December, he tallied the net allowable legal costs for Caroline and the children at £413, for Lowry at £186 3s, and for McGann at £208 14s.[33] Caroline's plea for a further extension in June 1870, along with the addition of William's costs of £179 2s, which had been held up by ongoing issues, resulted in an additional sum of around £309 for legal fees. Overall, legal fees ate up £1117 of the £14799 realised when the station, stock and chattels were sold.[34]

Caroline's experience with different bodies of law and the workings of the courts had expanded dramatically over the five years following Edward's death. William's actions in regard to Maria Ellen had led Caroline into the habeas corpus case, which she had won in a hearing in the Supreme Court in 1866. She had sought to claim insolvency in the insolvency court in 1869, then failed to turn up. Some time prior to that she had appeared in the Melbourne police court, charged with, and found guilty of, assault. Securing a final decision in *Kearney v. Lowry* must have taken much longer than she had ever imagined, stretching officially from the initial filing in March 1868 to June 1870, as Molesworth and the master of equity pushed the trustees to settle the estate, and judged successive pleas from Caroline, William, Lowry and McGann.

Edward's will, the conflict between William and the trustees, and Caroline's counterclaims were all publicised in the newspapers of the colony. By the time all the cases were settled, all of the four Supreme Court judges of Victoria, five barristers, including Melbourne's professor of political economy, and up to eight solicitors had been involved. The story of Edward's will, Lockhart Station and Caroline's struggle was assuredly part of conversations among the city's legal practitioners and of wider community gossip too. In Caroline's final legal intervention in *Kearney v. Lowry* she had won the battle, but not the war. In three months they would have to leave. She returned to Robe.

William had long been itching to depart. It was more than five years since he had arrived in Victoria with his retinue of Catholic relatives and workers. He had run Lockhart in the months leading up to Edward's death and for a while afterwards. His influence likely shaped the most troubling clause of Edward's will, the one requiring Caroline and the children to move to Ireland. His younger brother Patrick, the priest, was surely involved in that idea too. Since Edward's death he had pursued those goals and troubled the trustees as they sought to do their duty. Many of the expenses he incurred had been paid by the estate, including taking Maria Ellen to Geelong. He had successfully argued that 8 per cent interest should be paid on the legacies promised in Edward's will. That increased the value of his £100 legacy to £124 13s 4d. He expected compensation for his time as manager, and, after much haggling, was paid £110. William was not offering his services free to his brother and his family. Yet neither had he profited exorbitantly from his time in Australia. His was a battle about faith and control of the children's future more than money.

The £12 000 had been sent to the Irish trustees, of whom William was one. With this final settlement and his mission to force Caroline to leave apparently successful, he purchased a ticket on the iron clipper ship *Crusader*, due to leave on 25 June. His niece Mary Anne and her new husband Charles Mulrain joined him, thus forfeiting her claim to the £200 that Edward had promised her if she accompanied Caroline and the children to Ireland. Too much waiting for her too. She and Charles had married in Melbourne in September 1869. He was the Irish relative and worker who had taken out the suit against McGann for his Lockhart wages. Now Mary Anne was pregnant and they were keen to return and start their family in Ireland. The *Crusader* departed for London on 30 June. From there the newly married couple made their way home to County Westmeath. Their first daughter was born later that year and baptised at Moate, surely by the resident priest Patrick Kearney.[35] William had no doubt already reported to his brother that Caroline and the boys would soon arrive in Ireland. His mission had taken a long time, but in the end he had been successful.

Caroline and the five boys remained in Robe until late in August 1870. Then they sailed on the *Penola* as saloon passengers. This time Captain Snewin considered them healthy enough to mingle with his other passengers. They arrived in Melbourne on 28 August.[36] Young Edward's recollections again provide some insight into their last weeks in Australia. 'We stopped at Melbourne in the Clarence Hotel.' The Clarence Family Hotel was run by a Mrs Phair. Keeping a hotel was not among the occupations considered proper for middle-class women, but it was one domain where widows and wives could run successful businesses. It was on the south-east corner of Elizabeth Street and Flinders Lane. They were just three city blocks east of the Washington Hotel where Edward senior had died five years earlier, and back in urban haunts that were now familiar to Caroline. Edward's will had requested that the trustees 'outfit my family for the voyage home'. Caroline had the funds necessary to purchase all that they would require on the voyage ahead. Clothiers and passenger outfitters as well as grocers, wine and spirit merchants peppered the streets around the hotel. After years without access to spending money, Caroline had the liberty to shop. 'During this time, mother had an unlimited supply of money,' Edward remembered. 'We all got an outfit.'[37]

Mrs Phair advertised her establishment as a 'family hotel'. It was also a public space offering rooms to mining companies and other businesses for meetings. It housed men in town for a range of reasons. While the family was staying there, the guests included a Mr J. Brown, the mayor of Woods Point, a small town 179 kilometres north-east of Melbourne. It had sprung up after gold was discovered in the area in 1861. By 1870 the gold was pretty well played out and the population was falling.[38] The day before the Kearneys' departure, local newspapers reported that Mr Brown had tried to commit suicide by mixing grains of morphine with his drink. His attempt was described as resulting from 'indulgence in drink'. Given Caroline's penchant for tippling, I wonder if their paths crossed in the hotel; whether they had shared a drink, or life stories, and what else might have occurred. In my imagination I write a romance melodrama or the story of a brief liaison that ends with his attempted suicide and her departure. For this I have no historical evidence. Newspapers pragmatically reported that his stomach was vigorously pumped and he was expected to recover.[39]

For weeks the newspapers had announced that the *Hampshire* would depart for London, but the date kept being pushed forward. Finally, on 1 October 1870, after a month in the city, Caroline, Edward, Frank, William, Patrick and Charles made their way to the Sandridge Railway Pier, and from there boarded the splendid three-masted sailing vessel, built especially for the passenger trade between London and Melbourne. Edward's will had instructed the trustees to 'pay the expenses of the voyage in a first class Vessel or Vessels and to apply the monies accordingly and to ensure as far as possible the comfort and convenience of my family on such voyage'. Caroline and the boys travelled in style among the eighteen first class cabin passengers. Thirty-six other passengers travelled in second- and third-class cabins for prices starting at £15. The *Hampshire*'s saloon was 'very spacious'. Its cabins were large, well lit and ventilated, and 'fitted with fixed berths and toilet accessories'. This 1150-ton ship had been launched in March that year and made its first trip to Australia in late May from Gravesend to Plymouth to Melbourne. The *Hampshire* would sail back and forth between London or Plymouth and Melbourne many times over the next fifteen years. Its cargo included the usual staples exported from the colony: bales of wool and leather; cases of preserved meats, casks of tallow, bags of copper and diverse ores, cases of wine, and, on this trip, 4654 ounces (142 kilograms) of gold.[40]

Edward remembered it as 'a quick but very rough passage'.[41] For Caroline, then aged 36 and in her fifth year of widowhood, the 82 days to contemplate her past and her future surely felt long. She had failed to overturn Edward's demand that she and the children move to Ireland. In *Kearney v. Lowry*, Molesworth upheld the sanctity of her husband's intentions in his will over her claims of danger to her children's health. His decision confirmed dominant jurisprudence rather than setting new precedents. Caroline had demonstrated tenacity and determination in her legal and personal struggles. She also spent money fairly lavishly, tippled, was found guilty of a minor assault, and showed a tendency to stretch the truth in court and to play the part of the starving widow if she thought it would help her cause.

Caroline sailed from Australia with the knowledge that she would be much better off financially than her parents or most working-class and many middle-class widows. She could anticipate access to the promised annuity of £100 for herself, and further contributions for the education and support of her children. But this support was contingent on her remaining single, not conceiving a child out of wedlock and agreeing to live in whatever housing her brothers-in-law chose and furnished for her. It was nearly 20 years since she had left England in her teens. Now she was sailing 'home', but was obliged to continue on to another new country, with a different culture and dominant religion. Edward was now nearly fifteen, Frank was nearly fourteen and William ten. Patrick Edgar and Charles James were just eight and six. What would their futures look like, away from the station life that had shaped their early years? Caroline and her five boys were moving into the clutches of a family she had learned to mistrust and fear. She had good reason to dread living once again in close proximity to her brother-in-law William, and to meeting the rest of Edward's family.

# 7

# Arrivals and new challenges

The *Hampshire* docked in London on 20 December 1870. Caroline and her sons were back in the country of her birth. A short train ride and she could return to the town she had left nearly 20 years earlier. But there was to be no escape. They were met in London by Joseph Kearney, the second youngest of Edward's brothers. He shepherded them to Holyhead and across the Irish Sea to Dublin. Initially, according to young Edward, they stayed at Coffey's Hotel. It was on Upper Dominick Street in central Dublin. They seem to have lived in lodgings for a while until the trustees secured suitable housing, as required by Edward's will.[1] Shortly after they arrived Patrick Kearney came to see them. Over the six years since Edward's return visit he had become prominent as a promoter of Irish nationalism and of the expansion of Catholic institutions in County Westmeath and beyond. In 1867 he was made parish priest of the area around Moate, close to where he and his brothers were raised. Just four months before Caroline's arrival he returned from a trip to the eastern United States where he had successfully sought donations from Irish emigrants to fund his dream of building a new parish church in Moate.[2] The *Freeman's Journal* reported that his parishioners celebrated his return and his success in raising money. In Moate he was 'greeted by cheers, brass bands, flags waving. The reverend gentleman addressed the crowd calling for cheers for his friends at home and his Yankee friends. At the hour of eight o'clock there was not one house in the town but had their windows illuminated and dressed with laurel and box. The streets were crowded with people up to a late hour at night burning pitch barrels in every direction.'[3]

Flushed with his success abroad and assured that his beloved church project would be completed, Patrick may have anticipated that overseeing the educational and religious future of his five nephews, if not his sister-in-law, would be a relatively simple matter. As one of the guardians he shared responsibility for their housing and their education. Caroline and the boys hardly had time to recover from the lengthy sea voyage and their arrival in Dublin before, as young Edward recalled it, his 'uncle priest came to town and sent Bill, Frank and I to the French College Blackrock' (see image 10 in the picture section). It was only two weeks after her arrival, and Caroline did not yet have a place to live. Later, she contended that she had only agreed to Patrick's plan to place the older boys in boarding school as a temporary measure because she was a 'stranger in Dublin' and was worried about the boys running 'about the streets or in a hotel'. With the older boys safely in school for a while, she could focus on caring for her two youngest sons, whose health was 'extremely delicate'. She could also work on her plan to curtail the power that her three brothers-in-law held as co-guardians and the Irish trustees of Edward's will.[4]

This college, known today as Blackrock College, had been opened ten years earlier by members of the Congregation of the Holy Ghost, or Spiritans, a French order. It was then popularly known as the French College. The priests sought to provide the sons of the upper fractions of the Irish tenantry with a first-class Catholic education so they could enter university, become missionaries or take up positions in the civil service, which had only recently accepted Catholic candidates. By this time its reputation 'for the excellence of its teaching' had travelled across Ireland, attracting a growing number of pupils.[5] On 14 January, Patrick took his three nephews south down the coast from Dublin, past Sandymount and the Strand, and through what was then 'the straggling seedy village of Williamstown'. The approach to the college was 'along a shabby laneway' known as Castledawson Avenue, 'lined with dilapidated cottages on the College side'. The boys doubtless entered the locked entrance with foreboding. Edward, Frank and William had been educated by their mother and successive governesses. It was only in the short periods that they had spent in Robe with their teacher grandfather, or possibly while in Melbourne, that they would have attended a formal school.[6]

Edward's, Frank's and William's names were inscribed in the register of the college as the 558th, 559th and 560th pupils enrolled since it opened in 1860. Their ages were listed as fifteen, thirteen and eleven respectively. The section of the register for the names and addresses of their parents simply noted 'Mrs. Australia', rendering Caroline both invisible and absent. Clearly inscribed, in contrast, were the words: 'Uncle – V. Rev. Fr. Kearney, P.P Moate'. The Canon was clearly known and respected at the college. He had chosen the school judiciously. As one of the boys' trustees he could use his dead brother's assets to ensure that they received a good, Catholic education. Three months later in March he paid £45 4s 6d for 'pension and sundries' for the three boys, covering their costs until May 1871. A further £41 12s 9d was requested and paid for the following term. The superior education at the French College, like that at the Sacred Heart Catholic College that William had taken Maria Ellen to in Australia, was not cheap.[7]

When the boys arrived in January, classes were well underway. The school year began in September. A few students dribbled

173

in over subsequent months, but most would have been well settled this late in the school year. Another pupil of that time, Michael Tevlin, described his apprehension when on arriving he was interviewed in the Dean's office by Father Reffé. He had terrible trouble understanding his French accent. Tevlin made such 'a poor impression on the Dean' that he 'was relegated to the lowest English class'. The three Australian brothers are unlikely to have made a better impression! Their fellow schoolmates were mostly Irish Catholic boys and a few refugees from the Franco–Prussian war, which was waging at the time they arrived. Many, like them, were raised on farms, albeit very different ones from the stations of the Australian outback they had left. The school was by then one of the largest, if not *the* largest, Catholic boarding school in Ireland. Some 150 boarders jostled for space with day students and junior seminarians studying for the priesthood. Never would Caroline's sons have been surrounded by so many other boys and youths. Nor had they ever lived in such a structured environment.

Their fellow pupil Tevlin was struck by the 'spirit of study', 'love of language and literature' and 'interest in the Classics, modern and ancient' that prevailed. The school would go on to train some prominent Irish writers and politicians. Tevlin found the school 'very French'.[8] Almost all the priests were French and spoke English with accents. English, not Irish, was the language of instruction. The college's historian describes everything being 'done in French style'. 'Lacking the wines of France', they provided beer for the boys in champagne-type bottles, one for each table, so they learned how to act as they rose up in the world. Young Edward found it a very 'Roman Catholic place'. By 1870 there was a beautiful chapel. A large wing housed classrooms, a study room, the office of the dean of studies, and a dormitory, known as the 'Immaculate Heart Dormitory'. Recent additions included a hall for recreation, theatricals, debates and assemblies.

Construction and the growing numbers of students meant that the playing grounds – indeed, much of the college – was cramped. Every space was used.[9]

What a religious and cultural shock for the three eldest Kearney boys! They were used to galloping miles and miles to round up sheep and inspect outstations. They had learned to work hard to the rhythms of the days and the seasons. Their instruction by their mother and resident governesses had been intermittent. Here the days were rigidly organised into times for prayer, meals, lessons, study, sports, chapel and sleep. They 'were kept like prisoners', young Edward told his future wife.

After three months they bolted. It was Easter Monday, 10 April 1871. They had noticed that the 'big iron door' was open. The 'three of us darted out upsetting a priest in our way'. They ran and caught a train to Dublin. When some priests appeared in their carriage, they jumped off the train to evade them, then continued on to their 'mother's lodging place'. She was not there, he reported, with the judgmental sadness that pervades his references to Caroline in his memoir. She was in police court pursuing 'a char woman who had stolen a lot of things from her in the lodging house'.[10] That day Edward wrote a postcard to the head of the college. It informed the Reverand Julius Lehman in no uncertain terms that he did 'not intend to come back to the college, and likewise I am not going to change my religion for all the French colleges on earth; and besides I have been brought up in the Protestant religion, and so I intend to keep it, and if you like you can say what you will'.[11]

Caroline had anticipated problems. Soon after arriving in Dublin she approached Irish lawyers, seeking to have her sons made wards of the court. One month before the boy's escape her solicitor had presented a petition in her name to the Court of Chancery in Dublin with her request.[12] The Court of Chancery was the equivalent of the equity courts in Australia. Caroline had not succeeded in her main goal in *Kearney v. Lowry* in Melbourne, but she had gained considerable experience of the processes involved, and of the power of the judges and the master of equity to control the actions of trustees and guardians. Overseeing the guardianship of orphans, their education and their estates was one of the responsibilities of such equity courts. And they could remove or replace a ward's guardians if they deemed it wise.[13] Caroline was seeking to secure oversight of her children and of the administration of Edward's estate by court officials. This would curb the power of her brothers-in-law. She may also have doubted her own ability to raise her five sons in Ireland.

The boys' escape threw Caroline into yet another legal struggle with members of the Kearney family. Ten days later Patrick and William Kearney and Thomas McCormack filed a petition in the Court of Chancery in Dublin. In the written affidavits that launched their case, they blamed Caroline for the boys' departure. They claimed that she had taken them away for a 'short vacation' over Easter and failed to make them return. They implied that she was responsible for Edward's postcard explaining that he did not intend to return or to change his religion. Their narrative about the boys' departure from the school left no room for their nephews' agency in taking the initiative to escape from the school.[14] The uncles sought to force Caroline to return the boys to the college and to restrain her from instructing them in anything but the Roman Catholic faith.[15]

When the brothers' petition was delivered to the court, it was merged with her request that they be made wards of the court. Between 20 April and 8 May 1871 Dublin newspapers noted that petitions in *Re Kearneys, Minors* had been filed and would be heard shortly in the Court of Chancery.[16] Once again, the history and details of Edward's will, their marriage and the constraints placed on her as his widow were public news. Once again legal costs would be high. As was usual in chancery cases, each side secured the services of two Queen's Counsels. Mr Carleton and Mr Butt, acting for Caroline, were instructed by two solicitors, Mr Green and Mr Foley. William Kearney himself took on the task of instructing the trustees' two counsels, Mr John O'Hagan and Mr Palles, assisted by a Mr Carter.[17]

The case pitted the claims of Caroline's three Irish brothers-in-law, as both the boys' guardians and the Irish trustees of Edward's will, against hers as their mother and their other testamentary guardian. It was a key duty of guardians to ensure that children were properly educated 'in a religious and moral manner according to their expectations in life'. In earlier centuries in Ireland, as in England, English law forbade the education of wards in 'Romanist principles'. But jurisprudence and practice in the Courts of Chancery in Ireland and England had increasingly acknowledged that the guardians of children were the proper judges in matters relating to education and that they could raise them in any 'system of belief not contrary to law'.[18] Patrick had been fulfilling his role as a guardian and uncle by enrolling them in the college, and even in seeking to ensure that they were given a good Catholic education. Caroline's petition, the boys' refusal to return to the college and her support for their education as Protestants placed the profound religious differences between her and the other guardians, as well as the children's future, in the hands of the Court of Chancery. In *Re Kearneys, Minors*, Caroline was the defendant rather than the plaintiff as she had been in Melbourne.[19]

Things moved quickly. By 9 May 1871 the full case with Caroline's contestation of their claims was ready. The counsels for the boys' uncles and for Caroline presented vastly divergent stories, set out in competing affidavits. The lord chancellor of

Ireland, Lord O'Hagan (see image 11 in the picture section), presided over equity in the Court of Chancery. This was a political appointment. Until 1867 it was closed to Catholics. O'Hagan's appointment in 1868 made him the first Catholic to hold the position. The British prime minister, William Gladstone, chose him as part of his strategy of uniting the Liberal party and pacifying Ireland. This decision was virulently criticised by the unionist, conservative Lord Justice Jonathan Christian, who deplored the political nature of the post and O'Hagan's minimal experience in courts of equity. Yet, O'Hagan brought many years' legal experience to the position, though more in the Court of Common Pleas than in chancery. And he had already served as solicitor-general and attorney-general for Ireland.[20]

Thomas O'Hagan and the Kearney guardians shared some common goals for Ireland. This Belfast-born lawyer and politician was closely involved with the reforms in landlord–tenant relations that culminated in the *Land Act* of 1870, which provided compensation for evicted tenants. He fought for cost-effective legal structures to enable tenants to become landowners. He was a keen promoter of jury reform and of a well-funded national university, which, unlike Trinity, would admit Catholics and offer them an education as good as that which Protestants had benefitted from for so many years. Some legal observers assumed he would side with the Catholic plaintiffs. But both his commitment to Irish nationalism and his Catholicism were less dogmatic than the Kearneys'. O'Hagan was respected for his independent outlook. This skilled advocate and debater was also considered a 'kindly and humane man'.[21]

At the time of *Re Kearneys, Minors*, O'Hagan had been a peer for only one year. After initially refusing the honour, he had accepted being named Baron O'Hagan, of Tullahogue in the county of Tyrone in June 1870. This had placed him in the House of Lords when discussions on Irish land reform were underway.[22] O'Hagan was 58 years old and, like Edward and Caroline, had six children, though his were all girls. He, like Caroline, was widowed; his wife had died two years earlier. Shortly he would cement his recent elevation to the peerage along with his commitment to ongoing union with England by remarrying into the English gentry. His new wife, Alice Mary Towneley, was 34 years younger than him. She came from an ancient English Catholic family whose impressive home and estate in Lancashire dated back to at least the 15th century.[23]

In contrast to the Australian equity case regarding Edward's will and the three thick, rich bundles of documents it left, no archives of the Court of Chancery in Dublin have survived. They went up in smoke in June 1922, along with the other public documents so carefully consolidated over the previous century in the Record Treasury of the Public Record Office of Ireland. A year earlier the Anglo–Irish Treaty had established the Irish Free State as a Dominion within the British Empire, ending the Irish War of Independence. This did not go far enough for many Republicans. Anti-Treaty militants occupied the legal heart of Dublin – the Four Courts – and stored their ammunition close to the archives. As conflict degenerated into fighting and civil war, an explosion in the wing that housed the Public Record Office obliterated the details of this court case, along with virtually all of Ireland's legal and civil records. A statue of Lord O'Hagan was also destroyed.[24] Without these records, only the press reports allow us to piece together some of the details of this contest and of Caroline's and the boys' lives in Ireland.

Irish procedures in equity, like those in Australian colonies, were based largely on English ones. The process was familiar now to both Caroline and William: the petitions drawn up in the first person, with each paragraph referring to a distinct subject; the deponent's obligation to explain how they knew what they claimed to know; the filing of affidavits and responses all echoed *Kearney v. Lowry* in Australia.[25] Newspaper reports note that the Kearney brothers' statements professed to be based on their deceased brother's letters, 'statements, their knowledge of his principles' as well as Caroline's 'admissions and acts'. Yet the content of their affidavits suggests that they were making up information, lying, or that Edward had consistently deceived them about his family life. William claimed that Edward had always been a sincere Catholic, that Caroline became a Roman Catholic shortly after the marriage and 'complied with its religious requirements', including getting married again by a Catholic priest. 'All the children were baptized by Catholic priests.' William did admit that the closest Catholic Church to Lockhart was 180 miles away. He insisted that priests had visited the station 'three times a year', and that at those times the whole family 'attended Mass and approached the Sacraments of Confession and Holy Communion'. This may have been true while William was at Lockhart, but not earlier. The minimal religious structures and services of the Australian pastoral frontier were likely incomprehensible to parishioners and priests in the densely settled parishes of Ireland. Caroline, he argued, had continued to practise as a Catholic for two years after Edward's death. Now she refused to allow the boys to return to the college.[26]

Joseph Kearney affirmed that Caroline had agreed to the boys attending the Catholic college, but then took them away 'on the pretence of them going home for a visit'. Canon Kearney claimed that the children had never objected to him about the teaching they were receiving. The brothers' counsels produced letters from Edward senior to Patrick in which he told his brother that his wife was Protestant but received into the Catholic faith, that they had engaged a Catholic governess at Lockhart, and that he wished his brother William to 'take to a Christian land his children and their mother ... who was only lately turned to the blessed true church'.[27] O'Hagan might well have doubted the veracity of such letters sent home by a dying man keen to convince his own family of his adherence to their strict faith.[28]

Against this evidence, which wrongly identified Caroline's maiden name as Hamilton (the name of her sister's husband), and her religious affiliation as Presbyterian, rather than Anglican, Caroline's counsel, Mr Carleton QC and two of his colleagues presented her story. It asserted that she was 'an English Lady', and 'never was, nor professed to have become, a Roman Catholic'. She denied the Catholic marriage. Caroline offered a brief history of their moves as colonisers from Broom Station in South Australia to Lockhart, and stressed that she had educated the children herself as Protestants assisted by Protestant governesses. 'No Roman Catholic prayer book or version of the Bible was in their home'; she 'taught the children prayers from the Church of England prayer book'. Instructing the court through her affidavit about the lack of religious infrastructure in the outback, she explained that they travelled to the McLellans' station some four miles (six kilometres) away once every five weeks for Presbyterian worship. Furthermore, she insisted that Edward had known of this, gone with them sometimes, and never objected. He had held no strong religious convictions, Caroline argued. He had never given her directions about the children's religious upbringing. It was only when he became ill and returned from his visit to Ireland shortly before his death that Edward had renewed his Catholicism.[29]

Caroline's final assertions were the most dramatic – and they seem completely plausible to me. It was in the Irish equity court that she declared that Edward was so ill when his will was executed that 'he was incapable of understanding it'. Rather, it was 'prepared under the influence of his brother, William'. Had she been able to use and prove this earlier in the Melbourne case, she might have had a chance of overturning her forced departure from Australia. Now it was too late. William, she took pains to point out, had 'treated her with great unkindness and personal indignity' after Edward's death, including taking her daughter away without her consent. She then explained that she had only agreed to place the boys at the college as a temporary convenience, 'until they should be made wards of the court'.[30]

Unsurprisingly, Lord O'Hagan found it 'very hard to tell who had spoken the truth and who had not'.[31] The significant 'conflict as to the details in the affidavits' convinced him that he needed to talk to the boys. In proceedings in chancery, if the court was not 'satisfied by any evidence produced via a bill' it could 'require the production and oral examination of any witnesses or party to the cause'.[32] Young Edward was again sick. O'Hagan waited nearly a month until he was better.[33] He then conducted what he described as a 'most careful inquiry in lengthened interviews' with the three eldest boys. Edward recalled it as 'a long and stormy interview on the point of religion'. This conversation convinced O'Hagan that the boys had been 'taught Protestant prayers, instructed in the Protestant Bible and catechism, and attended Protestant worship'. He accepted their accounts of having been instructed by 'a succession of Protestant governesses and tutors' and their mother. He reported that they 'declared themselves Protestants and strongly desired to continue in the Protestant faith'.[34]

This, O'Hagan insisted, was their father's fault. Edward Kearney had failed to ensure their Catholic upbringing. In what might be read as a lesson on the dangers of emigration to Australia, he argued that Edward had 'left Ireland and went to Australia where he was out of reach of all religious discipline and the opportunity of cultivating the faith of his fathers'. His religious negligence had meant that 'for many years the children were directed by the mother, an intelligent woman and a Protestant. They said their prayers at her knee, and, in point of fact, this poor man did not look after his children as he ought to have done if he were in his own country.' Edward's neglect had allowed their mother 'to do what she pleased'. Perhaps she had done things 'now and then of which the father knew nothing, but on the whole, exercised control over these children from their birth'.[35]

Lord O'Hagan found Edward, Frank and William 'clever and intelligent'. He lauded the French College as a place of 'very great distinction', but accepted that they had not gone there of their own will and that the boys themselves had chosen to leave. His discussions with them convinced him that they had only 'exhibited outward conformity' with Roman Catholic worship and practices while there. He found them without instruction in the 'worship, discipline, or dogma of the Catholic Church'. As a result 'they were now without any tincture of Roman Catholicism'. To force them back to the school or into Catholicism, he decreed, was impossible. He feared that it would 'endanger the religious con-victions of those children, who were of age and capacity to have religious principles', if they were now educated differently. He would not risk leaving them 'without any fixed religious opin-ions', and losing 'all attachment to the Christian faith'.[36] Better Protestant than agnostic or atheist. Edward, Frank and William had secured the right to remain Protestant.

Not so Patrick Edgar and Charles James. At ages seven and nine, Lord O'Hagan considered them too young to have formed 'decided religious impressions'. Nothing would warrant the two young boys being educated 'otherwise than in the religion of their father'. So he directed that they be brought up as Roman Catholics, 'as strictly and carefully as [Edward] would have desired if he had still been alive'. In explaining his decision he argued that no opposition from a mother could ever override the principle that the wishes and religion of the father must be followed, except, as in the case of the older boys, when they already had clear religious beliefs. He dismissed concerns about the problems of raising offspring in one family in different faiths as 'one of the misfortunes which so often grow from mixed unions'. And, demonstrating paternal concern for the youngsters, he indicated that he would take advice about the fragile state of the health of the two youngest children from the eminent medical men who were attending them. The Kearney children clearly remained susceptible to ill health.[37]

*Re Kearneys, Minors* received some publicity. Newspapers across Ireland, England and Wales commented on its significance regarding children in mixed marriages. It was reported in the *Solicitor's Journal* in London and copied to the *American Law Review*. That commentary noted that 'zealous religionists – on either side – who respectively hoped and feared so much from Lord O'Hagan's known strong religious sympathies' had been disappointed. The Reverend Patrick Kearney and his co-guardians were likely among them. Thomas O'Hagan's decision was not shaped by his religious beliefs or any other religious or nationalist goals he might have shared with the Kearney uncles. Rather, it rested on the growing understanding in courts of equity that in conflicts between guardians about their wards' education or religious training, the wishes or religion of a deceased father had to be balanced against what was deemed in the best interest of the child. Most such cases involved 'mixed marriages', where the father had left no specific religious instructions and the surviving mother sought to raise her children in her own faith.[38]

This question of the religious education of infant wards of the Court of Chancery was increasingly debated at this time in England, Ireland, the United States and other common law colonies with equity courts. This was partially a result of the gradual lifting of some of the draconian restrictions the British had long placed on Catholics, including those forbidding guardians in Ireland to raise wards as Catholics, and those punishing priests who married a Catholic to a Protestant.[39] By the time of *Re Kearneys, Minors*, O'Hagan, along with other legal scholars, considered that the main principles were well established. Earlier that year they had been confirmed when the Appellate Court in London upheld the decision made in a recent case, *Hawkesworth v. Hawkesworth*. That widely cited judgment held that the child's welfare overrode any former right of deceased fathers to dictate what kind of religious education their children would receive.[40] It gave some autonomy to mothers and to children who held different religious beliefs than the dead father. This move away from an insistence that a father's religion inevitably determined that of their offspring in such cases resulted from broad cultural shifts including the growing sentimentalisation of domesticity and motherhood, and new understandings of childhood. A similar trend in the related, but different, area of child custody in cases of divorce also gave new emphasis to the rights of the child.[41]

Yet this was no revolution in mothers' or children's rights. *Hawkesworth v. Hawkesworth* upheld the 'absolute nature of the paternal right, qualified only by the clear interest' of the children. It did not undermine the power of men to dictate their children's religious futures in their wills or the understanding that normally children would follow their father's religion. Contemporaries understood that this could work a 'grievous hardship on a surviving mother' with different religious beliefs. In some jurisdictions in the United States, recent legislation gave surviving parents the right to choose the religion in which they would raise their children. This was not an option in England or Ireland. O'Hagan's decision made this very clear. The *American Law Review* lauded his decision as illustrating the general rule of the court as well as its principal exception, and as offering a good example of how the wide discretion vested in the Court of Chancery when it came to infants could be wisely exercised. His decision that the elder boys should remain Protestants was the exception. His decision regarding the two younger boys upheld the rule.[42]

Caroline may have considered the outcome of the case a minor triumph in her ongoing skirmishes with her brothers-in-law. Yet it was surely a pyrrhic victory. Her boys were to be raised in two different, warring Christian faiths. The animosity between the parties continued to seep into the chancery courts following the decision. William Kearney's counsel sought a direction from O'Hagan that Caroline 'should not interfere with the children'. Her counsel assured his Lordship that 'she has not the least wish' to interfere. The lord chancellor made it clear that he did not know 'whether she has or not; but if she has she ought to restrain it'. William also sought to avoid blame for the length of time it had taken for them to come to Ireland. O'Hagan insisted that he did not wish 'to throw the slightest blame on anybody'. He promised rapid action consistent with the children's safety.[43] Clearly Caroline's actions would be watched. Still, the boys' uncles had lost their attempt to force all the children into Catholicism. Their roles, not just as co-guardians of the boys, but as trustees of their estate, were now subject to the supervision of the Court of Chancery. Caroline had sought to place the boys under the supervision of that court. As wards of the court, their estates, their education and even their marriages required court administration, oversight and sanction.[44] The power of their uncles was curtailed. But so was hers.

The two younger boys were sent to a Roman Catholic school in Booterstown, run by a Miss Russell. Edward, Frank and William attended Santry Boarding School in the suburb of Santry, in the north of Dublin. It was part of a network of schools 'incorporated with the Society for Promoting Protestant Schools in Ireland'. Caroline appears to have been rubbing salt in the wounds of her Catholic brothers-in-law. Young Edward was not much happier there. He did not find it a 'very good place for young fellows'.[45] Santry, like the French College, had very high academic standards. It aimed to prepare its students for university studies at Trinity College, Dublin, or for a career in the civil service. Edward was, in his own words, 'a pretty good athlete', and 'trained to walk and jump'. Perhaps, like his uncle's brother Tom, he loved cricket and enjoyed playing it at the school. But its excessive focus on academic success did not nurture feelings of achievement in this boy, raised in such a different social and educational context.[46]

For any widow, raising five young boys through their teenage years on her own would be challenging and costly. Doing so in a foreign country under the watchful eye of trustees and the Court of Chancery was surely more so. Yet Caroline remained, in many ways, a very privileged widow. She was not homeless, and she did not have to pay for accommodation. However, she had to live where her brothers-in-law chose. They had 'full discretion as to renting, leasing or purchasing' a cottage or residence for the family. They were to keep it 'in a proper state of repair' until the youngest child turned 24 or the family and the trustees decided it made sense to leave it. Then Edward instructed them to sell or dispose of the dwelling, 'furniture and other effects and the sale monies shall then sink into and form part of the trust fund'.[47]

They fulfilled this wish, though it is unclear exactly when Caroline left temporary lodgings and settled into a permanent residence. It may just be a coincidence that the very day that Caroline and the boys arrived in London someone placed an advertisement in the Dublin paper the *Freeman's Journal* seeking 'a Modern HOUSE with good garden', at least four bedrooms and two sitting rooms. The notice specified that the house should be in 'Landsdowne, Sandymount, or Merrion Road or Clyde or Victoria Terrace'. These locations were all near Sandymount, the residential suburb and seaside resort four kilometres south of Dublin. It was there that at some point Caroline took up residence in a house at 2 Clyde Terrace. This was not far from either the French College or Booterstown, where the two youngest boys went to school. She was definitely living there later in the 1870s.[48]

Placing Caroline and the children in this middle-class locality, with its villas and terraced genteel housing, respected the spirit of Edward's directives to give them accommodation suitable to his status. The development of these southern suburbs over the century was fuelled by the 'gradual flight of wealth' from the north to the south of the city that left central Dublin grimy, unhealthy and home to the impoverished. Sandymount was far from the rough life and hotels and saloons of Dublin, which Patrick Kearney might have feared would appeal to Caroline. The train line that ran down the coast to Blackrock did not stop there. If she wished to visit the city she would need to take one of the omnibuses that had been serving the routes to the south since the 1840s, or hire a carriage.[49] Its seaside location promised a healthy environment for the illness-prone boys.

The houses on Clyde Terrace were a short walk inland from the Sandymount Strand and the beaches of South Dublin Bay. This small terrace of four two-storey houses ran off the north side of St John's road almost opposite the substantial Irish Anglican

Saint John's Church, Sandymount. Five years before Caroline and the boys arrived, the terrace was described as 'almost new', and 'built by an eminent building firm of Dublin'. These were substantial middle-class homes. Renovations at number two since its construction had included adding servants' quarters and a water closet. It had a large garden and a water tank. In 1911, the census enumerator categorised it as a first-class home. This classification included houses with solid walls made of stone, brick or cement; a slate, iron or tiled roof; between ten and twelve rooms, and five windows facing the street.[50]

Evidence suggests that the house was furnished very comfortably in a manner suited to the Kearneys' aspirations for gentility.[51] The hallway was graced by two carved mahogany chairs, a marble-topped hat, coat and umbrella stand, and an eight-day clock. Mahogany furniture signalled status in 19th-century urban middle-class society.[52] The drawing room included a cottage piano with a walnut case, a walnut drawing room suite and five spring-seat, oval-backed chairs as well as armchairs, easy chairs and couches. There was also an oval walnut table supported by a pillar and claw, a lady's work table and desk, and other tables. On the dining room floor was a Kidder carpet. That room housed a mahogany dining suite, a mahogany enclosed sideboard and six chairs, along with china, Delft pottery and glassware. One of the rooms boasted 'lofty mantelpiece glasses in gilt frames'. A Brussels carpet covered the stairs up to the second floor, where the four bedrooms were furnished with wardrobes, mahogany toilet tables, marble-topped stands, towel rails and commodes. The garden included a lean-to greenhouse, fruit trees, currant and gooseberry bushes, and space for several clothes lines.[53] The trustees seem to have set Caroline and the boys up in style in a house spacious enough to accommodate the whole family when the older boys were home from boarding school.

Young Edward was no happier at home than at school. He later described this stage of his life as one when 'things were going altogether wrong' at home. He told his future wife that alcohol had embittered all his 'young life', suggesting that Caroline continued to seek solace in drink. It is feasible that she became more dependent on drink as she faced the new challenges of life in Ireland.[54] As a keen temperance supporter, Canon Kearney would surely have sought to limit her access to ready money if she was drinking heavily. Within a year of the court case, she appeared before Lord O'Hagan again, claiming to have received insufficient support from the trustees. In July 1872, her solicitor, Mr Green, requested that the court pay her £349 17s that she expected but had not received. Newspapers reported that a sum of £280 a year had been calculated for the boys' support. This may have been paid directly to their schools, but Caroline should have been receiving her annuity, and also one-seventh of the net residue of the income from Edward's estate. The lord chancellor agreed. He requested that Caroline agree that should she spend more on the children's maintenance than allowed, it would be deducted from her claim on the estate.[55] As long as Caroline did not remarry or give birth to a child it looked as if she could secure the funds to support herself and the children, at a reasonable standard of living, with the support of the Court of Chancery.

These were significant sums. The £380 combined from her annuity and the support for the boys was more than double the £160 annually that Robert Morris, a British expert on 19th-century marriage, property and inheritance, estimates was 'just enough' for a widow to run 'an independent household with a servant' at this time.[56] Had the court records not been blown up it would be possible to better determine how the £12 000 sent to the Irish trustees from Australia was invested and deployed in the years following the family's arrival in Ireland. Were it possible to follow the money, it might be easier to explain Caroline's next moves.[57]

In March 1873 a Caroline Anne Kearney married a Doctor Richard Locke Johnson in London, England. The ceremony was held in the Saint Mary and Saint Joseph Catholic Church in the Poplar district of London.[58] For a long time I refused to believe that this was her. There were other Caroline Kearneys living in London at that time; surely it was one of them. Why would she marry, lose her promised support, and further compromise her relations with, and ability to care for, her five sons? Why would this woman who had experienced the divisiveness of marriage with a Catholic and supported her sons' desires to remain Protestant marry another Catholic? Had she and Richard Locke Johnson had a furtive fling, then decided to marry? Did he think he might benefit from her income and potential future share of the estate? This apparently impetuous move completely puzzled me. It still does. Certainly marriage might promise legitimate sex and possibly significant economic support. It would allow her to escape from the oversight of the boys' uncles and the courts. Yet to me, the losses for Caroline seem greater than any potential gains.

Could the years trying to shape her future in Australia and the constant struggles to free herself of the influence of her crusading Catholic brothers-in-law have worn Caroline down? She had shown prior to leaving Australia that she could spend an allowance of £100 quickly. In March 1873 she was in her late thirties and had been a widow for over seven years. Young Edward had turned seventeen in February. The other boys were between sixteen and nine. They had been in Ireland for just over two years. A remarriage could benefit two of her trustees, Brother Patrick and Thomas McCormack, who stood to inherit half of her portion of Edward's estate. Could they have pushed her into this? I don't think so.

Did the brothers even find out about the remarriage? I am now convinced that Richard and Caroline's wedding was not only very quiet, but also secret. They married by licence. This avoided all the publicity and time that the more usual announcement of banns in church over a three-week period entailed. For centuries securing a licence had been the recourse of couples wishing to marry privately or in a hurry because they feared family or community disapproval, were of different faiths, mismatched ages, or from elite families wishing for a private ceremony.[59] To obtain a marriage licence one of the spouses had to have lived in the parish where it was celebrated for at least a week. Both parties listed improbable addresses. His was given as Cross Street in the parish of Poplar, London. Yet both before and after this marriage, London's listings of inhabitants in the census and in city directories placed Richard at 6 Bedford Square in Bloomsbury. That middle-class residential area lay in the parish of Saint Giles, not Poplar. Caroline was said to live on Finchley Road, Upper Holloway, London. Were these fictitious addresses produced perhaps on the spur of the moment when they applied for the marriage licence? No members of their families or households witnessed their union. Two Poplar residents, William Hugget, a 24-year-old advertising agent, and his wife, Emma, served in that capacity.[60]

Much is mysterious about this marriage, but there is no question that the bride was indeed Caroline. The licence lists her as a widow, aged 38, and the daughter of William Bax, a supervisor of Inland Revenue. Had Caroline moved away from Dublin to London, the city that Richard had lived in since at least 1865? Probably not. Did she plan to live with him in London? What then about her income, which was to cease on remarriage? And what about her boys? Also, who was this man she was marrying? The last one is the only question to which I have some answers.

Richard Locke Johnson was born in Dublin and began his work life there as a brass founder and gasfitter. An irrepressible inventor, he patented several inventions in the 1850s. They aimed to improve the quality of gas lighting produced from peat. These were very well received by the shareholders of the Mullingar Gas Company and inhabitants of the town of Mullingar in County Westmeath, not far from where the Kearney brothers lived. The people of that town made a grateful public address to him in 1860, noting that the gas lighting exceeded their expectations. In the early 1860s he turned his quixotic mind to medicine, and trained and qualified as a surgeon at the Royal College of Surgeons in Edinburgh, obtaining diplomas in surgery and midwifery. He then moved to London, where he practised medicine for the rest of his life and continued to invent, research and publish articles. Titles published in the *Transactions of the Pathological Society of London* included 'Case of the gall stone, weighing 470 grains'; 'Catechu and opium in gonorrhoea;' 'Hydrophobia: a simple precaution in wounds from the bites of animals, etc.'[61]

It is not surprising that this inquisitive scientist–doctor chose to live in Bloomsbury, London's leading intellectual and medical quarter. His residential situation appears as maverick as his scientific interests. He was a boarder at 6 Bedford Square, the address listed for him in directories from 1871 until around 1876. When the census takers called in 1871, he was one of two male boarders in a three-generation family of women. Martha Hackwell was identified as the head of the household. She was aged 47 and married. There was no sign of any husband. Living with her were her 49-year-old widowed sister Harriet, and her thirty-year-old daughter Kate, as well as Kate's three-year-old daughter Elizabeth. Though Kate was noted as married in this census, for the rest of her life documents listed her as single.[62] Richard Locke Johnson was broadminded enough to accept lodgings in a house with an illegitimate child and women whose reputations were dubious by the standards of many of his middle-class medical peers.

Perhaps Caroline and Richard lived together briefly. They have left no traces of sharing an address. Wives invariably assumed their husband's name in 19th-century England and Ireland. No documents ever referred to her as Caroline Johnson. She and Richard may have hidden all evidence so that Caroline would not lose her annuity and her claim on Edward's estate. All evidence suggests the relationship was a temporary one. She returned to Ireland. Over the next nine years Johnson remained in London, working as a surgeon, publishing research papers and inventing. He patented a doorknocker in 1876 and improvements for the manufacture of respirators in 1878.[63] They may have both agreed they were not well suited. I presume she regretted the marriage. I hope she realised the enormity of leaving her sons behind in Ireland. Divorce was an expensive and very public option. Their apparent separation underlines the informal mechanisms that most couples used in the 19th century to end marriages.

If records existed of passengers sailing in either direction across the Irish Sea, we might be able to pin down the timing of Caroline's movements before and after this secretive marriage with more precision, but no such records were ever created.[64] Back in Dublin all the traces she left in directories and newspapers as well as court records identify her as a widow and as Mrs Kearney or Mrs Caroline Kearney. There is no hint in any newspaper reporting on the Court of Chancery proceedings that her remarriage was known to its officials. Nor does young Edward's memoir mention his mother remarrying. Edward was very frank in his writing about his disappointment with his mother, so it is hard to believe that he would have hidden the marriage from his future wife had he known about it. To me this circumstantial evidence suggests a secret marriage, quickly made, just as hastily regretted and carefully hidden by both spouses.

Still, it was later in the year of her remarriage that young Edward had had enough. His father had died when he was nine. At fourteen he had been forced to give up his favourite horse and saddle and leave the station he had hoped to inherit, and then Australia. He had successfully escaped the school run by French priests and avoided being forced into Catholicism. But he also disliked the Protestant school that he attended. As we have seen, he considered himself 'of a very sensitive nature'. He felt unloved and lacking 'encouragement as to a profession' from his mother. Now he was seventeen. 'So', as he explained later, he 'determined to leave home, and go to sea'. Edward signed up as a midshipman on the *Northumberland*. Built at Blackwall just two years earlier for the prominent British firm Money, Wigram & Sons, this screw steamer sailed regularly between London and Melbourne.[65]

Edward adjusted to life at sea. He 'got on very well' on his first trip. He had found a way to avoid his mother, support himself and to return to Australia, if not permanently. When he returned a year later, 'home was as usual.' He 'had a row with the Wigram Company', so signed up for three years as an apprentice with the Thomas Hilyard company. Apprenticeships in the merchant marine had changed since the early decades of the 19th century. Then sailing ships were required to train a certain number of boys to ensure that trained seamen were available for the navy. Apprentices were often young boys who would otherwise have been dependent on parish relief. By the 1850s owners were no longer required to take apprentices, and soon the rise of steam ships was transforming the labour required. At the time that Edward signed his indentureship in September 1874 apprenticeships were mostly 'officer recruitment' – training grounds for 'prospective masters and mates' for the shipping companies. Edward would train on the *Spool* under Captain Roberts. Two months after Edward signed this apprenticeship, his brother William, then aged fifteen, signed up for six years in Dublin to sail with Captain J. Edwards on the ship *William John*.[66] Edward remained a seaman, sailing over the rest of the decade to Japan, San Francisco, Peru, France and Australia. Every year or so he returned to take his leave in Sandymount, Dublin. It was there, after his first two years at sea, that he started courting his future wife Anna Cooke (see picture section, image 14).

Edward junior's cryptic retrospective comments about home being 'as usual' refer in part, I believe, to his concern about Caroline drinking and not providing the love and support that he craved. But they surely also reference the ongoing religious and legal battles with his uncles and further court interventions and conflicts. These continued. Between 1872 and 1874 notices that the court would consider the situation of the Kearney minors, issues regarding the accounts or settling the estate, and further attempts by Caroline to secure funds appeared in Irish newspapers. They contain frustratingly few, if any, details. In June 1874 Caroline again engaged the solicitor Mr Green. On 5 June newspapers reported that *Kearney v. Kearney* was on the list of cases to be heard in chancery that month. In contrast to *Re Kearney, Minors*, where she had been the defendant, accused of improperly preventing the boys from being Catholics, now she was the plaintiff. Once again she sought an accounting of the estate. This took chutzpah. Had anyone found out about the London marriage, she would surely have lost the possibility of future support. Or perhaps she had given up on support for herself, admitted to the remarriage, and sought justice for her sons.[67]

Five days later, the Irish trustees finally had Edward's will proved and registered at the Principal Registry in Dublin. They could have taken this action at any point after William's return in

1870, but they had not. Once again, Caroline faced the problem of executors who were slow to do their work. Had knowledge of Caroline's suit or pressure from the equity officials nudged them into action? The entry is extremely brief. 'The Reverend Patrick Kearney of St. Patrick's Moate, R.C.C., William Kearney of Williamstown and Thomas McCormack of Kilkenney West Drumreary [sic], all of the Country of Westmeath Esquires the Executors for Ireland' registered their oaths regarding the details of his will and his death. They claimed that his effects were worth under £5.[68] Was the amount so small because Edward's estate was so fully encumbered providing for Caroline and the children that there were no further assets? Or because the assets were effectively in the hands of the Court of Chancery officials? Lord O'Hagan had lost his position as lord chancellor with the defeat of Gladstone's liberals in February 1874. Caroline might well have expected a less sympathetic hearing from his replacement, Jonathan Christian, a man widely known, 'indeed notorious more widely for his vituperative language'.[69] He heard the counsels for Caroline and the trustees on 19 June and decreed that the three trustees should produce an account of the estate. As a result, in November that year Dublin papers called for Edward Kearney's creditors to present their claims.[70]

As with *Kearney v. Lowry* in Melbourne, *Kearney v. Kearney* resurfaced repeatedly over time. Two years later, in May 1876, Caroline again wanted money. This time she sought clarity on two main issues. She asked whether the £100 annuity that Edward had left her was payable from the date of his death or from when the funds reached Ireland. And she wanted to know how the remainder of his estate should be distributed. Caroline had again engaged Mr W. Green and Mr Foley. Her brothers-in-law seemed to change their legal counsel constantly, echoing the ways William had frustrated his Melbourne solicitors. This time a Mr Davies QC and Mr Honey represented them. The children were represented separately by Mr Lynch and Mr Perrot. Lord Christian decreed that the 'arrears of the annuity were to be computed from the date of the death of the testator'. This decision made Caroline eligible for at least £400. Whose portion of the estate this was to come from was left for further deliberation in court. 'His Lordship also made a decree declaring the rights of parties under the will,' the papers reported.[71] If only there were evidence of the content of that decree and the information on which it was based! It would show how Lord Christian deemed what remained of the £12000 sent to Ireland or any income it had generated should be distributed. In the frustrating absence of any such detail, very rough calculations and new questions must suffice.

Recall that Edward's will had required that his Irish trustees invest his assets, pay Caroline her £100 annuity and hold the residual income and proceeds in a trust. That trust was to be divided in seven parts, one for Caroline, the others for the six children. The income from the children's shares was to be used to support their maintenance and education until they reached the age of 24, or, in the case of his daughter, she attained that age or married.[72] As Maria Ellen had died, one of the issues regarding the will that Lord Christian may have decided was whether the estate should be divided in sixths, rather than sevenths. Had the Irish trustees known about Caroline's remarriage they would surely have insisted on the other clause of his will – cutting off her income, and making Patrick and her brother-in-law Thomas McCormack eligible for half of her portion each.[73] Patrick successfully completed a magnificent church in Moate and another in Mount Temple. These were costly projects, paid for in part through his fundraising abroad. Whether he received any assets through Edward's will or from other relatives remains unclear.[74]

Where did the money go? Were Edward's final wishes about the distribution of his estate followed as carefully as his command that Caroline and the children move to Ireland? The sale of Lockhart Station and its stock had produced over £15 000 after the mortgage was repaid. Once the debts and accounts were settled in Australia, some £14 799 8s remained.[75] Over £2500 had gone to support Caroline and the children and to cover the costs of the court case in Australia. Edward's will required that the money sent from Australia be invested in government or real securities in Ireland. The 1870s were volatile years for such investments. Interest rates had been high in the 1860s, but the world economic crisis of 1874, bank failures, then bad harvests in Ireland brought them plummeting down over the rest of the decade. Invested at 3.25 per cent, a rough average at the time, the £12 000 sent to Ireland might have generated as little as £390 annually.[76] This would only cover Caroline's £100 annuity and the £280 that the court had estimated was required for the boys' support. That support would include the cost of their housing and education. Unless the trustees or chancery officials were able to secure a much higher return, the capital would not have increased much in the years before the boys became eligible for their portions. None of the children were yet 24 in 1876, so if the dictates of Edward's will were being followed – as seems likely, given the oversight of chancery officials – maintenance should have been available for all five boys. If the capital had remained intact they might each expect to receive a minimum of between £1750 and £2000 when they turned 24. It doesn't sound very much. However, today these amounts translate to a purchasing power of between $200 800 and $229 000 Australian.[77] Such legacies might provide them with a new start in life. They would also make them attractive suitors!

In 1876 Caroline was definitely living at 2 Clyde Terrace. There was no hint of her remarriage. She was listed as Mrs Caroline

Kearney in that year's Dublin directory. Two of her sons had left home, seeking to shape their own lives. By then, Edward junior had been at sea for three years, William for two, returning to Sandymount between voyages.[78] On Edward's long trips away he brooded over his past life. It may well have been on one of his voyages that he wrote the memorandum about his childhood for his future wife. In that document he related to her how he envied his fellow sailors who received 'letters from their sweethearts at home'. He was pining 'for someone to love'. On his return home that year he went walking on the Sandymount Strand with his brother Frank. The Strand is perhaps the most famous beach in Irish fiction. Later it would feature in several episodes in James Joyce's *Ulysses*. This was where the young people of Sandymount walked, paraded and courted. Fresh from his lengthy voyage and the company of other crewmen, Edward was keen to meet women. 'Now if Bill was here he would introduce you to plenty of young ladies,' Frank told him, as the young sailor watched every woman who passed. In his account of his first encounter with the woman he would court and marry, Frank said to him:

'Ted, here comes the best and handsomest girl in Sandymount.' I saw a young lady crossing the road of very genteel appearance, with a black broad rimmed hat and a black and white thing around it. She passed me, I looked up, and I saw a regular vision of beauty. I watched till I saw her pass again. I said to Frank quite casually 'What's her name?' He said 'Miss Cooke'. I felt then in my inmost heart that I loved the same Miss Cooke. She always would rise up. I never tried to put her away, for I thought her beautiful to look at, and I felt a wild rapture in giving my heart to her, and I made a silent vow that if ever I got to know her, that I would tell her of my great love.[79]

Edward began courting Anna Cooke. Her family lived at 129 Strand Road, a quick walk towards the sea from Clyde Terrace. He poured all of his hopes into this romance. Much of their courting took place on the Sandymount Strand. There, Edward watched jealously as she interacted with other suitors from the neighbourhood, especially with one of the Cronhelm boys who lived just down the road from him, towards the sea on Tower Terrace. Rumour was that she was thinking of marrying one of them. Once he had been properly introduced and made her acquaintance, Edward was determined to marry her.[80]

Nothing in his own account of the torture he went through courting her suggests that he considered himself socially inferior to this well-educated middle-class woman. Edward was a handsome young man, with a striking Roman nose, piercing eyes and a hairline that was already receding when the couple first met. He considered himself mature for his years – hardly surprising, given his life history to date. He told Anna that he had never really had a childhood and felt older than many others who were his senior in years. Perhaps this was in part because she was three years older than him. Although he blamed his mother for not encouraging him to follow a profession, he had been raised sufficiently well to appeal to Anna, whose father, Hugh Cooke, Esquire, had legal training and worked as a rules clerk in the High Court in Dublin. Anna had two sisters and two brothers. They were a well-educated family with servants. She spoke French fluently and was a talented classical pianist.[81]

His efforts paid off. Edward and Anna were married by the Reverend B. C. Davidson on 5 February 1879 at St John's Church, Sandymount, a three- or four-minute walk from the Cookes' home on Strand Road, beside the sea, and a stone's throw from Caroline's house. Saint John's was a Church of Ireland institution, founded in 1850, and modelled on a 13th-century church in

Normandy. Anna and her family were members of that denomination. Edward's brother Frank and Cassie Atkinson, Anna's cousin and friend, served as witnesses. Anna was then 26 years old, Edward, 23. The marriage register identified both of Anna's parents, as was fairly usual. Edward was listed only as the eldest son of the late Edward Kearney, Esquire, of Lockhart, Victoria, Australia, deceased. No mention was made of Caroline there, or in the public announcement of their marriage. Was she present? Was Edward worried about how she would behave? He now listed his address as 7 Alfred Street in Cork. This was a lodging house.[82] It was to that coastal port that Anna and Edward moved after their week-long honeymoon.[83] Just over a year later their first daughter, Anna Violet Kearney, was born in Cork.[84]

Family reminiscences suggest that Edward avoided long sea voyages following his wedding, working instead for the Irish Lights Commission for a while. He would still be away for days on end checking coastal lighthouses and navigation markers, but he could spend more time at home than when away on trips to Australia. When he once again signed up for Australian trips, Anna moved back to Sandymount and lived with her parents. Their second daughter, Ida, was born there in July 1881. Long absences would characterise their family life for the next eight years. Edward was keen to take his young family back to Australia, but 'Anna was reluctant to leave' her aging parents.[85]

One by one Caroline's three other sons found ways to leave Dublin and Ireland. Most followed Edward and William, initially taking to the sea. This was one option, given their variable education. More importantly, it was a way to return to the colonies of their youth. Their father's will had forced them to leave Australia. It could not erase their sense of themselves as Australians or eliminate their love of the place. Patrick Edgar left for Scotland in the late 1870s or early 1880s. In April 1881, he was captured by the census taker as a lodger in Greenock, one of Scotland's main port cities serving the West and East Indies, Canada and Australia. He was then aged nineteen and serving an apprenticeship as a marine engineer. He and a shipmaster boarded in the home of a 73-year-old widow whose sixteen-year-old niece acted as her 'companion'.[86] Over the next eight to nine years Patrick sailed back and forth between Australia and England before settling in New South Wales.

Escaping Ireland on a more permanent basis began to look increasingly attractive to Frank as his romantic attraction to Margaret Kearney grew. Clearly the Kearney boys had met up with their relatives in County Westmeath. Margaret was one of the daughters of Francis and Anne Kearney of Renaun, Ballinahown. It was her sister Mary Anne who had gone to Australia with William senior, lived at Lockhart, warned Caroline of Maria Ellen's abduction, and whom Edward senior had hoped would accompany his family back to Ireland. After leaving Ireland, Mary Anne and Charles Mulrain had settled back in Ballymore, where they ran a shop. By 1876 they had three young children.[87] Frank and Margaret were first cousins. This was forbidden love within the Catholic Church, as it was in most faiths. Family members aware of the budding romance between Frank and Margaret sought to nip it in the bud.

In 1876 Margaret's father, Francis Kearney, was nearly 70, and likely unwell. His brother Patrick surely offered advice about what to do about his wayward daughter. This ardent advocate of temperance was also concerned that Francis's wife, like Caroline, liked to tipple. The Kearney brothers already had firsthand experience of the power of a man's final wishes to regulate unwanted behaviour. The presence of Caroline and the boys in Ireland was evidence of their partial success. In August that year Francis finalised his will. Patrick's influence seems clear throughout. As with

Edward's 1865 will, it fulfilled a husband's responsibility to provide shelter and financial support for his wife and a future for his children. Anne was to have the use of their farmhouse and furniture for the rest of her life as well as the income from his two houses in Athlone. His sons would inherit the farm and other properties. Provisions were made for his three married daughters, Mary Anne Mulrain, Kate Canton and Elizabeth Branagan, and their children. And he promised Margaret, his only daughter who was still single, significant support.[88]

Like his brother Edward, Francis attached conditions to virtually all these bequests. Margaret would not receive this inheritance if she married against 'the wish of her mother and her uncle' Patrick. In that case, she was to receive £100 and no more. To be fair, this may have reflected their hope that Margaret, as the only single daughter, would look after her mother in old age, as Irish daughters were expected to do. Yet it looks to me more like an attempt to police Margaret's liaison with Frank, who was not only her cousin, but also not a Catholic. Some of the bequests to Francis's wife were conditional on her leading a 'sober and regular life'. His sons Francis and Hugh would also lose some of the promised assets if their mother and Patrick did not approve of their marriage choices, or if they failed to live a sober life. But Margaret's loss of inheritance was to be much greater than theirs. The will gave Patrick extraordinary power over finances and family members' behaviour. He was named one of the three executors, alongside Charles Mulrain, Mary Anne's husband, and Thomas McCormack. But Thomas died before his elder brother.[89] Francis died seventeen months after writing his will, in January 1878. Within three months Charles Mulrain was also dead, leaving Mary Anne as a pregnant widow with three living children under five. In December that year the widowed Anne died. The two remaining trustees, the Reverend Kearney and McCormack, would oversee the actions of Francis and Anne's two unmarried sons and daughter.[90]

It is hard to imagine that young Frank Kearney could countenance the thought of the final wishes of another Kearney ruining his future. He and Margaret took things into their own hands. They headed to London and then, on 6 July 1881, boarded the *Lusitania*, bound for Plymouth, then Sydney and Melbourne. The transformations in the speed of travel had been dramatic in the decade since Frank had arrived in London from Australia. Their trip on the *Earl Grey* had taken eighty-two days. The *Lusitania*, 'one of the fleetest ships on the Orient line', completed the trip in half that time. She docked in Port Phillip on 21 August 1881. Margaret and Frank did not linger long. They may well have wanted to distance themselves from all of their relatives, expecting ongoing disapproval about their liaison. Two days later they boarded the steamer *Rotomahana*. It travelled regularly between Melbourne, Hobart and New Zealand ports. They travelled in steerage, stopped at Hobart and Bluff, then disembarked in Dunedin, New Zealand, on 30 August.[91]

Within less than two weeks they married in St Joseph's Church, a small brick building that was then the only Catholic church in that very Scottish Presbyterian town in the South Island.[92] Why New Zealand? Why Dunedin? Frank had relatives in Otago. His uncle Robert Steele had moved to Dunedin from Victoria in the 1850s. By 1881 he was living in the small Central Otago town of Arrowtown. Frank's cousins, the sons of James Allen and his mother's sister Esther, had returned from England. James senior had made a considerable fortune prior to his death. James junior had returned, married, 'inherited substantial property', and been elected to the Dunedin city council. He was becoming very prominent in the city. Later he would serve in national politics, including overseeing recruitment and much more during the First World

War. When Frank and Margaret arrived, James Allen was living in a house on Clyde Street, built around 1862 by Robert Steele. Clearly there were some links among these relatives, but I have no evidence that Frank and Margaret made contact with any of them during their brief stay in Dunedin.[93] Margaret and Frank Henry's marriage certificate listed him as a farmer and her as a spinster. Witnesses did not include his great uncle or his gifted, successful, conservative, wealthy first cousin. A labourer from Waikari, James O'Driscoll, and Rose Casey of Dunedin signed the certificate in front of M. Walsh, the officiating priest.[94] Soon Frank and Margaret moved to the Marlborough region at the north-eastern end of the South Island.[95]

As the decade of the 1880s opened, Caroline was almost an empty-nest widow. In 1881 she was still clearly identified in the Dublin listings of heads of households as living at 2 Clyde Terrace, Sandymount. The four-bedroom, two-storey house must have seemed increasingly empty. When she became a widow in 1865, she had six children to care for. Maria Ellen had now been dead for sixteen years. Had she lived she would have turned 26 in November 1880. Edward had left home seven years earlier. When he was not at sea he was now living with his wife, Anna, initially in Cork and then in Sandymount with their two daughters and her aging parents. By mid-1881 Caroline's second son, Frank, had eloped to New Zealand with Margaret. Two months after the couple married he turned 24. William had been working as an able seaman since starting his apprenticeship in 1874. His apprenticeship terminated in 1880. In 1882 a William Kearney, aged nineteen, likely him, was working as an able seaman on the *Grasmere* on the route between Sydney and Liverpool, UK. Patrick, as noted earlier, was also sailing between England and Australia. Only Caroline's youngest, Charles James, remained in Dublin. He turned sixteen in July 1880.[96]

One by one the boys were escaping Ireland and their mother. Late in August 1880, the substantial furniture and other contents of 2 Clyde Terrace were put up for auction. The newspaper advertisement carefully listed the furnishings of the house, from the elegant mahogany and walnut furniture through to the 'usual kitchen furniture and basement requisites, china, glass and delft etc'. The sale was announced first for Saturday 21 August, then for the 27th.[97] As we know, Edward's will had empowered his Irish trustees to buy or rent a cottage and to sell or dispose of it and its effects if the family or trustees deemed it expedient.[98] I assume that because the boys were wards of the court, chancery officials would have overseen this process.[99] Otherwise, one can imagine the tense and stormy discussions that might have erupted had Edward's brothers, some of the boys and Caroline sat down to seek a consensus on their futures. The final listing of Caroline as the occupant of 2 Clyde Terrace was in 1881.[100]

In late October 1881 the personal column of the *Irish Times* announced that Canon Kearney had accompanied Mrs and Master Kearney on the Kingstown mail steamer to England. Caroline was leaving Ireland, I presume with Charles James. She had spent a decade in Ireland under the thumb of her brothers-in-law. She may have quite simply had enough. Now that all her other sons had left home, she might have decided it was time to cut her ties with the Kearney family and escape from the country she had been forced to live in. Yet, if so, why did her brother-in-law accompany them? Had her drinking increased, accelerating perhaps from a way of escaping her worries into a habit, dependency and possibly addiction? Young Edward's memoirs certainly suggest that every time he returned from sea 'things were going altogether wrong' at home. A few weeks prior to his mother's departure he signed on as crew on the *Cotopaxi*, bound for Australia. He hoped that his wife, Anna, would agree to move there. Canon Kearney surely used diverse strategies to control excessive drinking in his family as well as in his parish. Had he decided that sending Caroline to England would limit further shame and trouble for his family? She had doubtless tested the patience of her brothers-in-law. Patrick Kearney was known for having a 'will and determination for success', being 'strong-minded, gruff' and short-tempered, and 'feared and at the same time loved, by his people'. One can imagine him insisting in his 'plain and blunt' way that it would be best for her to leave.[101]

Caroline had arrived in Ireland in early 1871 as a 36-year-old widow. She was still a relatively young widow at 47 as she sailed away from Ireland to Holyhead with sixteen-year-old Charles James and Patrick Kearney. The years of fighting against her husband's final wishes and members of his family had taken their toll on her and on her relationships with her sons. Lord Chancellor O'Hagan had found her an intelligent woman. He considered the three eldest boys clever and intelligent too. She had successfully supported Edward, Frank and William when they escaped from their college. Her secret marriage suggests impulsivity as well as impropriety. She was litigious, fighting back not only against her brothers-in-law, but also against the woman who stole possessions from her home. It is unlikely that Edward junior was alone in blaming alcohol and their mother's abuse of it for driving them to sea.[102] The boys' departures one after another speak eloquently to her failure to mother them in a way that led them to want to support her as she aged. They appear to have been keener to return to the Antipodes than to remain with Caroline.

Yet in conditions that were not at all of her making, she had sought to survive and to chart a course for her sons. Now she was finally leaving Ireland. Could she rebuild her life again? Return to Australia and her father and surviving siblings there? Could she ensure her youngest son a more secure future than the brothers working on ships sailing the route between Australia and England? What lay ahead of her?

# Part Three

# Later lives:
# Deaths and legacies

# 8

# Endings

Caroline had escaped the clutches of her brothers-in-law but not of booze. The next and last definite trace I have of her after she and Charles James were shepherded across the Irish Sea by Canon Kearney in the autumn of 1881 is her death. Four and a half years later, on 30 April 1886 she died in London. Her death certificate recorded the cause of death as 'cirrhosis dropsy'.[1] Years of stress, struggle and drinking had done irrevocable damage to her body just as they had damaged her relationships with her sons. None of her children were with her. Less than two years after arriving in England, Charles chose Australia over his mother. In May 1883 at the age of nineteen he made his way to Liverpool and sailed for Melbourne on the four-masted iron barque *Crofton Hall*. He was identified on the ship's list of passengers as a clerk. As his later life would prove, he was the only son whose education led directly into the world of white-collar work and a profession.[2]

Caroline did not return to Australia. She may have planned to join her sons and the siblings she had left over a decade earlier.[3] She might also have wondered whether she could rekindle her ties with the man she had married so furtively eight years earlier. Johnson had left his lodgings in Bedford Square three years after their marriage and taken up residence in a house at 2 Bury Place, a block to the west of Bloomsbury Square. This was a fairly respectable neighbourhood, though once again his living situation appears unorthodox. That year the enumerator copying the information from the forms left at the house identified him as married, and listed a 27-year-old Lilly Francis as his wife. This may have been a mistake. It noted her occupation as 'traveller's wife'. Perhaps Lilly, who had had three young children aged one to six, rented out rooms because her travelling salesman husband was so often away. For years Richard had suffered from deteriorating kidney disease. Perhaps he had engaged her to assist him in his final illness. Or had he hooked up with another woman? Might these have been his children? Probably not. They all bore the same surname as their mother.[4]

A year and a half later Richard was close to renal failure. He took up temporary quarters on Guilford Street, close to the cluster of hospitals that included the Great Ormond Street Hospital for Children, the Homeopathic Hospital, the Epileptic Hospital and others. There, perhaps in one of the area's boarding houses, known for their bad reputations, he set out his final wishes on 16 August 1882. They were simple. No mention of Caroline. No mention of Lilly or her children. All of his estate was to go to his two sisters in Dublin. He also named them his executors. He died a day later. He was only 50.[5]

Caroline was 51 when she died four years later at 16 Stratford Place in Kentish Town (see image 12 in the picture section). This was a far cry from the comfortable domesticity of Clyde Terrace in Sandymount, Dublin, with its open spaces and seaside strand. It is hard too to imagine an area more different from the flat and 'empty' country of the Wimmera around Lockhart Station, where she had raised her children. By the time Caroline moved into the area in the 1880s the railways had been transforming the neighbourhood for decades. In the early 1850s Irish workers had streamed in seeking construction and labouring work, first on the canals and then with the railroad companies. Many had congregated not far south of Stratford Place in what became a notorious slum, Agar Town. In 1851, Charles Dickens, a long-time resident of Camden Town, wrote a short story entitled 'A Suburban Connemara', in which the protagonist, shocked at the smells, poverty and 'wretched hovels', describes this area as a 'disgrace to the metropolis'. In the 1860s this reputation justified massive demolition of some 4000 homes to make space for the Midland Railway's St Pancras Station. Two other major railway companies' terminals and railway yards were also built in a vast area stretching south from St Paul's Road. Soot and grime seeped into lungs, onto clothing, through windows and into bricks. 'Vibration from the tunnels and sulphurous smoke from the ventilation shafts severely reduced the desirability of the area.'[6]

Yet Stratford Place was no slum. The street was laid out in the late 1840s as part of the planned, mixed community of New Camden Town. The goal was to attract a higher class of residents than those living in much of the area, especially to the grand houses constructed around Camden Square. Today, many of those have been gentrified, and are home to celebrities. Stratford Place – renamed Stratford Villas – runs south-west off the fashionable square. Its rows of plain but gracious three-storey homes were built to appeal to middle-class families. But railway construction had undermined these plans. The area and its reputation, like Caroline's life, had spiralled downwards since the mid-19th century.[7] House values and the social standing of the clientele and the neighbourhood fell. Speculators, owners and renters divided the single family homes into apartments, creating much-needed residential space for London's working classes.[8]

Caroline rented such a space. Sixteen Stratford Place, where she died, was occupied by an Irish-born builder, Richard Farrell, and his wife, Jane. In 1881 they were in their forties. Their household also included a 21-year-old live-in servant, and one lodger, a 67-year-old widow named Elizabeth Habb. Caroline likely replaced her as their lodger.[9] Fewer people were living at number sixteen than in most of the nearby houses. Other residents in this row of housing included several printers and clerks, a journalist, a cigar-maker, an upholsterer and skilled workers engaged by the railway companies. There were also other widowed women and married women without husbands. That year at least seven of the 24 household heads listed in the city directory on Stratford Place were women – yet another reminder of the significant presence of widows, single women and deserted wives in such urban spaces.[10] This house was assessed as of slightly higher quality than those around it. It was rated at £40 annual rent, most others at around £35.[11] A few years later, the anti-poverty activist Charles Booth and his team set out to measure poverty in London by assessing the quality of housing on the streets and cul-de-sacs of the city. They described Stratford Place as housing the 'very respectable working-class', in its three and a half-storey buildings. It was coded pink, which in his colour-coding scheme indicated 'Fairly comfortable. Good, ordinary earnings.'[12] Caroline was not living in luxury. Nor was she among the poorest of the city's residents. She ended her life as a boarder in the home of a skilled worker, far from the members of her birth family in Australia, and far from her sons in Australia, Ireland and on the seas.

Nausea; fluid retention leading to abdominal bloating and swollen legs; intense itchiness; jaundice – symptoms experienced in the late stages of cirrhosis vary. Dying of it is never painless and seldom rapid. The twinning of the terms cirrhosis and dropsy on Caroline's death certificate strongly suggests that her drinking had moved from dependency to alcoholism, causing cirrhosis that provoked the dropsy and other related symptoms. Within decades the term dropsy would disappear from medical descriptions of disease as no longer desirable in standardised international listings of causes of death. It was widely used across the 19th century to refer to the excessive retention of water in part of the body. It hints at the symptoms that surely confined Caroline increasingly to her room or rooms on Stratford Place and marked her final months and perhaps years.[13]

At some point Caroline or someone else in the household called in Dr Arthur Raynor for medical help. He had a practice nearby on Warden Road in Kentish Town, a 20-minute walk north of Stratford Place. There was little even the best doctor could do for most dying patients. Dr Arthur Raynor was no longer the brilliant medical man who had begun his career with aplomb as a West End consultant. His life, like Caroline's, was on a downward spiral. Born in 1849 to a Yorkshire linen and wool draper, he trained in medicine and became a registered medical practitioner at the age of 27. Soon he had a mansion in north-west London, and was well known for his smart dressing, and as an 'owner of racers and steeplechasers'. He began drinking heavily, 'becoming in a few years a hopeless drunkard'. Increasingly he associated with 'shady characters'. He was accused of bigamy, but escaped on a technicality. Somers Town police received a growing number of complaints of medical malpractice. By the time of Caroline's death he was attending victims of local accidents and crimes and performing post mortems to supplement his shrinking medical practice.[14] Later, long after Caroline's death, he was successfully charged with manslaughter after a woman in Kentish Town died following an abortion he performed. He died as an inmate in Pankhurst Prison of the Isle of Wight in 1908.[15]

I wonder whether Raynor and Caroline had crossed paths before he visited her during her final illness or certified the cause of her death. They may well have met in one of the drinking establishments that peppered the streets of Kentish Town. Or perhaps she sought his help soon after arriving from Ireland. She had shown great faith in doctors when her children fell ill. Had they met in some context that allowed them to share their life histories, they would have found they shared much: their keen interest in horses; their social decline; the devastating effects of excessive drinking; expensive tastes; and histories of unwise decision-making.

Caroline did not face her final illness or her death completely alone, despite the absence of her five sons. The ideal good death of the time took place at home, surrounded by family members. Though this was unattainable for many, it was assumed by English law, which gave the nearest relative of the deceased present at the death the responsibility of registering the death. It was only in the absence of such relatives in the household – or, failing that, in the wider neighbourhood – that someone else present at the death was required to inform the registrar. 'E. Fanning' attested to having been with Caroline when she died.[16]

The Fannings lived a fifteen-minute walk north-west of Stratford Place on Crown Court, off the Kentish Town Road in Camden Town. Michael and Johanna Fanning were Irish immigrants from Tipperary. They had arrived in London some years before they married there in 1858. By 1886 they had been living on Crown Court for over 25 years. It was a run-down street with some two-storey cottages, and some outhouses transformed into 'queer little one-room domiciles'. Charles Booth later categorised this area as a mixed one, with 'some comfortable and some poor'. Between Crown Court and Kentish Town Road were several blocks marked by dire poverty. Michael was an upholsterer, perhaps once a craftsman. But his trade suffered, as so many did, from competition from factory production. By 1871 he was making mattresses, probably in a factory or warehouse. In 1881 Michael and Johanna lived at 1 Court Place with six children: Catherine, aged nineteen; Edward, aged seventeen; Mary, sixteen; Robert, fifteen; Emily, eleven; and Ellen, ten. Emily and Ellen were still at school then. Theirs was a family economy. The earnings and other contributions of all Fanning family members kept them out of poverty. Johanna worked alongside her husband at mattress-making. In 1881 the four eldest children were working in an upholstering warehouse, while Mary found employment as a domestic servant. A year later, Ellen died. Soon Emily followed her elder sister into service. The 'E. Fanning' who signed Caroline's certificate was surely Emily.[17]

I presume that Emily was employed as a domestic servant by the Farrells, replacing earlier domestic servants. Turnover among domestics was always high. The year Caroline died, Emily turned seventeen. Caroline would have been sick for some time. I hope that Emily offered her support, and ensured that she did not die alone. Like other working-class Londoners, Emily was only too used to dealing with death and dying. After Caroline's death someone washed her body and laid it out. This was a female task, undertaken by family or community members. If she had friends in the city they may have visited her before her death or sat with her body afterwards.[18]

No burials were permitted until a death had been properly registered. A person who had been present at the death was legally required to visit the registrar of births and deaths in the next five days following a death and furnish him with the required details. Emily went to the office of Edward Hacker, the registrar for Kentish Town. This 78-year-old man, whose line engravings of animals and sporting prints are still available for sale on the internet, listened and recorded the location and date of Caroline's death. Emily, or perhaps Dr Raynor, knew enough about her to inform him that she was aged 51 and the widow of Edward Kearney, a sheep farmer. A registered medical practitioner who had attended the deceased during their last illness was required to 'state to the best of his knowledge and belief the cause of death', and to deliver the required certificate to the registrar. For Hacker, who had been acting in this position since at least 1843, this recording of information was routine; banal, perhaps. He matched this informant's report with the medical certificate that Dr Raynor had submitted, and recorded all the details in the required boxes on the death certificate.[19] Now Caroline could be laid to rest, though where she was buried I don't know. Extensive searching in the archives in Camden and on the growing number of internet sites that identify graves produced no results. Parish authorities arranged burials for paupers, often in unmarked graves.

News of Caroline's death travelled quickly to Ireland. One day after her decease the *Freeman's Journal* in Dublin noted, in the usually terse wording of such death notices, that she had died 'at her residence', Stratford Place, Camden Town, London. She was identified as the 'widow of the late Edward Kearney, Esq, Lockhart Station, Victoria', aged 51 and was 'deeply regretted'. No mention of her sons. Australian papers were requested to copy the notice. That took much longer. Five months later the Melbourne and Victoria-wide paper the *Argus* published details that suggest her sister Eleanor had arranged the notice. 'On the 20th of April, 1886, in London, Caroline Anne, widow of the late Edward Kearney of Broom Station, South Australia and Lockhart, Victoria. Sister to Mrs Hamilton, Bringalbert.' This final acknowledgment of her life located her explicitly within the geography of her time as a coloniser on the stations where she had begun her life with Edward, given birth to their children, and spent time visiting her parents and siblings. It highlighted her connection to her siblings while ignoring her offspring.[20]

This was the community of kin out of which Caroline had

been wrenched by her husband's final wishes. By 1886 the heart of the world of Bax relatives in Australia had shifted away from Robe to the Hamilton stations, Ozenkadnook and Bringalbert in the Wimmera country. Robe's golden days were over. The town declined dramatically over the 1870s and 1880s. William Bax senior had spent more and more time with Eleanor and James Hamilton and their three children following Caroline's departure, the termination of his teaching licence, and his wife's death in 1871. Shortly thereafter he moved in with them permanently. Mary, the youngest of the Bax girls, had remained single and living in Robe until 1875. That year, aged 38, she married William Robert Catt in the Robe house. The following year Catt was certified as the head teacher in Robe, and assumed ownership of the cottage. However, he died in 1884 and Mary then moved in with her elder sister Eleanor for a while. Documents written in 1886 and 1887 listed Mary as assistant housekeeper on their station. She would remarry briefly with a station labourer, Alfred Pain, but was soon a widow again.[21] The Bax home in Robe was sold to a labourer, John Bermingham. It is still known today as Bermingham Cottage. The history of its occupancy by the Bax family has disappeared.[22] William Thomas Bax, the eldest sibling, now widowed, still lived in Goroke. For a while, all of Caroline's surviving siblings, except Mary's twin, Robert, were living within 40 kilometres of each other. I have found no trace of Robert's whereabouts.

James Hamilton later described this era as one of 'changed circumstances'. He blamed the wave of newcomers, transformations in the forms of farming, unprecedented levels of sheep theft from Bringalbert and other stations, and a fall in the prices of wool and stock.[23] By 1886, much had indeed changed. In the Wimmera country, as on stations across Victoria and the other colonies, squatters were struggling in the face of legislation that opened up the land to selectors seeking to establish small farms. Eleanor and James Hamilton and his brothers had tried hard to hold on to what they could of their former life, work styles and property. For a while they had succeeded in purchasing some of their leased land freehold, and using the new laws to select portions of their former leases. Across the 1880s, Eleanor, James and their young-est son, as well as Janet, James's 75-year-old mother, William Bax senior and Mary Catt all selected roughly contiguous pieces of land. As age and ailments compounded other challenges, Eleanor and James found this whole process bureaucratic and frustrating. It required trips into the town of Horsham and other regional centres, and frequent letter-writing.[24] Ultimately their success was limited. Financial ups and downs, unwise investments, debts and accidents marked their final years.

Just a year before Caroline died, James Hamilton shot himself accidentally in the leg, which had to be amputated. Despite Eleanor's careful nursing, pain and ill health haunted him for the rest of his life. Within months of that accident William Bax senior died while on a trip back to Robe. Two years later, James's mother, Janet, died. Within a year, debt forced James to give up their remaining land and homestead at Bringalbert. He and Eleanor continued to try and 'stay afloat' for a while at Ozenkadnook, growing vegetables and running a few sheep on their small remaining acreage. Caroline's siblings were aging. After her second husband died, Mary left for Moonee Ponds, Melbourne. She died there in 1895 at 58.[25] Their brother William Thomas survived several bouts of illness in the 1880s, and spent time as a patient in the Maryborough and District Hospital in Avoca, some 200 kilometres east and south of Goroke. In early 1909 he went missing in the bush for three weeks, and was found dead under a tree, probably of a stroke. The notice of his death, like that for Caroline, identified him as Eleanor's sibling. He was buried in the private cemetery on the land of the Hamilton's former station, Ozenkadnook.[26] Eleanor survived him by less than two years; she was becoming disoriented and vague. In 1910 she burned herself badly standing close to a fire in her nightgown. She died on 14 June. She too was buried at Ozenkadnook.[27]

'My poor wife died in 1910, after our sojourn together of fifty years, and I am now a lonely old man,' James wrote two years later. He left the station, 'almost penniless', feeling his age, and with 'only one leg'. After one more attempt at grazing, he settled for a while by the ocean at Barwon Heights, south of Melbourne, and wrote his life story.[28] *Pioneering Days in Western Victoria* was well received then and has deservedly been republished since. That writing experience fuelled his wish to publish a broader history of colonialism in Australia. Sadly, that project was never completed. When his health declined he moved back to his former home and lived with his youngest son and namesake and his family for a while, then rented a house in the small town of Apsley, nearby. He died there in 1927 at the age of 91.[29] He had outlived all of his siblings, his wife, his wife's sisters, their husbands and his own eldest son, Francis, who had died a year earlier. His writing, his family's early arrival and his long life earned him historical recognition as a pioneer squatter – recognition that eluded his brother-in-law Edward Kearney.

Edward Kearney's will had ripped Caroline out of this supportive network of parents, siblings and their wider kin. William Thomas, Eleanor and Mary maintained those kinship links as they married, bore children, their spouses died and they grew old. James Charles Hamilton, his widowed mother and brothers had always run their stations as a shared family enterprise, and sheltered family members in need. Yet economically, the Hamilton family faced challenges that Edward Kearney escaped through his early death. Though Eleanor and James's youngest son and his family continued to live on the family's former station, Bringalbert, they did so as employees, not owners, earning meagre wages and living in a staff cottage, not their former station house. Family memories suggest they were too poor to fulfil James senior's wish that his funeral and burial be at Ozenkadnook, where so many of his family lay. His grave lies instead in Apsley.[30]

# 9

# The boys' adult lives

Edward's will had distanced Caroline and the five boys from Australia and from their network of Bax kin. But it was surely Caroline's own behaviour that distanced the boys from her as they grew up and shaped their own futures. In 1886, when Caroline died, they were scattered. Only Edward junior and William still resided in Ireland. Edward was keen to migrate to Australia, but his wife, Anna, would not desert her aging parents. Both brothers were away at sea more often than they were home. It was already five years since Frank and his cousin Margaret had eloped and escaped family surveillance by marrying and settling permanently in New Zealand. Charles James, the youngest of Caroline and Edward's sons, had been living in Sydney, Australia for three years and was making his living as a teacher.[1] Patrick Edgar had returned to Australia, possibly in 1882, more likely in 1886. He was seeking to make a living selecting land and running stock in the Clarence River Valley area of northern New South Wales, around the town of Grafton.

⁂

In 1886 it was twelve years since William had begun his apprenticeship at sea at fifteen. Six months before his mother's death, he had married a Dublin-born woman, Mary Theresa Sheridan, in Liverpool. Both spouses were aged 25. Both had lost their fathers as youngsters and been raised by their widowed mothers. Like Edward, William seems to have married surprisingly well, aided quite possibly by his share of his father's estate. Mary's father, Henry Sheridan, had been a merchant–manufacturer of agricultural machinery and supplies in Dublin. The newspaper announcement grandly identified her as the 'granddaughter of the late Edward Cavanagh, Drimna Castle, County Dublin'. Their union was sanctioned at the Catholic Oratory of Saint Philip Neri by special licence. Special dispensation was required to allow a Protestant to marry a Catholic.[2] Caroline was surely too ill to attend. Mary Theresa's mother, Margaret (née Cavanagh), was likely present. Her only brother, Walter Cavanagh, hosted the reception at his Liverpool home. This elderly bachelor uncle was a surgeon who had served in the Crimean War, and then the Shropshire militia before settling in Liverpool in 1865, running a private practice as well as serving as the surgeon for inmates of the Main Bridewell Prison in Liverpool.[3]

After their wedding William and Mary Theresa chose a home closer to her younger sister, Catherine Thomasina, her doctor husband, Patrick Matthias Poett, and their one-year-old daughter.[4] With kin nearby she would have company while William was absent at sea. The home they chose – Edenville Cottage – was located on Mount Merrion Avenue in Blackrock, not far from the French College from which William and his brothers had escaped fourteen years earlier. This was close to Sandymount, where Edward, Anna and their children were residing with her parents. The couple would have little time together. Nearly four years after their wedding, Mary Theresa was diagnosed with phthisis, the same disease that had killed William's father and that Caroline had always claimed her boys were susceptible to. Mary Theresa had likely been tired and weak, and coughing up blood for some time. Tuberculosis rates shot up in Ireland around this time, especially among women. Australia was understood to have a climate that helped cure the disease. Mary Theresa did not migrate. She died at home five days after Christmas in 1889. On 2 January, the *Freeman's Journal* announced the death of 'the dearly beloved wife of William Kearney and daughter of the late Henry Sheridan, Bridgefoot Street, after a short illness, deeply and deservedly regretted R.I.P.' Readers were informed that the funeral would leave their home at 9.30 the following morning and proceed to the Glasnevin Cemetery. I suspect that William was away at sea while Mary Theresa was ill, dying and buried. Irish law required that deaths be registered within five days by the closest relative living in the house, yet it was not until three weeks later that William informed officials at the Blackrock district office.[5] Grief, inattention to paperwork or his absence might explain this unusually long delay.[6]

A year and several months after his wife's death William was recorded by the English census taker residing temporarily in the home of an insurance clerk, his wife and child and a servant on Melbourne Grove, a comfortable middle-class street in Camber-well, London. He was 29, a mariner's mate in the merchant services, and widowed.[7] Melbourne Grove was a few minutes' walk from where his brother Charles James was then living. Presumably he was visiting his brother while in port.

Charles James had married Harriet Burnell in Sydney in October 1889. Their union was celebrated in Saint Patrick's Church, one of the city's earliest Catholic churches, and sanctioned by one of its resident Marist priests, Peter Piquet. Charles James was 25, Harriet was 20. Shortly after their wedding, Charles decided to change his career and become a doctor. Helped perhaps by Harriet's family, or drawing on his portion of his father's estate, they headed to England. There he trained in medicine.[8]

In London, they rented a comfortable house in the suburb of Camberwell. Their first daughter, May Burnell, was born in July 1890. It was nine months later that the census taker captured William Kearney's temporary residence nearby. Both brothers could afford rooms and homes in a middle-class area. Charles James, Harriet and little May were enumerated at 12 Ondine Road, a street that Charles Booth's researchers described as characterised by comfortable, semi-detached houses. Charles was identified as a medical student. They employed a seventeen-year-old live-in servant.[9] Their second daughter was born in July 1891. They named her Elizabeth Lockhart, after the station on which he had lived from birth to the age of five. Winnifred Laura was born in October 1894. That year Charles received his membership in the Royal College of Surgeons. A year later he was awarded his licentiate in the Royal College of Physicians.[10]

Within a decade Charles James and Edward, and possibly William, had joined Patrick Edgar in the area around Grafton, New South Wales. Edward and his family moved there in the early 1890s. In her study of siblings in England over this period, feminist historian and sociologist Leonore Davidoff highlights the importance of relations among brothers and sisters. As children and youth grow up and grapple with the issue of their identities, she suggests, a key question is who they can trust. For these brothers, whose lives had been transformed by their father's death and the provisions of his will, and whose mother had proved less and less reliable over time, one answer to that question was each other.[11] Like Caroline and her siblings, most of her sons chose to live close to one or more brothers at various times over their lives. Though no letters have survived, it is clear that they corresponded with each other, presumably sharing news of their lives, whereabouts and hopes and fears.

What attracted at least three of the brothers to the Clarence

River area of north-eastern New South Wales? The region bore little resemblance to the dry, hot, flat Wimmera plains that they had left after Lockhart Station was sold in 1869. Here the land was lush and hilly. The climate was subtropical and humid. These lands of the Bundjalung and Gumbaynggirr and Yaegi peoples were first invaded in the early 1830s, soon after an escaped convict spread news of the rich cedar forests of the area. They had struggled for over half a century with loss of their lands, attacks, diseases and other ravages wrought by settlers by the time the Kearney brothers arrived. As in the colony as a whole, their numbers were dropping dramatically. The census takers of 1891 counted only 225 Aboriginal people in all of Clarence County, though many no doubt succeeded in avoiding this accounting by the colonial state.[12]

In contrast to the monocultures of the Wimmera country, with its sheep stations succeeded by wheat farming, this was a diverse economy. Grafton in the 1890s was a bustling town with substantial hotels, churches, sugar mills and a growing reputation for its annual racing meet. Town blocks first went up for sale in 1851. Its population grew steadily: 2250 inhabitants in 1871; 3891 in 1881; and 4445 in 1891, around the time the Kearney brothers arrived. The wider area of Clarence County was home to over 15 000 inhabitants. Ship building, raising beef cattle, grow-ing maize and sugar and later dairying all flourished in the region. Historical geographer, D. N. Deans suggests that farmers had more options in this northern area than anywhere else in New South Wales in the years before 1900, because of the wide range of agricultural production possible there.[13]

The area thus offered diverse employment options that might fit the varied educational and work backgrounds of the Kearney brothers. The religious differences within the family could also be readily accommodated. The first Catholic Church on the north coast had opened in South Grafton in 1857. There was also a Catholic school. Anglican, Presbyterian, Lutheran, Baptist and Salvation Army churches and schools served the religiously heterogeneous population of the county.[14] Other Kearneys lived in the area too, though they were from Tipperary, and apparently not related to the brothers. Indeed, there were enough Kearneys in the area to form a Kearney Rifle Club. Edward would join it, and perhaps the other brothers too. A photograph of this group from the local archives shows 30 men and boys. Edward is there, sitting in the front row. Like the rest of the adult men in the image he holds his rifle over his left shoulder.[15] Of equal or more importance to the Kearney brothers was surely the community's passionate commitment to horseracing. The Clarence River Jockey Club and its annual horseraces dated back to the late 1850s. By the 1890s the July Grafton races were drawing crowds of up to 1000 from 'throughout the Clarence Valley, from Richmond and Tweed River districts, from the New England region and even from Sydney'. These were festive occasions. Men and women might concentrate on the races, bet on their choices or partake of the range of drinks on offer at the many publicans' booths. The Kearney brothers would surely have attended, laid their bets and perhaps raced too. Their wives and children would enjoy the shooting galleries, skittle alleys, merry-go-rounds and other entertainments that attracted young and old alike. Women dressed up in their most fashionable outfits and hats, some keen on the races, others on the sociability of the luncheon booths and lawns.[16]

Patrick Edgar set about making a living running stock in the rural area of Glenugie, south of Grafton. In 1889 he registered a brand for his cattle in the *New South Wales Gazette* and applied for a land lease at the Grafton land court. Between April 1890 and March 1891 he selected two smallish leases of 63 acres (25.5 hectares) close to Glenugie and larger leases of a further 620 acres (251 hectares) in Lanitza parish and 630 acres (255 hectares) slightly to the north in the neighbouring Lavadia parish.[17] But he was soon in trouble with the local police for drunkenness and 'willfully breaking three panes of glass at the Victoria Hotel.' This led to a fine, or possibly imprisonment. Heavy drinking ran in the family. The conditions of land selection required that properties be improved and fenced within a specified period. Patrick had trouble fulfilling these. As a result, his leases of the large acreages in Lanitza and Lavadia were declared forfeited in 1892. The next year he received conditional purchase and lease certificates for his two smaller properties, but had to appeal for further time to finish fencing them. He was allowed five months. He struggled on, managing to hold on to these smaller blocks through 1896. These were hard times for most of the colony as the effects of the 1893 collapse of banks in England rippled across the oceans, causing a worldwide economic crisis which destabilised colonial, local and family economies. In 1897 Patrick sold 113 acres (46 hectares) in Lanitza parish privately. Soon he was picking up odd contracts to clear away invasive prickly pear for the City Council. Then he left the area.[18]

Edward joined Patrick Edgar in the area when Anna finally agreed to migrate to Australia, after her parents died in 1889. Edward went on ahead, droving for a while in Queensland. On 3 January 1890 Anna, by then aged 37, and the two girls, Anna Violet, aged nine and Ida, eight, left Ireland, sailing for Melbourne on the SS *Liguria* of the Orient Line. Anna later recalled enjoying 'every minute of the journey', including the singing and dancing aboard ship.[19] Edward met them in Sydney. Comfortable steamers, run by the Clarence, Richmond & Macleay River Steam Navigation Company took passengers and some light freight up the 600 kilometres of Pacific coast of New South Wales north to Port Yamba at the mouth of the Clarence River. The next stage of the trip was a paddle steamer inland up the 65 kilometres of the Clarence, the 'largest and straightest' of Australia's coastal rivers, to Grafton. They stayed initially at the Tattersall Hotel on the banks of the Clarence River,[20] one of the main hotels in this thriving service centre. Soon the new arrivals from Ireland were exposed to one of the environmental hazards of this part of Australia. Rain poured down for days. The river burst its banks, stranding the Kearneys in the hotel. Young Anna Violet, or Vi as her family called her, later recalled that 'all the occupants of the hotel had to be supplied with food and provisions by a steam ferry which was able to be moored to the hotel balcony until the floodwaters receded.' The 1890 flood is still the largest recorded flood in the history of the town.[21]

Anna's recollections of this time suggest that her initial reaction on arrival was one of shock. The new home to which Edward took them was not in Grafton, but in the rural area of Glenugie, where Patrick had taken up land. This middle-class wife considered their first dwelling 'a hut with an earth floor'; 'Local aborigines still roamed the area and it was a lonely place.' There are echoes here, in Edward junior's immigrant wife's earliest Australian experiences, of those of his mother Caroline over 35 years earlier. Yet the Clarence River Valley area was much more settled than the areas Caroline had lived in. Anna learned to adjust and to 'calm the children's fears' and developed many new skills.[22] She had left her two married sisters behind in Ireland. Patrick Edgar had no wife for her to share her worries or hopes with. In June 1892 she gave birth to a baby boy. Drawing on family tradition and Kearney family names they called him Edward Francis Kearney. His nickname became Eddie.[23]

Four years later, the arrival of Charles James, his wife Harriet and their three daughters, May, Elizabeth and Winnifred, from England, meant Anna, Edward and the children had more

232

family company in the region. Charles James had decided to use his new qualifications to set up a medical practice in South Grafton, just 20 kilometres north-west of Glenugie. The couple and their daughters, aged five, four and one, settled into a house on Through Street, moving later to Wharf Street. He opened an office in town a short walk away. Local newspapers announced that he was available from 8.30 to 10 am, 2 to 3 pm and 7 to 8 in the evenings. In between he made house calls. He also offered his medical services voluntarily at the Grafton Hospital (see image 15 in the picture section).[24]

Charles and Harriet threw themselves exuberantly into life in Australia. In contrast to his brothers, Charles quickly became a prominent citizen. In addition to his medical work, he served as one of the judges for the Grafton races and became a member of the Jockey Club committee that organised the races and festivities. In 1898 he was elected to the Grafton Municipal Council and also appointed as a local magistrate. Over the next few years he served twice on the council, became president of the Rowing Club, vice-president of the Jockey Club and a member of diverse committees at the Grafton Hospital, the Grafton School of Arts and the Chamber of Commerce. Aged just one when his father had died, and five when they left Australia, he forged a professional and civic pathway in life that looks much more successful than his brothers'. He was said to be widely respected for his broad education, professional knowledge and 'natural courtesy of manner and refinement of character'. His 'winning smile and laughing blue eyes', wisdom and generosity earned him many friends. Raised Catholic from the age of seven he was seen by the people of Grafton as 'a devoted son of the Catholic Church' who worked hard for his parish and for Catholicism. Yet he was also praised as 'a wide-minded and tolerant thinker', who 'numbered hosts of friends among all denominations'.[25]

Even the well-respected Charles James showed signs of his father's quick temper and tendency to resort to physical violence. In February 1899 after a cab driver insulted his wife he called him a 'b—— crawling reptile', hit him so hard he went 'reeling to the ground about four yards away', and gave him a sound thrashing that left him screaming for help. Charles, himself one of the magistrates, pleaded guilty and paid his fine.[26] The altercation had little impact on his reputation in Grafton, though he did resign as an alderman a year later, pleading the demands of his profession. He was later described as having 'gained for himself the personal esteem of all who know him, while his medical attainments won a large practice throughout the district'.[27]

Harriet's arrival offered Anna the possibility of adult female companionship within the family and the chance for the teenage Vi and Ida to get to know their aunt, uncle and younger girl cousins. I imagine that despite the differences in their age and background, the two women found ways to share the challenges and joys of raising their children in this colonial setting that was so different from the cities of Dublin and London in which they had first become mothers. Within a year they shared tragedies too. In February 1897 four-year-old Eddie caught diphtheria. Charles James tried to help his nephew, but within a week the boy was dead. Edward and Anna buried him two days later in the Church of England Cemetery in South Grafton. Patrick Edgar acted as one of the two official witnesses of his burial, Charles James the other. Harriet was pregnant when Eddie died. In June that year she gave birth to a son. They named him Kenneth Ignatius Kearney. He lived only five months. On 26 November he died of pneumonia. Kenneth was laid to rest in the Roman Catholic cemetery in South Grafton. Religious differences resulting from the Irish chancery case meant these cousins did not share their final resting places.[28]

After Eddie's death Edward and Anna left the Glenugie area and moved Vi and Ida into Grafton, settling on Breimba Street, across the river from Charles James and Harriet's home. Town doubtless felt safer for Anna and took them all away from the site of their loss. On the anniversary of his death in both 1900 and 1901 they placed memorials to their 'only and beloved son', in the local paper. Both ended with a short quotation from the Bible. In 1900 it was 'Where your treasure is there will your heart be also', while in 1901 it was the more resigned, 'The Lord gave and the Lord hath taken away. Blessed be the name of the Lord.'[29]

A while after their move to town, Anna, Edward and the two girls dressed up in their good clothes and had a photograph taken (see image 16 in the picture section). Edward was now in his mid-forties – around the same age as his father had been when he died. He sports an impressive well-trimmed, curled handlebar moustache and beard that counterbalance his receding hair line. Anna, Vi and Ida look perky and intelligent, dressed in quite sensible but fashionable dark skirts and bodices with smallish leg-of-mutton sleeves.[30] The very middle-class appearance of the family in the photo belies the challenges Edward faced rebuilding a life in Australia.

In contrast to Charles James's easy integration into the civic, social, cultural and sporting life of the Clarence region, the other brothers seem to have drifted to varying degrees. Unlike their pioneering uncle, James Charles Hamilton, or even their father, they were starting as colonisers and adult settlers much too late to secure good land for large-scale stock or sheep raising. As in South Australia and Victoria, successive Land Acts had opened up property in New South Wales to selectors over the previous three decades. New arrivals without significant capital had access only to lands others had rejected.[31] All the boys had by now turned 24, and should have received their part of Edward's estate. Any capital they had not already spent might help had they hoped to farm, but was unlikely to go far. After years at sea, making a living on land would be a difficult transition for Edward, William and Patrick. Few of the skills they had developed transferred readily into land-based work opportunities, though their experience with horses and stock might.

Shreds of evidence suggest that Edward cobbled a living together in their first seventeen years back in Australia. I have found no indication that he selected or purchased land as his brother Patrick did, though when young Eddie's birth was registered he described himself as a grazier. In other documents he lists his occupation as farmer or builder. In 1902 the region's main newspaper noted that he was acting as Grafton agent for the colony-wide Tattersall's sweeps, the controversial company that profited from colonials' avid betting habits. Though this may have been a part-time job, it reflected the considerable reputation he was gaining in the region for his ability to judge horses' racing capacities. Years later his wife's death notice mentioned that he had practised as a veterinary surgeon in Grafton. It was not until 1906, 20 years after his mother's death, that he appears to have found satisfying employment.[32]

Edward's and Patrick Edgar's time in the Grafton area overlapped from 1890 until about 1903. Charles James remained in South Grafton from early 1896 until 1903. 'In spite of his splendid physique', his own health was not good. Like most of the boys he had been sick frequently as a child. As an adult he suffered from rheumatic fever, possibly a long-term result of childhood infections and illnesses. In 1903 he and Harriet decided that a dryer climate might improve his health. He sold his practice and they made plans to move inland to the town of Condobolin, to the south-west of Grafton and some 450 kilometres west of Sydney. The family had made many friends during their seven years in

Grafton. The Rowing Club held a special meeting in his honour and presented him with a gold medal. A public committee of residents mounted a massive departure party on 21 April, with food, dancing, musical entertainment and speeches at the School of Arts. The space was so crammed with friends and people for whom Charles James had served in public capacities that there was said to be sparse room for the dancing. Speakers waxed eloquent about his support of 'all things for the benefit and progress of the district'. They lauded his 'knowledge and judgment' as a doctor, and more generally. The mayor, colleagues and fellow citizens emphasised the contributions the whole family had made to the life of South Grafton. Winnie, their youngest daughter, was one of several performers. The eight year old demonstrated the latest dance moves to the audience. Charles James thanked all for the 'kindnesses' they had been shown. He concluded by suggesting that these had been 'the best seven years' of his life.[33]

The citizens of Grafton planned to present a plate to Harriet and give Charles James an illuminated version of the mayor's address. That speech concluded by wishing the couple and their family 'long life and happiness'.[34] But within two weeks, Harriet was taken into hospital, seriously ill with pneumonia. She died on 3 June 1903. The funeral was held a day later.

Charles James was soon also in hospital. While newspapers reported that 'little hope' was entertained for his recovery, he regained his health, and moved, as planned, to Condobolin with his three daughters, then aged twelve, eleven and eight.[35] There he opened a new medical practice and once again gained widespread respect for his public spirit, abilities and kind personality. It was no simple matter balancing work as a doctor with raising daughters heading into their adolescent years. Like so many widowers facing similar situations, he remarried. In 1906, at the age of 42, he married 23-year-old Rachel Naomi Margaret Tasker. After a few years his health deteriorated as his rheumatic fever flared up again and again. Rachel spent the later years of their nine-year marriage nursing him as he became increasingly crippled and unable to walk. After some time in a private hospital in Sydney and seeking cures in other locations, he died in Condobolin in May 1915. He was only 50 years old, a year younger than his mother had been in 1886 when, alone and suffering from dropsy and cirrhosis, she died in London.[36]

Twelve years after they lost their mother, the three girls had lost their father too. In contrast to Caroline, he died cared for and surrounded by kin and was widely mourned by family and friends. Rachel commissioned a solid marble tombstone for his grave. It was inscribed with the words, 'In loving memory of my beloved husband, Charles James Kearney, who died 23rd May 1915, Rest in Peace. One of the best that God could send, beloved by all – a faithful friend. His memory lives in the hearts of all who knew his worth.'[37]

Charles James's departure from Grafton after his first wife's death in June 1903, combined with the ongoing financial depression and personal factors, punctured the potential the Grafton area had seemed to offer the Kearney brothers who had reunited there. Patrick Edgar left and sought work in the sawmills of Milltown, north of Portland Bay. By 1907 only Vi – Edward and Anna's eldest daughter – remained near Grafton. She had married Walter Gerard in the Anglican Christ Church Cathedral late in 1905.[38] Walter's family was rooted in the region. Together they farmed at Glenugie for some years. Vi explained to her grandchildren later that she 'pioneered the land' there.[39]

In 1906 Edward's work life changed. He was appointed stock inspector for the Macleay River District. He and Anna left Grafton and set up their new home 180 kilometres to the south in the rural service centre, Kempsey. This position came with the considerable annual salary of £325 and travel and other expenses. At that time workers in manufacturing averaged just over £100 a year. He was in charge of counting the numbers of horses, sheep and cattle in the Macleay area, inspecting their health, offering advice, generally assessing the strength of the local stock economy and reporting to the government authorities. Now Edward could draw on his experience as a youngster raising sheep and stock with his father and uncle. His appointment suggests that he had indeed secured some experience or training as a veterinarian. From the 1880s on, several institutions began offering formal training for veterinarians. Older ways of learning through an apprenticeship with a working vet were increasingly frowned upon.[40]

It is ironic that he secured this position, given his father's run-ins with the sheep inspector when Edward was a toddler in South Australia. He became a respected and visible public official, travelling to stations and farms throughout the county. His advice on a range of stock-related issues appeared in the local papers. He offered information about how to treat cattle infected with the fatal disease known as blackleg. In 1911 he publicised his opinion that the spread of tuberculosis among humans and cattle in Australia resulted from its early reputation as a climate that was 'proof against the disease'. Citing his experience as a 'midshipman and officer', he reported having observed 'hundreds of fashionable consumptives crossing the ocean' in the hope of recovery. Their marriages into Australian families, he claimed, had increased the prevalence of the disease among settlers. Their spitting onto pastures had contaminated the cattle. He emphasised the importance of boiling milk, especially for infants. Scientists today might not concur with his analyses, but they demonstrate his concern for the health of the people as well as the animals of the region. Locals also sought him out for advice about racehorses. When rumours spread in 1908 that he was planning to leave the area, residents expressed their concern, then their relief when they discovered he was not. At the age of 50, Edward appears to have found his feet in Australia.[41]

Edward and Anna lived in Kempsey until his death. Their growing number of grandchildren were in visiting distance. In Grafton, Vi and Walter's first child, John Walter, was born in 1906; Caroline in 1907; Norah Violet in 1911; Alice in 1914; and George in 1916. (See image 17 in the picture section for a photograph of Anna, Edward, Vi, and three of the children.) Norah was apparently given an Irish name at the request of her grandfather, Edward. John Walter later described spending three months with his grandfather and enjoying his penchant for practical jokes, hoisting flags each morning and accompanying him in his buggy drawn by a 'beautiful bay mare' on his veterinary and stock-inspecting rounds. In 1911 Ida gave up her nursing career and married John Cartan Marks in Mudgee. She had moved to that town in the interior of New South Wales to serve as nursing matron at the Mudgee Hospital. His family ran a general merchant business in Mudgee. They married in the All Saints Church of England in West Kempsey. Local papers reported that her father, Edward, walked her up the aisle and gave her away. Her niece 'Miss Carrie [Caroline] Gerard', her sister Vi's daughter, was one of the two bridesmaids.[42] Ida and John Marks set up their home in Mudgee. She gave birth to five children in relatively quick succession: William in 1912; John in 1913; Molly in 1914; Frank in 1915; and then Thomas in 1917. John did not survive infancy. In August 1920 Ida gave birth to another son, Howard. It was a difficult childbirth complicated by pneumonia. She did not survive. Notices of her death in the newspaper reminded readers how well known and highly respected she was in Mudgee because of her work there as matron of the hospital.[43]

Few widowers left with young children were able to raise them themselves, unless they had an older daughter or widowed mother to help, and many remarried quickly. Ida and John's five surviving children including the new baby needed parenting, but John had to keep working. Widowers' children were often sent to orphanages. More were taken in by members of the extended family. Family members recall that the children were initially sent to live with members of the Marks family in Sydney, where 'they literally played in the "gutters" and picked up quite a lot of bad language'. Ida's sister Vi and her husband, Walter, decided to care for young Molly and Thomas. They were then living at Carr's Creek – 'a bicycle ride from Grafton'. In 1923 this extended family moved to a large, old farmhouse and dairy farm Walter had purchased at Nana Glen, north-west of Coffs Harbour. Theirs was an expansive, welcoming and loving household. At various times Walter's three brothers lived with them, helping with farm chores, gardening and entertaining the children. The farm had ample space for all. The seven cousins were brought up to enjoy fun, laughter and music as well as those other Kearney passions – horses and races. They created their own amusements, went by train to the beach at Coffs Harbour, and ran pretty free. The children ran circus productions for the locals, making money by charging entrance fees. They attended the local schools and church and did their share of the chores, feeding the pigs, collecting the hens' eggs and making sure that the fowls were sheltered at night from foxes.[44]

A few years after his daughter Ida died Edward Kearney's health deteriorated. For close to a decade he had suffered from cancer in his chest. Soon Anna could no longer care for him at home. He spent his final days in the Moorang Home in Ryde, part of the New South Wales Home for Incurables. This cancer care facility had opened a year earlier, with 24 beds for patients with malignant tumours. Edward died on 29 August 1925 at the age of 69.[45] The widowed Anna, by then in her early seventies, joined her daughter Vi and seven grandchildren at the farm. Her grandchildren remember her as a vital part of the Gerard family household and as a talented classical pianist. Her strictness – about 'good manners and good grooming' – contrasted dramatically with the freedom the very tolerant Vi and Walter gave the children, though she was remembered as more lenient with Ida's two than with the other grandchildren, no doubt feeling sorry for them.[46]

Anna lived with her daughter, son-in-law and the children of her two daughters for about five years. Rheumatism was making her increasingly uncomfortable, but her death came unexpectedly and suddenly in late December 1929. Her funeral was held in Grafton and she was buried there a day later. Vi, Walter and their family continued to work the farm at Nana Glen. After Walter died in 1945 at the age of 82, their daughter Carrie and her husband, Arthur Woodford, looked after the widowed Vi until her death in 1954. These two subsequent generations of widows were embraced within caring families as they faced their final years, unlike Caroline. They had developed deep roots in the region Anna and Edward Kearney had settled after returning to Australia.[47]

'Unsettled', not settled, was the word that William Kearney chose to describe his 'usual place of residence' in 1899. This is one of the most startlingly honest descriptions I have seen in official documents. While Charles James found his feet as a civically engaged, small town doctor, and Edward eventually found public recognition in his later years as a stock inspector, William and Patrick Edgar both seem to have lived 'unsettled' lives. William's movements in the decade following his first wife Mary Theresa's death in 1889 are hard to trace, a sure sign of the uncertainties of someone seeking to sort out their life and future. Perhaps he hoped things would change when he remarried in Yambuk in south-western Victoria in November 1899. His new wife, May Emily Isabella Moutray, was born and grew up with her five siblings in Yambuk. William was then living in the rural town of Heywood, 45 kilometres to the north-west. May's parents, Hercules Atkin Moutray and Caroline (née Jefferies) had migrated to Australia as newlyweds in 1859. Like William, May was one of six children. And like both William and his first wife, she had lost her father at an early age and been raised by her mother.[48]

Unlike Caroline Kearney, Caroline Moutray had been able to make a living to support her children. By 1899, she was in her sixties, widowed for 20 years and working as a nurse and midwife. She owned the six-roomed wooden house on a small plot where they kept a cow. Up to that point only her eldest child, Alexander, had married. That year three more did so, including May. She and William were married in Yambuk's small Anglican church. May was 24, William close to 40.[49]

William and May lived long lives, but their relationship was a rocky one. A year after their marriage, their first and only son, Edward Moutray Kearney, was born. May's mother Caroline acted as midwife.[50] For a while, William ran a paint shop in Yambuk on the same street as May's brother's saddlery. May worked as a dressmaker. By 1908 or 1909, however, she and William were living apart. When Victorian women were first inscribed on that state's electoral rolls in 1908, May was in Yambuk. William was back in Heywood, where he worked as a painter between 1908 and 1914. He then moved further away, settling about 100 kilometres away in Coleraine.[51]

As William distanced himself from his wife he moved closer to his brother Patrick Edgar, in Milltown. Between 1909 and 1914 the two brothers lived less than 12 kilometres apart in these small towns in the Wannon district of south-western Victoria. Once again Patrick seems to have cobbled together a living, mostly taking on labouring jobs for the city council and in the mills. He remained in Milltown well into his old age.[52]

In late March 1916 William made a move that distanced him even further from May and his failed marriage. He travelled to Ballarat to offer his services to the 39th Australian Infantry Battalion, formed there a month earlier, very late in Victoria's second major recruitment drive. William was 55. Initially the upper age limit for recruits was 38. Nine months before William sought to enlist it had been raised to 45. He lied about his age, stating that he was 44. He also lied about his birthplace and marital status, claiming to be a widower and born in Dublin. Australian authorities would have had trouble verifying the truth of his claims. Officials recorded the physical characteristics of Caroline's third son: 5 feet 11 inches tall (1.8 metres); 12 stone (76 kilograms); fair with blue eyes, thinning brown hair and excellent eyesight. Tattoos on his forearms and inside his left leg suggest legacies of his time at sea. The medical officer declared him fit for service.[53]

All recruits were asked to list their next of kin. William did not mention May. On his enlistment attestation he named his son, Edward Moutray, in Yambuk. On other military papers he listed his brother, Patrick Edgar Kearney, of Milltown. He obviously did not want May to receive any benefits as his wife or his widow. William and the 8th Battalion sailed out of Melbourne on 28 July 1916, then from Southampton to France in late November. He served mostly in France as a private with the 39th Battalion and the 3rd Australian Division. He survived and remained on active duty until mid-1918, but the trench warfare, mud, rain and cold were hard on his aging body, contributing to serious rheumatism. He was hospitalised several times in France, then sent to the Bulford Military Camp in Wiltshire, England, where he was treated for both VD and rheumatism. Deemed medically unfit for service, he sailed for Australia in December 1918. William arrived in

Melbourne in February 1919, and was discharged shortly there-after.[54] He returned to Yambuk. Perhaps May felt it her duty to stand by this man who had fought for king and country, survived and received the three medals offered all those who had served overseas. William remained in Yambuk for the next 20 years, working as his son did, as a painter. May became the town's assistant postmistress. When she wrote her will in April 1920, she promised all she had to their son.[55]

In their own ways the Kearney brothers sought to nurture the family ties broken for them by the early death of their father, their forced departure from Australia and the loss of their mother. Patrick in Milltown and William back in Yambuk were still in relatively easy visiting distance. In the mid-1920s, after his brother Edward died, William decided to introduce May to Edward's extended family in New South Wales. That he waited over 25 years after their wedding to do so surely confirms their incompatibility. A family photograph (see image 18 in the picture section) captures him sitting with his sister-in-law Anna, her daughter Vi and four of the children at Nana Glen. Anna's black clothing suggests she was still mourning Edward's death. She and William had known each other since their early twenties, when she and Edward were courting in Sandymount. William would have been around 66, and Anna about 74. This may have been their last visit. It was not an easy one. Family members report that Vi's second daughter Norah, then in her mid-teens, 'didn't like William's wife at all'. Her elder sister Caroline, in contrast, accepted William and May's invitation to visit them in Yambuk.[56]

May died in 1931 of asthma and heart failure.[57] By then, William had lost his youngest brother, Charles James, to rheumatic fever in 1915 and his eldest brother, Edward, to cancer ten years later. In May 1933 Frank died in New Zealand. He and Margaret had remained in the Wairau area of Marlborough throughout their adult lives. Frank found work labouring and as a hand in the flax mills. Like Patrick he too had run-ins with local police because of excessive drinking. In 1900 he was prohibited from purchasing alcohol in the district for twelve months. As he and Margaret headed into their seventies in the 1920s they faced old age with growing health problems. She died in February 1929 in her early 70s after several years of senility. When Frank died four years later, he was 77. The cause was listed as senile debility. Someone knew enough about his life to correctly identify the names of his parents and his place of birth on the Mosquito Plains of South Australia.[58] Perhaps they also wrote and informed his surviving brothers, Patrick and William.

With all their other brothers gone, death must have been on William's and Patrick Edgar's minds. When Frank died, the widowed William was nearly 73 and the elderly bachelor Patrick Edgar was 71. Patrick had remained in Milltown ever since William had departed for the war. He owned a small house in the town, valued at just £12, one of the lower valuations in the Shire of Portland. Living alone in old age is tough, especially for men. He is unlikely to have saved much over his life as a labourer. Whereas William was in contact with, and perhaps worked alongside, his son, Patrick had no children. His health deteriorated in the mid-1930s and in March 1935 he was admitted to hospital in nearby Hamilton with cancer of the bladder. They operated but he was discharged as incurable. On the recommendation of the priest of his parish he went to the home for the impoverished elderly that the Sisters of Nazareth had run in Ballarat since the 1880s. Old labourers without property or family to care for them were the prime clients of such institutions.[59]

He spent his last fourteen months in the three-storey, red-brick Victorian gothic institution which served as both mother-house and hospice.[60] His bladder had leaked since the operation, leaving him 'continually wet.' He developed bedsores. Most days he could get out of bed and sit in a chair for a few hours, but he became more and more feeble. Occasional visits from his brother William might have brought some cheer. He was already close to death on 18 May when he fell while getting out of bed and fractured his left thigh. He died three days later in the district hospital in Ballarat. The circumstances of his death were questionable enough for an inquest to be called. The coroner determined that no-one was to blame. The fall and shock had only hastened an imminent death.[61]

Nothing about Patrick's death prevented William from choosing shelter and care at the same home two years later. His choice is interesting. Lord O'Hagan's decision had deemed that William be raised a Protestant and Patrick a Catholic. Yet William's first wife was Catholic and they had married in a Catholic church in Liverpool. His second marriage was in the Anglican Church in Yambuk. When he enlisted in 1916 he reported his faith as Church of England. Yet the list of his personal effects included a rosary alongside his letters, postcards, a dictionary and a handkerchief. William, like Charles James, rejected the rigid sectarianism that had so scarred their lives as boys. By 1938 the rheumatism that had plagued him during and after the war had worsened. He had chronic bronchitis and heart disease. Had he had a daughter or daughter-in-law, she might have cared for him, but unmarried sons, like his Edward, rarely provided care for aging parents. In April 1938 he moved into the Nazareth Home. Two years later he died there. His death and war service were briefly acknowledged in the Melbourne newspaper the *Australasian*, which noted that he was a veteran of the 1914–18 war, had enlisted at the age of 55 and served with the 39th Battalion.[62]

The sectarian squabbles that had divided their family combined with the locations of their deaths to shape the final

Kearney resting places. Charles James's first wife, Harriet, was buried in Grafton. His second wife, Rachel, buried Charles James in the Catholic section of the Condobolin cemetery. The Nazareth sisters placed Patrick's body in a plot they owned in the Ballarat cemetery, listing his name with other deceased patients. William's name appears with May's on a headstone in the Port Fairy Cemetery, but he was buried close to Patrick in the Catholic section of the Ballarat cemetery; these two siblings, who had lived in close proximity in the years leading up to the First World War, were laid to rest in the same location. Their eldest brother Edward was buried in the Church of England cemetery known as the Field of Mars in Ryde, near where he died in New South Wales. Vi chose to bury her mother, Anna, in the South Grafton cemetery, close to where they had lived years earlier and not too far to visit from Nana Glen. Across the Tasman, both Frank and Margaret Kearney were laid to rest in the Catholic section of the beautiful Omaka cemetery, south of the town of Blenheim.[63]

⚜

The brothers' lives had been shaped by the contents of their father's will. They died in a different era. Women could vote. Their wives were listed on electoral rolls. More women took on paid labour and professions. Married women's property was understood to be separate from that of their husbands, if they had any. And in the years leading up to and following the First World War, a generation of feminists had generated public debate about the right of men to use their wills to dictate the future of their widows and children. First in New Zealand, and then in 1916 in New South Wales, legislators responded by passing legislation allowing courts to curtail or overturn a testator's power to name someone other than their surviving spouse as children's guardians, or to leave widows and children without economic support.[64] Caroline's chances of overturning Edward's final wishes would have been greater after this shift from protecting the testator's wishes towards the importance of providing for survivors.

The Kearney brothers understood some of the disadvantages of testamentary freedom. What were their final wishes? Only Charles James wrote a formal will. This is not surprising. People only make wills when they have property to distribute. Patrick Edgar was unlikely to have had anything to bequeath. Frank and Margaret faced old age and senility childless and with few resources. William Kearney likely passed his belongings informally to his son before moving into the Sisters of Nazareth's home. That Edward Kearney did not leave a will is more surprising. Anna was still alive, and there were his many grandchildren to think of. His death in a home for indigent cancer patients suggests he had few significant assets.

For Charles James, a will was essential. His three girls had lost their birth mother. They were aged between 20 and 24 when he died. All three were still single. Their stepmother, his younger wife, had nursed him through years of difficult illness. He knew he was dying. And, as a doctor, he had assets to bequeath. His will reflected his kindly character and the changing bequest patterns of the times. It contrasts dramatically with his father's will. Charles James placed no conditions on his bequests. He trusted his widow, Rachel, as the sole executor of the estate, and promised her all of his furniture, books and pictures, and his diamond ring. The rest of his estate was to go in four equal parts to her and each of his three daughters. Charles James opted for fair family provision over dictating draconian wishes from the grave.[65]

Their father's will had forced the boys to leave Australia, but he could not take Australia out of the boys. The brothers all chose to live out their adult lives in Australasia. All except Frank died and were buried in the country of their birth. Subsequent generations learned fragments of their story. They passed on to their descendants the importance of love and laughter over the sectarian conflict and harsh discipline that had marked their forebears' lives.[66]

# Coda

The events and dilemmas of the Kearneys' lives occurred well over a century ago. Yet they retain resonance today. Their story reminds us that past families were as complicated as current ones. Quarrels today are more likely to result from divorces than deaths, subjecting children to the effects of conflict between two living parents. Battles over custody that scar children are frequent. Stories of feuding parents absconding from particular countries with their children against the other parent's wishes reveal the ongoing ways in which children become pawns in adults' transnational fights. Inheritance squabbles and contested wills continue to divide families and to garner significant coverage in the press, especially when they involve the rich and famous. Today roughly four out of five Australian spouses leave all their property to their surviving spouse – something Edward resolutely avoided. Yet the tension 'between testamentary freedom and family support' continues, as recent Australian cases show.[1]

Caroline's experiences help explain why feminists fought so hard for wives to retain control of their own property and to have access to a much wider range of ways of earning a living and making money than Caroline or her contemporaries had. Matrimonial property regimes now acknowledge both partners' contributions to family fortunes in marriages and common-law relationships alike. Few courts today would allow a husband to force his widow and children to migrate elsewhere.

Yet forced migrations of diverse kinds continue across the world. Transportation and communications have speeded up. We understand that we live in a global age. The Kearneys' story also reminds us that mobility and a global world in which family members may live far apart are not new. This family history of how one man's final wishes forced his widow and children to leave Australia offers further evidence of the diverse ways relatively ordinary people lived out their lives and moved, both voluntarily and involuntarily, across different sites of empire and beyond in the past.

# Acknowledgments

I had no idea where exploring the lives of Caroline, Edward and their children would take me when I first began this project in 2012. Indeed when I presented my preliminary findings at a Feminist History Seminar at Melbourne University in 2013, I did not know whether Caroline and the children went to Ireland. My hunt for Caroline began, as I have recounted in the Introduction, when I read a report of her contest against Edward's will in the *Victoria Law Reports*. I was living in Toronto then, and vividly recall scrawling 'Wow, draconian patriarch', and then 'controlling father too' across my copy. Caroline's dilemma kept pushing into my thoughts. I began trying to explore how his will reflected the collision point of their life stories, what lay behind Edward's final wishes, and what happened to the family. I put aside the book I had been planning to write and focused on Caroline and the awful dilemma she faced.

Slowly, I pieced together evidence from the traces that Caroline, Edward and the children left in the courts, newspapers, legal journals, civil records and archives in Australia, Ireland and England. The explosion of genealogical family history websites and digitised documents and newspapers made this easier than it would have been in the past, especially as I was working initially from Canada and then from New Zealand. The full text of Edward's will and related probate documents are available through Victoria's Public Record Office website. The National Library of Australia's wonderful Trove website revealed newspaper reports of Maria Ellen Kearney's birth, some of their travels, Edward's problems with scabby sheep, the Aboriginal 'attack' on their station and the court case regarding Maria Ellen's abduction. None mentioned Edward aiming his gun at Coquata or Maria Ellen's death.

Caroline's story was more and more intriguing. Genealogical and family history websites revealed the Bax family migration to Australia in 1851 and further rich demographic details. Today, much can be researched online. But visits to archives and records offices remain essential. Archival digging in the Public Record Office in Melbourne led me to the original documents generated by *Kearney v. Lowry*. Historians have shown much more interest in criminal cases than civil ones like this, yet opening these equity court records was my greatest eureka moment. Here, tied up in three bundles, unopened perhaps since the pink ribbon was first tied around them, was a motherlode of information. Here I could read Caroline's affidavits and the counterclaims of the defendants. I could track the timing of the case. Here were notes from her lawyer about Caroline seeking to secure pictures that she claimed William Kearney had taken from the station. And here was an accounting of virtually every penny spent following Edward Kearney's death. The details allowed me to follow William Kearney as he took Maria Ellen to the convent in Geelong. Money owed gave information about the workforce on Lockhart Station and Caroline's spending. Habeas corpus files offered details on Caroline's struggle to have her daughter returned to her. Insolvency files revealed her bungled attempt to claim bankruptcy. Pastoral lease files gave details of the history of Lockhart Station. Similar records in the State Library of South Australia and State Archives contained Edward Kearney's own evidence regarding the hunt for Coquata as well as the concerns of the protector of Aborigines.

# Acknowledgments

Trips to the local history society in the Wimmera town of Kaniva, Victoria, to libraries in Naracoorte and Robe in South Australia and to the site of Lockhart and Broom stations added shards of information and gave me a sense of the landscapes in which they lived and worked as well as the histories of those areas. Further afield, digging in the Public Record Office in Kew, London and the Camden Local Studies and Archives Centre, London added shreds of evidence, solved particular puzzles and left many unresolved. Visiting Belfast and Dublin and their libraries and archives added some additional information. Had the majority of the civil and legal records of Ireland not blown up in 1922, they would have revealed more about Caroline and the boys' lives in Dublin and made it possible to better follow the money and the actions of court officials and Caroline's brothers-in-law.

I have found no single document that Caroline wrote herself that reveals her hopes or fears in her own words. Indeed, my only glimpse of her own handwriting is her signature on diverse court documents. With the exception of her son Edward's brief but evocative memorandum and her brother-in-law James Charles Hamilton's memoir, the family left few personal records that have survived – or that I have been able to locate. Had the documents stored in an old trunk at the family home at Nana Glen survived and included letters or diaries, more puzzles might be solved. They would surely have enriched the story and changed parts of the narrative. But I think the broad contours of my account would stand.

❧

Writing is usually a solitary activity. And it needs to be. But good research and good writing involve many collaborators. I could not have written *Caroline's Dilemma* without the support and feedback of many people and institutions. Profound thanks to Rosalind McLeod and Joe Palmer, two great-great-grandchildren of the couple at the heart of this book. We met. They became collaborators, sharing family stories and memories, documents, photographs and their own research and ideas about their ancestors' lives. Joe kindly transcribed the moving memorandum that young Edward penned for his future wife. They generously supported my desire to write a book about Caroline while giving me the liberty to write as I wished. They read a full version of the manuscript, offering valuable feedback, identifying mistakes and sharing their interpretations. Rosalind and Joe are proud of their great-great-grandmother Caroline, who ensured that her daughter was properly buried, and, as Ros put it, with all her faults stuck by those boys and brought them up as decent men, doing the best she could under the awful difficulties she faced. She achieved much, despite her drinking, and gave life a good shake.

I could not have researched the Irish side of the Kearney family history without the help of my Irish friends Kay MacKeogh, a formidable genealogist, and Proinnsias Breathnach, a skilled economic geographer. Two more collaborators had joined the hunt for Caroline. Guided by Proinnsias's careful mapping and Kay's research acumen, we sought what we thought was the site of Edward's older brother Francis's property, Renaun, in Ballinahown, County Westmeath. We were bowled over to discover it is the home of this generation's Francis Kearney, his wife Grainne Dunican and their children. Thanks to them and Francis's sisters, Olive and Marion, for receiving us so generously, sharing fabulous food, family photos and stories, and accompanying us to locate the original Kearney farmhouse, the graves of three of Edward's brothers, and his parents' headstones.

My daughter Anna helped me years ago, photocopying cases from the *Victoria Law Reports*. It was among these that I first found mention of Caroline and her husband's final wishes. My 'Hunt for Caroline' as my other daughter Emily calls it (echoing the title of New Zealand director Taika Waititi's 2016 film, *Hunt for the Wilderpeople*) had begun. Anna and Emily Bradbury and their husbands Matt Ropiha and Craig Coburn have listened with patience to new shreds of information and my retellings of the story, and provided me with two homes and love and laughter while researching Caroline's history in Melbourne. Emily acted as driver and research accomplice on my most recent exploration of the places Caroline lived as a daughter, wife and widow in South Australia and Victoria. At its most exciting, this involved driving at great speed in our cheap rental car across part of the former lands of Lockhart Station. We were following the farm truck of Mark Grosser, who grew up on the land there, as he showed us the site of the original homestead and of the early horseraces. Emily tells me that our car would have sunk into the ground's spongy surface had she not driven so quickly. We survived. And we better understood the characteristics of the local soil, along with the beauties of a western Wimmera sunset. Thanks to the Grosser family for giving us access to their land and for their interest in Caroline's story.

Staff at the Public Record Office in Melbourne, the State Library of Victoria, the State Library of South Australia, South Australia State Records, New South Wales Archives and Records, the National Archives, Dublin and the National Library, Dublin have helped me locate material. Thanks to Ross and Fran McDonald of the West Wimmera genealogical group in Kaniva, Victoria and to librarians at the Naracoorte and Robe libraries in South Australia. Claudette Brennan, archivist at Sacred Heart College in Geelong, and Jenny Glare, archivist at the MacKillop Family Services archives in South Melbourne, both welcomed me as I sought to understand Caroline's daughter Maria Ellen

Kearney's story. Dr Robert Foster, History Department, University of Adelaide, generously helped me locate the archival records detailing Edward Kearney's encounters with Indigenous peoples on whose land he was squatting. Thanks too to Caroline Mullin, archivist at Blackrock College, Dublin. Essential support for the project on marriage and inheritance in 19th-century white settler colonies from which this history developed came from the Canadian Social Science and Humanities Research Council and from grants to the Montreal History Group from the Fonds de Recherche du Québec – Société et Culture.

Feedback from many scholars and friends has been invaluable. Thanks to my colleagues in the Montreal History Group for the decades of fellowship, intellectual stimulation, research support and encouragement we have shared. Thanks too to members of the Feminist History Group in Melbourne for their feedback, the Toronto Legal History Group, the University of Adelaide's History Department, and workshop participants at the Historicizing Family Law Exceptionalism workshop organised by Janet Halley, Harvard Law School and Julia Stephens and Judith Surkis, History, Rutgers University. York University, Toronto has generously provided me with leave for research. My friends and colleagues there – Michele Johnson, Molly Ladd-Taylor, Kate McPherson, Anne Rubenstein and many others – have consistently shared enthusiasm and offered critical suggestions. In Wellington, Kate Hunter, Bronwyn Labrum, Charlotte Macdonald and Margaret Tennant have read versions of the manuscript and provided warm support and constructive feedback. For all of that, huge thanks. Further heartfelt gratitude to the anonymous reader solicited by NewSouth and to five other historian friends who read and commented on a draft of the book: Pat Grimshaw; Jarett Henderson; Craig Heron; Linda Kealey; and Andrée Lévesque. Huge thanks too to Jane Parkin in New

Zealand for helpful editorial suggestions. And special thanks to the wonderful NewSouth Publishing staff: Phillipa McGuinness for her support and wise editorial suggestions; Paul O'Beirne for shepherding the manuscript through the publication process; and all who worked on the design, printing and publicity. Finally, to all my friends, my sisters and wider family, and to members of my book club and walking groups who have encouraged me again and again by their interest in Caroline's story, I promise you I will find something else to talk about now. This would be a much weaker work without the input and feedback of all these generous people. Faults and mistakes remain my own.

# Bibliography

## Primary sources
### Family photos
Gerard, Anna Violet Gerard, recording, 1949, held by family members.

Gerard, John W, From Pictures Green to the Silver Screen, Coffs Harbour; 1984, held by family members.

Kearney, Edward, Memorandum, c.1876, transcribed by Joe Palmer, held by family members.

McLeod, Rosalind, History of the families of Walter Gerard and Anna Violet Kearney.


## Public, local and institutional archives
### Australia
### New South Wales State Archives (NSWSA)
NRS 5257, Immigration Board, Assisted immigrant passenger lists (4/4790), Microfilm, SR Reel 2136, 106; Passenger lists (4/4920), Microfilm, SR Reel 2462.

NRS 5257, Immigration Board, Reports by the Immigration Agent on the Condition of Immigrants and Ships on their Arrival (4/4699-703), Microfilm, SR Reel 2852.


### Public Record Office Victoria, Melbourne (PROV)
VPRS 16236/P/002, Roll of Barristers, 1841–1932.

VPRS 16237/P0001/1, Roll of Attorneys, 1841–1891.

VPRS 1697/P00000/3, 1860–1871, Equity Suit Books.

VPRS 24/ P0000/1308/1936/694, Proceedings of Inquest, Patrick Kearney, Ballarat, 4 June 1936.

VPRS 244, Pastoral Plans (microfiche).

VPRS 259/P0001/13, 1071, Equity Case Files, *Kearney v. Lowry*.

VPRS 267/P0007/141, 1867/2555, *Charles Mulrain v. William McGann Estate of Edward Kearney*, 1 January 1867.

VPRS 267/P/0007/181, 1869/742, *Bennett v. Kearney*, 8 March 1869.

VPRS 28/P0001/11, 5/461, Probate and Administration Files, In the Will of Edward Kearney, Will, Edward Kearney, 19 November 1865.

VPRS 3504 Microfilm, Inward Shipping Index, 1839–1900, Reel 2, L–Z.

# Bibliography

VPRS 37/P0000/8, 517, Habeas Corpus cases, In the Matter of Maria Ellen Kearney, 12 September 1866.

VPRS 4301/P0000/8, 13–16/71–75, Rate Books, Fitzroy, 1865.

VPRS 4301/P000/14, 1871–1872, Rate Books, Fitzroy.

VPRS 5357/P0000/002371, 406/121, Land Selection and Correspondence Files, Brockell, Brooksby.

VPRS 5357/P0000/002548, 25415/73/, Bringalbert, James Charles Hamilton.

VPRS 5825/ P0000/01–02, Pastoral Run Registers.

VPRS 5826, Pastoral Run Registers (microfiche).

VPRS 5920, Pastoral Run files (microfiche).

VPRS 759/P0000/215, 12474, Proceedings re Insolvency Estates, *In the matter of the Insolvency of Caroline Kearney*, 23 September 1869.

VPRS 7591/P0001/23, 5/461, Will, Edward Kearney, 30 September 1865.

VPRS 7592, Wills and Probate and Administration.

VPRS 809 P0001/1, Reports of Rents on Runs, 2nd half 1864.

**Sacred Heart College, Geelong, Victoria, Archives**

**Sisters of Nazareth, Ballarat, Victoria, Australia, Aged Care Resident Register**

**State Library, South Australia (SLSA)**
PRG497, Series 7, Roland Campbell, Series 6, A Short History of Robe and Guichen Bay, c.1930; Series 7, Research Notes on the South East.

**State Records, South Australia (SRSA)**
GRG24, Colonial Secretary's Office, from 1856 Chief Secretary's Office.

GRG24/6, Colonial Secretary's Office, Letters received, 1842–1982.

GRG35/4, Letters received – Commissioner of Crown Lands.

GRG35/518, Schedule of 14-year Depasturing Leases – Surveyor-General's Office.

GRG3519/1/1, Department of Lands, Registers of Pastoral Leases, 1851–1939.

GRG4/83/9, Local Court Robe.

GRG5/154/1, South Australia Police Department, Naracoorte Police Station Records.

MRG18/4, Assessment Books, District Council of Robe.

Map of Pastoral Lease Districts of South Australia/Compiled from Official Surveys in the Office of the Surveyor-General, c.1861, W. G. Harris, London, Holburn Hill and Crystal Palace: R. K. Burt, 1862, <www.southernflinders-midnorth.com.au/maps/map_pastoralleases1861-65main.htm, accessed 1 April 2019.

**England and Ireland**
**Blackrock College Archives, Dublin, Ireland**, Student Register, 1870.

*England & Wales, Criminal Registers, 1791–1892* (database online); Provo, UT, USA: <Ancestry.com>.

**Camden Local Studies and Archives Centre, London**
St Pancras Parish, Rate Assessments, Ward 3, 1882–1886, Stratford Place and
Stratford Villas, microfilm no. 803, 1885, Camden Road, 13, Stratford Place,
157; 1886, Camden Road, 13, Stratford Place, 162, Stratford Villas, 164.

**National Archives, United Kingdom (NA-UK)**
CUST 116/3/93, Excise Entry Papers, William Bax, 17 December 1825, 17 April
1826.
CUST 47/663, Excise Board and Secretariat: Minute Books, 9 May 1851, 239;
4 June 1851, 262.
*England & Wales, Criminal Registers, 1791-1892* [database on-line]; Provo, UT,
USA: <Ancestry.com>.

**National Archives of Ireland (NAI)**
Calendar of Wills and Administrations, 10 June 1874, 313, <www.willcalendars.
nationalarchives.ie/search/cwa/details.jsp?id=1639377692>.
NAI/CS/PS/1, Courts of Petty Sessions, Court Registers, County Westmeath,
14 November 1854; 22 December 1859; 20 July 1869; 7 and 14 September
1869.

**Public Record Office Northern Ireland (PRONI)**
D2777/7/4/52-132, MIC562/16; D27777/7/4/133-241, MIC562/17;
D27777/7/4/242-347, MIC 562/18: Papers Relating to Lord O'Hagan as
Chancellor Ireland, 1868–81.
D2777/5/80-89/40/1, MIC 562/25; D2777/59/41-53, MIC 562/26:
Correspondence with Individual Correspondents, 1859–84.
D2777/9/54-59/81/2, MIC 562/27: Correspondence with Individual
Correspondents, c.1850–1886.
D2777/9/82-113, MIC 562/26: Correspondence with Individual Correspondents,
c.1840–1884.

**City directories**
*Guy's Directory,* Dublin, 1875.
*London and Provincial Medical Directory*, 1865
Sands and McDougall, *Melbourne and Suburban Directory*, 1869, 1870, 1871.
*The Medical Directory,* London, 1875.
*Post Office Directory*, 1851, Cuckfield, West Surrey, <www.sussex-opc.org/
PostOffice1851/CuckfieldPostOffice1851.htm>.
*Post Office London Directory, 1882.*
*Slater's Royal National Commercial Directory of Ireland 1881.*
*Thom's Irish Almanac*, County Dublin, 1871–1880.
*Thom's Official Directory of the UK and Ireland,* 1873–1890.

# Newspapers and gazettes
**Australia**
(all accessed via Trove, <trove.nla.gov.au/newspaper/>)

# Bibliography

*Adelaide Observer*
*Adelaide Times*
*The Age* (Melbourne)
*The Argus* (Melbourne)
*Armidale Chronicle* (New South Wales)
*Australasian* (Melbourne)
*Bendigo Advertiser*
*Border Watch* (South Australia)
*Clarence and Richmond Examiner* (New South Wales)
*Clarence River Advocate* (New South Wales)
*Coff's Harbour Advocate* (New South Wales)
*Colonial Times* (Hobart)
*Courier* (Hobart)
*Daily Examiner* (Grafton)
*Empire* (Sydney)
*Evening Journal* (Adelaide)
*Geelong Advertiser and Intelligencer* (Victoria)
*Hamilton Spectator and Grange District Advertiser* (Victoria)
*Labour Call*
*Launceston Examiner* (Tasmania)
*Leader* (Melbourne)
*Macleay Chronicle* (New South Wales)
*Maitland Mercury and Hunter River General Advertiser* (New South Wales)
*Melbourne Punch*
*Mount Alexander Mail* (Victoria)
*Mudgee Guardian and North Western Representative* (New South Wales)
*Naracoorte Herald* (South Australia)
*New South Wales Gazette*
*Portland Guardian and Normanby General Advertiser* (Victoria)
*South Australian Register* (Adelaide)
*South Australian Weekly Chronicle*
*Sydney Gazette and New South Wales Advertiser*
*Sydney Morning Herald*
*Sydney Stock and Station Journal*

**England and Ireland**
(accessed via British Library Newspapers unless otherwise specified)
*Belfast Newsletter*
*Birmingham Market*
*Bradford Daily Telegraph*
*Cork Constitution*
*Derry Journal* (Ireland)
*Downpatrick Recorder* (Ireland)
*Drogheda Argus and Leinster Journal*
*Dublin Daily Express*
*Freeman's Journal* (Ireland)
*Irish Times*

*London Evening Standard*
*London Gazette*
*Saunders's News-Letter*
*Standard* (London, England)
*Times* (London, England), Times Digital Archive
*Waterford Standard*
*Westmeath Examiner*

**New Zealand**
(accessed via Papers Past, <paperspast.natlib.govt.nz/newspapers>)
*Auckland Star*
*Clutha Leader* (Otago)
*Marlborough Express*
*Otago Witness*

## Websites

Ancestry.com, <www.Ancestry.com>, for most births, census records, deaths, electoral rolls, marriages, voyages, etc.
Australian Data Archive, <http://hccda.ada.edu.au>, Census, South Australia, Census, 1855; Census, Victoria, 1857; Census, New South Wales, 1891.
Australian Institute of Aboriginal and Torres Islander Studies Map of Indigenous Australia, David R. Horton, Aboriginal Studies Press, AIATSIS, <aiatsis.gov. au/explore/articles/aboriginal-australia-map>.
Charles Booth Online Archive, Survey Notebook, B356, 150, © London School of Economics & Political Science, <booth.lse.ac.uk/>
Clarence River Historical Society, <www.clarencehistory.org.au/>.
Cricinfo, Australia, <www.espncricinfo.com/australia/content/player/6738. html>.
Darwin Online, <darwin-online.org.uk/.
eMelbourne, *The City Past & Present*, <www.emelbourne.net.au/biogs/ EM00845b.htm>.
Enlistment Standards, First World War, Australian War Memorial, <www.awm. gov.au/encyclopedia/enlistment/>.
Find My Past, <www.findmypast.com.au/> for births, deaths, marriages, city directories, etc.
Fitzroy State School No. 450, Victorian Heritage Database report, <vhd. heritagecouncil.vic.gov.au/places/103795/download-report>.
Founding of Dunedin Diocese, *Encyclopaedia of New Zealand*, 1966, <www. teara.govt.nz/en/1966/the-roman-catholic-church/page-5>.
Guide to Historic Shipwreck Trail on Victoria's West Coast, <www.pastmasters. net/uploads/2/6/7/5/26751978/shipwrecktrail_-_schomberg.pdf>.
History of Camden New Town, <www.camdenhistorywiki.org.uk/index. php?title=History_of_Camden_New_Town>.
Introduction to the O'Hagan Papers, Public Record Office of Northern Ireland (PRONI), <www.proni.gov.uk/introduction__o_hagan_papers_d2777.pdf>.

Irish Migration to Britain, <www.irish-genealogy-toolkit.com/Irish-immigration-to-Britain.html.

Jameson and District Historical Society, <home.vicnet.net.au/~jdhs/welcome.htm.

Library and Archives Canada, South African War, 1899–1902, <www.bac-lac.gc.ca/eng/discover/military-heritage/south-african-war-1899-1902/Pages/service-files-south-african-war.aspx>.

Map of the Province of South Australia/Compiled from official surveys in the office of the Surveyor-General, W. G. Harris, London, Holburn Hill and Crystal Palace: R. K. Burt, 1862, accessed, <www.southernflinders-midnorth.com.au/maps/map_pastoralleases1861-65main.htm>.

Measuring Worth, <www.measuringworth.com>.

Ozenkadnook Cemetery, <www.ianmarr.net.au/ozenkad.htm>.

Pioneer Land Surveyors of New Zealand via Survey and Spatial New Zealand, <www.surveyors.org.nz>.

Royal Rehab, <www.royalrehab.com.au/about-us/our-history/>.

Saint John the Evangelist, Sandymount, <sandymount.weebly.com/about-st-johnrsquos.html>.

SS *Ant*, <vhd.heritage.vic.gov.au/shipwrecks/heritage/33>.

Tindale's Catalogue of Australian Aboriginal Tribes, <archives.samuseum.sa.gov.au/tindaletribes/index.html>.

Western District Families. Stories of Pioneering Families from the Western District of Victoria, <westerndistrictfamilies.com/2013/03/28/passing-of-the-pioneers-20/>.

## Legal sources

*American Law Review*, 1871–72.

*Irish Reports, Equity Series*, 1870–81.

*Law Reports (Ireland), Chancery, 1878–1881.*

*Irish Reports and Law Reports (Ireland), Digest of Cases from 1867–1893.*

*Irish Law Times Digest of Cases Decided by the Superior Courts in Ireland, 1867–1893.*

*South Australian Law Reports*, 1863–1920.

*Victorian Law Reports*, 1874–1890.

*Wyatt and Webb's Reports* (Victoria), 1861–1863.

*Wyatt, Webb and A'Beckett's Reports* (Victoria), 1864–1869.

## Government publications

*Act to Make Provision for the Better Administration of Justice in the Colony of Victoria 1852* (Vic.).

New South Wales Statutes, accessed via Austlii, <www.austlii.edu.au/databases.html>.

Report from the Select Committee on State of Westmeath, and Nature of certain Unlawful Combinations, Great Britain. Parliament. House of Commons,

Parliamentary Papers, Session 1871, Vol. XIII, <https://archive.org/details/op1249739-1001>.

South Australia Heritage Committee, Register Research Programme, 1981/82, Bermingham's Cottage, Victoria Street, Robe, ref. no. 6823-10304.

South Australia Statutes, accessed via Austlii, <www.austlii.edu.au/databases.html>.

Victoria Hansard, 1870. Victoria Parliamentary Papers, 1867, no. 58, Report on the Condition, Management and Regulations at the Convent, Geelong, 1866, 3.

Victoria Parliamentary Papers, 1866, no. A13, Industrial Schools: Reports and Correspondence, 1866.

Victoria Statutes, accessed via Austlii, <www.austlii.edu.au/databases.html>.

## Books and articles

Adams, John, *The Doctrine of Equity: A Commentary on the Law as Administered by the Court of Chancery*, Philadelphia: T & J. W. Johnston & Co., 1873.

Anderson, Hugh, 'Clarke, William John (1805–1874)', *Australian Dictionary of Biography*, 1, 1966, <adb.anu.edu.au/biography/clarke-william-john-1902>.

Anderson, Michael, *Family Structure in Nineteenth-Century Lancashire*, Cambridge, Eng.: University Press, 1971.

Ashworth, William J., *Customs and Excise: Trade, Production and Consumption in England, 1640–1845*, Oxford: Oxford University Press, 2003.

Atherton, Rosalind, 'Expectation without right: testamentary freedom and the position of women in 19th-century New South Wales', *UNSW Law Journal*, 1988.

Baker, Christopher and Michael Gilding, *Inside Story*, 'Family matters', <insidestory.org.au/family-matters/>.

Ballantyne, Tony and Antoinette Burton, eds, *Moving Subjects: Gender, Mobility and Intimacy in an Age of Global Empire*, Urbana: University of Illinois Press, 2009.

Barnard, Jill and Karen Twigg, *Holding on to Hope. A History of the Founding Agencies of MacKillop Family Services 1854–1997*, Melbourne: Australian Scholarly Publishing, 2004.

Beer, Jane, Charles Fahey, Patricia Grimshaw and Melanie Raymond, *Colonial Frontiers and Family Fortunes*, Melbourne: Melbourne University Press, 1989.

Bell, Peter and Susan Marsden, 'Kingston SE – An overview history', <www.sahistorians.org.au/175/documents/kingston-se-an-overview-history.shtml>.

Bennett, J. M., *Sir William A'Beckett, First Chief Justice of Victoria, 1842–1857*, Sydney: Federation Press, 2009.

—— *Sir William Stawell, Second Chief Justice of Victoria, 1857–1886*, Sydney: Federation Press, 2004.

Benton, Lauren, *Law and Colonial Cultures: Legal Regimes in World History, 1400–1900*, Cambridge: Cambridge University Press, 2002.

Bermingham, Kathleen, *Gateway to the South East: A Story of Robetown and the Guichen Bay District*, Millicent, SA: South Eastern Times Ltd, 1961.

Blake, Leslie James, *Tattyara: A History of the Kaniva District*, Victoria: Shire of Kaniva, 1982.

——, *Wimmera*, Melbourne: Cypress Books, 1983.

Boothby, Josiah, *South Australia Almanac and Directory*, South Australia: Modbury, 1864.

Borchardt, D. H., 'Julian Edmund Tenison-Woods', *Australian Dictionary of Biography*, <adb.anu.edu.au/biography/tenison-woods-julian-edmund-4700>.

Bouchard, Gérard, *Quelques Arpents d'Amérique: Population, Economie, Famille au Saguenay, 1838–1971*, Montréal: Boréal, 1996.

Bradbury, Bettina, 'Colonial comparisons: rethinking marriage, civilization and nation in 19th-century white-settler societies', in *Rediscovering the British World*, Phillip Buckner and G. Frances, eds, Calgary: University of Calgary Press, 2005.

——, 'Elderly inmates and care-giving sisters: Catholic institutions for the elderly in nineteenth-century Montreal', in *On the Case: Case Files and Social History*, Franca Iacovetta and Wendy Mitchinson, eds, Toronto: University of Toronto Press, 1998.

——, '"In England a man can do as he likes with his property": migration, family fortunes and the law in nineteenth-century Quebec and the Cape Colony', in *Within and Without the Nation: Canadian History as Transnational History*, Adele Perry, Karen Dubinsky and Henry Wu, eds, Toronto: University of Toronto Press, 2015.

——, 'Troubling inheritances: an illegitimate, Māori daughter contests her father's will in the New Zealand courts and the Judicial Committee of the Privy Council', *Australia and New Zealand Legal History* (2012) E-Journal.

——, 'Twists, turning points and tall shoulders: studying Canada and feminist family histories', *Canadian Historical Review*, 96, 2, 2015, 257–85.

——, *Wife to Widow: Lives, Laws and Politics in 19th-Century Montreal*, Vancouver: University of British Columbia Press, 2011.

——, *Working Families: Age, Gender and Daily Survival in Working Class Montreal*, Toronto: McClelland & Stewart, 1993.

Breathnach, Proinnsias, 'The diffusion of the co-operative creamery system in Ireland, 1889–1920: a spatial analysis', PhD thesis, Department of Geography, National University of Ireland, Maynooth, 2006.

Brodbribb, William Adams, *Recollections of an Australian Squatter, 1835–1883*, Sydney: John Woods & Co., 1883, republished Sydney: John Ferguson, 1978.

Brouwer, Ruth Compton, *Modern Women Modernizing Men: The Changing Missions of Three Professional Women in Asia and Africa, 1902–69*, Vancouver: UBC Press, 2002.

——, *New Women for God: Canadian Presbyterian women and India Missions, 1876–1914*, Toronto: University of Toronto Press, 1990.

Buck, Andrew, '"A Blot on the certificate": dower and women's property rights in colonial New South Wales', *Australian Journal of Law and Society*, 4, 87, 1987.

———, John McLaren and Nancy E. White, eds, *Land and Freedom: Law, Property Rights and the British Diaspora*, Aldershot, UK: Ashgate, 2001.

Buettner, Elizabeth, *Empire Families: Britons and Late Imperial India*, Oxford: Oxford University Press, 2004.

Burton, V. B., 'Apprenticeship regulation and marine labour in the nineteenth-century British merchant marine', *International Journal of Maritime History*, vol. 1, 1989, 20–49.

Bushman, Richard, *The Refinement of America: Persons, Houses, Cities*, New York: Knopf, 1992.

Bynum, Helen, *Spitting Blood: The History of Tuberculosis*, Oxford: Oxford University Press, 2012.

Byrnes, Giselle, *Boundary Markers: Land Surveying and the Colonisation of New Zealand*, Wellington: Bridget Williams Books, 2001.

Carter, Sarah, *Imperial Plots: Women, Land, and the Spadework of British Colonialism on the Canadian Prairies*, Winnipeg: University of Manitoba Press, 2016.

———, *The Importance of Being Monogamous: Marriage and Nation Building in Western Canada*, Edmonton: Athabasca University Press, 2008.

Chambers, John David, *A Practical Treatise on the Jurisdiction of the High Court of Chancery over the Persons and Property of Infants,* London: Saunders and Benning, 1842.

Chilton, Lisa, *Agents of Empire: British Female Migration to Canada and Australia, 1860s–1930*, Toronto: University of Toronto Press, 2007.

Clark, David and Gerard McCoy, *Habeas Corpus: Australia, New Zealand, South Pacific*, Sydney: Federation Press, 2000.

Clark, Philip, 'The Aboriginal ethnobotany of the South-East of South Australia region, part 1: seasonal life and material culture', *Transactions of the Royal Society of South Australia*, vol. 139, no. 2, 2015.

Clarke, Michael, *'Big' Clarke*, Carlton, Victoria: Queensberry Hill Press, 1980.

Cleall, Esme, Laura Ishiguro and Emily J. Manktelow, Special Issue, 'Imperial relations: histories of family in the British empire', *Journal of Colonialism and Colonial History*, vol. 14, no. 1, 2013, 216–46.

Cliff, Andrew and Peter Hagget, 'Time, travel and infection', *British Medical Bulletin*, vol. 69, no. 1, 2004, 87–99.

Cockburn, Rodney, *Pastoral Pioneers of South Australia*, I, 2 vols, Blackwood, S.A.: Lynton Publications, 1974.

Cox, Liam, *Moate, County Westmeath: A History of the Town and District, Athlone*, n.p., 1981.

Damousi, Joy, 'Chaos and order: gender, space and sexuality on female convict ships', *Australian Historical Studies*, vol. 26, no. 104, 1995, 351–72.

Davidoff, Leonore, *Thicker than Water: Siblings and Their Relations, 1780–1920*, Oxford: Oxford University Press, 2012.

Davidoff, Leonore and Catherine Hall, *Family Fortunes: Men and Women of the English Middle Class, 1780–1850*, London: Routledge, 2002.

# Bibliography

Davies, Megan J., *Into the House of Old: A History of Residential Care in British Columbia*, Montreal: McGill–Queen's University Press, 2003.

De Serville, Paul, *Pounds and Pedigrees: The Upper Class in Victoria, 1850–1880*, Melbourne: Oxford University Press, 1991.

Dean, Arthur, *A Multitude of Counsellors: A History of the Bar in Victoria*, Melbourne: Cheshire for the Bar Council, 1968.

Deans, Dennis Norman, *An Historical Geography of New South Wales*, Sydney: Reed Education, 1972.

Dunn, Robert, *The Disputed Country: Australia's Lost Border*, South Australia: Bob Dunn and John Deckert, 2004.

Eid, Mushira, *The World of Obituaries: Gender across Cultures and Over Time*, Detroit: Wayne State University Press, 2001.

Elbourne, Elizabeth, 'The sin of the settler: the 1835–36 select committee on Aborigines and debates over virtue and conquest in the early nineteenth-century British white settler empire', *Journal of Colonialism and Colonial History*, vol. 4, no. 3, 2003.

Eustace, Nicole, Eugenia Lean, Julie Livingston, Jan Plamper, William M. Reddy and Barbara H. Rosenwein, 'AHR conversation: the historical study of emotions', *American Historical Review*, 2012, 1487–1531.

Evans, Julie, *Edward Eyre: Race and Colonial Governance*, Dunedin: Otago University Press, 2005.

Evans, Julie, Pat Grimshaw, David Philips and Shirley Swain, *Equal Subjects, Unequal Rights: Indigenous Peoples in British Settler Colonies, 1830–1910*, Manchester: Manchester University Press, 2003.

Evans, Tanya, *Fractured Families: Life on the Margins in Colonial New South Wales*, Sydney: NewSouth Publishing, 2015.

Fahey, Charles, '"Abusing the Horses and Exploiting the Labourer": the Victorian agricultural and pastoral labourer, 1871–1911', *Labour History*, vol. 65, 1993, 96–114.

Farragher, Seán P, CSSp, *The French College Blackrock, 1860–1896*, Dublin: Paraclete Press, 2011.

Fisher, Robert, Rick Hosking and Amanda Nettelbeck, *Fatal Collisions: The South Australian Frontier and the Violence of Memory*, Kent Town, SA: Wakefield Press, 2001.

Fitzpatrick, David, *Oceans of Consolation: Personal Accounts of Irish Migration to Australia*, Ithaca: New York, 1994.

Flynn, Michael P., *Genealogy of the Descendants of William Kearney and Mary Mulrain, Williamstown, Cornamaddy, Athlone, incorporating some Descendants of the Casey Family, the Strand, Walshetown, Mullingar, Compiled in 1994/1997*, Mullingar: Michael P. Flynn, 1997.

Forsyth, William, *A Treatise on the Law relating to Custody of Infants in Cases of Difference between Parents or Guardians*, Philadelphia: T & J. W. Johnston & Co., 1851.

Foster, Hamar, Benjamin L. Berger and A. R. Buck, eds, *The Grand Experiment: Law and Legal Culture in British Settler Societies*, Vancouver: Osgoode Society for Canadian Legal History and UBC Press, 2008. Foster, Robert and

Amanda Nettelbeck, *Out of the Silence: The History and Memory of South Australia's Frontier Wars*, Adelaide: Wakefield Press, 2011.

Foster, Robert and Paul Sendziuk, eds, *Turning Points: Chapters in South Australian History*, Adelaide: Wakefield Press, 2012.

Francis, Charles, Sir William Foster Stawell, *Australian Dictionary of Biography*, vol. 6, 1976, <adb.anu.edu.au/biography/stawell-sir-william-foster-4635>.

Fraser, Lyndon, 'The ties that bind: Irish Catholic testamentary evidence from Christchurch, 1876–1915', *New Zealand Journal of History*, vol. 29, no. 1, 1995: 67–82.

Fry, Daisy, *The Story of Tatiara, 1845–1947*, Bordertown: Tatiara Centenary Committee, 1947.

Gammage, Bill, *The Biggest Estate on Earth*, Sydney: Allen & Unwin, 2011.

——, 'Historical Reconsiderations: VIII. Who gained, and who was meant to gain from land selection in New South Wales?', *Australian Historical Studies*, April 1990: 104–122.

Gardiner, W. J., 'George Henry Moore', *Te Ara: The Encyclopedia of New Zealand*, <www.teara.govt.nz/en/biographies/1m52/moore-george-henry>.

Golder, Hilary and Diane Kirkby, 'Land conveyancing and the problem of the married woman in colonial Australia', in *Law, History, Colonialism: The Reach of Empire*, Diane Kirkby and Catharine Coleborn, eds, Manchester: Manchester University Press, 2001.

Gothard, Jan, *Blue China: Single Female Migration to Colonial Australia*, Melbourne: Melbourne University Press, 2001.

Grimshaw, Patricia, *Paths of Duty: American Missionary Wives in Nineteenth-century Hawaii*, Honolulu: University of Hawaii Press, 1989.

Grimshaw, Patricia and Andrew May, *Missionaries, Indigenous Peoples and Cultural Exchange*, Eastbourne, Brighton: Sussex Academic Press, 2010.

Grimshaw, Patricia, Charles Fahey, Susan Janson and Tom Griffiths, 'Families and selection in colonial Horsham', in *Families in Colonial Australia,* Patricia Grimshaw, Chris McConville and Ellen Mc Ewen, eds, Sydney: George Allen & Unwin, 1985.

Grimshaw, Patricia, Marilyn Lake, Ann McGrath and Marion Quartly, *Creating a Nation*, Ringwood, Vic.: McPhee Gribble, 1994.

Haggis, Jane, 'White women and colonialism: towards a non-recuperative history', in Clare Midgley ed., *Gender and Imperialism*, Manchester University Press, 1998.

Haigh, Gideon, *Stroke of Genius: Victor Trumper and the Shot that Changed Cricket*, Melbourne, Vic.: Penguin Random House, 2016.

Haines, David, 'In search of the "whaheen": ngai tahu women, shore whalers, and the meaning of sex in early New Zealand', in *Moving Subjects: Gender, Mobility and Intimacy in an Age of Global Empire*, Tony Ballantyne and Antoinette Burton, eds, Urbana: University of Illinois Press, 2009.

Haines, Robin, *Emigration and the Labouring Poor*, New York: St Martin's Press, 1997.

——, 'Indigent misfits or shrewd operators? Government-assisted emigrants from the United Kingdom to Australia, 1831–1860', *Population Studies*, vol. 48, 1994, 223–47.

# Bibliography

Hall, Catherine, *Civilising Subjects: Metropole and Colony in the English Imagination, 1830–1867*, Chicago: University of Chicago Press, 2002.

Halliday, Paul, *Habeas Corpus: From England to Empire*, Cambridge, Mass.: Belknap Press of Harvard University Press, 2010.

Hamilton, James Charles, *Pioneering Days in Western Victoria*, Melbourne: Exchange Press, 1913.

Hammerton, James, *Emigrant Gentlewomen: Genteel Poverty and Female Emigration, 1830–1914*, London: Croom Helm, 1979.

——, 'Gender and migration', in *Gender and Empire*, Philippa Levine, ed., Oxford: Oxford University Press, 2004.

Harfull, Liz, *Almost an Island: The Story of Robe*, South Australia: Wakefield Press, 2013.

Harrison, Richard, 'The legal profession in colonial Victoria: information in records of admission held by Public Record Office Victoria', *Journal of Public Record Office Victoria*, no. 13, 2014.

Hay, Douglas and Paul Craven, eds, *Masters, Servants, and Magistrates in Britain and the Empire, 1562–1955*, Chapel Hill, N.C.: University of North Carolina Press, 2004.

Hayes, David, 'A history of Camden Town 1895–1914', <www.tate.org.uk/art/research-publications/camden-town-group/david-hayes-a-history-of-camden-town-1895-1914-r1104374>.

Henderson, Alexander, *Early Pioneer Families of Victoria and Riverina: A Genealogical and Biographical Record*, Melbourne: McCarron, Bird & Co., 1936.

Hobsbawm, Eric and George Rude, *Captain Swing*, London: Lawrence and Wishart, 1969.

Hogan, Daire, 'Arrows too sharply pointed: the relations of Lord Justice Christian and Lord O'Hagan, 1868–1874', in *The Common Law Tradition: Essays in Irish Legal History*, J. F. McEldowney and Paul O'Higgins, eds, Blackrock, Ireland: Irish Academic Press, 1990.

Holcombe, Lee, *Wives and Property: Reform of the Married Women's Property Law in Nineteenth-Century England*, Toronto: University of Toronto Press, 1983.

Holmes, Katie and Kylie Mirmohamadi, 'Howling wilderness and promised land: imagining the Victorian mallee, 1840–1914', *Australian Historical Studies*, vol. 46, vol. 2, 2015, 191–213.

Homer, Sydney and Richard Sylla, *A History of Interest Rates*, Hoboken, N.J.: Wiley, 2005.

Hope, Ronald, *A New History of British Shipping*, London: John Murray, 1990.

Hunt, Tom, *Sport and Society in Victorian Ireland: The Case of Westmeath*, Cork: Cork University Press, 2007.

Hunter, Sylvester Joseph, *Elementary View of the Proceeds in a Suit of Equity*, 4th edn, London: Butterworths, 1867.

Ignatief, Noel, *How the Irish became White*, New York: Routledge, 1995.

Ignatius, Sister M., *The Wheel of Time: A brief Survey of the Ninety-six Years' Work of the Sisters of Mercy in Victoria, 1857–1953*, Melbourne: For the Sisters of Mercy, 1954.

Jalland, Pat, *Australian Ways of Death: A Social and Cultural History, 1840–1918*, Melbourne: Oxford University Press, 2002.

——, *Death in the Victorian Family*, New York: Oxford University Press, 1996.

Jones, Alan, *Tatiara. The First 140 Years, 1845–1985*, Netley, S.A.: District Council of Tatiara, 1985.

Jones, Helen, *In Her Own Name: Women in South Australian History*, South Australia: Wakefield Press, 1986.

Jones, Mrs, *Broad Outlines of Long Years in Australia*, London: Samuel Tinsley & Co., 1878.

Kenyon, Alfred S., *The Story of the Mallee: A History of the Victorian Mallee Read Before the Historical Society of Australia, 18 March 1912*, Rainbow, Vic.: Brentwood Publications, 1982.

Kercher, Bruce, *An Unruly Child: A History of Law in Australia*, Sydney: Allen & Unwin, 1998.

Kiddle, Margaret, *Men of Yesterday: A Social History of Western Victoria*, Melbourne: Melbourne University Press, 1961.

Killeen, Richard, *Historical Atlas of Dublin*, Dublin: Gill & Macmillan, 2009.

Kirkby, Diane and Hilary Golder, 'Marriage and divorce law before the Family Law Act, 1975', in *Sex, Power and Justice: Historical Perspectives on Law in Australia*, Diane Kirkby, ed., Melbourne: Oxford University Press, 1995.

——, 'Mrs Mayne and her boxing kangaroo: a married woman tests her property rights in colonial New South Wales', *Law and History Review*, vol. 21, no. 3, 2003, 585–605.

Kozub, Robert M., 'Evolution of taxation in England, 1700–1850: a period of war and industrialization', *Journal of European Economic History*, vol. 32, 2003, 363–87.

Laidlaw, Zoe, *Colonial Connections, 1815–1845: Patronage, The Information Revolution, and Colonial Government*, Manchester: Manchester University Press, 2006.

Lake, Marilyn, 'Frontier feminism and the marauding white man: Australia, 1890s to 1940s', in *Nation, Empire, Colony: Historicizing Gender and Race*, R. Pierson, Nupur Chaudhuri and Beth McAuley, eds, Indiana: Indiana Press, 1998.

Lambert, David and Alan Lester, eds, *Colonial Lives across the British Empire: Imperial Careering in the Long Nineteenth Century*, Cambridge: Cambridge University Press, 2006.

Landt, T. M., *The Story of the Kaniva District, 1845–1961*, Melbourne: Brown, Prior, Anderson Pty Ltd, 1961.

Learmonth, Noel F., *The Portland Bay Settlement, 1800–1851*, Melbourne: McCarron, Bird & Co., 1983.

Lee, Robert, *Linking a Nation: Australia's Transport and Communications, 1788–1970*, Canberra: Australian Heritage Commission, 2003.

Levitan, Kathryn, 'Redundancy, the "surplus woman" problem and the British census, 1851–1861', *Women's History Review*, vol. 17, no. 3, 2008, 359–376.

Lindsey, Kiera, *The Convict's Daughter: The Scandal that Shocked a Colony*, Sydney: Allen & Unwin, 2016.

Loyau, George E., *Notable South Australians*, Adelaide: Carey, Page & Co., 1935.

McConville, Chris, 'The Victorian Irish: emigrants and families, 1851–91', in *Families in Colonial Australia,* Patricia Grimshaw, Chris McConville and Ellen McEwen, eds, Sydney: George Allen & Unwin, 1985.

Macdonald, Charlotte, 'Land, death and dower in the settler empire: the lost cause of "the widow's third" in nineteenth-century New Zealand', *Victoria University Law Review*, vol. 41, 2010, 493–518.

——, *A Woman of Good Character: Single Women as Immigrant Settlers in Nineteenth-Century New Zealand*, Wellington: Bridget Williams Books, 1990.

MacGillivray, Leith, 'Land and people: European land settlement in the South East of South Australia, 1840–1940', PhD thesis, University of Adelaide, 1982.

——, '"We have found our Paradise": the South-East squattocracy, 1840–1870', *Journal of the Historical Society of South Australia*, vol. 17, 1989, 25–38.

Mackinolty, John, 'The Married Women's Property Acts', in *In Pursuit of Justice: Australian Women and the Law, 1788–1979*, Judy Mackinolty and Heather Radi, eds, Sydney: Hale & Iremonger, 1979.

Malcolm, Elizabeth and Dianne Hall, *A New History of the Irish in Australia*, Cork: Cork University Press, 2019.

McAloon, Jim, *No Idle Rich: The Wealthy in Canterbury and Otago, 1840–1914*, Dunedin: University of Otago Press, 2002.

McCann, Colum, *Let the Great World Spin*, New York: Random House, 2009.

McGibbon, Ian, 'James Allen', NZD, <www.teara.govt.nz/en/biographies/3a12/allen-james>.

McGrath, Ann, 'Consent, marriage and colonialism: Indigenous Australian women and colonizer marriages', *Journal of Colonialism and Colonial History*, vol. 6, no. 3, 2005.

——, *Illicit Love: Interracial Sex and Marriage in the United States and Australia*, Lincoln: University of Nebraska Press, 2015.

McKenzie, Kirsten, *Imperial Underworld: An Escaped Convict and the Transformation of the British Colonial Order*, Cambridge: Cambridge University Press, 2016.

——, *A Swindler's Progress: Nobles and Convicts in the Age of Liberty*, Cambridge: Harvard University Press, 2009.

McLaren, John, A. R. Buck and Nancy E. Wright, eds, *Despotic Dominion: Property Rights in British Settler Societies*, Vancouver: UBC Press, 2005.

McPherson, Kathryn, 'Home tales: gender, domesticity, and colonialism in the Prairie West, 1870–1900', in *Finding a Way to the Heart: Feminist Writings on Aboriginal and Women's History in Canada*, Robin Jarvis Brownlie and Valerie J. Korinek, eds, Winnipeg, MB: University of Manitoba Press, 2012.

Miller, Kerby A., *Emigrants and Exiles: Ireland and the Irish Exodus to North America*, New York: Oxford University Press, 1985.

Miller, Robert, 'George Henry Frederick Webb (1828–1891)', *Australian Dictionary of Biography*, <adb.anu.edu.au/biography/webb-george-henry-frederick-4822>.

Moodie, William, *A Pioneer of Western Victoria*, Mortlake, Vic.: The Editor, 1973.

Moore, George C. G., 'A biographical sketch of William Edward Hearn (1826–1888): a slightly "Irish" perspective', University of Notre Dame, Australia, School of Business, Research Online, 3–4, <https://researchonline.nd.edu.au/cgi/viewcontent.cgi?referer=https://www.google.com/&httpsredir=1&article=1015&context=bus_conference>.

Morris, R. J., *Men, Women and Property in England, 1780–1870: A Social and Economic History of Family Strategies amongst the Leeds Middle Class*, Cambridge: Cambridge University Press, 2005.

Mulvaney, Derek John, *Cricket Walkabout: The Australian Aboriginal Cricketers on Tour, 1867–8*, London: Melbourne University Press, 1967.

Murdoch, Judith and Heather Parker, *History of Naracoorte*, Naracoorte: Naracoorte Herald, 1963.

La Nauze, J. A., 'William Edward Hearn (1826–1888)', *Australian Dictionary of Biography*, <adb.anu.edu.au/biography/hearn-william-edward-3743/text5893>.

Nettelbeck, Amanda, 'Seeing to spread the truth: Christina Smith and the South Australian frontier', *Australian Feminist Studies*, vol. 16, no. 34, 2001.

Nettelbeck, Amanda, Russell Smandych, Louis A. Knafla and Robert Foster, *Fragile Settlements: Aboriginal Peoples, Law, and Resistance in South-West Australia and Prairie Canada*, Vancouver: UBC Press, 2016.

Ó Cormac, Gráda, 'Primogeniture and ultimogeniture in rural Ireland', *Journal of Interdisciplinary History*, vol. 10, 1979.

O'Farrell, Patrick, *The Irish in Australia*, Sydney: UNSW Press, 1986.

O'Hara, John, *Big River Racing: A History of the Clarence River Jockey Club, 1861–2001*, Sydney: UNSW Press, 1982.

Ó Maitiú, Séamus, *Dublin's Suburban towns, 1834–1930: Governing Clontarf, Drumcondra, Dalkey, Killiney, Kilmainham, Pembroke, Kingstown, Blackrock, Rathmines, and Rathgar*, Dublin: Four Courts, 2003.

Ollerenshaw, Philip, *Banking in Nineteenth Century Ireland: The Belfast Banks, 1825–1914*, Manchester, UK: Manchester University Press, 1987.

Parkinson, Charles, *Sir William Stawell and the Victorian Constitution*, Melbourne: Australian Scholarly Publishing, 2004.

Perry, Adele, *Colonial Relations: The Douglas–Connolly Family and the Nineteenth-century Imperial World*, Cambridge: Cambridge University Press, 2015.

——, *On the Edge of Empire: Gender, Race, and the Making of British Columbia, 1849–1871*, Toronto: University of Toronto Press, 2000.

Peel, Mark and Christina Twomey, *A History of Australia*, New York: Palgrave, 2011.

Pike, Douglas, *Paradise of Dissent: South Australia, 1839–1857*, Melbourne: MUP, 1957.

Proudfoot, Lindsay J. and Dianne Hall, *Imperial Spaces: Placing the Irish and Scots in Colonial Australia*, Manchester: Manchester University Press, 2011.

Reeves, Keir, '15 July 1851. Hargreaves discovers gold at Ophir: Australia's "golden age"', in *Turning Points in Australian History*, Martin Crotty and David Andrew Roberts, eds, Sydney: UNSW Press, 2009.

Reid, John, Keith H. Lovett and Les J. Blake, *Road Board to Restructure: The History of the Shire of Wimmera, 1862–1995*, Victoria, Australia: Joval Publications, Shire of Wimmera, 1996.

Renwick, Samantha, '"Responsibility to provide": family provision claims in Victoria', *Deakin Law Review*, vol. 18, no. 1, 2013, 149–90.

Reynolds, Henry, ed., *Aborigines and Settlers: The Australian Experience, 1788–1939*, Melbourne: Cassell Australia, 1972.

Richey, Alexander G. and Edmund T. Bewley, *The Chancery (Ireland) Act, 1867: And the General Orders and Regulations Thereunder, Copiously Annotated, with an Introduction, Schedules of Fees, and a Collection of Forms and Precedents*, Dublin: E. Ponsonby, 1868.

Robe District Council, *Robe: A Glimpse of Golden Days*, Robe: District Council of Robe, 1985.

Rollings-Magnusson, Sandra, *Heavy Burdens on Small Shoulders: The Labour of Pioneer Children on the Canadian Prairies*, Edmonton: University of Alberta Press, 2009.

Rothschild, Emma, *The Inner Life of Empires: An Eighteenth-Century History*, Princeton, N.J.: Princeton University Press, 2001.

Russell, Lynette, 'Introduction', in *Colonial Frontiers: Indigenous–European Encounters in Settler Societies*, Lynette Russell, ed., Manchester: Manchester University Press, 2001.

Russell, Penny, *A Wish of Distinction: Colonial Femininity and Gentility*, Carlton, Vic.: University of Melbourne Press, 1994.

——, *Savage or Civilized? Manners in Colonial Australia*, Sydney: UNSW Press, 2010.

Ruth, William, *The Romance of a Selection: Victoria's Western Border Country, 1850–1950*, Essendon, Vic.: Jim Ruth, 2001.

Sendziuk, Paul, 'No convicts here: reconsidering South Australia's foundation myth', in *Turning Points: Chapters in South Australian History*, Robert Foster and Paul Sendziuk, eds, Adelaide: Wakefield Press, 2012.

Serviceton Centenary Committee, *Serviceton: A Frontier Town on No Man's Land, 1887–1987*, Serviceton, Vic.: The Committee, 1987.

Sheehan, Jeremiah, *South Westmeath: Farm and Folk*, Dublin: Blackwater, 1978.

Sholl, Reginald, 'Sir Robert Molesworth (1806–1890)', *Australian Dictionary of Biography*, <adb.anu.edu.au/biography/molesworth-sir-robert-4217>.

Sinha, Mrinalini, *Colonial Masculinity: The Manly Englishman and the Effeminate Bengali in the Late Nineteenth Century*, Manchester: Manchester University Press, 1995.

Smith, Simon, ed., *Judging for the People: A Social History of the Victorian Supreme Court 1841–2016*, Sydney: Allen & Unwin, 2016.

Smith, W. Stephen, *The History of Sheep Scab in South Australia*, Adelaide: The Author, 1975.

Smyth, William J, 'Nephews, dowries, sons and mothers: the geography of farm and marital transactions in eastern Ireland, c.1820 – c.1870', in *Migration,*

*Mobility and Modernization*, David J. Siddle, ed., Liverpool: Liverpool University Press, 2000.

Statton, Jill, ed., *Biographical Index of South Australians, 1836–1885*, Adelaide: South Australian Genealogy and Heraldry Society, 1986.

Steel, Frances, *Oceania under Steam: Sea Transport and the Cultures of Colonialism*, Manchester: Manchester University Press, 2011.

Steiner, Marie, *Servants Depots in Colonial South Australia*, Kent Town, S.A.: Wakefield Press, 2008.

Stephens, Julia, 'An uncertain inheritance: the imperial travels of legal migrants, from British India to Ottoman Iraq', *Law and History Review*, vol. 32, no. 4, 2014, 749–72.

Stiles, Julie A., 'Nineteenth-century custody reform: maternal authority and the definition of the best interest of the child standard', *Probate Law Journal*, vol. 6, no. 5, 1984.

Stoler, Laura Ann, *Carnal Knowledge and Imperial Power: Race and the Intimate in Colonial Rule*, Berkeley: University of California Press, 2002.

Strange, Julie-Marie, *Death, Grief and Poverty in Britain, 1870–1914*, New York: Cambridge University Press, 2005.

———, '"She cried a very little": death, grief and mourning in working-class culture, c.1880–1914', *Social History*, vol. 27, no. 2, 2002, 143–61.

Swensen, Stephen, 'Mapping Poverty in Agar Town: Economic Conditions Prior to the Development of St Pancras Station', <eprints.lse.ac.uk/22539/1/0906Swensen.pdf>.

Taplin, G., *The Folklore, Manners, Customs and Languages of the South Australian Aborigines: Gathered from Inquiries Made by Authority of South Australian Government*, Adelaide: Government Printer, 1879.

Tennant, Margaret, 'Elderly indigents and old men's homes, 1880–1920', *New Zealand Journal of History*, vol. 17, no. 1, 1983, 3–20.

Thorpe, Osmund, 'Mary Helen MacKillop', *Australian Dictionary of Biography*, <adb.anu.edu.au/biography/mackillop-mary-helen-4112>.

Treloar, Lucy, *Salt Creek*, Sydney: Picador, 2015.

Van Kirk, Silvia, *Many Tender Ties. Women in Fur-Trade Society, 1670–1870*, Winnipeg: Watson & Dwyer Pub., 1980.

Veracini, Lorenzo, *Settler Colonialism: A Theoretical Overview*, London: Palgrave Macmillan, 2010.

Wanhalla, Angela, *In/visible Sight: The Mixed-Descent Families of Southern New Zealand*, Wellington: Bridget Williams Books, 2009.

———, *Matters of the Heart: A History of Interracial Marriage in New Zealand*, Auckland: Auckland University Press, 2013.

Ward, Ebenezer, *The South-Eastern District of South Australia: Its Resources and Requirements*, Adelaide: The Author, 1869.

Watts, John, Glen Turnbull and Kathleen Walsh, *Mercy Girls: The Story of Sacred Heart College Geelong, 1860–2010*, Newtown, Vic.: Sacred Heart College Geelong, 2010.

Weaver, John C., *The Great Land Rush and the Making of the Modern World, 1650–1900*, Montreal: McGill–Queen's University Press, 2003.

———, 'A pathology of insolvents: Melbourne, 1871–1915', *Australian Journal of Legal History*, vol. 8, no. 1, 2004, 109–32.

Weindling, Dick and Marianne Colloms, 'The downfall of a Kilburn doctor', *West Hampstead Life*, 5 December 2016.

Withers, Glen, Anthony M. Endres and Len Perry, 'Labour', in *Australian Historical Statistics: Labour Statistics*, Fairfax, Syme & Weldon Associates, 1987.

Wolski, Nathan, 'All's not quiet on the western front – rethinking resistance and frontiers in Aboriginal historiography', in *Colonial Frontiers: Indigenous–European Encounters in Settler Societies*, Lynette Russell, ed., Manchester: Manchester University Press, 2001, 216–33.

Woollacott, Angela, *Settler Society in the Australian Colonies: Self-Government and Imperial Culture*, Oxford: Oxford University Press, 2015.

Wright, Nancy, 'Local policy and legal decisions about dower in colonial New South Wales', *ANZLH E-Journal*, 2005, 226–33.

Zeigler, Sara L., 'Wifely duties: marriage, labor, and the common law in nineteenth-century America', *Social Science History*, vol. 20, no. 1, 1996, 63–96.

# Notes

## Introduction

1    *Argus* (Melbourne), 13 September 1865, 4; Victoria Department of Planning and Community Development, 'Guide to Historic Shipwreck Trail on Victoria's West Coast', <www.pastmasters.net/uploads/2/6/7/5/26751978/shipwrecktrail__schomberg.pdf>, accessed 3 April 2019.

2    Public Record Office Victoria (henceforth PROV), VPRS 7591/P0001/23, 5/461, Will, Edward Kearney, 30 September 1865.

3    PROV, Will, Edward Kearney, 30 September 1865.

4    Bettina Bradbury, '"In England a man can do as he likes with his property": migration, family fortunes and the law in nineteenth-century Quebec and the Cape Colony', in *Within and Without the Nation: Canadian History as Transnational History*, Adele Perry, Karen Dubinsky and Henry Wu, eds, Toronto: UTP, 2015, 145–67; Diane Kirkby and Hilary Golder, 'Marriage and divorce law before the Family Law Act, 1975', in *Sex, Power and Justice: Historical Perspectives on Law in Australia*, Diane Kirby, ed., Melbourne: Oxford University Press, 1995; Diane Kirkby and Hilary Golder, 'Mrs Mayne and her boxing kangaroo: a married woman tests her property rights in colonial New South Wales', *Law and History Review*, vol. 21, no. 3, 2003; Lee Holcombe, *Wives and Property: Reform of the Married Women's Property Law in Nineteenth-Century England*, Toronto: UTP, 1983; Helen Jones, *In Her Own Name: Women in South Australian History*, South Australia: Wakefield Press, 1986; John Mackinolty, 'The Married Women's Property Acts', in *In Pursuit of Justice: Australian Women and the Law, 1788–1979*, eds Judy Mackinolty and Heather Radi, Sydney: Hale & Iremonger, 1979; Sara L. Zeigler, 'Wifely duties: marriage, labor, and the common law in nineteenth-century America', *Social Science History*, vol. 20, no. 1, 1996.

5    Rosalind Atherton, 'Expectation without right: testamentary freedom and the position of women in 19th-century New South Wales', *UNSW Law Journal*, vol. 11, 1988, 155.

6    Atherton, 1988; Bettina Bradbury, *Wife to Widow: Lives, Laws and Politics in 19th-Century Montreal*, Vancouver: University of British Columbia Press, 2011; Jim McAloon, *No Idle Rich: The Wealthy in Canterbury and Otago, 1840–1914*, Dunedin: University of Otago Press, 2002, 81–89; Lyndon Fraser, '"The ties that bind": Irish Catholic testamentary evidence from Christchurch, 1876–1915', *New Zealand Journal of History*, vol. 29,

no. 1, 1995; R. J. Morris, *Men, Women and Property in England, 1780–1870: A Social and Economic History of Family Strategies amongst the Leeds Middle Class*, Cambridge: Cambridge University Press, 2005; Paul De Serville, *Pounds and Pedigrees: The Upper Class in Victoria, 1850–1880*, Melbourne: OUP, 1991.

7    Colum McCann, *Let the Great World Spin*, New York: Random House, 2009, 325.

8    *Empire* (Sydney), 8 December 1868, 2; *Argus*, 2 December 1868, 6.

9    Rosalind McLeod, email to author, 11 July 2013.

10   Edward Kearney, Memorandum, c.1876, transcribed by Joe Palmer, held by family members.

11   Charles James Hamilton, *Pioneering Days in Western Victoria*, Melbourne: Exchange Press, 1913; Teresa Hamilton, *A Squatting Saga*, Sorrento, Vic.: Arden Press, 1991, draws on personal papers and station journals to chronicle the Hamilton family's story in detail.

12   Michael P. Flynn, *Genealogy of the Descendants of William Kearney and Mary Mulrain: Williamstown, Cornamaddy, Athlone*, Mullingar: 1997.

13   Cf Kiera Lindsey, *The Convict's Daughter: The Scandal that Shocked a Colony*, Sydney: Allen & Unwin, 2016.

14   Bettina Bradbury, *Working Families: Age, Gender and Daily Survival in Industrializing Montreal*, Toronto: UTP, 2007; Bradbury, 2015; Bradbury, 'Twists, turning points and tall shoulders: studying Canada and feminist family histories', *Canadian Historical Review*, vol. 96, no. 2, 2015, 257–85; Tanya Evans, *Fractured Families: Life on the Margins in Colonial New South Wales*, Sydney: NewSouth Publishing, 2015; Kirsten McKenzie, *A Swindler's Progress: Nobles and Convicts in the Age of Liberty*, Cambridge: Harvard University Press, 2009; Kirsten McKenzie, *Imperial Underworld: An Escaped Convict and the Transformation of the British Colonial Order*, Cambridge: Cambridge University Press, 2016; Julia Stephens, 'An uncertain inheritance: the imperial travels of legal migrants, from British India to Ottoman Iraq', *Law and History Review*, vol. 32, no. 4, 2014.

15   Lisa Chilton, *Agents of Empire: British Female Migration to Canada and Australia, 1860s–1930*, Toronto: UTP, 2007; David Fitzpatrick, *Oceans of Consolation: Personal Accounts of Irish Migration to Australia*, Ithica: New York, 1994; Jan Gothard, *Blue China: Single Female Migration to Colonial Australia*, Melbourne: MUP, 2001; James Hammerton, 'Gender and migration', in *Gender and Empire*, Philippa Levine, ed., Oxford: OUP, 2004; Charlotte Macdonald, *A Woman of Good Character: Single Women as Immigrant Settlers in Nineteenth-Century New Zealand*, Wellington: Bridget Williams Books, 1990.

16   Julie Evans, Pat Grimshaw, D. Philips and Shirley Swain, *Equal Subjects, Unequal Rights: Indigenous Peoples in British Settler Colonies, 1830–1910*, Manchester: MUP, 2003; Lorenzo Veracini, *Settler Colonialism: A Theoretical Overview*, London: Palgrave Macmillan, 2010; Angela Woollacott, *Settler Society in the Australian Colonies: Self-Government and Imperial Culture*, Oxford: OUP, 2015.

17   Ruth Compton Brouwer, *New Women for God: Canadian Presbyterian Women and India Missions, 1876–1914*, Toronto: UTP, 1990; Brouwer, *Modern Women Modernizing Men: The Changing Missions of Three Professional Women in Asia and Africa, 1902–69*, Vancouver: UBC Press, 2002; Tony Ballantyne and Antoinette Burton, eds, *Moving Subjects. Gender, Mobility and Intimacy in an Age of Global Empire*, Urbana and Chicago: University of Illinois Press, 2009; Patricia Grimshaw, *Paths of Duty: American Missionary Wives in Nineteenth-century Hawaii*, Honolulu: University of Hawaii Press, 1989; Jane Haggis, 'White women and colonialism: towards a non-recuperative history', in *Gender and Imperialism*, Clare Midgley, ed., Manchester: MUP, 1998; Marilyn Lake, 'Frontier feminism and the marauding white man', *Journal of Australian Studies*, vol. 20, no. 49, 1996, 12–20; Philippa Levine, ed., *Gender and Empire*, Oxford: OUP, 2004; Adele Perry, *On the Edge of Empire: Gender, Race, and the Making of British Columbia, 1849–1871*, Toronto: UTP, 2000; Laura Ann Stoler, *Carnal Knowledge and Imperial Power: Race and the Intimate in Colonial Rule*, Berkeley: University of California Press, 2002; Angela Wanhalla, *Matters of the Heart: A History of Interracial Marriage in New Zealand*, Auckland: Auckland University Press, 2013, 45–75.

18   Elizabeth Buettner, *Empire Families: Britons and Late Imperial India*, Oxford: OUP, 2004; Sarah Carter, *The Importance of Being Monogamous: Marriage and Nation Building in Western Canada*, Edmonton: Athabasca University Press, 2008; Esme Cleall, Laura Ishiguro and Emily J. Manktelow, Special Issue, Imperial Relations: Histories of Family in the British Empire, *Journal of Colonialism and Colonial History*, online, vol. 14, no. 1, 2013; Jane Beer, Charles Fahey, Patricia Grimshaw and Melanie Raymond, *Colonial Frontiers and Family Fortunes*, Melbourne: MUP, 1989; Adele Perry, *Colonial Relations: The Douglas–Connolly Family and the Nineteenth-century Imperial World*, Cambridge: Cambridge University Press, 2015; Emma Rothschild, *The Inner Life of Empires: An Eighteenth-Century History*, Princeton, NJ: Princeton University Press, 2001.

19   Gérard Bouchard, *Quelques arpents d'Amérique: population, économie, famille au Saguenay, 1838–1971*, Montréal: Boréal, 1996; Bradbury, 2015; Morris, 2005; McAloon, 2002; Stephanie Wyse, 'Gender, Wealth and Margins of Empire: Women's economic opportunity in New Zealand cities, c.1890–1950', PhD thesis, King's College, University of London, 2008.

20   Lauren Benton, *Law and Colonial Cultures: Legal Regimes in World History, 1400–1900*, Cambridge: Cambridge University Press, 2002; A. R. Buck, John McLaren, and Nancy E. White, eds, *Land and Freedom: Law, Property Rights and the British Diaspora*, Aldershot, UK: Ashgate, 2001; Hamar Foster, Benjamin L. Berger and A. R. Buck, eds, *The Grand Experiment: Law and Legal Culture in British Settler Societies*, Vancouver: Osgoode Society for Canadian Legal History and UBC Press, 2008; Douglas Hay and Paul Craven, eds, *Masters, Servants, and Magistrates in*

*Britain and the Empire, 1562–1955*, Chapel Hill, NC: University of North Carolina Press, 2004; John McLaren, A. R. Buck and Nancy E. Wright, eds, *Despotic Dominion: Property Rights in British Settler Societies*, Vancouver: UBC Press, 2005.

21   Zoe Laidlaw, *Colonial Connections, 1815–1845: Patronage, the Information Revolution, and Colonial Government*, Manchester: MUP, 2006; David Lambert and Alan Lester, eds, *Colonial Lives across the British Empire: Imperial Careering in the Long Nineteenth Century*, Cambridge: Cambridge University Press, 2006.

22   Catherine Hall, *Civilizing Subjects: Metropole and Colony in the English Imagination, 1830–1867*, Chicago: University of Chicago Press, 2002, 17.

23   Hammerton, 2004, 161; Noel Ignatief, *How the Irish became White*, New York: Routledge, 1995; Lindsay J. Proudfoot and Dianne Hall, *Imperial Spaces: Placing the Irish and Scots in Colonial Australia*, Manchester: MUP, 2011; Patrick O'Farrell, *The Irish in Australia*, Kensington, NSW: NSW University Press, 1986.

24   Jane Beer, Charles Fahey, Patricia Grimshaw and Melanie Raymond, *Colonial Frontiers and Family Fortunes*, Melbourne: MUP, 1989; Leonore Davidoff and Catherine Hall, *Family Fortunes: Men and Women of the English Middle Class, 1780–1850*, London: Routledge, 2002.

25   Laidlaw, 2006; Lambert and Lester, eds, 2006; Patricia Grimshaw and Andrew May, *Missionaries, Indigenous Peoples and Cultural Exchange*, Eastbourne, Brighton: Sussex Academic Press, 2010; Ann McGrath, *Illicit Love: Interracial Sex and Marriage in the United States and Australia*, Lincoln: University of Nebraska Press, 2015; Ann McGrath, 'Consent, marriage and colonialism: Indigenous Australian women and colonizer marriages', *Journal of Colonialism and Colonial History*, vol. 6, no. 3, 2005; Perry, 2000; Stoler, 2002.

**1   Migrations and marriage**

1    SANSW, Assisted immigrant passenger lists, Reel 2136, 4/4790, 106; Passenger lists, Reel 2462, 4/4920; Chilton, *Agents of Empire: British Female Migration to Canada and Australia, 1860s–1930*, Toronto: University of Toronto Press, c.2007; Jan Gothard, *Blue China: Single Female Migration to Colonial Australia*, Melbourne: MUP, 2001; A. James Hammerton, *Emigrant Gentlewomen: Genteel Poverty and Female Emigration, 1830–1914*, London: Croom Helm, 1979; James Hammerton, 'Gender and migration', in *Gender and Empire*, Philippa Levine, ed., Oxford: OUP, 2004, 157; Charlotte Macdonald, *A Woman of Good Character: Single Women as Immigrant Settlers in Nineteenth-Century New Zealand*, Wellington: Bridget Williams Books, 1990.

2    'Post Office Directory, 1851, Cuckfield, West Surrey', <www.sussex-opc. org/PostOffice1851/CuckfieldPostOffice1851.htm>, accessed 8 March 2018.

3    Eric Hobsbawm and George Rude, *Captain Swing*, London: Lawrence and Wishart, 1969, 15, 34–35.

4   *London, England, Marriages and Banns, 1754–1921*, Ancestry.com, accessed 4 March 2019, citing Church of England Parish Registers, 1754–1921, London Metropolitan Archives; William Bax household, 1851 Census, England, Ancestry.com, accessed 29 March 2019; Teresa Hamilton, *A Squatting Saga*, Sorrento, Vic.: Arden Press, 1991, 20.

5   National Archives, Kew, UK, Excise Entry Papers, CUST 116/3/93, William Bax, 17 December 1825, 17 April 1826; NA, UK, Excise Board and Secretariat, Minute Books, CUST 47/683, 239, 262; 'Records of the Boards of Customs, Excise, and Customs and Excise, and HM Revenue and Customs', <www.rootschat.com/forum/index.php?topic=479375.0>, accessed 29 March 2019; William J. Ashworth, *Customs and Excise: Trade, Production and Consumption in England, 1640–1845*, Oxford: OUP, 2003, 118–23.

6   NA, UK, 'Excise Board and Secretariat: Minute Books', CUST 47/663/, 9 May 1851, 239.

7   Immigration historians suggest fearing loss of status was a more powerful reason to emigrate than poverty: see Robin F. Haines, *Emigration and the Labouring Poor*, New York: St Martin's Press, 1997, 22.

8   Robert M. Kozub, 'Evolution of taxation in England, 1700–1850: a period of war and industrialization', *Journal of European Economic History*, vol. 32, 2003, 363–87; NA, UK, 'Excise Board and Secretariat: Minute Books', CUST 47/663/, Wednesday 4 June 1851, 262.

9   Bettina Bradbury, *Working Families: Age, Gender and Daily Survival in Working Class Montreal*, Toronto: McClelland & Stewart, 1993; Michael Anderson, *Family Structure in Nineteenth-Century Lancashire*, Cambridge, Eng.: University Press, 1971.

10  Kathryn Levitan, 'Redundancy, the "surplus woman" problem and the British Census, 1851–1861', *Women's History Review*, vol. 17, no. 3, 2008; Macdonald, 1990; Gothard, 2001.

11  Robin Haines, 'Indigent misfits or shrewd operators? Government assisted emigrants from the United Kingdom to Australia, 1831–1860', *Population Studies*, vol. 48, 1994, 223–47.

12  *Otago Witness* (New Zealand), 7 November 1895, 51; *Clutha Leader* (Otago, New Zealand), 4 October 1895, 6.

13  Robin Haines, 1994, quote at 227. He estimates that 0.4% of assisted emigrants to New South Wales were professionals, and 0.3% in commercial occupations. Other estimates suggest a maximum of 2% fell into 'the Tertiary class', which would have included William Bax.

14  '1851 Britain: The Rail Network', <www.geog.cam.ac.uk/research/projects/occupations/britain19c/railways/railmap1-small.png>; <en.wikipedia.org/wiki/Great_Western_Railway>; <en.wikipedia.org/wiki/London,_Brighton_and_South_Coast_Railway>; <en.wikipedia.org/wiki/South_Devon_Railway_Company>; <www.britishempire.co.uk/article/plymouth/emigrationdepot.htm>; excerpt from *Sydney Mail*, 17 January 1885, <www.historic-shipping.co.uk/Emigration/buildings.html>, all accessed 3 April 2019; *Woolmer's Exeter and Plymouth Gazette*, 14 June 1851, 1.

15  SANSW, 'Passenger List, Earl Grey', October 1851, <indexes.records.nsw.
    gov.au/ebook/list.aspx?series=NRS5316&item=4_4790&ship=Earl Grey>,
    accessed 3 June 2019; SANSW, Assisted immigrant passenger lists, Reel
    2136, 4/4790, 106; Passenger lists, Reel 2462, 4/4920; David Fitzpatrick,
    *Oceans of Consolation: Personal Accounts of Irish Migration to Australia*,
    Ithica: New York, 1994, 57.
16  *Sydney Morning Herald*, 18 October 1851, 3; Andrew Cliff and Peter
    Hagget, 'Time, travel and infection', *British Medical Bulletin*, vol. 69,
    no. 1, 2004, 87–89; Ronald Hope, *A New History of British Shipping*,
    London: John Murray, 1990, 293.
17  Gothard, 2001, 129.
18  *Sydney Morning Herald*, 18 October 1851, 3.
19  Fitzpatrick, 1994, 51–52; Gothard, 2001, 3; Joy Damousi, 'Chaos and
    order: gender, space and sexuality on female convict ships', *Australian
    Historical Studies*, vol. 26, no. 104, 1995, 351–72.
20  SANSW, Passenger lists, Reel 2462, 4/4920.
21  'The gold fever in Australia', *Times* (London), 2 September 1851, 4, 5,
    'Times Digital Archive', accessed 18 August 2015; Keir Reeves, '15 July
    1851. Hargreaves discovers gold at Ophir: Australia's "golden age"', in
    *Turning Points in Australian History*, eds Martin Crotty and David Andrew
    Roberts, Sydney: UNSW Press, 2009.
22  William Adams Brodbribb, *Recollections of an Australian Squatter,
    1835–1883*, Sydney: John Woods & Co., 1883, republished Sydney: John
    Ferguson, 1978, 75; *Sydney Morning Herald*, 18 October 1851, 3.
23  *Sydney Morning Herald*, 24 October 1851, 3.
24  1851 is one of the few years for which records describing the placement
    of immigrants have not survived. The *Sydney Morning Herald*, 5 January
    1852, 2, and numerous other local papers list Mr and Mrs Bax, four Misses
    Bax, and a Master Bax.
25  *Colonial Times* (Hobart), 20 January 1852, 2.
26  Noel F. Learmonth, *The Portland Bay Settlement, 1800–1851*, Melbourne:
    McCarron, Bird and Co., 1983, 123–24; Charles James Hamilton,
    *Pioneering Days in Western Victoria*, Melbourne: Exchange Press, 1913,
    41–43.
27  Victoria, BDM, marriage, James Allen and Esther Bax, 3 May 1854,
    Portland, Victoria. Robert Steele witnessed the marriage.
28  *Adelaide Observer*, 25 September 1852, 5.
29  Jill Statton, ed., *Biographical Index of South Australians, 1836–1885*,
    Adelaide: South Australian Genealogy and Heraldry Society, 1986; James
    Allen and Charles Allen, Norwood, South Australia, birth registrations,
    <genealogysa.org.au/resources/online-databases.html>, accessed 12 January
    2017.
30  *Robe: A Glimpse of Golden Days*, Robe: District Council of Robe, 1985,
    18; Liz Harfull, *Almost an Island: The Story of Robe*, South Australia:
    Wakefield Press, 2013, 16.

31  Harfull, 2013, 15; SRSA, GRG24/6/1852/2765, Colonial Secretary's Office, Return of Robe Resident re supplies etc., 16 September 1852; Kathleen Bermingham, *Gateway to the South East: A Story of Robetown and the Guichen Bay District*, Millicent, SA: South Eastern Times Ltd, 1961, 50.
32  Leith MacGillivray, '"We have found our Paradise": the south-east squattocracy, 1840–1870', *Journal of the Historical Society of South Australia*, 17, 1989, 25–38, <www.sahistorians.org.au/175/documents/author/MacGillivray/we-have-found-our-paradise-the-south-east-squattoc.shtml>, accessed 1 April 2019; Bermingham, 1961, 113; Harfull, 2013.
33  Harfull, 2013, 66; District Council of Robe, 1985, 18.
34  South Australian Teachers, 1851–1962, <legacy.library.unisa.edu.au/condon/teachers/Teachers.asp?TeacherID=259>, accessed 3 August 2019.
35  Bermingham, 1961, 115, 140; she also reports that the first full-time customs officer, Mr Henry Dudley Melville, served from 1855 to 1869; earlier Robe had a sub-customs officer: Hamilton, 1991, 18.
36  Harfull, 2013, 66; Bermingham, 1961, 55, 213; SRSA, MRG18/4/0000/01, Assessment Books, District Council of Robe, 1870, show it was valued that year at £100; South Australia Register Research Programme 1981/82, Robe Interpretation Study, Register Research Programme 1981/82, 'Senior Historical Architect to South Australian Heritage Committee, 20 May 1982, re Bermingham Cottage', Item ref. no. 6823-10304, <data.environment.sa.gov.au/Content/heritage-surveys/3-Robe-Interpretation-Study-1983.pdf>, accessed 12 June 2019; *South Australian Advertiser*, 10 January 1860, 3. Known now as Bermingham Cottage, after a later owner, this building on Victoria Street has been renovated, recognised as one of the town's historic treasures, and listed on the South Australia Heritage Places database, ID# 16443, 28 Victoria Street, Robe. The allotments were sold by auction in December 1858. Bax first appears on Robe tax lists in 1870, but I believe he was its first occupant.
37  'South Australian Teachers, 1851–1962'; Bermingham, 1961, 85, 115, 213–14; *South Australian Register*, 4 January 1859, 3; SRSA, PRG497, series 6, Roland Campbell, 'Short history of Robe', 29.
38  Edward Kearney, Memorandum, 1, c.1876, transcribed by Joe Palmer, held by family members.
39  Alan Jones, *Tatiara, The First 140 Years, 1845–1985*, Netley, South Australia: District Council of Tatiara, 1985, 6; John C. Weaver, *The Great Land Rush and the Making of the Modern World, 1650–1900*, Montreal: McGill–Queen's University Press, 2003, 76 notes that in Australia squatters were exceptional in successfully promoting legislation giving them leases to land so that the 'squatter' label became respectable. Elsewhere a squatter was 'someone who violates formal rules to occupy land in order to originate an interest'.
40  SRSA, Map of Pastoral Lease Districts of South Australia, c.1861/Compiled from official surveys in the office of the Surveyor-General', W. G. Harris, London, Holburn Hill and Crystal Palace: R. K. Burt, 1862, <www.southernflinders-midnorth.com.au/maps/map_pastoralleases1861-65main.

htm>, accessed 1 April 2019; Rodney Cockburn, *Pastoral Pioneers of South Australia*, 2 vols, Blackwood, S.A.: Lynton Publications, 1974, I, 167 and II, 20; Judith Murdoch and Heather Parker, *History of Naracoorte*, Naracoorte: Naracoorte Herald, 1963, b14; Hamilton, 1913, 34; District Council of Robe, 1985, 26.

41 Ebenezer Ward, *The South-Eastern District of South Australia: Its Resources and Requirements*, Adelaide: The author, 1869, 23; 'SS *Ant*', <vhd.heritage.vic.gov.au/shipwrecks/heritage/33>, accessed 28 March 2019.

42 Harfull, 2013, 36.

43 Harfull, 2013, 36; Ward, 1869, 23; Murdoch and Parker, 1963, 47.

44 Hamilton, 1913, 34; Cockburn, 1974, I, 167.

45 Hamilton, 1913, 34–35. James Hamilton knew Roland Campion well enough to recall a conversation they had years earlier when he wrote his memoir; as noted, James Allen's run, Swede's Flat, was close to Campion's; SRSA, Map, Pastoral Leases in South-East, SA, c.1861.

46 Mrs Jones, *Broad Outlines of Long Years in Australia*, London: Samuel Tinslay & Co., 1878, 64–67 describes the welcome the Ormerods gave her and her husband in late 1857 or early 1858; Bermingham, 1961, 124–25; Marie Steiner, *Servants Depots in Colonial South Australia*, Kent Town, SA: Wakefield Press, 2008; SLSA, PRG497, series 6, Roland Campbell, 'Short history of Robe', 1855, 24–25.

47 South Australia, Census, 1855, County of Robe, <hccda.ada.edu.au/pages/SA-1855-census-01_1>, accessed 22 June 2019.

48 Jones, 1878, 24. Hamilton, 1913, 99, mentions that he was at Bendigo in 1854 at the diggings.

49 Fitzpatrick, 1994, 7.

50 Rosalind McLeod, History of the Families of Walter Gerard and Anna Violet Kearney, unpublished manuscript, held by family members, 7; Victoria, Death Register, 20 October 1865.

51 Kerby A. Miller, *Emigrants and Exiles: Ireland and the Irish Exodus to North America*, New York: OUP, 1985, 48; Proinnsias Breathnach, 'The diffusion of the co-operative creamery system in Ireland, 1889–1920: a spatial analysis', PhD thesis, Department of Geography, National University of Ireland, Maynooth, 2006.

52 Thanks to Proinnsias Breathnach, Maynooth, for his help identifying and mapping the Kearney properties. References to Kearney landholding are based on his analysis of the 1837 Ordinance Survey and the 1854 Griffith's Valuation of Athlone, mapped onto more recent maps.

53 William J. Smyth, 'Nephews, dowries, sons and mothers: the geography of farm and marital transactions in eastern Ireland, c.1820 – c.1870', in *Migration, Mobility and Modernization*, David J. Siddle, ed., Liverpool: Liverpool University Press, 2000, 19.

54 Michael P. Flynn, *Genealogy of the Descendants of William Kearney and Mary Mulrain: Williamstown, Cornamaddy, Athlone*, Mullingar: Michael P. Flynn, 1997; tombstone, Joseph, Francis and William Kearney, Cormagh Cemetery, County Westmeath; tombstone, William Kearney and Mary

Mulrain, Athlone Abbey, County Westmeath; Baptism, Edward Carny (sic), 25 Jun 1820, St Mary's Parish Church, Athlone, <registers.nli.ie/registers/vtls000632455#page/61/mode/1up>, accessed 1 April 2019.

55  The 1857 valuation of land and property holdings across Ireland undertaken by Griffith shows that William Kearney (probably the son) was the lessee (from Lord Castlemaine) of two parcels of land in Ballykeeran, one of 38 acres and the other of 17 acres which included a house and offices. The latter encompasses the Williamstown farmstead (parcel 23B), which is separated from the former, which is further to the ENE (parcel 23A). William Kearney also held 42 acres from Lord Castlemaine in the small townland of Clonagh immediately to the north of Williamstown and 38 acres (including a herdsman's house, again from Lord Castlemaine) in the townland of Garrynafela immediately to the west of Clonagh: <www.askaboutireland.ie/griffith-valuation>, accessed 1 April 2019.

56  Cormac Ó Gráda, 'Primogeniture and ultimogeniture in rural Ireland', *Journal of Interdisciplinary History*, vol. 10, no. 3, 1980, 494.

57  Flynn, 1997; Smyth, 2002, 19; Marriage William Kearney and Mary Malia, Ballymore, Westmeath, 30 October 1844, Ancestry.com, accessed 1 April 2019.

58  Victoria, Death Register, 20 October; *Irish Times*, 9 May 1871 states on p. 5 that he was believed to have emigrated in 1843.

59  National Archives of Ireland, CS/PS/1, Courts of Petty Sessions, Court Registers, County Westmeath, 14 November 1854; 22 December 1859; 20 July 1869; 7 and 14 September 1869.

60  Miller, 1985, 132–33; Ó Gráda, 1980, 491–97; Fitzpatrick, 1994; Chris McConville, 'The Victorian Irish: emigrants and families, 1851–91', in Patricia Grimshaw, Chris McConville and Ellen McEwen, eds, *Families in Colonial Australia*, Sydney: George Allen & Unwin, 1985, 2.

61  Fitzpatrick, 1994, 9.

62  Victoria, Death Register, 20 October 1865; *Irish Times*, 9 May 1871, 5; Passenger List, *Haidee*, Ancestry.com, accessed 1 April 2019; *Courier*, 2 September 1842, 2; *Sydney Gazette and New South Wales Advertiser*, 13 September 1842, 2; *Courier*, 8 January 1858, 2.

63  Jones, 1878, 7–8.

64  Jones, 1878, 8–9; evidence of Edward being on the lease appears in SRSA, GRG35 4/00004/3, Letters received – Commissioner of Crown Lands, R. Campion, Mosquito Plains to C. Bonney, Esq. Commissioner of Crown Lands, 31 August 1853; GRG35 4/00004/4, Letters received – Commissioner of Crown Lands, 1855–56, Edward Kearney to C. Bonney, Esq. from Broom Station, Mosquito Plains, 15 October 1855, no. 201–1855; Hamilton, 1913, 52–53.

65  Paul Sendziuk, 'No convicts here: reconsidering South Australia's foundation myth', in *Turning Points: Chapters in South Australian History*, Robert Foster and Paul Sendziuk, eds, Adelaide: Wakefield Press, 2012, 33–47; Hammerton, 2004.

66  MacGillivray, 1989, 25–38.

67    South Australia, 9 & 10 Vic, 1851; MacGillivray, 1989, 11; Douglas Pike, *Paradise of Dissent: South Australia, 1839–1857*, Melbourne: MUP, 1957, 305–309.

68    SRSA, GRG24/6/1851/2844, cited in Leith MacGillivray, 'Land and People: European Land Settlement in the South East of South Australia, 1840–1940', PhD thesis, University of Adelaide, 1982, 470; SRSA, GRG35 518/0000/1, Schedule of 14-year depasturing leases – Surveyor-General's Office, nos 1–486. Campion's run is listed as 36 square miles in the former and 33 in the latter sources.

69    SRSA, Schedule of 14-year leases, nos 1–486; SRSA, Map, Pastoral Leases in South-East, SA, c.1861.

70    'Map of Pastoral Lease Districts of South Australia/Compiled from official surveys in the office of the Surveyor-General, c.1861', W.G. Harris, London, Holburn Hill and Crystal Palace: R. K. Burt, 1862, <www.southernflinders-midnorth.com.au/maps/map_pastoralleases1861-65main.htm>, accessed 1 April 2019; SRSA, Schedule of 14-year leases, nos 1–486, 1851.

71    SRSA, Schedule of 14-year leases, nos 1–486, 156; Hamilton, 1913, 34. In 1855 Edward claimed he had been working the land for four years: SRSA, GRG35 4/00004/3, Letters received – Commissioner of Crown Lands, R. Campion, Mosquito Plains to C. Bonney, Esq. Commissioner of Crown Lands, 31 August 1853; GRG35 4/00004/4, Letters received – Commissioner of Crown Lands, 1855–56, Edward Kearney to C. Bonney, Esq. from Broom Station, Mosquito Plains, 15 October 1855, no. 201–1855; GRS 3519/1/1, Registers of Pastoral Leases, 1851–1939; MacGillivray, 1982, 470.

72    Harfull, 2013, 65; Cockburn, 1974, II, 20; District Council of Robe, 1985, 26–27; Hamilton, 1913, 34.

73    O'Farrell, 1986, 152; *Clarence and Richmond Examiner*, 25 May 1915, 8; Kearney, Memorandum, 1.

74    Helen Jones, *In Her Own Name: Women in South Australian History*, South Australia: Wakefield Press, 1986, 6–7; Fitzpatrick, 1994, 590; *Freeman's Journal* (Ireland), 9 May 1871, 6.

75    Margaret Kiddle, *Men of Yesterday: A Social History of Western Victoria*, Melbourne: Melbourne University Press, 1961, 111.

76    Bermingham, 1961, reports that the first church, a Free Presbyterian chapel, was completed in December 1858, 204; SRSA, PRG497 series 5–6, Roland Campbell, 'Short History of Robe', 21.

77    *Saunders's News-Letter*, 5 June 1871, 1; *Freeman's Journal*, 5 June 1871, 4; *Freeman's Journal*, 9 May 1871, 6; *Irish Times*, 9 May 1871, 5.

78    South Australia, Marriage Act, 12, 5 Vic, 1842, X, 4.

79    Smyth, 2000, 31. Had there been a marriage settlement, it should have been acknowledged in Edward's will.

80    South Australia, Census, 1855, County of Robe, <hccda.anu.edu.au/regions/SA>, accessed 1 April 2019, lists 221 single men and 114 single women among the 532 non-Aboriginal residents of the county.

81  Bettina Bradbury, 'Colonial comparisons: rethinking marriage, civilization and nation in 19th-century white-settler societies', in *Rediscovering the British World*, Phillip Buckner and G. Frances, eds, Calgary: University of Calgary Press, 2005, 135–58, 137; Lee Holcombe, *Wives and Property: Reform of the Married Women's Property Law in Nineteenth-Century England*, Toronto: UTP, 1983, 19; Jones, 1986, 2; John Mackinolty, 'The Married Women's Property Acts', in *In Pursuit of Justice: Australian Women and the Law, 1788–1979*, Judy Mackinolty and Heather Radi, eds, Sydney: Hale & Iremonger, 1979; Diane Kirkby and Hilary Golder, 'Marriage and divorce law before the Family Law Act, 1975', in *Sex, Power and Justice: Historical Perspectives on Law in Australia*, Diane Kirkby, ed., Melbourne: Oxford University Press, 1995; Diane Kirkby and Hilary Golder, 'Mrs Mayne and her boxing kangaroo: a married woman tests her property rights in colonial New South Wales', *Law and History Review*, vol. 21, no. 3, 2003; Sara L Zeigler, 'Wifely duties: marriage, labor, and the common law in nineteenth-century America', *Social Science History* vol. 20, no. 1, 1996.

**2  Broom Station, Mosquito Plains, South Australia, 1853–57**

1  *Saunders's News-Letter*, 9 May 1871, 1; Mrs Jones, *Broad Outlines of Long Years in Australia*, London: Samuel Tinslay & Co., 1878, 20 reports these as some of the questions she asked her future husband, Henry Jones.
2  *Otago Witness* (New Zealand), 7 November 1895, 51; Robert Fisher, Rick Hosking and Amanda Nettelbeck, *Fatal Collisions: The South Australian Frontier and the Violence of Memory*, Kent Town, SA: Wakefield Press, 2001, 7; Angela Woollacott, *Settler Society in the Australian Colonies: Self-Government and Imperial Culture*, Oxford: OUP, 2015, 9.
3  Peter Bell and Susan Marsden, 'Kingston SE – An Overview History', <www.sahistorians.org.au/175/documents/kingston-se-an-overview-history. shtml>, accessed 1 April 2019; MacGillivray, 1982, 220.
4  Jones, 1878, 79; Edward Kearney, Memorandum, 1, c.1876, transcribed by Joe Palmer, held by family members.
5  Pastoral Lease Map, c.1861.
6  Ebenezer Ward, *The South-Eastern District of South Australia: Its Resources and Requirements*, Adelaide: The author, 1869; MacGillivray, 1982, 79.
7  Pastoral Lease Map, c.1861; D Graves estimates that bullocks could pull carts at between 1.5 and 2 mph, <www.napoleon-series.org/cgi-bin/forum/ archive2009_config.pl?md=read;id=105473>, accessed 30 March 2018.
8  Jones, 1878, 68, 86.
9  Pastoral Lease Map, c.1861.
10  Ward, 1869, 6–7, 30–31; Lucy Treloar paints a grim picture of pioneer life north up the Coorong coast in her novel *Salt Creek*, Sydney: Picador, 2015.
11  See 'Australian Institute of Aboriginal and Torres Islander Studies Map of Indigenous Australia', David R. Horton, Aboriginal Studies Press, AIATSIS, <aiatsis.gov.au/explore/articles/aboriginal-australia-map>,

accessed 1 April 2019; Tindale names them Tanganekald peoples and offers more precision than seems likely about their location, given seasonal movement. He reports that they occupied the 'narrow coastal strip along Coorong from Middleton south to Twelve Mile Point (north of Kingston); inland only to about inner margin of first inland swamp and dune terrace, the Woakwine or 25 foot (7.5 m) terrace, usually no more than 5 to 10 miles (8 to 16 km)': 'Tindale's Catalogue of Australian Aboriginal Tribes', <archives.samuseum.sa.gov.au/tindaletribes/>, accessed 1 April 2019; Ward, 1869, 30.

12 Compare the areas identified on the 'AIATSIS Map' and 'Tindale's Catalogue'; Philip A. Clark, 'The Aboriginal ethnobotany of the South-East of South Australia region, part 1: seasonal life and material culture', *Transactions of the Royal Society of South Australia*, vol. 139, no. 2, 2015, 3, 5.

13 *Portland Guardian and Normanby General Advertiser* (Vic.), 4 December 1854, 3; Fisher et. al, 2001, 76.

14 Cockburn, *Pastoral Pioneers of South Australia*, I, Blackwood, S.A.: Lynton Publications, 1974, 117.

15 SRSA, GRG/24/6/1852/1430, Robert Lyon Milne, Border Inn, Mosquito Plains, Tatiara, to Colonial Secretary, 16 March 1852; *Adelaide Observer*, 25 May 1852, 7.

16 Fisher, Hosking and Nettelbeck, 2001, 76; Robert Foster and Amanda Nettelbeck, *Out of the Silence: The History and Memory of South Australia's Frontier Wars*, Adelaide: Wakefield Press, 2011; Robert Foster and Paul Sendziuk, eds, *Turning Points: Chapters in South Australian History*, Adelaide: Wakefield Press, 2012.

17 Jones, 1878, 86, 89.

18 Ward, 1869, 31–32.

19 Charles James Hamilton, *Pioneering Days in Western Victoria*, Melbourne: Exchange Press, 1913, 40, 41; Judith Murdoch and Heather Parker, *History of Naracoorte*, Naracoorte: Naracoorte Herald, 1963, 14–15; Pauline Henderson, 'The spatial evolution of Naracoorte', unpublished course paper, University of Adelaide, 1978, available at Naracoorte Library, South Australia, 8; Jones, 1878, 94.

20 Ward, 1869, 32; Cockburn, 1974, I, 116; Hamilton, 1913, 34.

21 MacGillivray, 1982, 113. The eastern border of lease 156 fell roughly along what is now the Riddoh Highway, just to the north of Padthaway; the western side was very irregular, as the map shows. A road named 'Edwards Road' now runs from the highway cutting north–south through the old lease area. Much of this block is planted with grape vines or grains, but on the western side of the highway, sheep still graze: SRSA, Fourteen Year Leases, no. 156.

22 *Naracoorte Herald*, 15 July 1931, 2; Cockburn, 1974, I, 116; MacGillivray, 1982, 465; Eliza born 1850; Janet born 1852; Mary born April 1854.

23 *Naracoorte Herald*, 15 July 1931, 2; 'Padthaway', <www.slsa.ha.sa.gov.au/manning/pn/m/m12.htm#mosquitoC>, accessed 2 April 2019.

24  Jones, 1985, 50, 82; Daisy Fry, *The Story of the Tatiara, 1845–1947*, Bordertown: Tatiara Centenary Committee 1947, 46; Jones, 1878, 98.

25  Marriage registration, James Allen and Esther Box (sic), Portland, Victoria, 3 May 1854, #1674; Hamilton, 1913, 18; Ward, 1869, 321; Jones, 1985, 62.

26  *Saunders's News-Letter*, 9 May 1871, 1; Kearney, Memorandum, 1.

27  MacGillivray, 1982, 477; SRSA, Fourteen Year Leases, nos 1–486'; Ward, 1869, 32; Marriage registration, James Allen and Esther Box (sic).

28  Jones, 1878, 91, 112.

29  Josiah Boothby, *South Australia Almanac and Directory*, 1864, 26; Jones, 1878, 90.

30  Post Office Directory, 1851, Cuckfield, West surrey, <www.sussex-opc.org/PostOffice1851/CuckfieldPostOffice1851.htm>, accessed 8 March 2018; *Portland Guardian*, 21 May 1855, 2 misidentifies Kearney's station as Brown rather than Broom.

31  Patricia Grimshaw, Charles Fahey, Susan Janson and Tom Griffiths, 'Families and selection in colonial Horsham', in *Families in Colonial Australia*, Grimshaw et. al, eds, 118–37; E. D. Calder, 'Early days in Wimmera', *Argus*, 24 June 1933, 4: William Ruth, *The Romance of a Selection: Victoria's Western Border Country, 1850–1950*, Essendon, Victoria: Jim Ruth, 2001.

32  Margaret Kiddle, *Men of Yesterday. A Social History of Western Victoria*, Melbourne: Melbourne University Press, 1961, 93.

33  Teresa Hamilton, *A Squatting Saga*, Sorrento, Vic.: Arden Press, 1991, 69, 112, 117–18; *Portland Guardian*, 4 December 1854, 3, 7 and 11 December 1854, 2.

34  Births, Edward Kearney, 26 February 1856; Frank Kearney, 26 November 1856, registered Robe, South Australia, 28 January 1858; James Allen, 10 February 1855; Charles Allen, 29 September 1856, registered South Australia, Norwood, Book 11/273, April 1858; Kiddle, 1961, 91–93.

35  Death, Mary Lawson, 27 December 1855, Ancestry.com, accessed 1 April 2019.

36  Kiddle, 1961, 45.

37  South Australia, Census, 1855, County of Robe, <hccda.anu.edu.au/regions/SA>, accessed 1 April 2019; Patricia Grimshaw, Marilyn Lake, Ann McGrath and Marion Quartly, *Creating a Nation*, Victoria, Australia: McPhee Gribble, 1994, 104, 114; Adele Perry, *On the Edge of Empire: Gender, Race, and the Making of British Columbia, 1849–1871*, Toronto: UTP, 2000.

38  Hamilton, 1913, 58; Les Blake, *Tattyara: A History of the Kaniva District*, Victoria: Shire of Kaniva, 1982, 5.

39  SRSA, GRG35 4/00004/4. Letters received by Crown Lands, 1855–56, Edward Kearney to C. Boney, Esq. from Broom Station, Mosquito Plains, 15 October 1855, no. 201–1855; SRSA, GRG 5/154/1, Naracoorte Police Station Journal, vol. 1, 1854–1857; SRSA, GRG5/35 2/0000/UNIT 23, File 3/1858, Mr Younghusband to Honourable Surveyor-General, South

Australia, 'That requested 14 year lease of Edward Kearney should not lapse'; South Australian Register, 22 January 1858, 3.

40 Kiddle, 1961, 50; *Portland Guardian*, 21 May 1855, 2.

41 Fisher, Hosking and Nettelbeck, 2001, 6.

42 SRSA, GRG 4/83/9, Local Court Robe, Box 1, Examination of Edward Kearney. A wether is a castrated male sheep.

43 Kiddle, 1961, 49; Bell and Marsden, 2019, describe Margaret Hutchison, who moved from the cattle farm she and her husband had worked near Melbourne after he died, set up a dairy at 'Dairy Range' near Robe, then in 1846 established Woolmit Station with Andrew Dunn, whom she married. The wealthy widow Mary Oliver, who had worked Hynam Station since 1850, purchased Morambro Station, close by, after her husband died in 1857, and furthered the wealth of this pioneering pastoralist family: *Daily Telegraph* (Sydney), 13 October 2012; MacGillivray, 1982, 478, 488.

44 Kiddle, 1961, 49; SRSA, GRG 4/83/9, Local Court Robe, Box 1, Examination of Edward Kearney, 25 April 1855; Examination of Edward Kearney, 11 May 1855; *Adelaide Times*, 21 May 1855, 3.

45 Amanda Nettelbeck, 'Seeing to spread the truth: Christina Smith and the South Australian frontier', *Australian Feminist Studies*, vol. 16, no. 34, 2001, 87–88; Foster and Nettelbeck, 2011, 97.

46 Clarke, 2015, 9.

47 Ward, 1869, 12; MacGillivray, 1982, 117, 149–50.

48 SRSA, Naracoorte Police Station Records, GRG 5/154/1, Naracoorte Police Station Journal, vol. 1, 25 September 1854–1857.

49 Reported in *Portland Guardian*, 21 May 1855, 2; *Adelaide Times*, 21 May 1855, 3; *Geelong Advertiser and Intelligencer*, 26 May 1855, 2; *Argus*, 26 May 1855, 5; *The Age* (Melbourne), 28 May 1855, 5; *Launceston Examiner*, 29 May 1855; *Sydney Morning Herald*, 31 May 1855, 1; *Mount Alexander Mail* (Victoria), 1 June 1855, 6; *Sydney Morning Herald*, 26 June 1855, 8. These accounts also misidentify Kearney's station as Brown rather than Broom.

50 Kathryn McPherson, 'Home tales: gender, domesticity, and colonialism in the prairie west, 1870–1900', in *Finding a Way to the Heart: Feminist Writings on Aboriginal and Women's History in Canada*, Robin Jarvis Brownlie and Valerie J. Korinek, eds, Winnipeg, MB: University of Manitoba Press, 2012, 224, 233, 232; Amanda Nettelbeck, Russell Smandych, Louis A. Knafla and Robert Foster, *Fragile Settlements: Aboriginal Peoples, Law, and Resistance in South-West Australia and Prairie Canada*, Vancouver: UBC Press, 2016, 131.

51 Henry Reynolds, ed., *Aborigines and Settlers: The Australian Experience, 1788–1939*, Melbourne: Cassell Australia, 1972, 8, 42; Nettelbeck et al., 2006, 178–79.

52 Fisher, Hosking and Nettelbeck, 2001, 7.

53 *Portland Guardian*, 21 May 1855, 2. I have found no evidence of a memorial among the Lieutenant Governor's papers.

54 SRSA, GRG 4/83/9, Local Court Robe, Box 1, Examination of Edward
Kearney, 25 April 1855; Examination of Appunwoonile, alias Paddy Smith,
10 May 1855; Indictment, 10 May 1855; Examination of Edward Kearney,
11 May 1855; GRG 4/83/9, Local Court Robe, Box 2, 1855; Warrant to
apprehend, 25 April 1855; Conviction of Coquata, 11 May 1855; GRG
24/6/1855/2124, Brewer, government resident, Robe to Moorhouse,
Protector of Aborigines, 28 June 1855.

55 Nettelbeck et al., 2006, 91–93, 96.

56 SRSA, GRG 5/154/1, Naracoorte Police Station Journal, vol. 1,
25 September 1854–1857; SRSA, GRG 4/83/9, Local Court Robe,
Box 1, Examination of Edward Kearney, 25 April 1855, 11 May
1855; Examination of Appunwoonile, alias Paddy Smith, 10 May
1855; Indictment, 10 May 1855; *Portland Guardian*, 21 May 1855, 2.
Interestingly, there is no report of this incident in the often very detailed
police journal.

57 Nettelbeck et al., 2006, 96.

58 Lucy Treloar offers a wonderful fictional account of the encounters between
a settler family and the Coorong in the Salt Creek area during this period in
her novel *Salt Creek*, Australia: Picador, 2015.

59 SRSA, GRG 4/83/9, Local Court Robe, Box 1, Examination of Edward
Kearney, 25 April 1855. A worley is a temporary shelter built of branches.

60 Eyre journals, 170, cited in Foster and Nettelbeck, 2011, 41; Julie Evans,
*Edward Eyre: Race and Colonial Governance*, Dunedin: Otago University
Press, 2005; Hall, *Civilizing Subjects*, 2002, 32–42.

61 Nettelbeck, 2006, 130; SRSA, GRG 4/83/9, Local Court Robe, Box 1,
Examination of Edward Kearney, 25 April 1855; *Portland Guardian*,
21 May 1855, 2.

62 Nettelbeck, 2006, 126, 130.

63 Ward, 1869, 28; Great Britain, Parliament, House of Commons, (1837),
*Report of the Select Committee on Aborigines (British Settlements), with
the Minutes of Evidence, Appendix and Index*, London: British Parliament;
Elizabeth Elbourne, 'The sin of the settler: the 1835–36 select committee
on Aborigines and debates over virtue and conquest in the early nineteenth-
century British white settler empire', *Journal of Colonialism and Colonial
History*, vol. 4, no. 3, 2003.

64 SRSA, GRG/24/6/1855/2882, documents forwarded by the protector of
Aborigines office to Captain Brewer, government resident, Robe, 31 May
1855; Brewer to M. Moorhouse, protector of Aborigines, 28 June 1855;
Moorhouse to Brewer, 14 September 1855; Moorhouse to Brewer,
19 September 1855; Foster and Nettelbeck, 2011, 71.

65 Nathan Wolski, 'All's not quiet on the western front – rethinking resistance
and frontiers in Aboriginal historiography', in *Colonial Frontiers:
Indigenous–European Encounters in Settler Societies*, Lynette Russell, ed.,
Manchester: Manchester University Press, 2001, 224–26.

66 *South Australian Register*, 31 January 1852, 3, lists diverse routes to
the goldfields from Adelaide. One alternative shorter route headed east

from Tilly's station to Ormerod's, then to the border; another was from Salt Creek via a 'straggling track' to Lawson's Station. See also <www.cornishvic.org.au/overlandgold/>, accessed 1 April 2019; Kathleen Bermingham, *Gateway to the South East: A Story of Robetown and the Guichen Bay District*, Millicent, SA: South Eastern Times Ltd, 1961, 107; Murdoch and Parker, 1963, 15–16.

67   *Portland Guardian*, 10 October 1856, 1; SRSA, PRG497, 'Roland Campbell', vol. 2, Research notes.

68   SRSA, GRG5 2/00000/3/34.5, Petition of Angelo Barnaby Rodriques, Shepherd to George Ormerod, Esq. re bushrangers at Mosquito Plains with Commissioner's reply to George Ormerod, 30 December 1853; SRSA, GRG5/154/1, Naracoorte Police Station Journal, vol. 1, 25 September 1854–57.

69   F. K. Crowley, 'Working Class Conditions in Australia, 1788–1851', PhD thesis, University of Melbourne, 214, cited in Kiddle, 1961, 63.

70   *Scab in Sheep Act 1840, 1841, 1844, 1846, 1852, 1853, 1854, 1855–6, 1859, 1863, 1867* (Vic.).

71   W. Stephen Smith, *The History of Sheep Scab in South Australia*, Adelaide: The Author, 1975.

72   *South Australian Register*, 19 June 1857, 3; 29 August 1857, 3.

73   Smith, 1975, 5, 8; *Border Watch* (Mount Gambier), 10 July 1863, 2–3; Hamilton, 1913, 50–51; Kiddle, 1961, 63; Hamilton, 1991, 13.

74   *South Australian Register*, 22 January 1858, 3; SRSA, GRG4/83/9, Local Court Robe, Box 1, Inspector of Sheep v. Edward Kearney, Scab Act; *South Australian Register*, 10 April 1858, 3.

75   *South Australian Register*, 19 June 1857, 3; 29 August 1857, 3; 22 January 1858, 3; 10 April 1858, 3; SRSA, GRG4/83/9, Local Court Robe, Box 1, Inspector of Sheep v. Edward Kearney, Scab Act.

76   *South Australian Register*, 22 January 1858, 3; Smith, 1975, 4; 'Obituary, Mr. H. T. Morris', *Chronicle*, (South Australia), 28 November 1911, 48; *South Australia Advertiser*, 8 September 1863, 3. In New Zealand, George Henry Moore's station Glenmark was so notorious for years as Canterbury's scabbiest run that its owner was widely referred to as 'Scabby Moore': W. J. Gardiner, 'George Henry Moore', *Te Ara: The Encylopedia of New Zealand*, <www.teara.govt.nz/en/biographies/1m52/moore-george-henry>, accessed 1 April 2019.

77   *South Australian Register*, 22 January 1858, 3.

78   *South Australian Register*, 22 January 1858, 3.

79   Hamilton, 1913, 58; Blake, 1982, 5.

80   SRSA, GRG35 4/00004/4, Letters received by Crown Lands, 1855–56, Edward Kearney to C. Boney, Esq. from Broom Station, Mosquito Plains, 15 October 1855, no. 201–1855; SRSA, GRG5/154/1, Naracoorte Police Station Journal, vol. 1, 1854–1857; SRSA, GRG5/35 2/0000/UNIT 23, File 3/1858, Mr Younghusband to Honourable Surveyor-General, South Australia, 'That requested 14 year lease of Edward Kearney should not lapse'.

81 Kearney, Memorandum, 1.

82 SRSA, GRG5/35 2/0000/UNIT 23, File 83/1858, Kearney to Commissioner of Crown Lands, 18 January 1858; Cockburn, 1974, I, 116–17.

83 Blake, 1982, 4; Hamilton, 1913, 34–35.

84 J. Wood Beilby, *Port Phillip Gazette*, 29 November 1849, 1 December 1849, cited in Robert Dunn, *The Disputed Country: Australia's Lost Border*, South Australia: Bob Dunn and John Deckert, 2004, 34–35.

85 Jane Beer, 'Highland Scots in Victoria's Western District', in Russell, 2001, 64–66; Sarah Carter, *Imperial Plots: Women, Land, and the Spadework of British Colonialism on the Canadian Prairies*, Winnipeg: University of Manitoba Press, 2016, 1.

86 Cockburn, 1974, I, 116–17; George E. Loyau, *Notable South Australians*, Adelaide: Carey, Page & Co., 1935, 259; *Border Watch*, 3 December 1863; Fry, 1947, 46 claims the house was not finished because Lawson 'bought out the man who was building the house'.

87 South Australia, Birth Registration, Charles Allen, 29 September 1856, registered 19 April 1858; Esther Mary Allen, New Zealand, Cemetery Records, 1800–2007, Southern Cemetery, Dunedin, <www.dunedin.govt.nz/services/cemeteries/cemeteries-search?recordid=92833&type=Burial>, accessed 1 April 2019; NZ Death Register, Esther Jane Allen, 6 February 1861; Hamilton, 1913, 56; Ian McGibbon, 'James Allen', NZDB, <www.teara.govt.nz/en/biographies/3a12/allen-james>, suggests that Esther died before they left South Australia, accessed 1 April 2019.

88 Hamilton, 1913, 13, 15, 29, 50, 96; *Portland Guardian*, 14 May 1860, 2; Hamilton, 1991, 19–21; Marriage Registration, 27 April 1860, Robe, South Australia, vol. 42, 300.

89 Australia Marriage Index, Victoria, 1856, no. 1272, Ancestry.com, accessed 1 April 2019; Public Record Office Victoria (henceforth PROV), VPRS 267/P/7, Unit 141, 1867/2555, Mulrain v. McGann, Affidavit of William, McGann, 29 July 1867.

90 *South Australian Register*, 4 January 1859, 7 December 1868, 3; 5 August 1861, 3; Bermingham, 1961, 214; Robe Parsonage minutes, 'Subscriptions paid in 1868', Robe Library and Visitor Information Centre, May 2018.

91 SRSA, GRG5/35 2/0000/UNIT 23, File 83/1858, Edward Kearney to Commissioner of Crown Lands, 18 January 1858; Birth Registration, Edward Kearney and Frank Henry Kearney, Robe, 28 January 1858: Blake, 1982, 4–5; *South Australian Register*, 10 April 1858, 3; 5 August 1861, 3.

92 Kearney, 'Memorandum', 1–2; *Saunders's News-Letter*, 9 May 1871, 1.

93 MacGillivray, 1982, 149–50, 152–53, 169; Hamilton, 1991, 15–16.

**3   Lockhart Station, Western Wimmera, Victoria, 1858–65**

1 A school opened at Horsham in 1857, 140 kilometres to the east.

2 Victoria, Census, 1857, Table I, 01-25; Table III, 01-26; Table 1, 02-11; Table VII, 02-23, 02-25; Table X, 04-21; Table 1, 04-75, <hccda.ada.edu.au/documents/VIC-1857-census>, accessed 3 April 2019; John Reid, Keith H. Lovett and Les J. Blake, *Road Board to Restructure: The History of*

*the Shire of Wimmera, 1862–1995*, Victoria, Australia: Joval Publications, Shire of Wimmera, 1996, 4, 19.

3   *Courier* (Hobart), 8 January 1858, 2, citing the *Normanby Guardian*. This is well over $1 000 000 Australian today.

4   Public Record Office Victoria (henceforth PROV), VPRS 5825, P0000/02, Pastoral Run Register, vols 1–2, 9, 11, 31; Bermingham, 1961, 130 reports that George Ormerod carried many of these early settlers over successive lean years without penalty or grievance.

5   Kiddle, Margaret, *Men of Yesterday: A Social History of Western Victoria*, Melbourne: Melbourne University Press, 1961, 177; Edward Kearney, Memorandum, 1, c.1876, transcribed by Joe Palmer, held by family members; James Charles Hamilton, *Pioneering Days in Western Victoria*, Melbourne: Exchange Press, 1913, 57.

6   Ebenezer Ward, *The South-Eastern District of South Australia: Its Resources and Requirements*, Adelaide: the Author, 1869, 31; Leslie James Blake, *Tattyara: A History of the Kaniva District*, Victoria: Shire of Kaniva, 1982, 5; Hamilton, 1913, 57; Alfred S. Kenyon, *The Story of the Mallee: A History of the Victorian Mallee Read before the Historical Society of Australia, 18 March 1912*, Rainbow, Vic.: Brentwood Publications, 1982, 3–21.

7   Robert Dunn, *The Disputed Country: Australia's Lost Border*, South Australia: Bob Dunn and John Deckert, 2004, 18, 27–35.

8   Kenyon, 1982, 26; Katie Holmes and Kylie Mirmohamadi, 'Howling wilderness and promised land: imagining the Victorian Mallee, 1840–1914', *Australian Historical Studies*, vol. 46, 2015, 197.

9   PROV, VPRS 5920, Pastoral Run Files (microfiche), Lockhart, #714, Baird and Hodgkins, Lockhart Station to the Commissioner of Crown Lands for the District of Wimmera, 23 August 1847; to Latrobe, 2 December 1850.

10  PROV, Pastoral Run Files (microfiche), Lockhart, #714.

11  Dunn, 2004, 86; Blake, 1982, 4 cites Lockhart as 56 080 acres and Coniay as 16 000; T. M. Landt, *The Story of the Kaniva District, 1845–1961*, Melbourne: Brown, Prior, Anderson Pty Ltd, 1961, 3, 17; *Horsham Times*, 3 November 1925, 1.

12  Dunn, 2004, 49, 74, 85; undated map of stations held by the Family History Society, Kaniva, c.1868.

13  Philip Clark, 'The Aboriginal ethnobotany of the South-East of South Australia region, part 1: seasonal life and material culture', *Transactions of the Royal Society of South Australia*, 2015, 4; AIATSIS Map, <aiatsis. gov.au/explore/articles/aboriginal-australia-map>, accessed 1 April 2019; Tindale's Catalogue of Australian Aboriginal Tribes, <archives.samuseum. sa.gov.au/tindaletribes/wotjobaluk.htm>, accessed 1 April 2019.

14  For more variants see <www.austkin.net/language/740>, accessed 1 April 2019.

15  Landt, 1961, 5; the reference is to Australian bush turkeys (*Alectura lathami*).

16  Blake, 1982, 9; Dunn, 2004, 42.

17  Kiddle, 1961, 47, 59, 124.

18  Kiddle, 1961, 126; Serviceton Centenary Committee, *Serviceton: A Frontier Town on No Man's Land, 1887–1987*, Serviceton, Vic.: The Committee, 1987, 12.

19  John Reid, Keith H. Lovett and Les J. Blake, *Road Board to Restructure: The History of the Shire of Wimmera, 1862–1995*, Victoria, Australia: Joval Publications, Shire of Wimmera, 1966, 77–78; Blake, 1982, 4.

20  Ward, 1869, 3; Kiddle, 1961, 59; William Ruth, *The Romance of a Selection: Victoria's Western Border Country, 1850–1950*, Essendon, Vic.: Jim Ruth, 2001, 51.

21  Serviceton, 1987, 12 and Blake, 1982, 4 are both unsure about whether Edward built the first station or renovated it. They were misled in part by a pencilled inscription of Mr Kearney's name and the date 20 June 1866 on the rafters of the limestone-walled cottage. As Edward senior was by then dead, this was surely young Edward Kearney recording his presence as his life fell apart around him following his father's death.

22  Blake, 1982, 5; Serviceton, 1987, 11, photo at 10.

23  *Argus*, 22 March 1869, 3.

24  The McLellan brothers ran Brimble Station, north of Lockhart, after purchasing it from Edward in 1860; *Saunders's News-Letter*, 9 May 1871, 1.

25  Kiddle, 1961, 50; PROV, VPRS 259/P/0001, Unit 13, no. 1071, *Kearney v. Lowry*, Affidavit of Henry Wallace Lowry, 9 September 1869; *Freeman's Journal*, 9 May 1876, 6.

26  *Argus*, 24 June 1933, 4.

27  Kearney, Memorandum, 1.

28  Hamilton, 1913, 19; Sandra Rollings-Magnusson, *Heavy Burdens on Small Shoulders: The Labour of Pioneer Children on the Canadian Prairies*, Edmonton: University of Alberta Press, 2009.

29  Serviceton, 1987, 12; Kearney, Memorandum, 3; Daisy Fry, *The Story of Tatiara, 1845–1947*, Bordertown: Tatiara Centenary Committee, 1947, 56.

30  Kearney, Memorandum, 3.

31  Kearney, Memorandum, 1; Mrs Jones, *Broad Outlines of Long Years in Australia*, London: Samuel Tinslay & Co., 1878, 99.

32  Kearney, Memorandum, 2.

33  Kearney, Memorandum, 2.

34  *South Australian Weekly Chronicle*, 4 October 1862, 8.

35  Woollacott, 2015, 189, 198, 202.

36  Kiddle, 1961, 50; PROV, *Kearney v. Lowry*, Affidavit of Henry Wallace Lowry, 9 September 1869.

37  *Hamilton Spectator*, 21 April 1869, 3; Blake, 1982, 5; Serviceton, 1987, 11; William Moodie, *A Pioneer of Western Victoria*, Mortlake, Vic.: The Editor, 1973, 62.

38  *Argus*, 22 March 1869, 3; Hamilton, 1913, 38, 61; Moodie, 1973, 60–61; PROV 9704/P2, Shire of Wimmera, District of Horsham, Assessment of

General District Rate, 11 February 1869. Cove and Brimble were valued at £547 for the land and £103 for the improvements, Lillimur at £381 and £55. Compare with Dugald McPherson's Nihill station at £1678 and £90, or James Campbell Telford's Mt Elgin at £1628 and £98. Today £558 translates to $64 680 in purchasing power, Measuring Worth, <www.measuringworth.com/calculators/australiacompare/relativevalue.php>, accessed 1 April 2019.

39 Photo board, Geraldine Historical Museum, Geraldine, New Zealand.
40 Kiddle, 1961, 132–34.
41 *Star* (Ballarat), 26 October 1859, 3; 29 October, 4; 19 November, 4.
42 PROV, Pastoral Run Files, Lockhart, #714, Baird and Hodgkins, Lockhart Station to the Commissioner of Crown Lands for the District of Wimmera, 23 August 1847; Serviceton, 1987, 11; Blake, 1982, 1; Holmes and Mirmohamadi, 2015, 192; Kenyon, 1982, 26.
43 *Courier*, 3 May 1858, 2.
44 *Adelaide Observer*, 4 December 1858, 1S; *Labor Call*, 12 November 1914, 8.
45 Hamilton, 1913, 57; Blake, 1982, 5.
46 *Argus*, 22 March 1869, 3.
47 Blake, 1982, 5; PROV, Equity Case Files, *Kearney & others v. Lowry*, Affidavit of Thomas Trollope, 19 April 1869.
48 Hamilton, 1913, 58; Blake, 1982, 5.
49 PROV, VPRS 5920, Edward Kearney to Commissioner of Crown Lands, Wimmera District, 19 July 1860; John Pearson to Wright, Commissioner of Crown Lands, Wimmera district, 3 January 1860 and 25 April 1860, Lockhart, Pastoral Runs Files; Blake, 1982, 5.
50 Blake, 1982, 5; Serviceton, 1987, 13; 'Old Wimmera Stations', *Horsham Times*, 23 August 1927, 10.
51 Hamilton, 1913, 58; Blake, 1982, 4; Serviceton, 1987, 11; *Horsham Times*, 23 August 1927, 10. Its second owner, Hunter, had been murdered by one of his shepherds. Little two-year-old Janet McFarlane, whose father Daniel came to Lockhart from London in mid-1852 to work for John McKellar, had died after suffering severe burns. Her older brother still worked on the station at times. Her grave beside a gum tree to the west of the homestead was a reminder to beware of accidents.
52 Kearney, Memorandum, 1.
53 Mark Peel and Christina Twomey, *A History of Australia*, New York: Palgrave, 2011.
54 Kearney, Memorandum, 1.
55 Hugh Anderson, 'Clarke, William John (1805–1874)', *Australian Dictionary of Biography*, <adb.anu.edu.au/biography/clarke-william-john-1902>, accessed 15 June 2019.
56 Anderson, 'Clarke, William John (1805–1874)', 205; Michael Clarke, *'Big' Clarke*, Carlton, Vic.: Queensberry Hill Press, 1980, 113, citing G. C. Mundy, *Our Antipodes or: Residence and Rambles in the Australian Colonies, with a Glimpse of the Goldfields*, London: Richard Bentley,

1855, 538–40; PROV, Kearney v. Lowry, Bill from W. J. Trollope for assisting Lowry and McGann, attendance 10 January 1872.

57 PROV, *Kearney v. Lowry*, Affidavit of Thomas Trollope, 19 April 1869.

58 Kearney, Memorandum, 2.

59 Kearney, Memorandum, 2.

60 Kearney, Memorandum, 2.

61 Kearney, Memorandum, 2.

62 'The Little Desert ... Some Old Stations', *Australasian*, 31 October 1925, 6–9.

63 Kearney, Memorandum, 2; VPRS 3506, reel 31, Outward Passenger lists, May–December 1864, *True Briton*, April 1864, PROV, VPRS 948 P1, 27, Microfilm 3506, May–August 1864; *Mercury* (Hobart), 4 May 1864, 2.

64 Report from the Select Committee on State of Westmeath, and Nature of Certain Unlawful Combinations, Great Britain. Parliament. House of Commons, Parliamentary Papers, Session 1871, vol. XIII, consulted at <archive.org/details/op1249739-1001>, accessed 13 April 2016; Jeremiah Sheehan, *South Westmeath: Farm and Folk*, Dublin: Blackwater, 1978, 122–24.

65 Sheehan, 1978, 138; *Westmeath Examiner*, 24 February 1883, 4.

66 Chris McConville, 'The Victorian Irish: emigrants and families, 1851–91', in *Families in Colonial Australia*, eds Patricia Grimshaw, Chris McConville and Ellen McEwen, Sydney: George Allen & Unwin, 1985, 2. When Joseph married Harriet Gaynor on 21 February 1868 he was identified as Farmer, Williamstown, Cornamaddy: Ireland, *Catholic Parish Registers*, 1655– 1915, Marriage, Joseph Kearney and Harriet Gaynor, Westmeath, 21 February 1868. He was listed as aged 43, Harriet as 22; Marriage, William Kearney and Mary Malia, 30 October 1844, Ballymore, Westmeath, Ancestry.com, accessed 15 June 2019. Michael P. Flynn, *Genealogy of the Descendants of William Kearney and Mary Mulrain*: Williamstown, Cornamaddy, Athlone, Mullingar: Michael P. Flynn, 1997, 5, 21.

67 Griffith's Valuation, 1854, <www.askaboutireland.ie/griffith-valuation/>, accessed 25 July 2018; family members report that seven generations of Kearneys lived in Williamstown.

68 Sheehan, 1978, 137.

69 *Westmeath Examiner*, 24 February 1883, 4, and 30 August 1913, 8; Sheehan, 1978, 137–38; Tom Hunt, *Sport and Society in Victorian Ireland: The Case of Westmeath*, Cork: Cork University Press, 2007, 14.

70 Kearney, Memorandum, 2; Father Tom Murray, archivist, Diocescan archives, Diocese of Ardagh and Clonmacnois, Ireland, reports that there are no records there or at St Patrick's Church.

71 *Westmeath Examiner*, 24 February 1884, 4; *Westmeath Examiner*, 30 August 1913, 8; *Freeman's Journal*, 25 August 1870, 5.

72 PROV, Microfiche VPRS 7668, 7667, Victoria, Inward Overseas Passenger Lists, *Great Britain*, February 1865, Fiche #242, 10; *Irish Times*, 9 May 1871, 5.

73  *Freeman's Journal*, 9 May 1871, 6.

74  Kearney, Memorandum, 2.

75  *Saunders's News-Letter*, 9 May 1871, 1; *Freeman's Journal*, 6; a Miss Cunningham received pay from the estate in May and June 1866, PROV, *Kearney v. Lowry*, Affidavit of William McGann, 30 June 1869. Woods was the most influential Catholic in the area, alongside his significant work as a geologist.

76  PROV, *Kearney v. Lowry*, Affidavit of William Kearney, 20 July 1869.

77  D. H. Borchardt, 'Julian Edmund Tenison-Woods', *Australian Dictionary of Biography*, <adb.anu.edu.au/biography/tenison-woods-julian-edmund-4700m>, accessed 12 June 2019; Osmund Thorpe, 'Mary Helen MacKillop', *Australian Dictionary of Biography*, <adb.anu.edu.au/biography/mackillop-mary-helen-4112>; *South Australian Register*, 5 October 1858, 1. MacKillop became Australia's first saint in 2010.

78  *Argus*, 13 September 1865, 4 listed a Mr and Mrs Kearney, as well as a Mr Kearney. I presume these were Edward, Caroline and William because the timing and departure from Guichen Bay, Robe, fits so well: *South Australian Register*, 6 October 1865, 2; *Argus*, 17 October 1865, 4; <www.flotilla-australia.com/adsteam.htm>, accessed 3 April 2019; Liz Harfull, *Almost an Island: The Story of Robe*, South Australia: Wakefield Press, 2013, 50.

79  Sands and McDougall, *Melbourne Directory*, 1865, 18–19; Penny Russell, *A Wish of Distinction: Colonial Femininity and Gentility*, Carlton, Vic.: University of Melbourne Press, 1994, 66.

80  In 1860, James Vincent Hughes failed to secure a licence at least twice. Those opposing the application stated that the house 'was not wanted and had insufficient accommodation'. The police report of the house was also unsatisfactory: *Argus*, 7 March 1860, 1; 22 September 1865, 2; 19 October 1865, 8; 2 November 1865, 7; 8 August 1866, 1 – 'wanted a clean little girl as a nurse'. The Royal Melbourne Hospital was located at the corner of Lonsdale and Swanston streets, about a 15-minute walk away. Kennedy's tenure was brief. In November 1866 it was taken over by a Thomas Lang. His licence appears to have lapsed a month later: PROV, Index to Defunct Hotel Licences.

81  St Francis' Catholic Church remains a block away at the corner of Lonsdale and Elizabeth streets; *Freeman's Journal*, 6 May 1871, 6; eMelbourne, 'The City Past and Present', <http://www.emelbourne.net.au/biogs/EM01301b.htm>, accessed 16 June 2019.

82  PROV, Will, Edward Kearney, 30 September 1865; Sands and McDougall, *Melbourne Directory*, 1865, 18; Atherton, 1988. On this process, see Bettina Bradbury, 'Troubling inheritances: an illegitimate, Māori daughter contests her father's will in the New Zealand courts and the Judicial Committee of the Privy Council', *Australia and New Zealand Legal History* (2012) E-Journal.

83  PROV, *Kearney v. Lowry*, Affidavit of Thomas Trollope, 19 April 1869.

84  PROV, Will, Edward Kearney, 30 September 1865, 2–3; VPRS 28/P1/ 11, Will, Edward Kearney, proved 10 November 1865.

85   *Freeman's Journal*, 9 May 1871, 6.

86   Lee Holcombe, *Wives and Property: Reform of the Married Women's Property Law in Nineteenth-Century England*, Toronto: UTP, 1983; Bettina Bradbury, '"In England a man can do as he likes with his property": migration, family fortunes and the law in nineteenth-century Quebec and the Cape Colony', in *Within and Without the Nation: Canadian History as Transnational History*, eds Adele Perry, Karen Dubinsky and Henry Wu, Toronto: UTP, 2015; Christopher Baker and Michael Gilding, 'Family matters', *Inside Story*, <insidestory.org.au/family-matters/>, accessed 3 April 2019 highlights the ongoing tension between the two approaches.

87   Victoria, Statutes, 1864, no. 268, An Act to Consolidate the Laws relating to Marriage and to Divorce and Matrimonial Causes.

88   John Mackinolty, 'The Married Women's Property Acts', in *In Pursuit of Justice: Australian Women and the Law, 1788–1979*, Judy Mackinolty and Heather Radi, eds, Sydney: Hale & Iremonger, 1979; Diane Kirkby and Hilary Golder, 'Marriage and divorce law before the Family Law Act, 1975', in *Sex, Power and Justice: Historical Perspectives on Law in Australia*, Diane Kirkby, ed., Melbourne: Oxford University Press, 1995; Bettina Bradbury, 'Colonial comparisons: rethinking marriage, civilization and nation in 19th-century white-settler societies', in *Rediscovering the British World*, Phillip Buckner and G. Frances, eds, Calgary: University of Calgary Press, 2005; Victoria, 'An Act to amend the Law Relating to the Property of Married Women', 29 December 1870, *Hansard*, Victoria, 1870, vol. 11, 115, 218–19, 232, 250, 398–408, 531, 643–46, citations at 219, 406.

**4   Edward's death, his final wishes and religious warfare**

1   Death registration, Edward Kearney, District of South Melbourne, Victoria, 20 October 1865; Helen Bynum, *Spitting Blood: The History of Tuberculosis*, Oxford: OUP, 2012, 15.

2   Pat Jalland, *Australian Ways of Death: A Social and Cultural History, 1840–1918*, Melbourne: OUP, 2002, 128–29, 66; *Freeman's Journal*, 6 May 1871, 6.

3   Death registration, Kearney, 20 October 1865; Charles James Hamilton, *Pioneering Days in Western Victoria*, Melbourne: Exchange Press, 1913, 58; Edward Kearney, Memorandum, 2, c.1876, transcribed by Joe Palmer, held by family members.

4   Penny Russell, *A Wish of Distinction: Colonial Femininity and Gentility*, Carlton, Vic.: University of Melbourne Press, 1994, 120–21; Jalland, 2002, 130–31.

5   Public Record Office Victoria (henceforth PROV), *Kearney v. Lowry*, Affidavit of Thomas Trollope, 19 April 1869 lists outlays of £500 in the three months following Edward's death.

6   *Wife to Widow. Lives, Laws and Politics in 19th Century Montreal*, Vancouver: University of British Columbia Press, 2011, 205–10.

7   Russell, 1994, 123; Jalland, 2002, 130.

8   *Argus,* 22 January 1863, 5; *Argus,* 21 October 1865, 4; Death registration, Kearney, 20 October 1865.
9   PROV, *Kearney v. Lowry,* Affidavit of Henry Wallace Lowry, 19 October 1869.
10  *Argus,* 26 October 1865, 4; *Australasian,* 21 and 28 October 1865, 8; Mushira Eid, *The World of Obituaries: Gender across Cultures and Over Time,* Detroit: Wayne State University Press, 2001; Bradbury, 2015, 215.
11  PROV, VPRS P/2, Affidavit of Thomas Trollope, 19 April 1869; Kearney, Memorandum, 3; *Freeman's Journal,* 9 May 1871, 6.
12  Noall identified his address as 34 Collins Street, McGann, as 60 Collins Street – the same address as Thomas Pavey, the solicitor whose clerk witnessed the will: PROV, Will, Edward Kearney, 30 September 1865; Sands and McDougall, *Melbourne Directory,* 1861, 310 locates Noall at 48 Collins Street West.
13  PROV, Will, Edward Kearney, 30 September 1865.
14  PROV, Will, Edward Kearney, 30 September 1865, 2–3.
15  PROV, Will, Edward Kearney, 30 September 1865, 5–6, 9.
16  Kearney, Memorandum, 2.
17  Rosalind Atherton, 'Expectation without right: testamentary freedom and the position of women in 19th-century New South Wales', *UNSW Law Journal,* vol. 11, 1988, 136.
18  *Argus,* 24 October 1865, 7; PROV, VPRS 28, P0001, Unit 11, 5/461, Probate and Administration Files, Will of Edward Kearney.
19  Teresa Hamilton, *A Squatting Saga,* Sorrento, Vic.: Arden Press, 1991, 25; Bruce Kercher, *An Unruly Child: A History of Law in Australia,* Sydney: Allen & Unwin, 1998, 141–42;
20  *Shaw v. Salter* (1865), 2 Wyatt, Webb and A'Beckett's Reports, Equity (Vic.), 159–71; *English v. English* (1866), 3 Wyatt, Webb and A'Beckett's Reports, Equity (Vic.), 170–73; *Hoyle v. Edwards,* (1869), 6 Wyatt, Webb and A'Beckett's Reports, Equity (Vic.), 48–58; Hilary Golder and Diane Kirkby, 'Land conveyancing and the problem of the married woman in colonial Australia', in *Law, History, Colonialism. The Reach of Empire,* Diane Kirkby and Catharine Coleborn, eds, Manchester: MUP, 2001, 208, 212; Nancy Wright, 'Local policy and legal decisions about dower in colonial New South Wales', *ANZLH E-Journal,* 2005, 226–33; Charlotte Macdonald, 'Land, death and dower in the settler empire: the lost cause of "the widow's third" in nineteenth-century New Zealand', *Victoria University Law Review,* 41, 2010, 493–518; Andrew Buck, '"A Blot on the Certificate": dower and women's property rights in colonial New South Wales', *Australian Journal of Law and Society,* vol. 4, 87 (1987).
21  *Real Property Statute* 1864 (Vic.), pt III, s. 59, states: 'Where a husband shall devise any land out of which his widow would be entitled to dower ... to or for the benefit of the widow such widow shall not be entitled to dower ... unless a contrary intention shall be declared in the will.'
22  PROV, *Kearney v. Lowry,* Lowry response to Caroline Kearney's bill, 1 May 1868 and Affidavit of Thomas Trollope, 19 April 1869; PROV,

VPRS 5825, Pastoral Run Register, vol. 1, 11, 31, 81; vol. 2, 199.
23  *Freeman's Journal*, Ireland, 6; PROV, *Kearney v. Lowry*, Account of the monies disbursed by William Kearney after the decease of Edward Kearney, 29 June 1869; Affidavit of Henry Wallace Lowry, 19 October 1869.
24  *Freeman's Journal*, 6.
25  Kearney, Memorandum, 2.
26  PROV, VPRS 37 P0000/8, Habeas Corpus cases, #517, *In the Matter of Maria Ellen Kearney*, Affidavit of Caroline Kearney, filed 12 September 1866; *Argus*, 13 September 1866, 6.
27  John Watts, Glen Turnbull and Kathleen Walsh, *Mercy Girls: The Story of Sacred Heart College Geelong, 1860–2010*, Newtown, Vic.: Sacred Heart College Geelong, 2010; Jill Barnard and Karen Twigg, *Holding on to Hope: A History of the Founding Agencies of MacKillop Family Services 1854–1997*, Melbourne: Australian Scholarly Publishing, 2004, 20–21; *Westmeath Examiner*, 30 August 1913, 8.
28  PROV, Will, Edward Kearney, 30 September 1865, 9; PROV, *Kearney v. Lowry*, An Account of the monies disbursed by William Kearney after the decease of Edward Kearney, 29 June 1869.
29  Jill Barnard and Karen Twigg, *Holding on to Hope: A History of the Founding Agencies of MacKillop Family Services 1854–1997*, Melbourne: Australian Scholarly Publishing, 2004, 21–22; Sister M. Ignatius, *The Wheel of Time: A Brief Survey of the Ninety-six Years' Work of the Sisters of Mercy in Victoria, 1857–1953*, Melbourne: For the Sisters of Mercy, 1954; Watts et al., 2010, 24.
30  *Argus*, 15 September 1866, 6; PROV, *Kearney v. Lowry*, An Account of the monies disbursed by William Kearney after the decease of Edward Kearney, 29 June 1869. His accounts reveal that he paid £5 5s for her clothing along with four different expenses related to travelling that totalled £32.
31  Register, Convent School Geelong, Archives, Sacred Heart College, Geelong.
32  Sister M. Ignatius, 1954, 89; Watts et al., 2010.
33  Watts et al., 2010, 10; PROV, *Kearney v. Lowry*, Affidavit of McGann, 4 August 1869; *Argus*, 15 September 1866, 6.
34  Robert Miller, 'George Henry Frederick Webb (1828–1891)', *Australian Dictionary of Biography*, <adb.anu.edu.au/biography/webb-george-henry-frederick-4822>, accessed 12 June 2019; PROV, Habeas Corpus cases, #517, Maria Ellen Kearney; PROV, *Kearney v. Lowry*, Affidavit of McGann, 4 August 1869; David Clark and Gerard McCoy, *Habeas Corpus: Australia, New Zealand, South Pacific*, Sydney: Federation Press, 2000, 4; Paul D. Halliday, *Habeas Corpus: From England to Empire*, Cambridge, Mass.: Belknap Press of Harvard University Press, 2010.
35  PROV, Habeas Corpus cases, #517, Maria Ellen Kearney.
36  *Argus*, 13 September 1866, 6.
37  PROV, Habeas Corpus cases, #517, Maria Ellen Kearney, Affidavit of James Hamilton, 12 September 1866.
38  Simon Smith, ed., *Judging for the People: A Social History of the Victorian*

*Supreme Court 1841–2016*, Sydney: Allen & Unwin, 2016.

39  J. M. Bennett, *Sir William Stawell, Second Chief Justice of Victoria, 1857–1886*, Sydney: Federation Press, 2004, 4–6, 87–90, 126; Charles Parkinson, *Sir William Stawell and the Victorian Constitution*, Melbourne: Australian Scholarly Publishing, 2004, quote at xi, 1; Charles Francis, 'Sir William Foster Stawell', *Australian Dictionary of Biography*, <adb.anu.edu.au/biography/stawell-sir-william-foster-4635>, accessed 12 June 2019.

40  Clark and McCoy, 2000, 127–28; *Argus*, 15 September 1866, 6.

41  *Argus*, 15 September 1866, 6–7.

42  Quotation from *Argus*, 15 September 1866, 6; 13 September 1866, 6; 15 September 1866, 6–7; *Bendigo Advertiser*, 14 September 1866, 3; *Sydney Morning Herald*, 17 September 1866, 6; *Maitland Mercury and Hunter River General Advertiser*, 22 September 1866, 3. The current website for the school highlights the 'tale of Mary [sic] Ellen Kearney', though the archivist, Claudette Brennan, had no idea that she had subsequently died: <www.shcgeelong.catholic.edu.au/archives/the-curious-case-of-mary-ellen-kearney> [sic], accessed 25 October 2017.

43  *Melbourne Punch*, 20 September 1866, 13.

44  *Saunders's News-Letter*, 9 May 1871, 1; PROV, VPRS 37 P0000/8, Habeas Corpus cases, #517, Maria Ellen Kearney.

45  Kearney, Memorandum, 2; *Geelong Advertiser*, 13 October 1866, 2; *Geelong Advertiser*, 17 November 1866, 2; *The Age*, 8 December 1866, 5.

46  Victoria Parliamentary Papers, 1866, no. A13, Industrial Schools: Reports and Correspondence, 1866, 11; VPARL, 1867, no. 58, Report on the Condition, Management and Regulations at the Convent, Geelong, 1866, 3; Report of the Inspector of Industrial Schools for the year 1867, vol. 5, no. 3.

47  PROV, *Kearney v. Lowry*, Bill, Caroline Kearney, 30 March 1868; *The Age*, 8 December 1866, 5.

48  Victoria, Death certificate, Maria Ellen Kearney, 29 November 1866; Kearney, Memorandum, 2.

49  PROV, *Kearney v. Lowry*, Bill of Caroline Kearney, 30 March 1868; Kearney, Memorandum, 2.

50  *McGann (executor) v. Kearney*, reported in *Argus*, 10 September 1867, 6; 11 September 1867, 6; PROV, *Kearney v. Lowry*, Lowry, response to Caroline Kearney's bill, 1 May 1868, *Kearney v. Lowry*; PROV, VPRS 267/P7/181, 1869/742, *John Barter Bennett v. Kearney*; John Barter Bennett, Parliament of Victoria, Former Members, <https://www.parliament.vic.gov.au/index.php?option=com_fabrik&view=list&listid=23&Itemid=1135&limitstart23=0>, accessed 13 June 2019.

51  PROV, *Kearney v. Lowry*, Roll of Proceedings and Affidavit of Henry Wallace Lowry, 19 October 1869; *Kearney v. Lowry* (1868), 5 Wyatt, Webb and A'Beckett's Reports, Equity (Vic.), 202–208, at 204; Hamilton, 1913, 58; PROV, VPRS 5825, P0000/02, Pastoral Run Register, vol. 1, 11, 31, 81; vol. 2, 199.

52  PROV, *Kearney v. Lowry*, Lowry, response to Caroline Kearney's bill,

1 May 1868; Affidavit of Thomas Trollope, 19 April 1869; Affidavit of Henry Wallace Lowry, 19 October 1869.

53 PROV, *Kearney v. Lowry*, Affidavit of Thomas Trollope, 19 April 1869.

54 Kearney, 'Memorandum', 2.

### 5 Learning legal procedures

1 Public Record Office Victoria (henceforth PROV), VPRS 267/P/0007/Unit 141, 1867/2555, *Charles Mulrain v. William McGann*, Affidavit of Joseph Hardingham, 20 August 1867; *McGann (Executor) v. Kearney, Argus*, 20 August 1867, 5; 10 September 1867, 4, 6; *Queen v. Pohlman, Argus*, 11 September 1867, 6.

2 PROV, *Mulrain v. McGann*, Affidavit of Joseph Hardingham, 20 August 1867.

3 PROV, *Mulrain v. McGann*, Judgment and Remittance, 7 August 1867.

4 Penny Russell, *A Wish of Distinction: Colonial Femininity and Gentility*, Carlton, Vic.: University of Melbourne Press, 1994, 8.

5 Kearney, Memorandum, 2; image held by family members; Victoria, Death certificate, Maria Ellen Kearney, 29 November 1866; PROV, *Kearney v. Lowry*, Affidavit of Thomas Trollope, 19 April 1869; Affidavit of Henry Wallace Lowry, 30 June 1869; Affidavit of William McGann, 30 June 1869.

6 eMelbourne, 'The City Past and Present', <www.emelbourne.net.au>, accessed 3 April 2019; Arthur Dean, *A Multitude of Counsellors: A History of the Bar in Victoria*, Melbourne: Cheshire for the Bar Council, 1968, 21.

7 PROV, VPRS 16237/P1, Roll of Attorneys, unit 1, 37; *Catalogue of the Library of the Supreme Court of Victoria*, Melbourne: Lucas Printer, 1861, xxxii; Richard Harrison, 'The legal profession in colonial Victoria: information in records of admission held by Public Record Office Victoria', *Journal of Public Record Office Victoria*, vol. 13, 2014.

8 *Catalogue of the Library*, 1861, n.p.; *Argus*, 31 January 1870; *Act to Make Provision for the Better Administration of Justice in the Colony of Victoria* 1852 (Vic.); Lee Holcombe, *Wives and Property: Reform of the Married Women's Property Law in Nineteenth-Century England*, Toronto: UTP, 1983, 3, 37; PROV, Law of Equity, research guide.

9 Sylvester Joseph Hunter, *Elementary View of the Proceeds in a Suit of Equity*, 4th edn, London: Butterworths, 1867, 15–22; PROV, *Kearney v. Lowry*, Plaintiff's Costs. The master in equity notes that he first gave advice about drawing up the bill in the Hilary Term, 1867.

10 PROV, Roll of Proceedings, *Kearney & Others v. Henry Wallace Lowry*, William Kearney and William McGann.

11 Sands and McDougall, *Melbourne Directory*, 1870 locates Garrard and James at 22 Collins Street, East; PROV, *Kearney v. Lowry*, Affidavit of Henry Wallace Lowry, Moneys paid on account of the estate; Kearney, Memorandum, 2–3.

12 PROV, *Kearney v. Lowry*, Authority by Best Friend, 30 March 1868.

13 PROV, *Kearney v. Lowry*, Bill, Caroline Kearney, 30 March 1868; Hunter, 1867, 12–18.

14   PROV, *Kearney v. Lowry*; Hunter, 1867, 22.
15   PROV, *Kearney v. Lowry*; Harrison, 2014.
16   PROV, *Kearney v. Lowry*, Answer, Lowry, 1 May 1868.
17   John Barter Bennett, Parliament of Victoria, Former Members, <www. parliament.vic.gov.au/index.php?option=com_fabrik&view=list&listid =23&Itemid=1135&limitstart23=0>, accessed 13 June 2019; Sands and McDougall, *Melbourne Directory*, 1863, 348; 1868, 543; *Argus*, 2 January 1865, 4.
18   PROV, *Kearney v. Lowry*, Answer, William Kearney, 18 May 1869.
19   PROV, *Kearney v. Lowry*, Answer, William McGann, 18 May 1869.
20   Harrison, 2014.
21   PROV, *Kearney v. Lowry*, Costs, defendant Lowry.
22   PROV, *Kearney v. Lowry*, Claim, William Ainslie, Drapers and Outfitters, Quartz Reefs, Pleasant Creek, 3 April 1869.
23   Serviceton Centenary Committee, *Serviceton: A Frontier Town on No Man's Land, 1887–1987*, Serviceton, Vic.: The Committee, 1987, 13–14.
24   PROV, *Kearney v. Lowry*, Affidavit of McGann, 30 June 1869.
25   PROV, *Kearney v. Lowry*, Affidavit of Francis Beaver Oliver, storekeeper, Bordertown, 21 March 1869 for purchases 29 June 1868.
26   PROV, *Kearney v. Lowry*, Affidavit of Walter Moore Miller, 1 August 1868; Plaintiff's costs, starting Hilary Term, 1867.
27   PROV, *Kearney v. Lowry*, Affidavit of Caroline Kearney, 4 August 1868; Affidavit of Henry Wallace Lowry and Schedule of Costs, 9 September 1869.
28   Harrison, 2014; Dean, 1968, 5–6.
29   J. A. La Nauze, 'William Edward Hearn (1826–1888)', *Australian Dictionary of Biography*, <adb.anu.edu.au/biography/hearn-william-edward-3743>, accessed 13 June 2019.
30   Sands and McDougall, *Melbourne Directory*, 1869, 595; J. M. Bennett, *Sir William A'Beckett, First Chief Justice of Victoria, 1842–1857*, Sydney: Federation Press, 2009.
31   PROV, *Kearney v. Lowry*, Costs, Lowry, *Argus*, 28 October 1868, 4.
32   *The Age*, 1 December 1868, 3; Hunter, 1867, 81; Reginald R. Sholl, 'Sir Robert Molesworth (1806–1890)', *Australian Dictionary of Biography*, <adb.anu.edu.au/biography/molesworth-sir-robert-4217>, accessed 13 June 2019.
33   Sholl, 'Sir Robert Molesworth'; Russell, 1994, 115–18, quote at 115; Bennett, 2004, 156.
34   Russell, 1994, 118.
35   *The Age*, 1 December 1868, 3; *Argus*, 1 December, 5.
36   *The Age*, 2 December 1868, 2, 3; *Argus*, 2 December 1868, 4, 6.
37   *Empire* (Sydney), 8 December 1868, 2; *Leader* (Melbourne), 5 December 1868, 13; *Australasian*, 5 December 1868, 22; Hugh Anderson, 'Clarke, William John (1805–1874)', *Australian Dictionary of Biography*, <adb. anu.edu.au/biography/clarke-william-john-1902>, accessed 3 April 2019.

38  *Argus*, 2 December 1868, 6; George C. G. Moore, 'A biographical sketch of William Edward Hearn (1826–1888): a slightly "Irish" perspective', University of Notre Dame, Australia, School of Business, Research On-Line, 3–4, <researchonline.nd.edu.au/cgi/viewcontent.cgi?referer=www.google.com/&httpsredir=1&article=1015&context=bus_conference>, accessed 2 April 2019.

39  *Argus*, 2 December 1868, 6; *Kearney v. Lowry* (1868), 5 Wyatt, Webb and A'Beckett's Reports, Equity (Vic.), 206.

40  *Argus*, 2 December 1868, 6.

41  Kearney, Memorandum, 2; PROV, *Kearney v. Lowry*, Affidavit of Henry Wallace Lowry, 9 September 1869.

42  Rosalind Atherton, 'Expectation without right: testamentary freedom and the position of women in 19th-century New South Wales', *UNSW Law Journal*, vol. 11, 1988, 144–45, 147; *In the Will of Anne Neeson* (1869), 6 Wyatt, Webb and A'Beckett's Reports, Equity (Vic.), 319–21; *Argus*, 12 October 1869, 6.

43  *Kearney v. Lowry* (1868), 5 Wyatt, Webb and A'Beckett's Reports, Equity (Vic.), 113, 201.

44  *Argus*, 2 December 1868, 6.

45  PROV, *Kearney v. Lowry*, Decree; *Argus*, 18 December 1868, 6.

46  PROV, *Kearney v. Lowry*, Costs, William Kearney under Order dated 12 November; Affidavit of Walter Moore, 11 March 1869.

47  PROV, Will, Edward Kearney, 30 September 1865, 2.

48  *Argus*, 20 March 1869, 3; 22 March 1869, 3; 23 March 1869, 3; 24 March 1869, 2; 27 March 1869, 3.

49  *Argus*, 5, 7, 9, 12, 13, 14, 16; 17 April 1869, 3; *Hamilton Spectator*, 21 April 1869, 3.

50  <westerndistrictfamilies.com/2017/01/30/passing-of-the-pioneers-51/>, accessed 16 June 2019; *Horsham Times*, 22 March 1938, 10; 12 October 1937, 3; PROV 9704/P2, Rate Books, Shire of Wimmera, District of Horsham, Assessment of General District Rate, 1869–1870.

51  *Argus*, 6 May 1869, 4; Charles James Hamilton, *Pioneering Days in Western Victoria*, Melbourne: Exchange Press, 1913, 58; PROV, *Kearney v. Lowry*, Costs, McGann, 17 June 1870; Costs, William Kearney, 12 November 1869.

52  PROV, *Kearney v. Lowry*, Affidavit of Henry Wallace Lowry, 19 October 1869. The International Institute of Social History website reports that average weekly wages in Victoria in 1869 were around £1 2s: <www.iisg.nl/hpw/>, accessed 14 April 2016. The Measuring Worth website reports that a simple purchasing power, real wage or real wealth conversion of this to 2019 Australian dollars would make the relative value $1 750 000.

53  PROV, Will, Edward Kearney, 30 September 1865.

**6    Leaving Lockhart Station**

1   Edward Kearney, Memorandum, 3, c.1876, transcribed by Joe Palmer, held by family members. Liz Harfull, *Almost an Island: The Story of Robe*, South Australia: Wakefield Press, 2013, 189.

2    Public Record Office Victoria (henceforth PROV), *Kearney v. Lowry*, Affidavit of Henry Wallace Lowry, 17 September 1869.

3    PROV, *Kearney v. Lowry,* Affidavit of Caroline Kearney, 6 September 1869; 'Glass Terrace', <vhd.heritagecouncil.vic.gov.au/places/457/download-report>, accessed 3 April 2019.

4    Charles James Hamilton, *Pioneering Days in Western Victoria*, Melbourne: Exchange Press, 1913, 78; Australian Aboriginal Cricketers, 1867, photograph by Patrick Dawson, <www.portrait.gov.au/portraits/2009.134/australian-aboriginal-cricketers>, accessed 6 September 2018; Gideon Haigh, *Stroke of Genius: Victor Trumper and the Shot that Changed Cricket*, Melbourne: Penguin Random House, 2016; Derek John Mulvaney, *Cricket Walkabout: The Australian Aboriginal Cricketers on Tour, 1867–8*, Melbourne: MUP, 1967; Teresa Hamilton, *A Squatting Saga*, Sorrento, Vic.: Arden Press, 1991, 48–55.

5    PROV, VPRS 4301/P000/14, Rate Book, Fitzroy, 1871–72, fo. 41; Sands and McDougall, *Melbourne Directory*, 1869, 1870, 180; 1871, 187; *Melbourne History Resources*, 177, <omeka.cloud.unimelb.edu.au/melbourne-history/items/show/11>, accessed 3 April 2019; Cricinfo, Australia, <www.espncricinfo.com/australia/content/player/6738.html>, accessed 3 April 2019.

6    Fitzroy State School, no. 450, Victorian Heritage Database report, <vhd.heritagecouncil.vic.gov.au/places/103795/download-report>, accessed 3 April 2019.

7    Sylvester Joseph Hunter, *Elementary View of the Proceeds in a Suit of Equity*, 4th edn, London: Butterworths, 1867, 127.

8    PROV, *Kearney v. Lowry*, Affidavit of Caroline Kearney, 8 September 1869; Affidavit of William Kearney, 9 September 1869.

9    PROV, *Kearney v. Lowry*, Costs, William Kearney, 12 November 1869; Costs, Caroline Kearney, 9 September 1869; Affidavit of Henry Wallace Lowry, 19 October 1869.

10   PROV, *Kearney v. Lowry*, Costs, defendant, Caroline Kearney, 9 September 1869; *Argus*, 10 September 1869, 7.

11   Bettina Bradbury, *Working Families: Age, Gender and Daily Survival in Industrializing Montreal*, Toronto: UTP, 2007; Pat Jalland, *Australian Ways of Death: A Social and Cultural History, 1840–1918*, Melbourne: OUP, 2002, 133.

12   PROV, *Kearney v. Lowry*, Affidavit of Henry Wallace Lowry, 19 October 1869; VPRS, 759/ P/215, #12474, Proceedings in Insolvent Estates, *In the Matter of the Insolvency of Caroline Kearney*, 29 September 1869.

13   PROV, Insolvency of Caroline Kearney, 29 September 1869; Kearney, Memorandum, 2.

14   *Argus*, 25 September 1869, 5, 6; PROV, Insolvency of Caroline Kearney; *Argus*, 6 October 1869, 6; PROV, *Kearney v. Lowry*, Affidavit of Henry Wallace Lowry.

15   John C. Weaver, 'A pathology of insolvents: Melbourne, 1871–1915', *Australian Journal of Legal History*, vol. 8, no. 1, 2004, 109, 110.

16  *Argus*, 6 October 1869, 6; PROV, Insolvency of Caroline Kearney; Sands and McDougall, *Melbourne Directory*, 1869, 735.

17  PROV, *Kearney v. Lowry*, Costs, Lowry, William Kearney, 19 September 1869; Affidavit of Henry Wallace Lowry, 19 October 1869.

18  PROV, *Kearney v. Lowry*, Costs, Plaintiff, Lowry, McGann, William Kearney, 1869; Hunter, 1867, 186.

19  Hunter, 1867, 189.

20  *Argus*, 3 November 1869, 1.

21  PROV, *Kearney v. Lowry*, Before Justice Molesworth, 12 November 1869.

22  PROV, *Kearney v. Lowry*, Affidavit of Caroline Kearney, 20 June 1870.

23  SRSA, MRG18/4/0000/01, Robe District Council Assessment Book, 1869 to 1887, section 4, 1870–1875; Kathleen Bermingham, *Gateway to the South East: A Story of Robetown and the Guichen Bay District*, Millicent, SA: South Eastern Times Ltd, 1961, 151, 184; Harfull, 2013, 65–67, 186, 189; SRSA, PRG 497, series 7, Roland Campbell, Research Notes.

24  PROV, *Kearney v. Lowry*, Bill, Trollope for assisting McGann and Lowry, 1869–70.

25  Bermingham, 1961, 214–16; PROV, *Kearney v. Lowry*, Affidavit of Henry Wallace Lowry, 19 October 1869; SRSA, MRG 18/9/00000/1, Robe, Miscellaneous letters, Clerk, Robe to Education Office Adelaide, 20 September 1870; SRSA, PRG497, series 6, Campbell, Short History of Robe, 47–48; *South Australian Advertiser*, 10 January 1860, 3; *Border Watch*, 11 March 1871, 2.

26  Kearney, Memorandum, 3.

27  Hamilton, 1991, 35–39; Kearney, Memorandum, 3.

28  PROV, *Kearney v. Lowry*, Bill, Trollope for assisting McGann and Lowry, 1869–71; telegram dated 27 April 1870.

29  PROV, *Kearney v. Lowry*, Affidavit of Caroline Kearney, 13 June 1870; Affidavit of James Mustarde, 20 June 1870; Affidavit of Frederick Snewin, 9 June 1870.

30  PROV, *Kearney v. Lowry*, Bill, Trollope, June 1870.

31  PROV, *Kearney v. Lowry*, Before Molesworth, 12 November 1869; 17 June 1870; *Argus*, 18 June 1870, 6.

32  *Kearney v. Lowry* (1868), 5 Wyatt, Webb and A'Beckett's Reports, Equity (Vic.), 205.

33  Hunter, 1867, 185, 187; PROV, *Kearney v. Lowry*, Certificate of Costs, Master in Equity, 8 December 1869.

34  PROV, *Kearney v. Lowry*, Costs, Plaintiffs, Lowry, McGann, William Kearney.

35  PROV, *Kearney v. Lowry*, Costs, McGann, Lowry, William Kearney, 1869; Victoria, Marriage Registration, #2948, 6 September 1869; PROV, Index to Outward Passengers to Interstate UK, NZ and Foreign Ports (digitised copy); *Argus*, 22 June 1870, 1; *Ireland, Select Births and Baptisms, 1620–1911*, Birth and Baptism, Ann Mulrean, 3 November 1870, Ancestry.com, accessed 1 April 2019.

36  *Australasian*, 3 September 1870, 13; *Leader (Melbourne)*, 3 September 1870, 13.

37 Kearney, Memorandum, 3; 'Melbourne's Hotels in 1870; in the heyday', Melbourne: Museline Maps, 2003; 'Sands & McDougall's Melbourne and Suburban Directory for 1870', 13, 30, *Melbourne History Resources*, <omeka.cloud.unimelb.edu.au/melbourne-history/items/show/10>, accessed 2 April 2019; PROV, Will, Edward Kearney, 30 September 1865. While Caroline was there, a resident advertised in the *Argus* hoping someone had found a 'blue-silk panier' they lost somewhere between Gertrude Street and the hotel, located at the corner of Elizabeth and Collins Street. Could this have been Caroline, revisiting the street where she had lodged formerly? If so, was she so stressed or inebriated that she was distracted and losing things? The finder was promised a reward on bringing the basket to the Clarence Hotel: *Argus*, 17 September 1870, 1.

38 *Argus*, 15 September 1870, 6; Jamieson and District Historical Society, 'Woods Point', <home.vicnet.net.au/~jdhs/8woodspoint.htm>, accessed 1 April 2019.

39 PROV, Will, Edward Kearney, 30 September 1865; *Argus*, 1 October 1870, 18.

40 *Argus*, 3 September 1870, 4; 14 September 1870, 4; 17 September 1870, 4; 28 September 1870, 4; PROV, Will, Edward Kearney, 30 September 1865; *Argus*, 19 September 1870, 1; 20 August 1870, 2; 1 October 1870, 4; *Australasian*, 1 October 1870, 18; *Argus*, 3 October 1870, 4.

41 Kearney, Memorandum, 2.

**7   Arrivals and new challenges**

1 Edward Kearney, Memorandum, c.1876, 3, transcribed by Joe Palmer, held by family members; *Irish Times*, 9 May 1871, 5.

2 Liam Cox, *Moate, County Westmeath: A History of the Town and District*, Athlone: n.p. 1981, 141; Kearney, Memorandum, 3.

3 *Freeman's Journal*, 25 August 1870, 5.

4 Kearney, 'Memorandum', 3; *Saunders's News-Letter*, 9 May 1871, 1.

5 Seán P Farragher CSSp, *The French College Blackrock, 1860–1896*, Dublin: Paraclete Press, 2011, 1–3, 7.

6 Farragher, 2011, 2.

7 Blackrock College, Archives, Student Register, Kearney, Edward; Kearney, William; Kearney, Francis Henry, 1870; Payment register, 1870, 131.

8 Farragher, 2011, 8, 7, 125, 7, 8, 14; they included the politician Eamon de Valera and writer, Flann O'Brien.

9 Farragher, 2011, 2, 5, 7; Kearney, Memorandum, 3.

10 Kearney, Memorandum, 3. Unfortunately, Petty Sessions records do not exist for Dublin or Sandymount between 1871 and 1881. There is no mention of this event in the *Irish Times* or the *Evening Mail* court reporting for around that date.

11 Kearney, Memorandum, 3; *Standard* (Ireland), 10 May 1871, 5.

12 *Drogheda Argus and Leinster Journal*, 10 June 1871, 3.

13 John David Chambers, *A Practical Treatise on the Jurisdiction of the High Court of Chancery over the Persons and Property of Infants*, London: Saunders & Benning, 1842, 24–25; John Adams, *The Doctrine of Equity:*

*A Commentary on the Law as Administered by the Court of Chancery*;
William Forsyth, *A Treatise on the Law relating to Custody of Infants in
Cases of Difference between Parents or Guardians*, Philadelphia: T &
J. W. Johnston and Co., 1851.

14   *Saunders's News-Letter*, 20 April 1871, 2; *Saunders's News-Letter*,
29 April 1871, 2.

15   *Irish Times*, 9 May 1871, 5; *Freeman's Journal*, 9 May 1871, 6.

16   *Saunders' News-Letter*, 29 April 1871, 2; 6 May 1871, 2; 8 May 1871, 2;
*Irish Times*, 5 May 1871, 5.

17   *Saunders's News-Letter*, 9 May 1871, 1.

18   Chambers, 1842, 116, 137.

19   Sylvester Joseph Hunter, *Elementary View of the Proceeds in a Suit of
Equity*, 4th edn, London: Butterworths, 1867, 21–23.

20   PRONI, 'Introduction to the O'Hagan Papers', <www.nidirect.gov.uk/
publications/introduction-ohagan-papers>, accessed 2 April 2019; Daire
Hogan, 'Arrows too sharply pointed: the relations of Lord Justice Christian
and Lord O'Hagan, 1868–1874', in *The Common Law Tradition. Essays in
Irish Legal History*, J. F. McEldowney and Paul O'Higgens, eds, Blackrock,
Ireland: Irish Academic Press, 1990, 61–62.

21   PRONI, D2777/5/80–89/40/1, MIC 562/25, O'Hagan Papers,
Correspondence with individual correspondents, 1859–84, O'Hagan to
Lord Hartingdon, n.d. 1873; PRONI, D27777/7/4/133–241, MIC562/17,
John Francis Maguire to Lord Chancellor O'Hagan, 4 April 1872.

22   Hogan, 1990, 64.

23   PRONI, 'Introduction to the O'Hagan Papers;' *Tamworth Herald*
(Tamworth, England), 18 June 1870, 3, no. 98, consulted via British
Library Newspapers, Part III: 1780–1950.

24   'Destruction of the Irish Chancery Rolls (1304–1922)', <chancery.tcd.
ie/content/destruction-irish-chancery-rolls-1304-1922>, accessed 3 April
2019; Hogan, 1990.

25   Alexander G. Richey and Edmund T. Bewley, *The Chancery (Ireland) Act,
1867: And the General Orders and Regulations Thereunder, Copiously
Annotated, with an Introduction, Schedules of Fees, and a Collection of
Forms and Precedents*, Dublin: E. Ponsonby, 1868, xxxiii–xviii.

26   *Standard* (London), 10 May 1871, 5; *Irish Times*, 9 May 1871, 5;
*Freeman's Journal*, 9 May 1871, 6l; *Saunders's News-Letter*, 9 May, 1.

27   *Freeman's Journal*, 9 May 1871, 6; *Saunders's News-Letter*, 9 May
1871, 1.

28   *American Law Review*, vol. 6, 1872, 193.

29   *Irish Times*, 9 May 1871, 5; *Standard*, 10 May 1871, 5; *Irish Times*, 9 May
1871, 5; *Standard*, 10 May 1871, 5; *Saunders's News-Letter*, 9 May 1871, 1.

30   *Irish Times*, 9 May 1871, 5; *Standard*, 10 May 1871, 5; *Saunders's
News-Letter*, 9 May 1871, 1.

31   *Saunders's News-Letter*, 5 June 1871, 1.

32   Richey and Bewley, 1867, xiv.

33   *Freeman's Journal*, 5 June 1871, 6.

34 *Freeman's Journal*, 5 June 1871, 6; *Saunders's News-Letter*, 5 June 1871, 1; *American Law Review*, 1872, 192–94; Kearney, Memorandum, 3.

35 *Freeman's Journal*, 5 June 1871, 6; *Saunders's News-Letter*, 5 June 1871, 1; *American Law Review*, 1872, 192–94.

36 *Freeman's Journal*, 5 June 1871, 6; *American Law Review*, 1872, 192–94; *Saunders's News-Letter*, 5 June 1871, 1.

37 *American Law Review*, 1872, 193; *Freeman's Journal*, 5 June 1871, 6.

38 O'Hagan's decision was widely copied, including in the *Cork Constitution*, 9 May 1871, 3 and 5 June 1871, 2, 3; *Waterford Standard*, 7 June 1871, 3; *London Evening Standard*, 10 May 1871, 5, and 6 June 1871, 5; *Birmingham Market*, 10 June 1871, 3, 4; *Bradford Daily Telegraph*, 6 June 1871, 4; *American Law Review*, 1872, 193.

39 *American Law Review*, 1872, 192; Chambers, 1842, 137.

40 *American Law Review*, 1872, 192–94; Forsyth, 1851.

41 Julie A. Stiles, 'Nineteenth-Century child custody reform: maternal authority and the development of the best interest of the child standard', *Probate Law Journal*, vol. 6, no. 5, 1984, 5, 7, 10–11, 21.

42 *American Law Review*, 1872, 192. Interestingly, there is no mention of the case in *The Irish Reports, Equity Series*, 1870–81; *The Law Reports (Ireland), Chancery*, 1878–1881; R. D. Murray and G. Y. Dixon, compilers, *The Irish Reports and Law Reports (Ireland): Digest of Cases from 1867–1893*, Dublin: Edward Ponsonby, 1899; William Cotter Stubbs, compiler, *The Irish Law Times Digest of Cases decided by the Superior Courts in Ireland, 1867–1893*, Dublin: John Falconer, 1895. The *American Law Review* took its information from the London-based *Solicitors' Journal and Reporter*.

43 *Saunders's Newsletter*, 5 June 1871, 1, 4.

44 Chambers, 1842, 24–25.

45 *Downpatrick Recorder*, 16 February 1867, 4; *Saunders's News-Letter*, 23 July 1870, 4; *Dublin Daily Express*, 13 August 1832, 2; *Freeman's Journal*, 13 August 1873, 3; *Belfast Newsletter*, 30 December 1882, 1; *Belfast Newsletter*, 15 August 1883, 1; Kearney, Memorandum, 3.

46 Kearney, Memorandum, 3.

47 Public Record Office Victoria (henceforth PROV), PROV, VPRS 28/P1, Unit 11, Will, Edward Kearney, 19 November 1865, 4.

48 *Thom's Irish Almanac*, County Dublin, 1876, 1649; 1878, 1666; 1879, 1670; 1880, 1674; *Slater's Royal National Commercial Directory of Ireland 1881*, 97; *Freeman's Journal*, 13 March 1878, 7.

49 *Freeman's Journal*, 20 December 1870; Richard Killeen, *Historical Atlas of Dublin*, Dublin, Gill and Macmillan, 2009, 114; Séamas Ó Maitiú, *Dublin's Suburban towns, 1834–1930: Governing Clontarf, Drumcondra, Dalkey, Killiney, Kilmainham, Pembroke, Kingstown, Blackrock, Rathmines, and Rathgar*, Dublin: Four Courts, 2003, 38.

50 *Irish Times*, 6 September 1866, 2; Ireland, Census, 1911, <www.census.nationalarchives.ie/reels/nai000114284/>, accessed 3 April 2019.

51 *Irish Times*, 27 August 1880, 8; *Irish Times*, 23 February 1875, 1.

52    Richard Bushman, *The Refinement of America: Persons, Houses, Cities*, New York: Knopf, 1992, 19.

53    *Irish Times*, 27 August 1880, 8.

54    Kearney, Memorandum 4.

55    *Irish Times*, 2 July 1872, 5; PROV, Will, Edward Kearney, 19 November 1865, 5.

56    R. J. Morris, *Men, Women and Property in England, 1780–1870: A Social and Economic History of Family Strategies amongst the Leeds Middle Class*, Cambridge: Cambridge University Press, 2005, 35.

57    NAI, Calendar of Wills and Administrations, 1874, 313, <www.willcalendars.nationalarchives.ie/search/cwa/details.jsp?id=1639377692>, accessed 2 April 2019; *Freeman's Journal*, 9 May 1871, 6.

58    England, Marriage certificate, Caroline Anne Kearney and Richard Locke Johnson, 18 March 1873, no. 174.

59    'Marriage Allegations, Bonds and Licences in England and Wales', <https://www.familysearch.org/wiki/en/Marriage_Allegations,_Bonds_and_Licences_in_England_and_Wales>, accessed 23 June 2019.

60    England, Marriage certificate, Caroline Anne Kearney and Richard Locke Johnson, 18 March, 1873, no. 174; *London and Provincial Medical Directory*, 1865, 108; England, Census, 1871, RG10, Piece 348, folio 76, 51, accessed 21 June 2018, Ancestry.com, accessed 1 April 2019; *London Gazette*, 6 December 1872, #23926, 6170, accessed 14 April 2017; Post Office London Directory, 1875, 2163; England, Census, 1881, Poplar, London, <booth.lse.ac.uk/map/15/-0.1863/51.5398/100/0?marker=526006.936,185128.434>, accessed 2 April 2019.

61    *London Gazette*, 2 November 1855, #21808, 4047; *London Gazette*, 5 February 1856, #21846, 429; *Freeman's Journal*, 14 December 1855, 3; 25 February 1860, 1; 21 April 1863, 3; *Medical Directory*, London, 1875, 126, Ancestry.com, accessed 20 June 2018.

62    England, Census, 1871; England, Census, 1891; England, Census, 1901; Workhouse discharge records, Lewisham Parish, 1900, 1904, Ancestry.com, accessed 3 April 2019.

63    *London Gazette*, 31 October 1876, #24377, 5087; *London Gazette*, 15 March 1878, #24563, 2022, accessed 14 April 2017; England, Census, 1881, St Giles, St George Bloomsbury, Class RG11, piece 321, folio 145, 3, accessed 7 December 2013, Ancestry.com, accessed 1 April 2019.

64    'Irish migration to Britain', <www.irish-genealogy-toolkit.com/Irish-immigration-to-Britain.html>, accessed 3 April 2019 notes that 'one crucial feature of Irish immigration to Britain', is that 'there are no passenger lists of people who crossed the Irish Sea by ship'.

65    Kearney, Memorandum, 3–4; NA-UK, BT 99/892, Records of the Registrar General of Shipping and Seamen, Crew Lists and Ships Agreements, #65640, *Northumberland*; PROV, VPRS 3504, Microfilm, Inward Shipping Index, 1839–1900, Reel 2, L–Z; Ronald Hope, *A New History of British Shipping*, London: John Murray, 1990, 313–14 reports that it used both

sail and steam, was fitted with 300 horsepower engines and capable of 10.5 knots when sailing.

66 Kearney Memorandum, 7; V. B. Burton, 'Apprenticeship regulation and marine labour in the nineteenth-century British merchant marine', *International Journal of Maritime History*, vol. 1, 1989, 20–49; NA-UK, BT 151, 'Indexes of apprentices registered in the Merchant Navy, 1824–1910', Ancestry.com, accessed 1 April 2019; 'Register of UK apprentices indentured in the Merchant Navy, 1824–1910', Edward Kearney, 19 September 1874; William Kearney, 7 November 1874.

67 *Freeman's Journal*, 5 June 1874, 7; 9 June 1874, 7; 19 June 1874, 7; *Irish Times*, 20 June 1874, 3; *Freeman's Journal*, 13 November 1874, 4; 18 July 1874, 6; 18 November 1874, 3.

68 NAI, Calendar of Wills and Administrations, 1874, 313.

69 Hogan, 1990, 61.

70 *Irish Times*, 20 June 1874, 3; *Freeman's Journal*, 13 November 1874, 4.

71 *Irish Times*, 2 July 1872, 5; *Freeman's Journal*, 3 May 1876, 3; 30 November 1876, 2.

72 *Irish Times*, 2 July 1872, 5.

73 PROV, Will, Edward Kearney, 30 September 1865, 5–6.

74 I have sought evidence of how Edward's money was spent and whether any went towards Patrick's projects, without success. The archivist for the diocese of Ardagh and Clonmacnois, which includes the part of County Westmeath in which St Patrick's Church is located, informs me that they have no archives and he does not think there is any documentation at the church.

75 PROV, *Kearney v. Lowry*, Affidavit of Henry Wallace Lowry, 19 October 1869.

76 PROV, VPRS 7591/P1/23, 5/461, Will, Edward Kearney, 30 September 1865, 2; Sydney Homer and Richard Sylla, *A History of Interest Rates*, Hoboken, N.J.: Wiley, 2005, 179–80; Philip Ollerenshaw, *Banking in Nineteenth Century Ireland: The Belfast Banks, 1825–1914*, Manchester, UK: MUP, 1987, 109–14.

77 Calculations from <www.measuringworth.com/calculators/australiacompare/>, accessed 19 June 2018.

78 *Thom's Official Directory of the UK and Ireland*, 1876, 104; *Freeman's Journal*, 13 March 1878, 7.

79 Kearney, Memorandum, 4.

80 Kearney, Memorandum, 4–5.

81 Rosalind McLeod, History of the Families of Walter Gerard and Anna Violet Kearney, unpublished manuscript, held by family members, 17.

82 *Freeman's Journal*, 6 February 1879, 1; Kearney, Memorandum, 6; Ireland, Marriage Certificate, 5 February 1879, Saint John's, Sandymount. The boarding house was run by a Mrs Mary Ann Sumner, *Guy's Directory*, 1875; *Slater's Directory*, 1881.

83 Mr and Mrs Kearney are among the passengers listed as departing

from Kingstown on the Royal Mail Steamer and returning a week later: *Freeman's Journal*, 7 February 1879, 5; *Irish Times*, 14 February 1879, 3.

84   *Irish Times*, 11 March 1880, 1.

85   McLeod, History of the Families of Walter Gerard and Anna Violet Kearney, 15; recording, Anna Violet Gerard, 1949, in possession of Joe Palmer; New South Wales, Australia, Unassisted Immigrant Passenger Lists, 1826–1922, Ancestry.com, accessed 2 April 2019; NSW State Records, online Index to Vessels Arrived 1837–1925.

86   Edgar Kearney, aged 19, Scotland, Census, 1881, 7 Lynedoch Street, Greenock, Renfrewshire, Apprentice Marine Engineer, Ancestry.com, accessed 26 June 2015. The census was taken on 3 April 1881.

87   Births, Anne, 3 November 1870; Eliza, 21 October 1872; Mary Margaret, 6 May 1875; Francis Joseph, 17 July 1877: Ireland, Select Births and Baptisms, 1620–1911, Ancestry.com, accessed 1 April 2019.

88   NAI, Calendar of Wills and Administrations, Grant of Probate, 8 August 1878, Will of Francis Kearney, 21 August 1876.

89   NAI, Calendar of Wills and Administrations, Grant of Probate, 8 August 1878, Will of Francis Kearney, 21 August 1876.

90   NAI, Civil Deaths Index, 1864–1958, accessed via Ancestry.com, accessed 1 April 2019; Francis Kearney, 15 January 1878; Charles Mulrain, 6 May 1878; NAI, Calendar of Wills and Administrations, 1858–1927, <www.willcalendars.nationalarchives.ie>, accessed 3 April 2019, Francis Kearney, Letters of Administration to Patrick Kearney, 8 August 1878; Charles Mulrean, Letters of Administration to Mary Anne Mulrain, 8 June 1878.

91   PROV, VPRS 7666, Victoria Assisted and Unassisted Inward Passenger Lists, 1839–1923, *Lusitania*, 9 July 1881; *Sydney Morning Herald*, 26 August 1881, 4; Victoria Australia, Outward Passenger Index, 1852–1915, *Rotomahana*, August 1881.

92   Marriage Registration, Frank Henry Kearney and Margaret Kearney, Dunedin, 11 September 1881, no. 45; 'Founding of Dunedin Diocese', *Encyclopaedia of New Zealand*, 1966, <www.teara.govt.nz/en/1966/the-roman-catholic-church/page-5>, accessed 3 April 2019.

93   McGibbon, 'James Allen', *Dictionary of New Zealand Biography*, <www.teara.govt.nz/en/biographies/3a12/allen-james>, accessed 14 June 2019; Obituary, Robert Steele, *Otago Witness*, 7 November 1895, 51.

94   Marriage Registration, Frank Henry Kearney and Margaret Kearney, Dunedin, 11 September 1881, no. 45.

95   Electoral rolls, Blenheim, Ward, Wairau, 1901–1928, Ancestry.com, accessed 16 April 2016.

96   *Slater's Royal National Commercial Directory of Ireland 1881*, 97; NSW, List of Crew and Unassisted Passengers, *Grasmere*, Liverpool–Sydney, arrived 10 August 1882, Ancestry.com, accessed 19 June 2018.

97   *Irish Times*, 21 August 1880, 8; *Irish Times*, 27 August 1880, 8.

98   PROV, VPRS 7591/P1/23, 5/461, Will, Edward Kearney, 30 September 1865, 4.

99   Chambers, 1842, 24–25.

100 In Charles Dickens' *Bleak House*, for example, the Lord Chancellor oversaw young Richard Carstone's successive choices of potential professions: *Slater's Royal National Commercial Directory of Ireland 1881*, 97.

101 *Irish Times*, 24 October 1881, 7; *Westmeath Examiner*, 30 August 1913, 8; Jeremiah Sheehan, *South Westmeath: Farm and Folk*, Dublin: Blackwater, 1978, 138, 141; SRNSW, List of the Crew and Passengers, *Cotopaxi*, 9 December 1881, Ancestry.com, accessed 5 January 2016; *Argus*, 24 November 1881, 6.

102 Kearney, Memorandum, 4.

**8    Endings**

1 Death certificate, Caroline Kearney, dated 3 May 1886, secured through General Register Office, England.

2 Victoria, Australia, Assisted and Unassisted Passenger Lists, 1839–1923, *Crofton Hall*, departed Liverpool 26 May 1883, Ancestry.com, accessed 20 June 2018.

3 SRSA, MRG18/4/0000/01, Robe District Council Assessment Book, 1869 to 1887, lists a Mrs Kearney as the owner of their cottage in Robe the year after her death.

4 *London Gazette*, 15 March 1878; England, Census, 1881, RG11, Piece 321, fo. 145, p. 3, GSU roll, 134109, accessed Ancestry.com, accessed 21 June 2018; General Register Office, England, Death Certificate, Richard Locke Johnson, 17 August 1882.

5 Will, Richard Locke Johnson, 16 August 1882, proved 3 October 1882, London, England, General Registrar Office; England and Wales, National Probate Calendar, 1882, 120, accessed via Ancestry.com, accessed 21 June 2016; Charles Booth Online Archive, Booth Walk with Police Constable Robert Turner, District 2 (Strand and St Giles), 13 July 1898, © London School of Economics & Political Science, <booth.lse.ac.uk>, accessed 18 June 2019; General Register Office, England, Death Certificate, Richard Locke Johnson, 17 August 1882.

6 *Household Words*, cited by Stephen Swensen, 'Mapping poverty in Agar Town: economic conditions prior to the development of St. Pancras Station', <eprints.lse.ac.uk/22539/1/0906Swensen.pdf>, accessed 2 April 2019; 'History of Camden Town', <www.camdenhistorywiki.org.uk/index.php?title=History_of_Camden_New_Town>, accessed 2 April 2019.

7 'History of Camden Town', <www.camdenhistorywiki.org.uk/index.php?title=History_of_Camden_New_Town>, accessed 18 June 2019.

8 David Hayes, 'A History of Camden Town 1895–1914', <www.tate.org.uk/art/research-publications/camden-town-group/david-hayes-a-history-of-camden-town-1895-1914-r1104374>, accessed 2 April 2019.

9 Camden Local Studies and Archives Centre, London, Rate Assessments, microfilm no. 803, 1885, Camden Road, 13, Stratford Place, 157; 1886, Camden Road, 13, Stratford Place, 162, Villas, 164. England, Census, 1881, RG11: piece 209, fo. 79, p. 61; GUS roll: 1341046. Ancestry.com, accessed 14 June 2013.

10  *Post Office London Directory*, 1882, Part 1, 616.
11  Camden Local Studies and Archives Centre, St Pancras Parish, Rate assessments, Ward 3, 1882–1886, Stratford Place and Stratford Villas.
12  Charles Booth Online Archive, Survey Notebook, B356, 150, <booth.lse. ac.uk>, accessed 3 April 2019.
13  Death certificate, Caroline Kearney, dated 3 May 1886, secured through General Register Office, England; *Manual of the International List of Causes of death: As adapted for Use in England and Wales. Based on the Second Decennial Revision by the International Commission, Paris*, 1909.
14  *Auckland Star*, 10 October 1908, 15; Dick Weindling and Marianne Colloms, 'The downfall of a Kilburn doctor', *West Hampstead Life*, 5 December 2016, 1; England and Wales, Criminal Registers, 1791–1892, Class: HO 27, Piece 207, p. 175, 21 November 1887, Ancestry.com, accessed 10 August 2018; Web: London, England, Proceedings of the Old Bailey and Ordinary's Accounts Index, 1674–1913, London, 10 December 1906, Ancestry.com, accessed 10 August 2018.
15  England and Wales, Criminal Registers, 1791–1892, Class: HO 27, Piece 207, p. 175, 21 November 1887, Ancestry.com, accessed 10 August 2018; London, England, Proceedings of the Old Bailey and Ordinary's Accounts Index, 1674–1913, 10 December 1906, <https://www. oldbaileyonline.org/browse.jsp?id=t19061210-18&div=t19061210-18&terms=Arthur_Raynor#highlight>, accessed 19 June 2019; *Auckland Star*, 10 October 1908, 15; Weindling and Colloms, 2016, 1.
16  Pat Jalland, *Death in the Victorian Family*, New York: OUP, 1996; Julie-Marie Strange, *Death, Grief and Poverty in Britain, 1870–1914*, New York: Cambridge University Press, 2005; *Births and Deaths Registration Act 1874* (England), c. 88, ss 10, 12, 20.
17  Marriage of Johanna Harman and Michael Fanning, 1858; England, Census 1871, 1881, 1901, 1911; Electoral Rolls, London, Michael Fanning, 1876–1885; England, Andrews Newspaper Index Cards, 1790–1976, Ancestry.com, all accessed 2 April 2019; Booth B/356, 45, Booth Online Archive.
18  Julie-Marie Strange, '"She cried a very little": death, grief and mourning in working-class culture, c. 1880–1914', *Social History*, vol. 27, no. 2, 2002, 145–46, 152.
19  *Births and Deaths Registration Act 1874* (England), c. 88, ss 10, 12, 20; *Post Office London Directory*, 1843, 47.
20  *Freeman's Journal*, 1 May 1886, 1; *Argus*, 6 September 1886, 1.
21  *Border Watch*, 11 March 1871, 2; Kathleen Bermingham, *Gateway to the South East: A Story of Robetown and the Guichen Bay District*, Millicent, SA: South Eastern Times Ltd, 1961, 214; SRSA, MRG18/4/0000/01, Robe District Council Assessment Book, 1869 to 1887; 'South Australian Teachers, 1851–1962', online database, <http://legacy.library.unisa.edu.au/ condon/teachers/Teachers.asp?TeacherID=405>, accessed 22 June 2019; Hamilton, 1991, 42, 91; *Border Watch*, 23 January 1875, 2; Marriage Mary Bax and William Catt, 14 January 1875, Robe, South Australia,

vol. 102, 96; William Catt, Robe Cemetery, 8 December 1884; Public Record Office Victoria (henceforth PROV), VPRS 5357/P0000/002371, 406/121, Brockell, Brooksby, Land Selection and Correspondence Files, Re: *Land Act* of 1884, Grazing Area, Allotment 90, County of Lowan, Parish of Booroopki, 20 August 1886, 26 March 1887; J. Weldon Power to Secretary of Lands, Victoria, cites 3 May 1890 as the marriage date for Mary Catt and Alfred Pain. He died in April 1894. She died a year later: PROV, VPRS 28/P0/1022/80/066 and P2/588/80/066, letters of administration, Mary Pain, 1901.

22  Bermingham Cottage, South Australia Heritage Places database, ID#16443, 28 Victoria Street, Robe; Liz Harfull, *Almost an Island: The Story of Robe*, South Australia: Wakefield Press, 2013, 42–44.

23  Charles James Hamilton, *Pioneering Days in Western Victoria*, Melbourne: Exchange Press, 1913, 108–109; Victoria, *Land Act* 1884.

24  PROV, VPRS 5357/P/002371, 406/121, Brockell, Brooksby, Land Selection and Correspondence Files; Victoria Gazette, 1890, Applications for Leases approved, Victoria, *Land Act 1890*, s. 2, 5065.

25  Teresa Hamilton, *A Squatting Saga*, Sorrento, Vic.: Arden Press, 1991, 104–105, 107, 111; PROV, VPRS 28/P0/1022/80/066 and P2/588/80/066, letters of administration, Mary Pain, 1901.

26  Hospital Record, Avoca, 9 November 1886, 29 April 1887, 19 October 1887, Genealogical Society of Victoria; *Argus*, 21 January 1909, 6; *Horsham Times*, 22 January 1909, 3; *Chronicle*, 30 January 1909, 41.

27  Hamilton, 1991, 123; Ozenkadnook Cemetery listing, <www.ianmarr.net. au/OZENKAD.HTM>, accessed 23 June 2018.

28  Hamilton, 1913, 109.

29  Hamilton, 1991, 125–26.

30  Hamilton, 1991, 126; Ozenkadnook Cemetery Listing, <www.ianmarr.net. au/OZENKAD.HTM>, accessed 3 April 2019; Apsley cemetery, <www. findagrave.com/memorial/138889588/j-c-hamilton>, accessed 3 April 2019.

9    **The boys' adult lives**

1    Public Record Office Victoria (henceforth PROV), VPRS 7666, Australia, Assisted and Unassisted Passenger Lists, 1839–1923, Series: Ancestry. com, accessed 1 April 2019; *Clarence and Richmond Examiner*, 25 May 1915, 8.

2    *Irish Times*, 17 October 1885, 7; England and Wales, FreeBMD Marriage Index, 1837–1915, Ancestry.com, accessed 1 April 2019.

3    *Irish Times*, 17 October 1885, 7; *British Medical Journal*, 29 March 1890, 757.

4    Ireland, Death certificate, Mary Teresa (sic) Kearney, registered 23 January 1890, Rathdown, Blackrock, Dublin. Her sister married into a military family. Her husband's father, John Joseph Poett, served in the British Army in India and had married his mother there: *Thom's Official Directory of the UK and Ireland*, 1884, 4 Carlisle Terrace; *Thom's Official Directory of the*

*UK and Ireland*, 1883, 1884, 1885, 1900; Census, Ireland, 1901, Ancestry. com, accessed 17 April 2017.

5   Death certificate, Mary Teresa (sic) Kearney, 23 January 1890; *Freeman's Journal*, 2 January 1890, 1; *Amendment of Births and Deaths Registration Act 1880* (Ireland), 43 & 44 Vict., c. 13, s. 10.

6   William was listed at Edenville Cottage in the directories of 1889 and 1890: *Thom's Official Directory*. I have been unable to trace his movements in any listing of ships' crews or passengers in these months between his selection of land in New South Wales in May 1889 and her death.

7   Census, England, 1891, Ancestry.com, accessed 17 April 2017.

8   New South Wales, Marriage Index, Registration no. 1430; *Sydney Morning Herald*, 24 October 1889, 11; Saint Patrick's History – Early Years, <stpatschurchhill.org/st-patricks-history-early-years/>, accessed 3 April 2019; *Clarence and Richmond Examiner*, 25 May 1915, 8.

9   Census, England, 1891, Ancestry.com, accessed 17 April 2017; Charles Booth online archive, notebooks, Ondine Road, B375, 36–37.

10  *Australian Medical Directory and Handbook*, 1896, 4; England and Wales, Civil Registration, Birth Index, Camberwell, London, Q3, July–September 1889; Q3, July–September 1891; Q4, October–December 1894; England, Census, 1891; Passenger List, *Austral*, 20 September 1895, Ancestry.com, all accessed 18 November 2016.

11  Leonore Davidoff, *Thicker than Water: Siblings and Their Relations, 1780–1920*, Oxford: OUP, 2012, 7.

12  New South Wales, Census, 1891, Table VI, Number of Persons, Males and Females, in each County, distinguishing the Chinese and Aboriginal population, also the Area of each County and the Number of Persons per Square Mile, <http://hccda.ada.edu.au/pages/NSW-1891-census-02_732>, accessed 21 June 2019. This table reports the total numbers of Aboriginal men and women in NSW as 8280.

13  New South Wales, Census, 1891, Table IX, Showing Towns, Villages, and specified Localities, in Alphabetical order, with Population at the date of each Census, 1861–1891, <http://hccda.ada.edu.au/pages/ NSW-1891-census-02_749>; Table VIII, Population, Urban and Rural respectively, in each County (exclusive of Aborigines), <hccda.ada.edu.au/ pages/NSW-1891-census-02_746>; Table IX, Numbers and Percentages of Breadwinners, including both Sexes, under various Sub-divisions of Occupations in each County (exclusive of Aborigines), <hccda.ada.edu.au/ pages/NSW-1891-census-02_640>.

14  'Timeline Links', Clarence River Historical Society, <www.clarencehistory. org.au/html/timeline.html>, accessed 3 April 2019.

15  Photo, The Kearney Rifle Club, Grafton, n.d., (c.1890–96?), held by the Clarence River Historical Society, Grafton, NSW.

16  John O'Hara, *Big River Racing: A History of the Clarence River Jockey Club, 1861–2001*, Sydney: University of New South Wales Press, 1982, 44–45, 228; *Clarence and Richmond Examiner*, 23 June 1896, 5; 12 December 1896, 8.

17  *New South Wales Gazette*, July–September 1889, 5595; *Clarence and Richmond Examiner*, 6 December 1889, 8; 1 March 1890, 3; 5 April 1890, 8; 3 May 1890, 8; 26 July 1890, 8; 17 December 1890, 8; 20 December 1890, 8; 24 March 1891, 4.

18  *Clarence and Richmond Examiner*, 9 February 1892, 4; 15 February 1896, 8; 9 December 1893, 3; 23 December 1893, re extension; 15 February 1896, 8; 23 October 1897, 4; 19 March 1898, 2; 23 April 1898, 2; New South Wales Electoral Roll, South Grafton, 1903, Ancestry.com, accessed 17 April 2017.

19  Ireland, Civil Registration Deaths Index, Hugh Cooke, 9 July 1889; Ellen Cooke, July–September 1889, vol. 2, 418; UK Outward Passenger List, *Liguria*, 3 January 1890, Ancestry.com, accessed 17 April 2017, Rosalind McLeod, History of the Families of Walter Gerard and Anna Violet Kearney, unpublished manuscript, held by family members, 2; recording, Anna Violet Gerard.

20  Robert Lee, 'Linking a nation: Australia's transport and communications, 1788–1970', <https://webarchive.nla.gov.au/awa/20060820101024/http://ahc.gov.au/publications/linking-nation/chapter-2.html>, accessed 21 June 2019; McLeod, History of the Families of Walter Gerard and Anna Violet Kearney, 16.

21  McLeod, History of the Families of Walter Gerard and Anna Violet Kearney, 2.

22  McLeod, History of the Families of Walter Gerard and Anna Violet Kearney, 16.

23  In Memorium, *Clarence and Richmond Examiner*, 2 February 1901, 1; genealogical information from *Ancestry.com*, accessed 17 April 2017; New South Wales, Census, 1891, Clarence County, lists a Patrick E. Kearney, though he is noted as 41 years old. Patrick would have been 29.

24  UK Outward Passenger List, *The Austral*, departed London 20 September 1895, Ancestry.com, accessed 1 April 2019; *Australian Medical Directory and Handbook*, 1896, 76; *Clarence and Richmond Examiner*, 7 November 1899, 2; 23 May 1903, 5.

25  *Clarence and Richmond Examiner*, 1 February 1898, 1; *Sydney Morning Herald*, 18 June 1898, 12; *Clarence and Richmond Examiner*, 7 November 1899, 2; 25 May 1915, 8.

26  *Clarence River Advocate*, 24 February 1899, 5.

27  *Clarence and Richmond Examiner*, 25 May 1915, 8.

28  NSW, Death Certificate, Edward Francis Kearney, 1276/1897; NSW, Death Certificate, Kenneth Ignatius Kearney, 11806/1897.

29  *Clarence and Richmond Examiner*, 3 February 1900, 1; 2 February 1901, 1.

30  Family photo, Anna, Anna Violet, Ida and Edward, Grafton c.1898–1905.

31  Bill Gammage, 'Historical reconsiderations: VIII. Who gained, and who was meant to gain from land selection in New South Wales?', *Australian Historical Studies*, vol. 24, no. 94, 1990, 104–22.

32  Recording, Anna Violet; NSW, Birth Certificate, Edward Kearney,

14927/1892; NSW, Death Certificate, Edward Kearney, 1276/1897; *Clarence and Richmond Examiner*, 13 September 1902, 5; *Sydney Morning Herald*, 22 March 1930, 2; *Armidale Chronicle*, 21 November 1908, 4; Grafton Electoral Roll, 1903–04, Ancestry.com, accessed 1 April 2019; *Coff's Harbour Advocate*, 13 August 1954, 3.

33  *Clarence and Richmond Examiner*, 23 May 1903, 5.

34  *Clarence and Richmond Examiner*, 23 May 1903, 5; *Clarence River Advocate*, 12 June 1903, 5.

35  *Clarence River Advocate*, 5 June 1903, 5; 12 June 1903, 5; *Freeman's Journal*, 13 June 1903, 18.

36  *Clarence and Richmond Examiner*, 25 May 1915, 8.

37  New South Wales, Will Books, #70316, Will, Charles James Kearney, Ancestry.com, accessed 5 November 2015; Tombstone image, Condobolin Cemetery, RC1, E18.

38  McLeod, History of the Families of Walter Gerard and Anna Violet Kearney dates the wedding as 2 January 1905; Australia Marriage Index, Grafton, NSW, 1906, reg. no. 1347.

39  *Coff's Harbour Advocate*, 13 August 1954, 3; recording, Anna Violet Gerard.

40  *Sydney Stock and Station Journal*, 1 May 1906, 5; Glen Withers, Anthony M. Endres and Len Perry, *Australian Historical Statistics: Labour Statistics*, Fairfax, Syme & Weldon Associates, 1987, 154, 161; today, the £325 translates to nearly A$43 000 in income: *Official Municipal Year Book and Shires Directory*, NSW, 1907, 88; *Macleay Chronicle*, 10 February 1910, 3; 8 February 1911, 4; *Clarence and Richmond Examiner*, 4 February 1913, 6.

41  *Macleay Chronicle*, 17 July 1908, 10; 8 February 1911, 4; 13 August 1908, 8; *Armidale Chronicle*, 21 November 1908, 4.

42  *Macleay Chronicle*, 15 November 1911, 4; John W. Gerard, *From Pictures Green to the Silver Screen*, Coff's Harbour: 1984, 12, held by family members.

43  *Mudgee Guardian and North-Western Representative*, 18 January 1912, 18; 9 August 1920, 9; McLeod, History of the Families of Walter Gerard and Anna Violet Kearney, 4.

44  *Mudgee Guardian and North-Western Representative*, 9 August 1920, 9; personal communication, Rosalind McLeod, 28 November 2016; McLeod, History of the Families of Walter Gerard and Anna Violet Kearney, 3; Obituary, Norah Violet Palmer, <jjhc.info/palmernorahvioletgerard2009>, accessed 2 April 2019; *Sydney Mail*, 27 September 1927, 48.

45  Death Certificate, Edward Kearney, New South Wales, 29 August 1925, no. 12762/1925; *Sydney Morning Herald*, 31 August 1925, 8; <www.royalrehab.com.au/about-us/our-history/>, accessed 2 April 2019; *Daily Examiner* (Grafton), 30 August 1925, 4; *Coff's Harbour Advocate*, 10 December 1929, 2.

46  McLeod, History of the Families of Walter Gerard and Anna Violet Kearney, 3–4; communication with Rosalind McLeod, 29 November 2016.

47    *Coff's Harbour Advocate*, 10 December 1929, 2; *Sydney Morning Herald*, 22 March 1930, 2; communication with Rosalind McLeod, 29 November 2016.

48    Victoria, Marriage registration, William Kearney and May Emily Isabella Moutray, 1 November 1899, Port Fairy District; Births, deaths, migration and marriage of Moutray family members, Ancestry.com, accessed 17 April 2017. Hercules Moutray died in 1879. May, the youngest, was only four years old.

49    Moutray migration and marriage, Ancestry.com; *Sydney Mail and NSW Advertiser*, 29 July 1899, 298; *Derry Journal (Ireland)* 8 September 1899, 1; New South Wales, Marriage registration Anne Moutray and Albert Duncan Austin, 18 July 1899; Victoria, Marriage registration, Hercules Moutray and Sara Atkins, 11 October 1899, Port Fairy District; William Kearney and May Moutray, 1 November 1899, Port Fairy District.

50    Birth registration, Victoria, Yambuk, 308, Edward Moutray Kearney, 6 November 1900.

51    Victoria Electoral Rolls, 1899–1908, Ancestry.com, accessed 17 April 2017.

52    Victoria Electoral Rolls, 1903–1934, Ancestry.com, accessed 1 April 2019; *Portland Guardian*, 16 January 1907, 3; Yambuk Book Committee, *Yambuk and District, 1839–1994*, Yambuk: Collett, Bain & Gaspars, 1994, 47; Aged Care Resident Register, Sisters of Nazareth, Ballarat, Patrick Edgar Kearney, 26 March 1935 – 21 May 1936.

53    Victoria Electoral Rolls, 1914, 1915, Ancestry.com, accessed 1 April 2019; Australia Military Records, William Kearney, Ancestry.com, accessed 1 April 2019.

54    Australia, Military Records, William Kearney, Ancestry.com, accessed 1 April 2019; Australian Commonwealth Military Forces, <www.aif.adfa.edu.au>, accessed 3 April 2019.

55    Electoral Rolls, 1919–1937, Ancestry.com, accessed 1 April 2019; PROV, VPRS 7591/P2, Unit 855, 243/809.

56    McLeod, History of the Families of Walter Gerard and Anna Violet Kearney, 13; Rosalind McLeod, emails to author, 6 October 2016, 7 January 2019.

57    Victoria Electoral Rolls, 1919–1937, Ancestry.com, accessed 1 April 2019; Death registration, May Emily Isabella Kearney, 23 July 1931, Port Fairy, Victoria, no. 11105.

58    New Zealand Electoral Rolls, 1890–1922, Find My Past and Ancestry.com, accessed 1 April 2019; *Marlborough Express*, 15 November 1900, 2; New Zealand, Death Certificate, Wairau district, Margaret Kearney, 23 February 1929; Death Certificate, Wairau district, Frank Henry Kearney, 16 May 1933, 1933–2423.

59    Victoria Electoral Rolls, 1909–1934; *Portland Guardian*, 31 October 1932, 4; PROV, VPRS 24/P/1308/1936/694, Inquest Deposition Files, Patrick Kearney, Ballarat, 4 June 1936; Megan J. Davies, *Into the House of Old: A History of Residential Care in British Columbia*, Montreal: McGill–Queen's University Press, 2003; Bettina Bradbury, 'Elderly inmates

and care-giving sisters: Catholic institutions for the elderly in nineteenth-century Montreal', in *On The Case: Case Files and Social History*, Franca Iacovetta and Wendy Mitchinson, eds, Toronto: UTP, 1998, 129–55; Margaret Tennant, 'Elderly indigents and Old Men's Homes, 1880–1920', *New Zealand Journal of History*, vol. 17, no. 1, 1983, 3–2.

60 Sisters of Nazareth, 'History', <www.sistersofnazareth.com/who-we-are/history/>, accessed 3 April 2019.

61 Death Certificate, Patrick Kearney, Victoria, 21 May 1936, Ballarat, no. 1762; Aged Care Resident Register, Sisters of Nazareth, Ballarat, Patrick Edgar Kearney, 26 March 1935 to 21 May 1936; PROV, VPRS 24/P/1308/1936/694, Inquest Deposition Files, Patrick Kearney, Ballarat, 4 June 19360.

62 Aged Care Resident Register, Sisters of Nazareth, Ballarat, William Kearney, 5 April 1938 – 28 August 1940; William Kearney, First Australian Imperial Force Personnel Dossiers, 1914–1920, Ancestry.com, accessed 1 April 2019; Death Certificate, William Kearney, Ballarat, Victoria, 4238, 28 August 1940; *Australasian*, 14 September 1940, 24.

63 Ancestry.com, accessed 1 April 2019, Billiongraves index, and other searches.

64 Atherton, Rosalind, 'Expectation without Right: Testamentary freedom and the position of women in 19th-century New South Wales', *UNSW Law Journal*, 1988, 156.

65 Will, Charles James Kearney, probated 20 August 1915, New South Wales Will Books, no. 70136.

66 Rosalind McLeod and Joe Palmer, emails to author.

## Coda

1 Christopher Baker and Michael Gilding, *Inside Story*, 'Family matters', <insidestory.org.au/family-matters/>, accessed 21 July 2018.

# Index

# Index